HOPELESS

BARACK OBAMA AND THE POLITICS OF ILLUSION

Edited by Jeffrey St. Clair and Joshua Frank

AK PRESS

EDINBURGH · OAKLAND · BALTIMORE

Advance praise for *Hopeless*

"It could have been the best of times for progressives: the collapse of financial deregulation, two failed wars, an election mandate to repeal Republican policies, and, most of all, a Democratic president whose name would not be Clinton. Yet, this book explains, three years after Obama's election, as political mobilization has shifted toward the Tea Party, the White House helps banks no less than Robert Rubin, and worships free trade and American Empire as fervently as Al Gore."—**Serge Halimi**, *Le Monde Diplomatique*

"In their captivating collection of essays, Jeffrey St. Clair and Joshua Frank have skillfully smoked out the real Barack Obama—Obama the smirk-free George W. Bush, more intelligent, more articulate, and, therefore, much more dangerous. They mindfully unveil Obama the technofascist military strategist disguised as a Nobel Peace Laureate, but owned, operated, and controlled by Wall Street, Corporate America, and the Pentagon."—**Thomas H. Naylor**, Professor Emeritus of Economics at Duke University; co-author of *Affluenza, Downsizing the USA, and the Search for Meaning*

"In a world of fact-averse pitbulls attacking Obama from the right and morally challenged liberal lapdogs defending the administration, more than ever we need this honest assessment from the left. Important reading to gird ourselves for the 2012 presidential charade."—**Robert Jensen**, author of *All My Bones Shake: Seeking a Progressive Path to the Prophetic Voice* and *The Heart of Whiteness: Confronting Race, Racism and White Privilege*

"*Hopeless* constitutes the most sustained critical analysis yet of the rightward turn of the Obama administration. The writers assembled here hit hard, with accuracy, and do not pull punches."—**Marcus Rediker**, author of *The Slave Ship: A Human History*

"If you're still weeping with post-Bush, multicultural joy for the 2008 election of Barack Obama—or have somehow managed to pull the wool over your eyes regarding his record on Wall Street, the environment, militarism, democracy, leadership, health care, and human rights—read *Hopeless* and weep again."—**Chellis Glendinning**, Ph.D., author of *Off the Map: An Expedition Deep into Empire and the Global Economy*

"Those who feel that like lemmings they are being led over a cliff would be well-advised not to read this book. They may discover that they are right."—**Noam Chomsky**

"Jeffrey St. Clair and Joshua Frank bring thoughtful analysis and passionate arguments to the debate over the Obama presidency. This book is a crucial intervention for progressives engaged in electoral politics."—**Jordan Flaherty**, author of *Floodlines: Community and Resistance from Katrina to the Jena Six*

"Like all Presidents, Barack Obama lied his way into office and betrayed his constituency even before he took the oath. Like most presidents, he proceeded to tinker with the policies of his predecessor, and where he did meddle, he often moved toward even more reactionary, repressive positions. There has been no president in my lifetime less inclined to budge from the monstrous center of standard American policies, foreign and domestic, no president more callous in dismissing the needs of citizens or more eager in advancing the aims of corporate thugs and military bullies. This book is a fitting tombstone for whatever promise his election seemed to offer. Read it and then get back to work building the decent America and civilized world he's done his best to prevent."—**Dave Marsh**, author of *Two Hearts: The Bruce Springsteen Story*

"Open this book and step into an alternative universe in which political commentary values honesty and insight over deference to power. Here's a focus on the latest individual we've handed imperial power, but a focus that takes the facts for what they are and places them in the context of forces reshaping our society in the interests of the Pentagon and the plutocracy. If our televisions talked like this reads, I'd have a use for words like 'hope' and 'change.'"—**David Swanson**, author of *War Is A Lie*

"Candidate Barack Obama svengali-ed his way across the country, speaking and inspiring hope. A new generation of young voters and many older progressives believed the message. Now this hope has vaporized. St. Clair and Frank's eye-opening book reveals that President Obama is just another custodian of oligarchy and empire, a spokesperson for Wall Street, the gated community that controls U.S. politics."—**Missy Comley Beattie**, Gold Star Families for Peace

"St. Clair and Frank are to be thanked for compiling a timely and sweeping assay of the Obama era, and a dreadful reckoning it makes, at home and abroad. This damning statement of account clears the ground for the next task—root and branch renovation of the American commonwealth."—**Iain Boal**, co-author of *Afflicted Powers: Capital and Spectacle in a New Age of War*

"Yes, Obama has become the latest front-man for endless war and corporate imperialism, at home and abroad. What you will learn, page after page, in *Hopeless* is that the man from 'yes we can' is more concerned with defending US torture chambers, than health care for the people who need it most, and that he'd much rather be known as the Commander and Chief, than the Commander of a peace time economy: Tax Cuts for the Rich, and a new war in Libya for the corporate oil Barons. This book is the perfect 'counterpunch' to the big lies coming out of the corporate media."—**Dennis J. Bernstein**, Executive Producer of *Flashpoints*, syndicated on Pacifica Radio

Hopeless: Barack Obama and the Politics of Illusion
© 2012 Jeffrey St. Clair and Joshua Frank

This edition © 2012 AK Press (Oakland, Edinburgh, Baltimore)
ISBN: 978-1-84935-110-2 | eBook ISBN: 978-1-84935-111-9
Library of Congress Control Number: 2012933063

AK Press   AK Press
674-A 23rd Street   PO Box 12766
Oakland, CA 94612   Edinburgh EH8 9YE
USA   Scotland
www.akpress.org   www.akuk.com
akpress@akpress.org   ak@akedin.demon.co.uk

The above addresses would be delighted to provide you with the latest AK Press distribution catalog, which features the several thousand books, pamphlets, zines, audio and video
products, and stylish apparel published and/or distributed by AK Press. Alternatively, visit
our websites for the complete catalog, latest news, and secure ordering.

Visit us at:
www.akpress.org
www.akuk.com
www.revolutionbythebook.akpress.org

Printed in the USA on acid-free, recycled paper.
Cover design by Tim Simons (timsimonsgraphics.net).

Contents

Barack Obama, Changeling

By JEFFREY ST. CLAIR and JOSHUA FRANK

> Damaged goods, send them back
> I can't work, I can't achieve, send me back
> Open the till, give me the change
> You said would do me good
> Refund the cost
> You said you're cheap, but you're too much
> —"Damaged Goods," Gang of Four

Barack Obama was in Brasilia on March 19, 2011, when he announced with limited fanfare the latest war of his young presidency. The bombing of Libya had begun with a hail of cruise missile attacks and air strikes. It was something of an impromptu intervention, orchestrated largely by Hillary Clinton, Susan Rice and the diva of vengeance Samantha Powers, always hot for a saturation bombing in the name of human rights.

Obama soon upped the ante by suggesting that it was time for Qaddafi to go. The Empire had run out of patience with the mercurial colonel. The vague aims of the Libyan war had moved ominously from enforcing "a no-fly zone" to seeking regime change. Bombing raids soon targeted Qaddafi and his family. Coming in the wake of the extra-judicial assassination of Osama Bin Laden in a blood-spattered home invasion, Qaddafi rightly feared Obama wanted his body in a bag, too. (In the end, Qaddafi's butchered body was put on public display in a Benghazi meat locker.)

Absent mass protests against the impending destruction of Tripoli, it fell to Congress to take some tentative steps to challenge the latest unauthorized and unprovoked war. At an earlier time in the history of the Republic, Obama's arrogant defiance of Congress and the War Powers Act of 1973 might have provoked a constitutional crisis. But these are duller and more attenuated days, where such vital matters have been rendered down into a kind of hollow political theater. All the players duly act their parts, but everyone, even the cable news audience, realizes that it is just for show. The wars will proceed. Congress will fund them. The people will have no say in the matter. As Oscar Wilde quipped: "All the world's a stage, badly cast."

That old softy John Boehner, the teary-eyed barkeep's son, sculpted a resolution demanding that Obama explain his intentions in Libya. It passed the House overwhelmingly. A competing resolution crafted by the impish gadfly Dennis Kucinich called for an immediate withdrawal of US forces from operations in Libya. This radically sane measure garnered a robust 148 votes. Obama dismissed both attempts to downsize his unilateralist approach to military operations, saying with a chill touch of the surreal that the 14,000-and-counting sorties flown over Libya didn't amount to a "war."

This is Barack Obama, the political moralist? The change agent? The constitutional scholar? Listen to that voice. It is petulant and dismissive. Some might say peevish, like the whine of a talented student caught cheating on a final exam.

Yes, all the political players were acting their parts. But what role exactly had Obama assumed?

Obama, the Nobel laureate, casts himself as a New Internationalist, a chief executive of the global empire, more eager to consult with European heads of state than members of Congress, even of his own party. Indeed, his co-conspirators in the startling misadventure in Libya were David Cameron and Nikolas Sarkozy, an odd troika to say the least. Even Obama's own Defense Secretary, Robert Gates, seems to have been discreetly cut out of the decision loop.

We are beginning to see why Obama sparks such a virulent reaction among the more histrionic precincts of the libertarian right. He has a majestic sense of his own certitude. The president often seems captivated by the nobility of his intentions, offering himself up as a kind of savior of the eroding American Imperium.

While Obama sells pristine idealism to the masses, he is at heart a calculating pragmatist, especially when it comes to advancing his own ambitions. Obama doesn't want to be stained with defeat. It's one reason he has walked away from pushing for a Palestinian state, after his Middle East envoy George Mitchell resigned in frustration. It's why Obama stubbornly refused to insist on a public option for his atrocious health care bill. It's why he backed off cap-and-trade and organized labor's card check bill and the DREAM Act.

Obama assumed the presidency at a moment when much of the nation seemed ready to confront the unwelcome fact that the American project had derailed. Before he died, Norman Mailer lamented that the American culture was corroding from a bad conscience. The country was warping under the psychic weight of years of illegal wars, torture, official greed, religious prudishness, government surveillance, unsatisfying Viagra-supplemented sex, bland genetically engineered food, crappy jobs, dismal movies, and infantile, corporatized music—all scrolling by in an infinite montage of annoying Tweets. Even the virtual commons of cyberspace had gone solipsistic.

Corporate capitalism just wasn't delivering the goods anymore. Not for the bottom 80 percent, any way. The economy was in ruins, mired in what appeared to be a permanent recession. The manufacturing sector had been killed from the inside-out, with millions of well-paying jobs outsourced and nothing but dreary service-sector positions to take their place. Chronic long-term unemployment hovered at more than 10 percent, worse, much worse, in black America. Those who clung to their jobs had seen their wages stagnate, their home values shrivel and were suffocating under merciless mounds of debt. Meanwhile, capital moved in ever-tightening circles among a new odious breed of super-rich, making sweat-free billions from the facile movement of digital money.

By 2008, the wistfulness seemed to have evaporated from the American spirit. The country had seen its own government repeatedly prey on its citizens' fear of the future. Paranoia had become the last growth industry. From the High Sierras to the Blue Ridge, the political landscape was sour and spiteful, the perfect seed-ground for the sprouting of the Tea Party and even ranker and more venomous movements on the American right. These were not the ideological descendents of the fiery libertarian Barry Goldwater. The tea-baggers lacked Goldwater's western innocence and naïve idealism. These suburban populists, by and large, were white, unhappy and aging. Animated by the grim nostalgia for a pre-Lapsarian fantasyland called the Reagan administration, many sensed their station in society slipping inexorably away. They wanted their country back. But back from whom?

Instead of blaming corporate outsourcers or predatory bankers, they directed their vindictive impulse toward immigrants and blacks, government workers and teachers, scientists and homosexuals. There's something profoundly pathetic about the political fatalism of this new species Know-Nothings. But, it must be said, their wrath was mostly pure. This strange consortium of discontent seethed with an inchoate sense of alienation, an acidic despair at the diminished potentialities of life in post-industrial America.

No, these were not fanatical idealists or even ante-bellum utopians. They were levelers, of a sort, splenetic and dread-fuelled levelers, conspiratorialists with a Nixonian appetite for political destruction. Primed into a frenzy by the cynical rantings of Glenn Beck and Rush Limbaugh, mass gatherings of Tea Partiers across the summer of 2009 showed signs of a collective psychopathy, as if the enervating madness from decades of confinement in the hothouse of the American suburbs had finally ruptured in primetime for all the world to watch over-and-over again on YouTube with mounting mortification. Right there on the National Mall could be heard the vapid gibberish of Michele Bachmann and the new American preterite, those lost and bitter souls who felt their culture had left them far behind.

With his sunny disposition and Prospero-like aptitude for mystification, Obama should have been able to convert them or, at least, to roll over them. Instead, they kicked his ass. How?

Obama is a master of gesture politics, but he tends to flinch in nearly every pitched battle, even when the odds and the public are behind him. His political instincts drive him to seek cover in the middle ground. He is a reflexive compromiser, more Rodney "Can't We All Just Get Along" King than Reverend King. Even when confronted by bumbling hacks like John Boehner and Eric Cantor, Obama tends to wilt.

Perhaps Obama had never before been confronted with quite this level of toxic hostility. After all, he'd lived something of a charmed life, the life of a star-child, coddled and pampered, encouraged and adulated, from Indonesia to Harvard. Obama was the physical and psychic embodiment of the new multiculturalism: lean, affable, assured, non-threatening. His vaguely liberal political ideology remained opaque at the core. Instead of an over-arching agenda, Obama delivered facile jingoisms proclaiming a post-racial and post-partisan America. Instead of radical change, Obama offered simply managerial competence. This, naturally, the Berserkers of the Right interpreted as hubris and arrogance and such hollow homilies served only to exacerbate their rage. The virulent right had profiled Obama and found him to be the perfect target for their accreted animus. And, even better, they had zeroed-in on an enemy so innately conflict-averse that even when pummeled with racist slurs he wouldn't punch back.

Of course, Obama's most grievous political wounds were self-inflicted, starting even before his election when he rushed back to Washington to help rescue Bush's Wall Street bailout. This was perhaps the first real indication that the luminous campaign speeches about generational and systemic change masked the servile psyche of a man who was desperately yearning to be embraced by the nation's political and financial elites. Instead of meeting with the victims of Wall Street predators or their advocates, like Elizabeth Warren and Ralph Nader, Obama fist-bumped with the brain trust of Goldman Sachs and schmoozed with the crème de la crème of K Street corporate lobbyists. In the end, Obama helped salvage some of the most venal and corrupt enterprises on Wall Street, agreed to shield their executives from prosecution for their financial crimes and, predictably, later got repaid with their scorn.

Thus the Obama revolution was over before it started, guttered by the politician's overweening desire to prove himself to the grandees of the establishment. From there on, other promises, from confronting climate change to closing Gitmo, from ending torture to initiating a nationalized health care system, proved even easier to break.

Take the issue that had so vivified his campaign: ending the war on Iraq. Within weeks of taking office, Obama had been taken to the woodshed by Robert Gates and General David Petreaus and had returned to the White House bruised and humbled. The withdrawal would slowly proceed, but a sinister force would remain behind indefinitely, a lethal contingent of some 50,000 or so CIA operatives, special forces units, hunter-killer squads and ruthless private security details. Bush's overt war quietly became a black op under Obama. Out of sight, out of mind.

By the fall of 2009 even the most calloused Washington hands had grown weary over how deeply entangled the US occupation of Afghanistan had become. The savage rhythms of the war there had backfired. Too many broken promises, too many bombed weddings and assassinations, too many dead and mutilated children, too much cowardice and corruption in the puppet satrapy in Kabul. The tide had irrevocably turned against the US and its squalid policies. Far from being terminally crippled, the Taliban was now stronger than it had been at any time since 2001. But instead of capitalizing on this tectonic shift of sentiment by drawing down American troops, Obama, in a cynical ploy to prove his martial meddle, journeyed to West Point and announced in a somber speech that he was raising the stakes in Afghanistan by injecting a Petreaus-sanctioned surge of forces into the country and unleashing a new campaign of lethal operations that would track and target suspected insurgents across the Hindu Kush and into Pakistan.

That night Obama spoke in a stern cadence, studded with imperious pauses, as if to suggest that he, unlike the fickle George W. Bush, was going to wage the Afghan war until it was won. But he knew better. And so did his high command—even Stanley McChrystal and David Petreaus, who had trademarked the counter-insurgency strategy. There was nothing to win in Afghanistan. Out on that distant rim of the world, there weren't even any standards to gauge military success. This was meant to be a punitive war, pure and simple, designed to draw as much blood as possible, an obscene war fought largely by remote-controlled drones attacking peasant villages with murderous indiscretion.

Afterwards, the American peace movement could only bray in impotent outrage. But as Obama's wars spread from Afghanistan and Iraq to Pakistan and Yemen, Somalia and Libya, outside of the redoubtable Catholic Workers and Quakers and a few Code Pinkers—the last flickering moral lights in the nation—even those empty yawps of protest dissipated into whispered lamentations, hushed murmurs of disillusionment. Could it be that the American Left had gone extinct as any kind of potent political force and it took the election of Barack Obama to prove it?

And what of Obama's spellbound followers, those youthful crusaders who saw him illumined in the sacral glow of his ethereal rhetoric and cleaved to him during the hard slog of two campaigns with a near-religious devotion? What was running through their minds when the mists finally parted to reveal that Obama was implementing cunning tracings of Bush-era policies on everything from the indefinite detention of uncharged prisoners in the war on terror to raids on medical marijuana distributors in states where medical pot has been legalized? What, indeed.

Illusions die hard, especially when shattered by cruise missiles.

Marketing Hope
The Birth of the Hero

By KEVIN ALEXANDER GRAY

My wife, Sandra, warned me, "Don't be hating." Now San (as we call her), who has worked in retail sales, selling ladies shoes, throughout her working life, is not an overtly political person. She is one of those old-timey, "salt of the earth" types. But when she doesn't like a person, there is usually something wrong with that person. For instance, before it became evident that Al Sharpton's effort in South Carolina was going nowhere fast, she coined the now-popular phrase "scampaign" to refer to the reverend's run. I know it is ill-advised not to take heed of her warning.

With San's admonition in mind, I tried to table her (and my) Oprah-tainted, media-hyped preconception of Barack Obama so that I could read *The Audacity of Hope* with an open mind and with the same hopeful spirit as the title seeks to portray.

But the book is like those two solid yellow lines on a two-lane mountain road. They're just there in the middle and never-ending, with a stop sign as the only relief.

He offers no boldness. Dr. King set out to change the social, economic, and political structures of this country. He described the change as a "third way" beyond capitalism and socialism. King's "third way" is far different than Bill Clinton's "third way," promoted by Obama and all those around Hillary, who tout the Clintons as the second and third coming of Camelot.

The Clinton "third way" is Republican Party politics in slow motion. Under Bill Clinton, US troops weren't trapped in Iraq, but just as many, if not more, Iraqis died as a result of his policies. His destruction of the welfare system, his embrace of capital punishment and other punitive and discriminatory crime policies, his bowing to Wall Street all made him palatable to Republicans.

The hope in Obama's title is for a mixture of Kennedyism, Reaganism, and Clintonism packaged as the new face of multicultural America. At its core, this is what *The Audacity of Hope* promotes, instead of any fundamental progressive change.

Nonetheless, it comes as no surprise that *The Audacity of Hope* was a *New York Times* bestseller. The book arrived amidst the hype of an upcoming and wide-open Presidential race, the collective angst over the country moving in the wrong direction, an economy that working people know isn't as good as they are being told it is, and a war that has washed away—at home and abroad—the country's preexisting false sense of moral superiority. As the line in Ethan and Joel Cohen's 2000 movie, *Oh Brother Where Art Thou?*, goes, "Everybody's looking for answers."

Yet, does Obama's book provide any real answers? Is there anything in it that will help stimulate measurable change? Or, is it all just talk, posturing, and positioning for personal political goals? Is it an orchestrated, consciously plotted pretext to inoculate a politician from the perceived liabilities of race, lineage and inexperience?

The answers are no, no, yes, yes.

I can agree with Obama on the need for a new kind of politics. But he suggests that what's broken can be fixed versus being replaced altogether. He opines that if we would all just recognize our "shared understanding," "shared values," and "the notion of a common good" that life (or politics) in the United States would be better.

Take, for instance, his praise of Reagan, hedged as it is by criticism of Reagan's "John Wayne, *Father Knows Best* pose, his policy by anecdote, and his gratuitous assault on the poor." Writes Obama: "I understood his appeal. It was the same appeal that the military bases back in Hawaii always held for me as a young boy, with their tidy streets and well-oiled machinery, the crisp uniforms and crisper salutes.… Reagan spoke to America's longing for order, our need to believe that we are not subject to blind, impersonal forces, but that we can shape our individual and collective destinies. So long as we rediscover the traditional values of hard work, patriotism, personal responsibility, optimism, and faith."

Obama gets a lot wrong from start to finish. While people may indeed have a shared reality—which means we witness the same things—we don't always feel, understand, process or react to what we witness in the same way. The simplest example of not having a "shared understanding" is the difference in how blacks and whites view the police.

What is lacking here is devotion to principles, which Obama constantly sacrifices on the altar of "shared values." And of course the issue is not of shared values. It's how we rank our values. Many people value religion, but which religion has more value? In this country we all know the answer to that question. As proof that the United States government values Christians over Muslims, consider that the United States is at war with an Islamic country. Consider that Muslims in this country are subject to increased government scrutiny and racial, ethnic and religious profiling. No one in their right mind could believe that the United States places a Muslim on an equal footing with a Christian or Jew. The daily body count dispels that notion.

At the top of Obama's shared values matrix is his Christian faith, his heterosexual family, the American flag, and the Democratic Party. "Shared values" and "the notion of a common good" pretty much amounts to the same thing in Obamaspeak. It all sounds pleasant, but it's surely not new. It's somewhat reminiscent of Jesse Jackson's "common ground" theme that he built his '88 campaign around. Clinton picked up the phrase, and it is now a standard part of the political lexicon.

But the use and meaning of Jackson's phrase has changed over the years since Clinton co-opted it. Jackson's "common ground" meant bringing together a coalition of workers, women, men, blacks, progressive whites, gays and lesbians, environmentalists, anti-apartheid activists, those opposed to Ronald Reagan's illegal war in Central America, farmers, Latinos, Arab-Americans and other traditionally underrepresented or unrepresented groups. With Jackson's phrase, all could demand a seat at the Democratic Party table.

By contrast, Clinton wanted the Democratic Party to renew its "common ground" with those who left the party with Strom Thurmond and the Dixiecrats and those who jumped ship when Ronald Reagan rose to power: white men. Clinton's "common ground" was with the Democratic Leadership Council. Clinton's "common ground" pushed aside those whom Jackson brought to the party. And *The Audacity of Hope* places Obama squarely in the DLC camp, even if he never applies for a membership card.

As a political tome, *The Audacity of Hope* is kind of a new and improved, better-written version of Clinton's long-winded speech at the '88 Democratic Convention in book form. Obama touches all the hot button words like the "nuclear option," "strict constructionists," and the like, but never really says anything deep or brave or new other than to remind us that the hot buttons are really hot.

Give Obama credit for copping to the fact that his "treatment of the issues is often partial and incomplete." Overall, the treatise reads like a very, very long speech of sound bites and clichés arranged by topic and issue and connected by conjunctions, pleasantries, and apologies. Pleasantries like wishing for a return to the days when Republicans and Democrats "met at night for dinner, hashing out a compromise over steaks and cigars." Or, leading with apologias to describe painful parts of United States history or softening a rightfully deserved blow as when he describes racist southern Senator Richard B. Russell as "erudite." Or accusing his mom of having a "incorrigible, sweet-natured romanticism" about the '60s and the civil rights era as he waxes romantically about Hubert Humphrey's Democratic Party. It's like he did not have a clue about the 1964 struggles of Fannie Lou Hamer and the Mississippi Freedom Democratic Party.

The shame of Obama's lack of depth is that Hamer's conflict over representation pretty much set the table for how the Democratic Party deals with blacks today. But of course he was only three years old and living in Hawaii when Lyndon Johnson went on national television to give a speech so that Hamer's image and the MFDP challenge would be off the airwaves. Hamer's fight was a precursor to the candidacy of Shirley Chisholm, the first black to seriously run for President in 1972 (if you exclude Dick Gregory's 1968 bid). Chisholm continued Hamer's fight for a greater black and female voice in politics and government.

Throughout, Obama proffers an unnaturally romantic view of the Democratic Party for a person of his age. His appreciation of party seems at times deeper than his understanding of the civil rights movement, which comes across as antiseptic. And he goes out of his way to comfort whites with a critique of black Americans that could tumble out of the mouth of William Bennett. "Many of the social or cultural factors that negatively affect black people, for example, simply mirror in exaggerated form problems that afflict America as whole: too much television (the average black household has the television on more than eleven hours per day), too much consumption of poisons (blacks smoke more and eat more fast food), and a lack of emphasis on educational attainment," he writes. "Then there's the collapse of the two-parent black household, a phenomenon that … reflects a casualness towards sex and child rearing among black men."

The book has no soul. That perhaps explains why some (with motives good and bad) in the black community complain that he "is not black enough," or "he has no respect or appreciation for the past," or "he is the amalgamation of everything white folk want a black man to be," or "he's a white boy being scripted by smart-ass white boys."

The book is surprisingly short on substance. Given all the policy disasters of the Bush Administration, what troubles Obama about the Bush era is not so much the policies Republicans championed but "the process" or lack of process "by which the White House and its Congressional allies disposed of opposing views." In the end, all he offers is the promise of a "hope" that he will manage the process better than the other guy or gal.

So then, why write the book?

Obama's face is everywhere. And, there is no shortage of opinion about him, which makes it difficult to read his book and sort things out without atmospheric bias. But *The Audacity of Hope* plays on the creation of a Kennedy-like mystique. I've spoken to a couple of writer friends who attended an Obama event and in both conversations the comparison to John Kennedy was bandied about. On cue, Obama plays the Kennedy-card throughout his book, tossing in passages from *Profiles in Courage*.

Although we now know that John F. Kennedy did not write *Profiles in Courage*, the book is one you have on your shelf that you might look through on occasion and actually enjoy rereading. *Profiles in Courage* is a historical marker in a way *Audacity of Hope* will never be. Not that I am a fan in the slightest regard of the early John and Robert Kennedy. There was much to dislike about them even before the days when they authorized then-FBI director J. Edgar Hoover to bug Dr. King, after which the top cop and closet cross dresser (no disrespect to cross dressers) in turn authorized his agents to try to prod King into killing himself.

Not everyone writes a book before running for the Presidency. But some do, and those books reveal things about the person and the time. Jackson's

Straight from the Heart, of which many people contributed to, still holds up as a record of where progressives stood at a particular point and where many progressives stand today. Ross Perot's *United We Stand* at least tried to confront some familiar problems such as the federal debt. And he actually wrote of reforming the system of campaign finance, increasing electoral participation, and eliminating the Electoral College.

The title of a book usually tells the story. Sometimes it may take reading the entire book, down to the last page before you realize how telling or appropriate a title is. *The Audacity of Hope*. You can't chant it in a crowd like, well, *"Keep Hope Alive!"* or *"Keep the Faith, Baby!"* or *"Power to the People!"* And while the book is technically well-written with aspirations to inspire, Obama falls far short of the mountaintop. In the end, the feels trapped in a valley of buzzwords, catch-phrases, and insider jargon with words like "halcyon" thrown in for good measure.

So, if you are searching Obama's book for hints or even the language of the kind of change that means something in a structural and systemic way, it's not there.

Kevin Alexander Gray is lead organizer of the Harriet Tubman Freedom House Project in Columbia, South Carolina, which focuses on community-based political and cultural education. He is also a contributing editor to Black News *in South Carolina. Gray served as 1988 South Carolina coordinator for the Presidential campaign of Jesse Jackson and as 1992 southern political director for Iowa Senator Tom Harkin's Presidential bid. His book,* Waiting for Lightning to Strike, *is published by CounterPunch/AK Press.*

Obama's Money Cartel

By PAM MARTENS

Wall Street, known variously as a barren wasteland for diversity or the last plantation in America, has defied courts and the Equal Employment Opportunity Commission (EEOC) for decades in its failure to hire blacks as stockbrokers. Now it's marshalling its money machine to elect a black man to the highest office in the land. Why isn't the press curious about this?

Walk into any of the largest Wall Street brokerage firms today and you'll see a self-portrait of upper management's racism and sexism: women sitting at secretarial desks outside fancy offices occupied by predominantly white males. According to the EEOC, as well as the recent racial discrimination class actions filed against UBS and Merrill Lynch, blacks make up between 1 percent to 3.5 percent of stockbrokers—this after thirty years of litigation, settlements and empty promises to do better by the largest Wall Street firms. The first clue to an entrenched white male bastion seeking a black male occupant in the oval office (having placed only five blacks in the US Senate in the last two centuries) appeared in February on a chart at the Center for Responsive Politics website. It was a list of the twenty top contributors to the Barack Obama campaign, and it looked like one of those comprehension tests where you match up things that go together and eliminate those that don't. Of the twenty top contributors, I eliminated six that didn't compute. I was now looking at a sight only slightly less frightening to democracy than a Diebold voting machine. It was a Wall Street cartel of financial firms, their registered lobbyists, and go-to law firms that have a death grip on our federal government.

Why is the "yes, we can" candidate in bed with this cartel? How can "we," the people, make change if Obama's money backers block our ability to be heard?

Seven of the Obama campaign's top fourteen donors consisted of officers and employees of the same Wall Street firms charged time and again with looting the public and newly implicated in originating and/or bundling fraudulently made mortgages. These latest frauds have left thousands of children in some of our largest minority communities coming home from school to see eviction notices and foreclosure signs nailed to their front doors. Those scars will last a lifetime.

These seven Wall Street firms are (in order of money given): Goldman Sachs, UBS AG, Lehman Brothers, JP Morgan Chase, Citigroup, Morgan Stanley and Credit Suisse. There is also a large hedge fund, Citadel Investment Group, which is a major source of fee income to Wall Street. There are five large corporate law firms that are also registered lobbyists; and one is a corporate law firm that is no longer a registered lobbyist but does legal work for Wall Street. The cumulative total of these fourteen contributors through February 1, 2008, was $2,872,128, and we're still in the primary season.

But hasn't Senator Obama repeatedly told us in ads and speeches and debates that he wasn't taking money from registered lobbyists? Hasn't the press given him a free pass on this statement?

Barack Obama, speaking in Greenville, South Carolina on January 22, 2008:

Washington lobbyists haven't funded my campaign, they won't run my White House, and they will not drown out the voices of working Americans when I am president.

Barack Obama, in an email to supporters on June 25, 2007, as reported by the *Boston Globe*:

Candidates typically spend a week like this—right before the critical June 30th financial reporting deadline—on the phone, day and night, begging Washington lobbyists and special interest PACs to write huge checks. Not me. Our campaign has rejected the money-for-influence game and refused to accept funds from registered federal lobbyists and political action committees.

The Center for Responsive Politics website allows one to pull up the filings made by lobbyists, registering under the Lobbying Disclosure Act of 1995, with the clerk of the US House of Representatives and secretary of the US Senate. These top five contributors to the Obama campaign have filed as registered lobbyists: Sidley Austin LLP; Skadden, Arps, et al; Jenner & Block; Kirkland & Ellis; Wilmerhale.

Is it possible that Senator Obama does not know that corporate law firms are also frequently registered lobbyists? Or is he making a distinction that because these funds are coming from the employees of these firms, he's not really taking money directly from registered lobbyists? That thesis seems disingenuous when many of these individual donors own these law firms as equity partners or shareholders and share in the profits generated from lobbying.

Far from keeping his distance from lobbyists, Senator Obama and his campaign seem to be brainstorming with them.

The political publication, *The Hill*, reported on December 20, 2007 that three salaried aides on the Obama campaign were registered lobbyists for dozens of corporations. (The Obama campaign said they had stopped lobbying since joining the campaign.) Bob Bauer, counsel to the Obama campaign, is an attorney with Perkins Coie. That law firm is also a registered lobbyist.

What might account for this persistent (but non-reality based) theme of distancing the Obama campaign from lobbyists? Odds are it traces back to one of the largest corporate lobbyist spending sprees in the history of Washington whose details would cast an unwholesome pall on the Obama campaign, unless our cognitive abilities are regularly bombarded with abstract vacuities of hope and change and sentimental homages to Dr. King and President Kennedy.

On February 10, 2005, Senator Obama voted in favor of the passage of the Class Action Fairness Act of 2005. Senators Biden, Boxer, Byrd, Clinton, Corzine, Durbin, Feingold, Kerry, Leahy, Reid and sixteen other Democrats voted against it. It passed the Senate 72–26 and was signed into law on February 18, 2005.

Here is an excerpt of remarks Senator Obama made on the Senate floor on February 14, 2005, concerning the passage of this legislation:

> Every American deserves their day in court. This bill, while not perfect, gives people that day while still providing the reasonable reforms necessary to safeguard against the most blatant abuses of the system. I also hope that the federal judiciary takes seriously their expanded role in class action litigation, and upholds their responsibility to fairly certify class actions so that they may protect our civil and consumer rights.

Three days before Senator Obama expressed that fateful yea vote, fourteen state attorneys general, including Lisa Madigan of Senator Obama's home state of Illinois, filed a letter with the Senate and House, pleading to stop the passage of this corporate giveaway. The AGs wrote: "State attorneys general frequently investigate and bring actions against defendants who have caused harm to our citizens.... In some instances, such actions have been brought with the attorney general acting as the class representative for the consumers of the state. We are concerned that certain provisions of S.5 might be misinterpreted to impede the ability of the attorneys general to bring such actions."

The Senate also received a desperate plea from more than forty civil rights and labor organizations, including the NAACP, Lawyers Committee for Civil Rights Under Law, Human Rights Campaign, American Civil Liberties Union, Center for Justice and Democracy, Legal Momentum (formerly NOW Legal Defense and Education Fund), and Alliance for Justice. They wrote as follows:

> Under the [Class Action Fairness Act of 2005], citizens are denied the right to use their own state courts to bring class actions against corporations that violate these state wage and hour and state civil rights laws, even where that corporation has hundreds of employees in that state. Moving these state law cases into federal court will delay and likely deny justice for working men and women and victims of

discrimination. The federal courts are already overburdened. Additionally, federal courts are less likely to certify classes or provide relief for
violations of state law.

This legislation, which dramatically impaired labor rights, consumer
rights and civil rights, involved five years of pressure from 100 corporations,
475 lobbyists, tens of millions of corporate dollars buying influence in our
government, and the active participation of the Wall Street firms now funding the Obama campaign. "The Civil Justice Reform Group, a business alliance comprising general counsels from Fortune 100 firms, was instrumental
in drafting the class-action bill," says Public Citizen.

One of the hardest working registered lobbyists to push this corporate
giveaway was the law firm Mayer-Brown, hired by the leading business lobby
group, the US Chamber of Commerce. According to the Center for Responsive Politics, the Chamber of Commerce spent $16 million in just 2003, lob-
bying the government on various business issues, including class action reform.

According to a 2003 report from Public Citizen, Mayer-Brown's class
action lobbyists included "Mark Gitenstein, former chief counsel to the Senate Judiciary Committee and a leading architect of the Senate strategy in
support of class-action legislation; John Schmitz, who was deputy counsel
to President George H.W. Bush; David McIntosh, former Republican congressman from Indiana; and Jeffrey Lewis, who was on the staffs of both Sen.
John Breaux (D-La) and Rep. Billy Tauzin (R-La)."

While not on the Center for Responsive Politics's list of the top twenty
contributors to the Obama presidential campaign, Mayer-Brown's partners
and employees are in rarefied company, giving a total of $92,817 through
December 31, 2007, to the Obama campaign. (The firm is also defending
Merrill Lynch in court against charges of racial discrimination.)

Senator Obama graduated Harvard Law magna cum laude and was the
first black president of the *Harvard Law Review*. Given those credentials,
one assumes that he understood the ramifications to the poor and middle
class in this country as he helped gut one of the few weapons left to seek
justice against giant corporations and their legions of giant law firms. The
class action vehicle confers upon each citizen one of the most powerful rights
in our society: the ability to function as a private attorney general and seek
redress for wrongs inflicted on ourselves as well as for those similarly injured
that might not otherwise have a voice.

Those rights should have been strengthened, not restricted, at this dangerous time in our nation's history. According to a comprehensive report from
the nonprofit group United for a Fair Economy, over the past eight years the
total loss of wealth for people of color is between $164 billion and $213
billion for subprime loans, which is the greatest loss of wealth for people of
color in modern history:

According to federal data, people of color are more than three times
more likely to have subprime loans: high-cost loans account for 55
percent of loans to blacks, but only 17 percent of loans to whites.

If there had been equitable distribution of subprime loans, losses for
white people would be 44.5 percent higher and losses for people of color
would be about 24 percent lower. "This is evidence of systemic prejudice and
institutional racism."

Before the current crisis, based on improvements in median household
net worth, it would take 594 more years for blacks to achieve parity with
whites. The current crisis is likely to stretch this even further.

So, how should we react when we learn that the top contributors to the
Obama campaign are the very Wall Street firms whose shady mortgage lenders buried the elderly and the poor and minority under predatory loans? How
should we react when we learn that on the big donor list is Citigroup, whose
former employee at CitiFinancial testified to the Federal Trade Commission
that it was standard practice to target people based on race and educational
level, with the sales force winning bonuses called "Rocopoly Money" (like
a sick board game) after "blitz" nights of soliciting loans by phone? How
should we react when we learn that these very same firms, arm in arm with
their corporate lawyers and registered lobbyists, have weakened our ability to
fight back with the class action vehicle?

Should there be any doubt left as to who owns our government? The very
same cast of characters making the Obama hit parade of campaign loot are
the clever creators of the industry solutions to the wave of foreclosures grip-
ping this nation's poor and middle class, effectively putting the solution in the
hands of the robbers. The names of these programs (that have failed to make a
dent in the problem) have the same vacuous ring: Hope Now; Project Lifeline.

Senator Obama has become the inspiration and role model to millions
of children and young people in this country. He has only two paths now: to
be a dream maker or a dream killer. But be assured of one thing: this country
will not countenance any more grand illusions.

* * *

The Obama phenomenon has been likened to that of cults, celebrity groupies
and Messiah worshipers. But what we're actually witnessing is ObamaMania
(as in tulip mania), the third and final bubble orchestrated and financed by
the wonderful Wall Street folks who brought us the first two: the Nasdaq
tech bubble and a subprime-mortgage-in-every-pot bubble.

To understand why Wall Street desperately needs this final bubble, we
need to review how the first two bubbles were orchestrated and why.

In March of 2000, the Nasdaq stock market, hyped with spurious claims
for startup tech and dot.com companies, reached a peak of over 5,000. Eight

years later, it's trading in the 2,300 range and most of those companies no longer exist. From peak to trough, Nasdaq transferred over $4 trillion from the pockets of small mania-gripped investors to the wealthy and elite market manipulators.

The highest monetary authority during those bubble days, Alan Greenspan, chairman of the Federal Reserve, consistently told us that the market was efficient and stock prices were being set by the judgment of millions of "highly knowledgeable" investors.

Mr. Greenspan was the wind beneath the wings of a carefully orchestrated wealth transfer system known as "pump and dump" on Wall Street. As hundreds of court cases, internal emails, and insider testimony now confirm, this bubble was no naturally occurring phenomenon any more than the Obama bubble is.

First, Wall Street firms issued knowingly false research reports to trumpet the growth prospects for the company and stock price; second, they lined up big institutional clients who were instructed how and when to buy at escalating prices to make the stock price skyrocket (laddering); third, the firms instructed the hundreds of thousands of stockbrokers serving the mom-and-pop market to advise their clients to sit still as the stock price flew to the moon or else the broker would have his commissions taken away (penalty bid). While the little folks' money served as a prop under prices, the wealthy elite on Wall Street and corporate insiders were allowed to sell at the top of the market (pump-and-dump wealth transfer).

Why did people buy into this mania for brand new, untested companies when there is a basic caveat that most people in this country know, i.e., the majority of all new businesses fail? Common sense failed and mania prevailed because of massive hype pumped by big media, big public relations, and shielded from regulation by big law firms, all eager to collect their share of Wall Street's rigged cash cow.

The current housing bubble bust is just a freshly minted version of Wall Street's real estate limited partnership frauds of the '80s, but on a grander scale. In the 1980s version, the firms packaged real estate into limited partnerships and peddled it as secure investments to moms and pops. The major underpinning of this wealth transfer mechanism was that regulators turned a blind eye to the fact that the investments were listed at the original face amount on the clients' brokerage statements long after they had lost most of their value.

Today's real estate related securities (CDOs and SIVs) that are blowing up around the globe are simply the above scheme with more billable hours for corporate law firms.

Wall Street created an artificial demand for housing (a bubble) by soliciting high interest rate mortgages (subprime) because they could be bundled and quickly resold for big fees to yield-hungry hedge funds and institutions. A major underpinning of this scheme was that Wall Street secured an artificial rating of AAA from rating agencies that were paid—by Wall Street—to provide the rating. When demand from institutions was saturated, Wall Street kept the scheme going by hiding the debt off its balance sheets and stuffed this long-term product into mom-and-pop money markets, notwithstanding that money markets are required by law to hold only short-term investments. To further perpetuate the bubble as long as possible, Wall Street prevented pricing transparency by keeping the trading off regulated exchanges and used unregulated over-the-counter contracts instead. (All of this required lots of lobbyist hours in Washington.)

But how could there be a genuine national housing price boom propelled by massive consumer demand at the same time there was the largest income and wealth disparity in the nation's history? Rational thought is no match for manias.

That brings us to today's bubble. We are being asked to accept on its face the notion that after more than two centuries of entrenched racism in this country, which saw only five black members of the US Senate, it's all being eradicated with some rousing stump speeches.

We are asked to believe that those kindly white executives at all the biggest Wall Street firms, which rank in the top twenty donors to the Obama presidential campaign, after failing to achieve more than 3.5 percent black stockbrokers over thirty years, now want a black populist president because they crave a level playing field for the American people.

The number one industry supporting the Obama presidential bid, by the start of February—the crucial time in primary season—according to the widely respected, nonpartisan Center for Responsive Politics, was "lawyers/law firms" (most on Wall Street's payroll), giving a total of $11,246,596.

This presents three unique credibility problems for the yes-we-can-little-choo-choo-that-could campaign: (1) these are not just "lawyers/law firms"; the vast majority of these firms are also registered lobbyists at the Federal level; (2) Senator Obama has made it a core tenet of his campaign platform that the way he is going to bring the country hope and change is *not* taking money from federal lobbyists; and (3) with the past seven ignoble years of lies and distortions fresh in the minds of voters, building a candidacy based on half-truths is not a sustainable strategy to secure the west wing from the right wing.

Yes, the other leading presidential candidates are taking money from lawyers/law firms/lobbyists, but Senator Obama is the only one rallying with the populist cry that he isn't. That makes it not only a legitimate but a necessary line of inquiry.

The Obama campaign's populist bubble is underpinned by what on the surface seems to be a real snoozer of a story. It all centers around business classification codes developed by the US government and used by the Center for Responsive Politics to classify contributions. Here's how the Center explained its classifications in 2003: "The codes used for business groups follow the general guidelines of the Standard Industrial Classification (SIC) codes initially designed by the Office of Management and Budget and later replaced by the North American Industry Classification System (NAICS)."

The Akin Gump law firm is a prime example of how something as mundane as a business classification code can be gamed for political advantage. According to the Center for Responsive Politics, Akin Gump ranks third among all Federal lobbyists, raking in $205,225,000 to lobby our elected officials in Washington from 1998 through 2007. The firm is listed as a registered federal lobbyist with the House of Representatives and the Senate; the firm held lobbying retainer contracts for more than 100 corporate clients in 2007. But when its non-registered law partners, the people who own this business and profit from its lobbying operations, give to the Obama campaign, the contribution is classified as coming from a law firm, not a lobbyist.

The same holds true for Greenberg Traurig, the law firm that employed the criminally inclined lobbyist, Jack Abramoff. Greenberg Traurig ranks ninth among all lobbyists for the same period, with lobbying revenues of $96,708,249. Its partners and employee donations to the Obama campaign of $70,650 by February 1—again at that strategic time—appear not under lobbyist but the classification lawyers/law firms, as do thirty other corporate law firm/lobbyists.

Additionally, looking at Public Citizen's list of bundlers for the Obama campaign (people soliciting donations from others), twenty seven are employed by law firms registered as federal lobbyists. The total sum raised by bundlers for Obama from these twenty seven firms till February 1: $2,650,000. (There are also dozens of high powered bundlers from Wall Street working the Armani-suit and red-suspenders cocktail circuits, like Bruce Heyman, managing director at Goldman Sachs; J. Michael Schell, vice chairman of Global Banking at Citigroup; Louis Susman, managing director, Citigroup; Robert Wolf, CEO, UBS Americas. Each raised over $200,000 for the Obama campaign.)

Senator Obama's premise and credibility of not taking money from federal lobbyists hangs on a carefully crafted distinction: he is taking money, lots of it, from owners and employees of firms registered as federal lobbyists but not the actual *individual* lobbyists.

But is that dealing honestly with the American people? According to the website of Akin Gump, it takes a village to deliver a capitol to the corporations:

> The public law and policy practice [lobbying] at Akin Gump is integrated throughout the firm's offices in the United States and abroad. As part of a full-service law firm, the group is able to draw upon the

experience of members of other Akin Gump practices—including bankruptcy, communications, corporate, energy, environmental, labor and employment, health care, intellectual property, international, real estate, tax and trade regulation—that may have substantive, day-to-day experience with the issues that lie at the heart of a client's situation. This is the internal component of Akin Gump's team-based approach: matching the needs of clients with the appropriate area of experience in the firm ... Akin Gump has a broad range of active representations before every major committee of Congress and executive branch department and agency.

When queried about this, Massie Ritsch, communications director at the Center for Responsive Politics, says: "The wall between a firm's legal practice and its lobbying shop can be low—the work of an attorney and a lobbyist trying to influence regulations and laws can be so intertwined. So, if anything, the influence of the lobbying industry in presidential campaigns is undercounted."

Those critical thinkers over at the *Black Agenda Report* for the *Journal of African American Political Thought and Action* have zeroed in on the making of the Obama bubble:

> The 2008 Obama presidential run may be the most slickly orchestrated marketing machine in memory. That's not a good thing. Marketing is not even distantly related to democracy or civic empowerment. Marketing is about creating emotional, even irrational bonds between your product and your target audience.

And slick it is. According to the Obama campaign's financial filings with the Federal Election Commission (FEC) and aggregated at the Center for Responsive Politics, the Obama campaign has spent over $52 million on media, strategy consultants, image building, marketing research and telemarketing.

The money has gone to firms like GMMB, whose website says its "goal is to change minds and change hearts, win in the court of public opinion and win votes" using "the power of branding—with principles rooted in commercial marketing," and Elevation Ltd., which targets the Hispanic population and has "a combined experience of well over 50 years in developing and implementing advertising and marketing solutions for Fortune 500 companies, political candidates, government agencies." Their client list includes the Department of Homeland Security.

There's also the Birmingham, Alabama based The Parker Group which promises: "Valid research results are assured given our extensive experience with testing, scripting, skip logic, question rotation and quota control ... In-house list management and maintenance services encompass sophisticated geo-coding, mapping and scrubbing applications." Is it any wonder America's brains are scrambled?

The Wall Street plan for the Obama-bubble presidency is that of the cleanup crew for the housing bubble: sweep all the corruption and losses, would-be indictments, perp walks and prosecutions under the rug and get on with an unprecedented taxpayer bailout of Wall Street. (The corporate law firms have piled on to funding the plan because most were up to their eyeballs in writing prospectuses or providing legal opinions for what has turned out to be bogus AAA securities. Lawsuits naming the Wall Street firms will, no doubt, shortly begin adding the law firms that rendered the legal guidance to issue the securities.) Who better to sell this agenda to the millions of duped mortgage holders and foreclosed homeowners in minority communities across America than our first, beloved, black president of hope and change?

Why do Wall Street and the corporate law firms think they will find a President Obama to be accommodating? As the *Black Agenda Report* notes, "Evidently, the giant insurance companies, the airlines, oil companies, Wall Street, military contractors and others had closely examined and vetted Barack Obama and found him pleasing."

That vetting included his remarkable "yes" vote on the Class Action Fairness Act of 2005, a five-year effort by 475 lobbyists, despite appeals from the NAACP and every other major civil rights group. Thanks to the passage of that legislation, when defrauded homeowners of the housing bubble and defrauded investors of the bundled mortgages try to fight back through the class action vehicle, they will find a new layer of corporate-friendly hurdles.

I personally admire Barack Obama. I want to believe Obama is not a party to the scheme. But corporate interests have had plenty of time to do their vetting. Democracy demands no less of we, the people.

Pam Martens worked on Wall Street for twenty one years; she has no securities position, long or short, in any company mentioned in this article. She has been writing in the public interest for CounterPunch *since she retired from Wall Street in 2006.*

Obama's Kettle of Hawks

By JEREMY SCAHILL

Barack Obama has assembled a team of rivals to implement his foreign policy. But while pundits and journalists speculate endlessly on the potential for drama with Hillary Clinton at the State Department and Bill Clinton's network of shady funders, the real rivalry that will play out goes virtually unmentioned. The main battles will not be between Obama's staff, but rather against those who actually want a change in US foreign policy, not just a staff change in the War Room.

When announcing his foreign policy team, Obama said: "I didn't go around checking their voter registration." That is a bit hard to believe, given the sixty-three-question application to work in his White House. But Obama clearly did check their credentials, and the disturbing truth is that he liked what he saw.

The assembly of Hillary Clinton, Robert Gates, Susan Rice and Joe Biden is a kettle of hawks with a proven track record of support for the Iraq war, militaristic interventionism, neoliberal economic policies and a world-view consistent with the foreign policy arch that stretches from George H. W. Bush's time in office to the present.

Obama has dismissed suggestions that the public records of his appointees bear much relevance to future policy. "Understand where the vision for change comes from, first and foremost," Obama said. "It comes from me. That's my job, to provide a vision in terms of where we are going and to make sure, then, that my team is implementing." It is a line Obama's defenders echo often. The reality, though, is that their records do matter.

We were told repeatedly during the campaign that Obama was right on the premiere foreign policy issue of our day—the Iraq war. "Six years ago, I stood up and opposed this war at a time when it was politically risky to do so," Obama said in his September debate against John McCain. "Senator McCain and President Bush had a very different judgment." What does it say that, with 130 members of the House and 23 in the Senate who voted against the war, Obama chose to hire Democrats who made the same judgment as Bush and McCain?

On Iraq, the issue that the Obama campaign described as "the most critical foreign policy judgment of our generation," Biden and Clinton not only supported the invasion, but pushed the Bush administration's propaganda and lies about Iraqi WMDs and fictitious connections to Al Qaeda. Clinton and Obama's hawkish, pro-Israel chief of staff, Rahm Emanuel, still refuse to renounce their votes in favor of the war. Rice, who claims she opposed the Iraq war, didn't hold elected office and was not confronted with voting for or against it. But she did publicly promote the myth of Iraq's possession of WMDs, saying in the lead up to the war that the "major threat" must "be dealt with forcefully". Rice has also been hawkish on Darfur, calling for "strik[ing] Sudanese airfields, aircraft and other military assets".

It is also deeply telling that, of his own free will, Obama selected President Bush's choice for Defense Secretary, a man with a very disturbing and lengthy history at the CIA during the cold war, as his own. While General James Jones, Obama's nominee for National Security Adviser, reportedly opposed the Iraq invasion and is said to have stood up to the neocons in Donald Rumsfeld's Pentagon, he did not do so publicly when it would have carried weight. *Time* magazine described him as "the man who led the Marines during the run-up to the war—and failed to publicly criticize the operation's flawed planning". Moreover, Jones, who is a friend of McCain's, has said a timetable for Iraq withdrawal, "would be against our national interest".

But the problem with Obama's appointments is hardly just a matter of bad vision on Iraq. What ultimately ties Obama's team together is their unified support for the classic US foreign policy recipe: the hidden hand of the free market, backed up by the iron fist of US militarism to defend the America First doctrine.

Obama's starry-eyed defenders have tried to downplay the importance of his cabinet selections, saying Obama will call the shots, but the ruling elite in this country see it for what it is. Karl Rove, "Bush's Brain", called Obama's cabinet selections, "reassuring", which itself is disconcerting, but neoconservative leader and former McCain campaign staffer Max Boot summed it up best. "I am gobsmacked by these appointments, most of which could just as easily have come from a President McCain," Boot wrote. The appointment of General Jones and the retention of Gates at Defense "all but puts an end to the 16-month timetable for withdrawal from Iraq, the unconditional summits with dictators and other foolishness that once emanated from the Obama campaign."

Boot added that Hillary Clinton will be a "powerful" voice "for 'neoliberalism' which is not so different in many respects from 'neoconservativism.'" Boot's buddy, Michael Goldfarb, wrote in the *Weekly Standard*, the official organ of the neoconservative movement, that he sees "certainly nothing that represents a drastic change in how Washington does business. The expectation is that Obama is set to continue the course set by Bush in his second term."

There is not a single, solid anti-war voice in the upper echelons of the Obama foreign policy apparatus. And this is the point: Obama is not going to fundamentally change US foreign policy. He is a status quo Democrat. And that is why the mono-partisan Washington insiders are gushing over Obama's new team. At the same time, it is also disingenuous to act as though Obama is engaging in some epic betrayal. Of course these appointments contradict his campaign rhetoric of change. But move past the speeches and Obama's selections are very much in sync with his record and the foreign policy vision he articulated on the campaign trail, from his pledge to escalate the war in Afghanistan to his "residual force" plan in Iraq to his vow to use unilateral force in Pakistan to defend US interests to his posturing on Iran. "I will always keep the threat of military action on the table to defend our security and our ally Israel," Obama said in his famed speech at the American Israel Public Affairs Committee last summer. "Sometimes, there are no alternatives to confrontation."

Jeremy Scahill is the author of Blackwater: The Rise of the World's Most Powerful Mercenary Army.

Obama's Israel Problem

By JOSHUA FRANK

As President-Elect Barack Obama vacationed in Hawaii on December 26, stopping off to watch a dolphin show with his family at Sea Life Park, an Israeli air raid besieged the impoverished Gaza Strip, killing at least 285 people and injuring over 800 more.

It was the single deadliest attack on Gaza in over twenty years and Obama's initial reaction on what could be his first real test as president was "no comment." Meanwhile, Israel has readied itself for a land invasion, amassing tanks along the border and calling up 6,500 reserve troops.

On *Face the Nation*, Obama's Senior Adviser David Axelrod explained to guest host Chip Reid how an Obama administration would handle the situation, even if it turned for the worst:

> Well, certainly, the president-elect recognizes the special relationship between United States and Israel. It's an important bond, an important relationship. He's going to honor it ... And obviously, this situation has become even more complicated in the last couple of days and weeks. As Hamas began its shelling, Israel responded. But it's something that he's committed to.

Reiterating the rationale that Israel's bombing of Gaza was an act of retaliation and not of aggression, Axelrod, on behalf of the Obama administration, continued to spread the same misinformation as President George W. Bush: that Hamas was the first to break the ceasefire agreement, which ended over a week ago, and Israel was simply responding judiciously.

Aside from the fact that Israel's response was anything but judicious, the idea that it was Hamas who broke the six-month truce is a complete fabrication.

On the night of the US election, Israel fired missiles on Gaza that were aimed at closing down a tunnel operation they believed Hamas was building in order to kidnap Israeli soldiers. The carnage left in the wake of Israel's bombing of Gaza over the six-week period that followed killed dozens of Palestinians.

"The escalation towards war could, and should, have been avoided. It was the State of Israel which broke the truce, in the 'ticking tunnel' raid ... two months ago," the Israeli peace group Gush Shalom wrote in a press release. "Since then, the army went on stoking the fires of escalation with calculated raids and killings, whenever the shooting of missiles on Israel decreased."

Over the last seven years only seventeen Israeli citizens have been killed by Palestinian rocket fire, which makes it extremely difficult for Israeli politicians, which are in the midst of an election, to argue that their response has been proportionate or defensible in any way.

The asymmetry of the conflict leaves an opening for harsh criticism from soon-to-be President Barack Obama. He has every right to oppose Israel's belligerence. The international community and public opinion are on his side. Certainly he knows Israel's disproportionate response has inflicted pain on Palestinians beyond what the blockade has done by keeping vital medical and other supplies from reaching Gaza, where hundreds have died as a result of inadequate medical treatment.

While bombs fall on a suffocating Palestinian population and Israeli forces prepare for a ground invasion, Obama is monitoring the situation from afar after a talk with Secretary of State Condoleezza Rice and other Bush administration officials. This isn't leadership; it's a continuation of a policy that has left Palestinians with little recourse, let alone hope for lasting peace.

"The president-elect was in Sderot last July, in southern Israel, a town that's taken the brunt of the Hamas attacks," David Axelrod told Chip Reid on *Face the Nation*. "And he said then that, when bombs are raining down on your citizens, there is an urge to respond and act and try and put an end to that. So, you know, that's what he said then, and I think that's what he believes."

From Oscar Grant to Barack Obama

By RON JACOBS

I was out in Oakland for a friend's birthday. Naturally, I visited Telegraph Ave. in Berkeley—my old stomping grounds—while I was there. Things have changed there while remaining the same. The area is certainly much more ethnically diverse. Gentrification has slithered in, but its presence is quite minimal when compared to other sections of Berkeley, Oakland or San Francisco.

Peoples Park looks better than it has in years, with native plant life dominating the east and west ends of that small piece of turf where so many battles have been fought. Doorways that used to shelter street people have been blocked off and some benches have been removed from areas where those same folks used to relax.

In short, the presence of corporate America was greater than it used to be some thirty years ago, but the character of those few blocks that was carved during the 1960s and 1970s remains as its essence despite numerous attempts by city and university officials and businessmen and women to convert the strip into just another pedestrian mall.

The politics expressed on t-shirts for sale and in posters pasted on fences and shop windows were less radical then I remember. Indeed, the overwhelming number of Obama images came as a bit of a surprise to me, especially when compared to the very small number of posters reacting to the Israeli invasion of Gaza and massacre of Palestinian children.

Yet, the most interesting juxtaposition of political imagery appeared in a shop window that featured a poster of Obama and several leaflets calling for protests against the murder of a young black man by the BART transit police.

For those of you who don't know, the facts of this case are these. Early New Year's morning an argument on a BART train erupted into a fight. Several passengers involved in the fight were removed from the train at Oakland's Fruitvale station. Several transit police took those involved off the train, cuffed some of them and forced them all to squat near a wall in the station.

One young man, named Oscar Grant, was lying face down on the station floor with his hands behind his back when a police officer took out his gun and shot him. He died several hours later.

This is my interpretation of the events derived from viewing at least two cellphone videos taken by other passengers and posted on the internet. It is an interpretation shared by thousands of other (if not millions) viewers. In fact, it is the opinion apparently held by the prosecutor involved in the case, as the officer was indicted for murder and turned himself in January 14th, 2009.

The reaction on the street to Grant's murder was definite and quick. People around the Bay Area saw the video and saw murder. Protests were organized by a variety of groups, including churches and radical political sects. The first protest on January 7th attracted a thousand or so people and ended with a small riot in downtown Oakland and the arrest of more than a hundred protesters. Most people were not just angry about the murder, but also that no charges or arrests had been made in the case even though a week had passed since the shooting.

Then there is Barack Obama. If the state of black America could be summed up with the life of one individual, which of these men would we choose to represent that state? Barack Obama or Oscar Grant, whose life was ended by a police bullet on January 1st, 2009? The very fact of Grant's death shows the world that there is no post-racial America. In fact, it reminds us all that, despite the gains in the area of race in the United States, Obama is the significant exception to the rule.

This fact is not a denial of the hopes his election has raised for African-Americans and the nation, but it is a cold reminder that making a black man president is a long way from ending the very real fact of the systemic racism that made this nation what it is. The death of Oscar Grant, like the presence of so many African-Americans in the US prison system, is an even harsher reminder of how that racism plays itself out in the daily lives of so many of its citizens.

Racism will end in this country when it no longer serves the interests of the elites that run it. The presence of a black family in the White House may be a symbolic victory for the forces opposed to racism, but the men and women chosen by Obama to help him rule represent the real nature of his presidency. Malcolm X once said that "An integrated cup of coffee isn't sufficient pay for four hundred years of slave labor."

Well, neither is a black man in the White House sufficient enough to forget the death of Oscar Grant and the many other African-Americans whose lives have been destroyed by the very system soon to be governed by President Obama.

Ron Jacobs is author of The Way the Wind Blew: A History of the Weather Underground *(Verso)*.

AIG and the System
By JEFFREY ST. CLAIR

The first clue that something was terribly amiss with the insurance giant AIG should have been made manifest when the conglomerate began offering products—and financial products at that. What exactly does an insurance company produce? The short and nasty answer is that AIG manufactured precisely what it was meant to guard against. Namely, risk. Extreme risk.

Ultimately, AIG was cashiered on several trillion dollars of risky financial products, sewn together by Ivy League math whizzes and aces in the arcane art of arbitrage. These were fanciful consolidations of debt that no sane insurer would ever have indemnified. When the company crashed in the dismal autumn of 2008, it turned sheepishly to the insurer of last resort for rescue: the US government. The disgraced executives made the case that the rot in AIG was spreading and was threatening to go systemic. Too big to fail became the mantra of the bailout. AIG, perhaps the most recklessly managed company in the world, was so thoroughly enmeshed in nearly every sector of the American—and even global—economy that to let it sunder would be to risk the crash of the nation. Or so they said.

Both the Bush and the Obama teams—themselves thoroughly marinated in the AIG mindset—quickly capitulated to financial extortion and infused the company with more than $182 billion in taxpayer cash—a sum that continues to rise each month with the inexorability of a lava dome inside an active volcano. Thus did the Obama administration in one of its first official acts endorse the remorseless logic of throwing good billions after bad.

The Treasury Department and AIG's management were so harmonious that Timothy Geithner allowed AIG's executives to continue to run the company even after the bailout. The top brass at AIG had successfully duped Geithner and his political puppet master Larry Summers into buying the far-fetched idea that the collapse of AIG had been perpetrated by a handful of rogue traders operating out of satellite offices in distant London and suburban Wilton, Connecticut.

Indeed, Geithner and Summers were so sympathetic to the plight of these corporate titans that they sanctioned more than $450 million in executive bonuses to managers at AIG, including the disgraced Financial Products Division.

Of course, AIG had, among other giants of Wall Street, insured Goldman Sachs, which had made its own dementedly bad investments in subprime loans to the tune of tens of billions of dollars. And there was no way in hell that Geithner, Summers or Hank Paulson was going to let Goldman Sachs eat those loans. And that bit of political sleight-of-hand seems to have paid off handsomely for Goldman Sachs, which just posted record quarterly profits of $700 million only a brief nine months after it seemed like the investment house was on the verge of an ignominious collapse. In other words, the $54 billion in direct payments the feds had lavished on Goldman, Merrill-Lynch and the other Wall Street firms was just the icing on a very rich cake.

In a sense, it's only fitting that the government ended up as the ultimate guarantor for those furious seasons of Wall Street greed. After all, by consciously dismantling the regulatory framework that tended to constrain the felonious instincts that come naturally to the Wall Street player (such as the Glass-Steagall Act), the government played a decisive role in fostering the rampant financial criminality and looting that reached its apogee in 2008, crashing the global economy, draining retirement funds and pension accounts and casting millions from their homes and millions more into the perdition of long-term unemployment. All of this coming down in an era of extreme government austerity, typified by over-burdened and underfunded social welfare programs. As with the defunct regulations to restrain corporate crimes, so too had the economic safety net been sheared away—its tethers sliced by Reagan, the Bushes and Clinton—long before the economy cratered. Now there is nothing to cushion the blow on the long fall to the bottom.

The architects of this economic deregulation achieved a truly fearful bipartisan symmetry that persists to this day. Even now, amid the rubble of Wall Street's collapse, the neo-liberals and neo-conservatives remain as uniform as conjoined twins in their devotion to a broadly deregulated market. Any talk of bringing back forceful correctives such as a new and improved Glass-Steagall Act was immediately squelched by Obama, flanked by John McCain and Mitch McConnell, as well. If the crash of AIG—the largest in history—was in the sclerotic parlance of the times a "teachable moment" it is apparent that while much was ventured, nothing was learned.

The problem is that the government bailout, which some accounts now estimate will eventually top $24-cap T—for Trillion—flowed almost entirely in the wrong direction. Instead of helping to mend the lives of Wall Street's victims—the unemployed, the uninsured, the destitute and homeless—Bush and Obama rewarded the perpetrators. They even gave them bonuses.

* * *

As the financial writer Michael Lewis explains in a fascinating article on the AIG FP division in *Vanity Fair,* the financial products offered by AIG were little more than complex iterations of the bizarre financial instruments designed in the 1980s by Drexel, Burnam, Lambert—the company that brought us the junk bond and other improvised explosive devices of high finance.

The young turks at AIG FP, led by Joseph Cassano, improved on the Drexel, Burnham model—or at least mutated it for their own purposes. The game was all about swallowing risk—hiding it, hedging it and repackaging it as, yes, a financial product and not a liability. In other words, something to swap, buy, sell and make money on. Lots and lots of money.

And it worked—for a while. Soon Cassano's division was piling up $300 million a year in profits and making the platoon of financial tricksters themselves hugely wealthy. Bonuses of more than $25 million a year were commonplace. The executives were making a killing in looting their own hedge funds by skimming 35 percent of the profits, a self-asserted gratuity that would shame even the most rapacious personal injury lawyer.

All through the high-flying 90s, the AIG risk-swallowing business continued to defy gravity, posting amazing profits on ever more opaque financial confabulations. Then in 2002 came the first whiff of rot. AIG insiders told Michael Lewis that the decomposition began to gnaw away at the FP Division the very moment Cassano replaced his mentor Tom Savage as CEO of the subsidiary. Of course, this retrospective was almost certainly motivated in large measure by post-fall ass-covering. But there's no question that Cassano was an abrasive personality and not, like many of the traders, an Ivy Leaguer with a DNA profile shaped by generations of old money.

Like AIG's former CEO, Hank Greenberg, who had been chased out of the company by Eliot Spitzer, Cassano was viewed by his rivals and subordinates as a reckless bully, who ruled the company through the humiliation of nearly everyone he encountered from secretaries to junior executives. Cassano's father was a police officer and the son brought the brute mentality and creepy paranoia of the street cop into the executive suites and the trading room floor. He ruled the London office by fear and did not countenance any contrarian opinions, even as the trading instruments passing before the insurers became more fantastical and the economic perils ever more extreme.

Lewis's AIG confidants blame the terminal descent of their company on Cassano's over-weening arrogance and his rather crude understanding of the very products his FP Division was manufacturing.

In other words, Cassano simply didn't have the head for the complex math at play in those deep derivatives. He didn't see the pitfalls, trapdoors and inevitable apocalypse at the end of the road. And his team of math geniuses—many with minds minted by MIT and Harvard—went along for the ride, swallowing his torrents of abuse, glossing over the hollow core of the hedge funds. Why? Because, naturally, they were making too much money to object and Cassano, despite his tyrannical fits, was dishing out eight-figure bonuses for Christmas. Indeed, many of the top AIG traders did worse than merely endure Cassano's abuse—both personal and organizational. They coddled his worst financial impulses and sucked up to him. In other words, they did their damnedest to suppress their consciousness of guilt.

In the aftermath of the wreckage, Cassano's supervisors back at AIG HQ in Manhattan have worked sedulously to create the impression that they scarcely knew the man running their hottest division. From Hank Greenberg to Edward Libby, the top brass has sought to portray Cassano and his team as an out-of-control unit that had somehow fled the reservation.

This won't wash. Not for those in the know, anyway. The man who was running AIG's darkest appendage had been installed as boss of the division by Greenberg himself, who saw in Cassano a man who shared his own despotic management style in playing billion-dollar shell games with other people's money. When Eliot Spitzer brought down Greenberg in 2005 for the executive's accounting high-jinks, some inside AIG thought that Cassano might eventually end up taking his place. Others in the company believed that he should've been slapped in leg irons. Opinions on Cassano four years ago were divided, but there was no shortage of them. Now Cassano is suddenly the man no one knew about.

According to his colleagues in London, Cassano was ascetic in his total commitment to the company he was steadily destroying. So devoted, in fact, that Cassano recycled most of his $38.5 million salary right back into AIG and its toxic products. The remainder of his AIG trove—estimated at some $238 million—he cached in that most timid of financial parking lots, the US Treasury Bill. Say this for Cassano, he was no preening financial playboy. He dressed casually, drove a modest car and lived to work—and terrorize his staff. "Without AIG FP, he had nothing," one trader told Lewis.

* * *

With Greenberg and Savage by his side, Joseph Cassano turned AIG FP into a kind of recycling station for toxic financial properties held by corporations, equity firms, banks and institutional hybrids, those freaks and sports of the post-Glass-Steagall era. Cassano opened the gates of AIG FP to them, one and all, eventually absorbing $450 billion in corporate credit-default swaps and another $75 billion in the fatal subprime mortgages. He became Wall Street's one-stop waste manager, insuring and amalgamating bad debts of every stripe, from credit cards to student loans, corporate buyouts to commercial mortgages, transmuting this junk into big new packages with a glossy veneer that masked the entropic nature of the whole enterprise.

After the attacks of 9/11 and subsequent nosedive of the global economy, AIG's business began to pick up, as troubled executives desperately scrambled for someplace to dump their risky debts. Cassano and Co. were happy to provide the landfill services, charging a very healthy tipping fee.

But gradually, almost imperceptibly, the weight of the debt-load began to shift, tilting away from traditional corporate investments and decisively toward the necrotic subprime mortgages. By 2005, AIG FP's consumer loan insurance portfolio consisted of 95 percent subprime mortgages. The seeds of destruction had been sown. When housing prices began to plummet, AIG was doomed.

But is Cassano the arch villain of this particular chapter in the annals of American capitalism or was he, in the end, Wall Street's willing dupe?

To reach a plausible assessment it's vital to remember that AIG was digesting what the big Wall Street houses fed it. Often these packages were artful mixes of consumer and corporate debt. So artful, in fact, that AIG's brain trust wasn't entirely clear what they were bonding. The risks were blended, sliced and pressurized into indecipherable collages of debt, like mutual funds from Mars. One top analyst thought that AIG's credit-default packages consisted of no more than 10 percent subprime loans. Another put the figure at 20 percent, tops. Cassano, it appears, had no clue about the real number and didn't care. In his mind, there was simply no way the housing market would go bust—not across the board, anyway. And his Wall Street clients at Goldman Sachs and Merrill-Lynch backed him up in this delusion. After all, what did they have to lose?

In 2007, Cassano, as blissfully ignorant of the peril immediately before him as Wile E. Coyote ten feet off the cliff, boasted in a talk to a seraglio of investors that it was hard for him to even imagine a scenario "that would see us losing one dollar on any of these transactions."

Less than six months later, it was all over. Cassano had been evicted from AIG (though he continued to get paid $1 million a month as a consultant without portfolio) and Goldman Sachs was knocking at the door of the company demanding that AIG compensate the investment firm for its own landslide of bad debts. AIG was in no position to pay up, naturally, but Goldman Sach's man at Treasury, its former CEO Hank Paulson, did—dollar for dollar.

In for a dollar, in for a trillion.

It has been said by Wall Street apologists that the crash of AIG was an aberration, a singularity of greed run amok. No one could have predicted the fall, they say. Wall Street analysts were beguiled by the blizzard of prospectuses and portfolios on AIG operations that were, they claimed, as immune from explication as the most arcane passages in *Finnegans Wake*. So too with the business press, which was apparently so mesmerized by these chimerical reports that they completely missed the financial fun-and-games transpiring inside AIG FP.

The regulators at the SEC have also connived to claim ignorance about the true condition of AIG and its more malign operations as it veered toward the cliff of no return, fooled, they claimed, by the company's diction of deceit. Somehow missing the daily bulletins of impending ruin, the regulators have tried to offload all the blame on Cassano and his traders for perverting the system.

This is all nonsense. AIG operated at the very heart of the system, a system enabled by the SEC and its political overlords. Indeed, AIG served as the system's great backstop, its failsafe. What happens when the failsafe fails?

So now the bills from this tableau of financial debauchery have come due. That $182 billion payout wasn't a final call, but merely an opening bid. Tens of trillions may yet follow.

No, AIG didn't pervert the system. It was a creature of a perverse system. One that it is literally consuming itself from the inside out. A mighty leveling looms.

Orwell in Baghdad
By CHRIS FLOYD

It would be superfluous of us to point out that a plan to "end" a war which includes the continued garrisoning of up to 50,000 troops in a hostile land is, in reality, a continuation of that war, not its cessation. To produce such a plan and claim that it "ends" a war is the precise equivalent of, say, relieving one's bladder on the back of one's neighbor and telling him that the liquid is actually life-giving rain.

But this is exactly what we are getting from the Obama Administration on Iraq. Word has now come from on high—that is, from "senior administration officials" using "respectable newspapers" as a wholly uncritical conduit for government spin—that President Obama has reached a grand compromise with his generals (or rather, the generals and Pentagon poobahs he has inherited—and eagerly retained—from George W. Bush) on a plan to withdraw some American troops from the country that the United States destroyed in an unprovoked war of aggression. Obama had wanted a sixteen-month timetable for the partial withdrawal; his potential campaign rival in 2012, General David Petraeus, wanted twenty three months; so, with Solomonic wisdom, they have now split the difference, and will withdraw a portion of the American troops in nineteen months instead.

But the plan clearly envisions a substantial and essentially permanent American military presence in Iraq, dominating the politics and policy of this key oil nation—which was of course one of the chief war aims of the military aggressors in the Bush Administration all along. By implementing his war continuation plan, Obama will complete the work of Bush and his militarist clique. From the *New York Times:*

> Even with the withdrawal order, Mr. Obama plans to leave behind a "residual force" of tens of thousands of troops to continue training Iraqi security forces, hunt down foreign terrorist cells and guard American institutions.

And a "senior military officer" dispatched to pipe the spin to the *Los Angeles Times* added another potential role for the remaining American troops: fighting Iraq's war for it. He was also refreshingly frank on the plan's ultimate intentions:

> "The senior officer said the troops also could help protect Iraq from outside attack, something the Iraqis cannot yet do.... When President Obama said we were going to get out within 16 months, some people heard, 'get out,' and everyone's gone. But that is not going to happen," the officer said.

No indeed, that is "not going to happen." One of the most remarkable aspects of Obama's "war lite" plan is its brazen and absolute disregard for the agreement signed between the US and the supposedly sovereign Iraqi government guaranteeing the complete withdrawal of all American troops by the end of 2011. Of course, this "agreement" was always considered a farce by everyone—except for the American corporate media, which kept reporting on the "tough negotiations" as if the pact would have any actual meaning in the real world. The agreement contained escape clauses allowing the Iraqi government to "request" a continued American military presence after the 2011 deadline—and considering that any Iraqi government in place in 2011 will be helplessly dependent on American guns and money to maintain its power, such a "request" has always been a dead certainty. So I suppose we must admire the Obama Administration's candor in dropping all pretense that US forces are going to leave Iraq at any time in the foreseeable future.

But the hypocrisy—the literally murderous hypocrisy—of claiming that this plan "leaves Iraq to its people and responsibly ends this war," as Obama asserted in his State of the Union speech, is sickening. It does no such thing, and he knows it.

Instead, it entrenches the United States more and more deeply in a "counter-insurgency" war on behalf of whichever clique or faction of sectarian parties in Iraq is most effective in adhering to America's dominationist agenda in the region. It sends an apparently endless stream of American troops to die—and, in even greater numbers, to kill—in a criminal action that has helped bankrupt our own country while sending waves of violent instability and extremism around the world. It will further enfilth a cesspool of corruption and war profiteering that has already reached staggering, world-historical proportions.

All of this is what the Obama-Petraeus plan will do. But what it won't do is "end this war"—"responsibly" or otherwise. When Obama says it will—as he said last night to a rapt national audience—he is, quite simply, and very deliberately, lying.

Chris Floyd is an American writer and frequent contributor to CounterPunch. *His blog, Empire Burlesque: High Crimes and Low Comedy in the American Imperium, can be found at www.chris-floyd.com.*

A Redneck View of Obamarama
By JOE BAGEANT

When it comes to expressing plain truths, few are as gifted as American rednecks. During recent travels in the Appalachian communities of West Virginia, Tennessee and Kentucky I've collected scores of their comments on our national condition and especially President Barack Obama.

In America, all successful politicians are first and foremost successfully marketed brands. In fact, the Obama campaign was named Advertising Age's 2008 marketer of the year. George W. Bush's brand may have "collapsed," as they say on Madison Avenue, but things don't change much. Rednecks instinctively know this:

> It don't matter who gets to warm his butt in the White House chair," says a West Virginia trucker. "The top dogs eat high on the hog and the little dogs eat the tails and ears. That's what them bailouts is all about, and that's the way it is no matter who's president. So you might as well vote for the guy who looks like the most fun because you gonna be watching his ass on television for the next eight years.

Yup. Rednecks do have a way of getting right down to the bone of the matter. For example, the news shows us Obama in an auto plant. We see Obama talking to the troops in Iraq. Obama ladling out grubs in a soup kitchen. That's the stuff of urban liberal wet dreams. But a fellow over in the mountains of Mineral County West Virginia, a guy named Pinch who sells fence posts, poles and firewood out of his back yard, puts it like this:

> Nothing against Obama, mind you, but the last time I looked, the car plants was dead meat. Obama has never even come close to serving in the military, except for serving up that batch of hash in Baghdad. And there he was with his wife in a soup kitchen for god sake! Things has got so bad that we've got soup kitchens all over this country now. So, two millionaires in their armored limo drop by a soup kitchen, and this is supposed to make me feel good about my country?

To be sure, the Obama brand is a feel good brand. Like those Hallmark talking digital greeting cards we geezers send one another that say "You're still sexy baby!" Or "How's it hanging stud?" we know of course, the only things hanging are our beer bellies and the fat on our upper arms. But it makes us feel good anyway. For about ten seconds.

What makes us feel good in the long term is getting back to the true meaning of being an American—buying stuff and racking up debt. Still, who'd have ever thought we'd see the president of the US on television telling us, "There's never been a better time to refinance our homes," or buy a car?—which is exactly what he did last month.

Hawking home refis seems a bit unpresidential, to some of us. But then too, this is America, where, by orders of President Bush, we struck back hard at the 9/11 terrorists by going shopping. In any case, a local mortgage lender here in Winchester, Virginia is running ads with pictures of Obama and quoting him on the virtue of debt. That lender is one cast iron Obama hating Republican. So maybe Obama is truly a uniter after all.

As to America's working class debt serfdom, some of us were resigned to that a long time ago. My former neighbor, Fat Larry (whose real name is Myron, and is thus happy enough to be called Fat Larry) says: "Hey, look, I don't care if Obama is putting us in debt. I was already in hock for the rest of my life before they started hollering about a 'debt crisis.'" Nor is he opposed to accepting a handout: "Obama can let a smidgen of them trillions land in my poke anytime. Right now I got no problems fifty thousand bucks wouldn't fix."

Not to worry Larry! According to our media, the cavalry is on the way to our rescue. Arrival time is estimated to be in two years. That's when employment is supposed to start coming back, after another year or so of continued job losses.

Meanwhile, Obama is humping the pump in an effort to re-inflate an economy that looks more every day like a balloon with a 55 caliber bullet hole in it. He's even tried to get some of the escaped air back into the balloon by making corporations return a few billion dollars of the trillions in bailout money that disappeared the minute it crossed their paws. "Seems to me," says Fat Larry, "he should'a give the money back to me. It was mine to start with."

Personally, I really cannot bitch too much about Obama's giveaways. At the end of this month he's sending me a $250 check—stimulus money being handed out to us retirees—which is about the only good thing I have encountered so far about getting old.

Indeed, it's cause for celebration. So I'm gonna call ole Larry and we're going out to get so damned stimulated we can't walk home.

Postscript: Aw hell! The front page of today's newspaper tells me the $250 stimulus payment is only a loan from the government, and that I will have to pay it back next April. In this new America, we are all issued debt, whether we ask for it or not *(sigh)*.

Joe Bageant was a frequent contributor to CounterPunch. *His books include* Dear Hunting with Jesus *and* Rainbow Pie: A Redneck Memoir. *He died in 2011.*

Obama and Abortion Rights

By SHARON SMITH

As soon as the news surfaced that President Barack Obama had been invited to speak at the University of Notre Dame's 2009 commencement ceremony, the fanatical wing of the nation's anti-abortion crusade began assembling the smoke and mirrors needed to masquerade as a mass movement. Media savvy crackpot Randall Terry, who boasts a long record of confrontation with the enemies of the Christian Right, immediately took the lead. With great fanfare, he announced his plan to "make a circus" out of the pro-choice Obama's speech—the kind of grandiose threat guaranteeing a prominent spot on the evening news.

Terry is perhaps best known for his role as a media representative for the parents of Terri Schiavo and a key proponent of "Terri's Law" in Florida, a bill passed in 2003 that temporarily blocked the removal of their daughter's feeding tube as she lay in a prolonged vegetative state. At the time, Terry organized angry protests outside husband Michael Schiavo's home because he wished to have the feeding tube removed. The media lapped it up.

But Terry's pet cause is opposing abortion. He founded Operation Rescue in 1987, which specialized in whipping anti-abortion fanatics into a collective frenzy as they blockaded abortion clinics across the country during the following decade. As *Washington Post* staff writer Michael Powell wrote in 2004, "Subtlety wasn't Terry's thing—he described Planned Parenthood's founder, Margaret Sanger, as a 'whore' and an 'adulteress' and arranged to have a dead fetus presented to Bill Clinton at the 1992 Democratic National Convention."

In the weeks before Obama's May 17th speech, Terry et al worked hard to create the illusion that they represented a groundswell of outrage at Notre Dame's betrayal. Money was apparently no object, since Terry spent $50,000 saturating the campus with photos of bloody "aborted fetuses"—which, as usual, looked suspiciously like newborn babies covered in ketchup. These doctored photos appeared and reappeared on placards, on the sides of semi-trailers that circled the university, and even on so-called "Truth Banners" streaming from low flying "Abortion Planes" above Notre Dame.

Anti-abortion activists pushed strollers with plastic baby dolls covered in red paint through neighborhoods as horrified residents tried to calm their frightened toddlers. On May 1st, Terry and a small group of these stroller pushers achieved their first well-publicized arrest on Notre Dame's campus. Many more arrests would follow in the coming weeks.

As graduation day approached, rumors circulated that up to 20,000 protesters would descend on campus for commencement weekend. A student organization calling itself Notre Dame Response was formed, claiming it was a coalition of campus groups planning to protest Obama's speech. When the day arrived, however, the anti-abortion masses never appeared. Only twenty six seniors and their families—out of a graduating class of 2,900—skipped commencement to protest Obama' presence. And twenty three student groups actually endorsed Obama's invitation to speak. No students were counted among the dozens arrested over the weekend (many of them repeat offenders), while a mere 150 off-campus protesters demonstrated against Obama's speech.

* * *

Yet curiously, no pro-choice demonstration took place at Notre Dame that weekend to combat all the anti-abortion hype. A handful of students did line up holding "Pro-Obama" signs, but "choice" never made its way into the campus discourse. It seems that the established pro-choice organizations preferred to let Obama represent their side of the debate.

He did not. On the contrary, his speech called for those on opposing sides of the abortion debate to find "common ground … to work together to reduce the number of women seeking abortions by reducing unintended pregnancies, and making adoption more available, and providing care and support for women who do carry their child to term." Obama's speech never articulated his own support for women who choose abortion to end an un-wanted pregnancy. His speech was so conciliatory to abortion opponents that even the Pope expressed delight. The Vatican newspaper *L'Osservatore Romano* praised Obama's speech and noted that Obama had stated at a recent press conference that passing a Freedom of Choice Act, which would protect women's right to choose, was not high on his list of priorities.

As such, Randall Terry was able to transform Notre Dame into ground zero for the most maniacal wing of the anti-choice movement without ever being forced to debate a coherent defense of the right to choose.

Shortly before Notre Dame's commencement, a new Gallup poll was released claiming that for the "first time a majority of U.S. adults have identi-fied themselves as pro-life since Gallup began asking this question in 1995." The poll found 51 percent describing themselves as "pro-life," up 7 points from a year ago. To be sure, the same poll showed that 53 percent of re-spondents also believe that abortion should be legal in certain circumstances. But this severe erosion of support for choice—which stood at 75 percent in 1973—should be a wake-up call for abortion rights advocates.

Obama appears intent on replaying the Clinton-era scenario, in which the pro-choice presidential candidate promises supporters that he will pass the Freedom of Choice Act while on the campaign trail. Once elected, his enthusiasm vanishes and, when pro-choice supporters do not protest this be-trayal, the legislation never materializes. Indeed, the pro-choice movement's silence during Clinton's two terms allowed the passage of a wide array of an-ti-abortion restrictions in states around the country—including mandatory parental consent and notification laws for minors, twenty-four-hour waiting periods and anti-abortion "counseling"—allowing abortion rights to recede under the watch of a pro-choice president.

Entrusting politicians to defend legal abortion has proven a disaster for the pro-choice movement. The movement embarked on this calamitous strategy in the late-1980s, when the leaders of the largest pro-choice organizations, including the National Abortion Rights Action League (now called NARAL Pro-Choice America) decided to adapt their argument for choice to one more acceptable to rightward moving Democrats. NARAL issued a "talking points" memo to its affiliates in 1989, instructing staffers not to use phrases such as "a woman's body is her own to control" and to reshape the right to choose as a "privacy" issue.

In so doing, the politically passive pro-choice movement allowed the more aggressive anti-abortion crusade to successfully hijack the very definition of "life" in the abortion debate. Removing women's rights from the debate allowed the rights of embryos to supersede those of living, breathing women desperate to end an unintended pregnancy.

Since Clinton's election in 1992, the anti-abortion crusade has remained defiant while the pro-choice movement has been in steady retreat. This is the only way to understand how a small but dedicated army of religious zealots has managed to successfully transform the political terrain in its favor—and why a figure as ridiculous as Randall Terry is now regarded as legitimate within the political mainstream.

* * *

Those who specialize in doctoring photos of babies care little about saving women's lives. But large numbers of women die when abortion is illegal, because they are forced to undergo unsafe procedures performed in unsanitary conditions. If they develop an infection, they are often reluctant to go to the hospital for fear of arrest. In 2003, the World Health Organization estimated that 78,000 women around the world die from unsafe abortions every year. The death toll during the century when abortion was illegal in the US is unknown, but the number is certainly large — and some estimates are as high as 10,000 each year. A University of Colorado study done in the late 1950s reported that 350,000 women experienced postoperative complications each year from illegal abortions in the US

One in every three US women—including one in every three practicing Catholics—has an abortion in her lifetime. Indeed, the abortion rate has been rising as the economy worsens in the current recession, while the National Network of Abortion Funds told the *New York Times* that calls to its hotline requesting financial help are almost four times higher than a year ago. The majority of women who undergo abortions are young and low-income. So legal abortion is not a marginal issue but an urgent need for millions of women.

Women bear the ultimate responsibility for carrying an unwanted pregnancy to term—often as single parents, earning wages that are much lower
than men's. It is not a coincidence that female-headed households are the
most likely families to be living in poverty in the US today. For all these
reasons, the decision whether to terminate a pregnancy should belong to the
pregnant woman alone.

The Supreme Court's *Roe v. Wade* decision that made abortion legal in
1973 was the greatest victory of the women's liberation movement—and it
was the product of struggle. If support for abortion has declined in recent
years, it is not because the right to choose is any less necessary. On the contrary, there is an urgent need to build a new pro-choice movement that rein-
serts women into the abortion debate and wages an uncompromising fight
for abortion without apology.

Sharon Smith is the author of Women and Socialism *and* Subterranean
Fire: A History of Working-Class Radicalism in the United States.

From State Secrets to War to Wiretaps

By SIBEL EDMONDS

"In politics we presume that everyone who knows
how to get votes knows how to administer a city
or a state. When we are ill … we do not ask for the
handsomest physician, or the most eloquent one."

—Plato

During the campaign, amid their state of elation, many disregarded presidential candidate Senator Barack Obama's past record and took any criticism of these past actions as partisan attacks deserving equally partisan counterattacks. Some continued their reluctant support after candidate Obama became grand finalist and prayed for the best. And a few still continue their rationalizing and defense, with illogical excuses such as "He's been in office for only twenty days, give the man a break!" and "He's had only fifty days in office, give him a chance!" and currently, "be reasonable—how much can a man do in 120 days?!" I am going to give this logic, or lack of, a slight spicing of reason, then, turn it around, and present it as: If "the man" can do this much astounding damage, whether to our civil liberties, or to our notion of democracy, or to government integrity, in "only" 120 days, may God help us with the next [(4 X 365)—120] days.

I know there are those who have been tackling President Obama's changes on change; they have been challenging his flipping, or rather flopping, on issues central to getting him elected. While some have been covering the changes comprehensively, others have been running right and left like headless chickens in the field—pick one hypocrisy, scream a bit, then move on to the next outrageous flop, the same, and then to the next, basically, looking and treating this entire mosaic one piece at a time.

Despite all the promises Mr. Obama made during his campaign, especially on those issues that were absolutely central to those whose support he garnered, so far the President of Change has followed in the footsteps of his predecessor. Not only that, his administration has made it clear that they intend to continue this trend. Some call it a major betrayal. Can we go so far as to call it a "swindling of the voters"?

On the State Secrets Privilege

Yes, I am going to begin with the issue of State Secrets Privilege; because I was the first recipient of this "privilege" during the now gone Administration; because long before it became "a popular" topic among the "progressive experts," during the time when these same experts avoided writing or speaking about it; when many constitutional attorneys had no idea we even had this "law"—similar to and based on the British Official Secret Act; when many journalists did not dare to question this draconian abuse of Executive Power; I was out there, writing, speaking, making the rounds in Congress, and fighting this "privilege" in the courts. And because in 2004 I stood up in front of the Federal Court building in DC, turned to less than a handful of reporters, and said, "This, my case, is setting a precedent, and you are letting this happen by your fear-induced censorship. Now that they have gotten away with this, now that you have let them get away, we'll be seeing this 'privilege' invoked in case after case involving government criminal deeds in need of cover up." Unfortunately I was proven right.

So far the Obama administration has invoked the state secrets privilege in three cases in the first 100 days: *Al Haramain Islamic Foundation v. Obama, Mohammed v. Jeppesen Dataplan*, and *Jewel v. NSA*.

In defending the NSA illegal wiretapping, the Obama administration maintained that the State Secrets Privilege, the same draconian executive privilege used and abused voraciously by the previous administration, required the dismissal of the case in courts.

Not only has the new administration continued the practice of invoking SSP to shield government wrongdoing, it has expanded its abuses much further. In the Al Haramain case, Obama's Justice Department has threatened to have the FBI or federal marshals break into a judge's office and remove evidence already turned over in the case, according to the plaintiff's attorney. Even Bush didn't go this far so brazenly. In a well-written disgust-provoking piece Jon Eisenberg, one of the plaintiffs' attorneys, poses the question: "The president's lawyers continue to block access to information that could expose warrantless wiretapping. Is this change we can believe in?"

This is the same President, the same well-spoken showman, who went on record in 2007, during the campaign shenanigans, and said the following:

> When I am president we won't work in secret to avoid honoring our laws and Constitution.

Yes, this is the same President who had frowned upon and criticized the abuses and misuse of the State Secrets Privilege.

On NSA Warrantless Wiretapping

The new Administration has pledged to defend the Telecommunications Industry by giving them immunity against any lawsuit that may involve their participation in the illegal NSA wiretapping program. In 2007, Obama's office released the following position of then Senator Obama: "Senator Obama unequivocally opposes giving retroactive immunity to telecommunications companies … Senator Obama will not be among those voting to end the fili-buster." But then Senator Obama made his 180 degree flip, and voted to end the filibuster. After that, along with other colleagues in Congress, he tried to placate the critics of his move by falsely assuring them that the immunity did not extend to the Bush Administration—the Executive Branch who did break the law. Another flip was yet to come, awaiting his presidency, when Obama's Justice Department defended its predecessor not only by using the State Secrets Privilege, but taking it even further, by astoundingly grant-ing the Executive Branch an unlimited immunity for any kind of "illegal" government surveillance.

Let me emphasize, the Obama Administration's action in this regard was not about "being trapped" in situations created and put in place by the previous administration. These were willful acts fully reviewed, decided upon, and then implemented by the new president and his Justice Department.

Accountability on Torture

President Obama's action and inaction on Torture can be summarized very clearly as follows: First give an absolute pass, under the guise of "looking forward not backward," to the ultimate culprits who had ordered it. Next, absolve all the implementers, practitioners and related agencies, under the excuse of "complying with orders without questioning," and then start giv-ing the drafters of the memos an out by transferring the decision for action to the states.

After granting the "untouchable" status to all involved in this shame-ful chapter in our nation's dangerous downward slide, he now refuses to release the photos, the incriminating evidence, and is doing so by using the exact same justification used repeatedly by his predecessors: "Their release would endanger the troops," as in "the revelation on NSA would endanger our national security" and "stronger whistleblower laws would endanger our intelligence agencies" and so on and so forth.

Not only that, he goes even further to shove his secrecy promotion down other nations' courts throat. In the case of Binyam Mohamed, an Ethiopian citizen and a legal resident in Britain who was held and tortured in Guantanamo from 2004 to 2009, and filed lawsuits in the British courts to have the evidence of his torture released, Mr. Obama's position has been to threaten the British Government in order to conceal all facts and related evidence. This case involves the brutal torture and so very "extraordinary" rendition practices of the previous administration, the same practices that "in words" were strongly condemned by the President during his candidacy.

Now he and his administration unapologetically maintain the same Bush Administration position on extraordinary rendition, torture, and related secrecy to cover up. Here is Ben Wizner's—the attorney who argued the case for the ACLU—response "We are shocked and deeply disappointed that the Justice Department has chosen to continue the Bush administration's practice of dodging judicial scrutiny of extraordinary rendition and torture. This was an opportunity for the new administration to act on its condemnation of torture and rendition, but instead it has chosen to stay the course." Yes indeed, President Obama has chosen to protect and support the course involving torture, rendition and the abuse of secrecy to cover them all up.

The Revival of Bush Era Military Commission

After all the talk and pretty speeches given during his presidential campaign on the "failure" of Bush era military tribunals of Guantanamo inmates, Mr. Obama has decided to revive the same style military commission, albeit with a little cosmetic tweak here and there to re-brand it as his own. Many former supporters of Mr. Obama, who've been vocal and active on Human Rights fronts, have expressed their "total shock" by this move and its pretense of being different and improved, "As a constitutional lawyer, Obama must know that he can put lipstick on this pig—but it will always be a pig," said Zachary Katznelson, legal director of Reprieve.

Thankfully the "on the record" statements of Candidate Obama in 2008 on this issue, contradicting his action today, are accessible to all:

> It's time to better protect the American people and our values by bringing swift and sure justice to terrorists through our courts and our Uniform Code of Military Justice.

> Suspect terrorists (emphasis on "suspect") cannot have just trials consistent/in line with our "courts and Uniform Code of Military Justice" via military commissions. It's an oxymoron! And if you add to that the other Obama-approved ingredients such as secrecy, rendition, and evidence obtained under torture, what have we got? Anything resembling our courts and Uniform Code of Military Justice system?

On War and Bodies Piling Up

Here is the first paragraph in a *New York Times* report on May 15, 2009:

> The number of civilians killed by the American air strikes in Farah Province last week may never be fully known. But villagers, including two girls recovering from burn wounds, described devastation that officials and human rights workers are calling the worst episode of civilian casualties in eight years of war in Afghanistan.

> The report also includes the disagreement over the exact number of civilian casualties in Afghanistan by our military airstrike:

Government officials have accepted handwritten lists compiled by the villagers of 147 dead civilians. An independent Afghan human rights group said it had accounts from interviews of 117 dead. American officials say that even 100 is an exaggeration but have yet to issue their own count.

Does it really matter—the difference between 147 and 117 or just 100 when it comes to children, grandmothers ... innocent lives lost in a war with no well-defined objectives or plans? If for some it indeed does matter, then here is a more specific and detailed report:

A copy of the government's list of the names, ages and father's names of each of the 140 dead was obtained by Reuters earlier this week. It shows that 93 of those killed were children—the youngest eight days old—and only 22 were adult males.

Maybe releasing the photographs of the nameless victims of these airstrikes should be as important as those of torture. Because, from what I see, they and their loss of lives have been reduced to some petty number to fight about.

When I was around twelve years old, in Iran, during the Iran-Iraq war, my father, a surgeon in charge of a hospital specializing in burns and reconstructive surgery, decided to take me to the hospital to teach me an unforgettable lesson on war. I think one of the factors that prompted him was my new obsession with classic war movies; you know, ones like *The Great Escape*. Anyhow, he took my hand and we entered a transition ICU Unit. In that room, on a standard size hospital bunk bed, laid an infant of eight or nine months of age, or what was remaining of her. Over 80 percent of her body was burned; to a degree that the skin had melted and absorbed the melting clothing on top—impossible to remove without removing the skin with it. Instead of a nose two holes were drilled in the middle of her face with tubes inserted allowing breathing, the upper eyelids were melted and glued to the lower ones, and ... I am not going to go further, I believe you get the picture.

This baby was the victim of an air strike, a bombing that killed her entire family and leveled her modest home to the ground. My father pointed at this heartbreaking baby and said, "Sibel, this is war. This is the real face of war. This is the result of war. Do you think anything can justify this? I want to replace the glamorous exciting phony images of those war movies in your head. I want you to remember this for the rest of your life and stand against this kind of destruction."

And I do. This is why I am offended by those petty numbers when it comes to civilian deaths. This is the reason I believe some may need pictures of these atrocities as much as those of torture to replace those "Shock & Awe" images fed to them by our MSM.

All this death and destruction is carried out while the administration's Afghan policy is still murky and confused, and its strategy ambiguous. Sure, our so-called new Afghan strategy includes more troops and asks for a much larger budget allocation; nothing new there. It is another war with no time table. It is the continuation of the same abstract War on Terror without any definition of what would constitute an accomplished mission. One minute there is pondering on possible reconciliation with the Taliban, and the next minute seeking to topple it. In fact, to confuse the matter even further, we now hear this distinction between "Good Taliban, Bad Taliban, and the Plain Ugly Taliban." As stated by Karzai on *Meet the Press* on May 10, 2009, apparently not all Taliban are equal!

I can go on listing cases of Mr. Obama's change on change. Whether it is his reversal on protection for whistleblowers, despite his campaign promise to the contrary, or his expansion of the Un-American title of "czardom," where we now have more czars than ever: border czar, energy czar, cyber security czar … car czar … maybe even a bicycle czar! But for now I'll stick with the major promises that were central to him getting elected, all of which he has flipped on in less than 150 days in office, a track record indeed.

What I want the readers to do is to read the extremely important cases above, step back in time to those un-ending campaign trail days, and answer the following questions:

How would Senator McCain have acted on these same issues if he had been elected? How would Senator Hillary Clinton? Do you believe there would have been any major differences? Weren't their records almost identical to Senator Obama's on these issues? If you are like me, and answer same, same, no, and yes, then, why do you think we ended up with these exact same candidates, those deemed viable and sold to us as such?

With too much at stake, too many unfinished agendas for the course of our nation, and too many skeletons in the closet in need of hiding for self-preservation, the permanent establishment made certain that they took no risk by giving the public, via their MSM tentacles, a coin that no matter how many times flipped would come up the same—heads, heads.

Sibel Edmonds is the founder and director of National Security Whistleblowers Coalition (NSWBC). Ms. Edmonds worked as a language specialist for the FBI. During her work with the bureau, she discovered and reported serious acts of security breaches, cover-ups, and intentional blocking of intelligence that had national security implications. After she reported these acts to FBI management, she was retaliated against by the FBI and ultimately fired in March 2002. Since that time, court proceedings on her case have been blocked by the assertion of "State Secret Privilege"; the Congress of the United States has been gagged and prevented from any discussion of her case through retroactive re-classification by the Department of Justice. Ms. Edmonds is fluent in Turkish, Farsi and Azerbaijani; and has a MA in Public Policy and International Commerce from George Mason University, and a BA in Criminal Justice and Psychology from George Washington University. PEN American Center awarded Ms. Edmonds the 2006 PEN/Newman's Own First Amendment Award.

Obama and the Man in the Hat

By JEFFREY ST. CLAIR

Although America's greatest Interior Secretary, Harold Ickes, who had the post for nearly a decade under FDR, was from Chicago, the playbook for presidential transitions calls for picking a Westerner for Interior, as long as the nominee isn't a Californian. Pick someone from Arizona or New Mexico or Colorado. Of course, Colorado has produced two of the worst recent Interior Secretaries: James Watt and Gale Norton. Ken Salazar may make it three.

And why not? After all, Salazar was one of the first to endorse Gale Norton's nomination as Bush's Interior Secretary.

By almost any standard, it's hard to imagine a more uninspired or uninspiring choice for the job than professional middle-of-the-roader Ken Salazar, the conservative Democrat from Colorado. This pal of Alberto Gonzalez is a meek politician, who has never demonstrated the stomach for confronting the corporate bullies of the West: the mining, timber and oil companies who have been feasting on Interior Department handouts for the past eight years. Even as attorney general of Colorado, Salazar built a record of timidity when it came to going after renegade mining companies.

The editorial pages of Western papers largely hailed Salazar's nomination. The common theme portrayed Salazar as "an honest broker." But broker of what? Mining claims and oil leases, most likely.

Less defensible were the dial-o-matic press releases faxed out by the mainstream groups, greenwashing Salazar's dismal record. Here's Carl Pope, CEO of the Sierra Club, who fine-tuned this kind of rhetorical airbrushing during the many traumas of the Clinton years:

> The Sierra Club is very pleased with the nomination of Ken Salazar to head the Interior Department. As a Westerner and a rancher, he understands the value of our public lands, parks, and wildlife and has been a vocal critic of the Bush Administration's reckless efforts to sell-off our public lands to Big Oil and other special interests. Senator Salazar has been a leader in protecting places like the Roan Plateau and he has stood up against the Bush administration's dangerous rush to develop oil shale in Colorado and across the West.
>
> Senator Salazar has also been a leading voice in calling for the development of the West's vast solar, wind, and geothermal resources. He will make sure that we create the good-paying green jobs that will fuel our economic recovery without harming the public lands he will be charged with protecting.

Who knew that strip-mining for coal, an industry Salazar resolutely promoted, was a green job? Hold on tight, here we go once more down the rabbit hole.

The Sierra Club had thrown its organizational heft behind Mike Thompson, the hook-and-rifle Democratic congressman from northern California. Obama stiffed them and got away with it without enduring even a whimper of disappointment.

In the exhaust-stream, not far beyond Pope, came an organization (you can't call them a group, since they don't really have any members) called the Campaign for American Wilderness, lavishly endowed by the centrist Pew Charitable Trusts, to fete Salazar. According to Mike Matz, the Campaign's executive director, Salazar "has been a strong proponent of protecting federal lands as wilderness.... As a farmer, a rancher, and a conservationist, Sen. Salazar understands the importance of balancing traditional uses of our public lands with the need to protect them. His knowledge of land management issues in the West, coupled with his ability to work with diverse groups and coalitions to find common ground, will serve him well at the Department of the Interior."

Whenever seasoned greens see the word "common ground" invoked as a solution for thorny land use issues in the Interior West it sets off an early warning alarm. "Common ground" is another flex-phrase like, "win-win" solution that indicates greens will be handed a few low-calorie crumbs while business will proceed to gorge as usual.

In Salazar's case, these morsels have been a few measly wilderness areas inside non-contentious areas, such as Rocky Mountain National Park. Designating a wilderness inside a National Park is about as risky as placing the National Mall off-limits to oil drilling.

But Salazar's green gifts haven't come without a cost. In the calculus of common ground politics, trade-offs come with the territory. For example, Salazar, under intense pressure from Coloradoans, issued a tepid remonstrance against the Bush administration's maniacal plan to open up the Roan Plateau in western Colorado to oil drilling. But he voted to authorize oil drilling off the coast of Florida, voted against increased fuel-efficiency standards for cars and trucks and voted against the repeal of tax breaks for Exxon-Mobil when the company was shattering records for quarterly profits.

On the very day that Salazar's nomination was leaked to the press, the Inspector General for the Interior Department released a devastating report on the demolition of the Endangered Species Act under the Bush administration, largely at the hands of the disgraced Julie MacDonald, former Deputy Secretary of Interior for Fish and Wildlife. The IG report, written by Earl Devaney, detailed how MacDonald personally interfered with thirteen different endangered species rulings, bullying agency scientists and rewriting biological opinions. "MacDonald injected herself personally and profoundly in a number of ESA decisions," Devaney wrote in a letter to Oregon Senator Ron Wyden. "We determined that MacDonald's management style was abrupt and abrasive, if not abusive, and that her conduct demoralized and frustrated her staff as well as her subordinate managers."

What McDonald did covertly Salazar attempted openly in the name of, yes, common ground. Take the case of the white-tailed prairie dog, one of the declining species that MacDonald went to nefarious lengths to keep from enjoying the protections of the Endangered Species Act. Prairie dogs are viewed as pests by ranchers and their populations have been remorselessly targeted for elimination on rangelands across the Interior West.

Ken Salazar, former rancher, once threatened to sue the Fish and Wildlife Service to keep the similarly imperiled black-tailed prairie dog off the endangered species list. As a US senator, Salazar also fiercely opposed efforts to inscribe stronger protections for endangered species in the 2008 Farm Bill.

"The Department of the Interior desperately needs a strong, forward looking, reform-minded Secretary," says Kieran Suckling, executive director of the Tucson-based Center for Biological Diversity. "Unfortunately, Ken Salazar is not that man. He endorsed George Bush's selection of Gale Norton as Secretary of Interior, the very woman who initiated and encouraged the scandals that have rocked the Department of the Interior. Virtually all of the misdeeds described in the Inspector General's expose occurred during the tenure of the person Ken Salazar advocated for the position he is now seeking." As a leading indicator of just how bad Salazar may turn out to be, an environmentalist need only bushwhack through the few remaining daily papers to the stock market pages, where energy speculators, cheered at the Salazar pick, drove up the share price of coal companies, such as Peabody, Massey Energy and Arch Coal. The battered S&P Coal index rose by 3 percent on the day Obama introduced the coal-friendly Salazar as his choice to head Interior.

Say this much for Salazar: he's not a Clinton retread. In fact, he makes Clinton Interior Secretary Bruce Babbitt look like Ed Abbey.

As Hot Rod Blagojevich demonstrated in his earthy vernacular, politics is a pay-to-play sport. Like Ken Salazar, Barack Obama's political underwriters included oil-and-gas companies, utilities, financial houses, agribusiness giants such as Archer Daniels Midland, and coal companies. These bundled campaign contributions dwarfed the money given to Obama by environmentalists, many of whom backed Hillary in the Democratic Party primaries.

Environmentalists made no demands of Obama during the election and sat silently as he promoted off-shore oil drilling, pledged to build new nuclear plants and sang the virtues of the oxymoron known as clean-coal technology. Obama probably felt he owed them no favors. And he gave them none. The environmental establishment cheered never-the-less.

* * *

Of all of Barack Obama's airy platitudes about change, none were more va-
porous than his platitudes about the environment and within that category
Obama has had little at all to say about matters concerning public lands and
endangered species.

As Interior Secretary, Ken Salazar wasted no time in turning the department into a hive of his homeboys. This group of lawyers and former colleagues
earned the nickname the Colorado Mafia, Version Three. It's Version Three
because Colorado Mafia Version One belonged to James Watt (a Colorado
transplant) and his Loot-the-West zealots from the Mountain States Legal
Fund. The Version Two update came in the form of Gale Norton and her
own band of fanatics, some of whom remain embedded in the Department's
headquarters, just down the hall from Salazar's office.

Beyond a perverse obsession with Stetson hats, Salazar and Watt share
some eerie resemblances. For starters, they look alike. There's a certain fleshy
smugness to their facial features. Who knows if Salazar shares Watt's apoca-
lyptic eschatology (Why save nature, Watt once quipped, when the end of
the world is nigh.), but both men are arrogant, my-way-or-the-highway
types. Watt's insolent demeanor put him to the right even of his patron Ronald Reagan and ultimately proved his downfall. (Salazar may well meet the
same fate.) Most troubling, however, is the fact that both Watt and Salazar
hold similar views on the purpose of the public estate, treating the national
forests and Bureau of Land Management lands not as ecosystems but as
living warehouses for the manufacture of stuff: lumber, paper, wedding rings,
meat, energy.

With this stark profile in mind, it probably came as no big shock that the
man Salazar nominated to head the Fish and Wildlife Service, the agency
charged with protecting native wildlife and enforcing the Endangered Species Act, viewed those responsibilities with indifference if not hostility. For
the previous twelve years, Sam Hamilton ran the Southeast Region of the
Fish and Wildlife Service, a swath of the country that has the dubious distinction of driving more species of wildlife to the brink of extinction than
any other.

From Florida to Louisiana, the encroaching threats on native wildlife are
manifest and relentless: chemical pollution, oil drilling, coastal development,
clearcutting, wetland destruction and a political animus toward environmental laws (and environmentalists). And Sam Hamilton was not one to stand up
against this grim state of affairs.

A detailed examination of Hamilton's tenure by Public Employees for
Environmental Responsibility revealed his bleak record. During the period
from 2004 through 2006, Hamilton's office performed 5,974 consultations
on development projects (clearcuts, oil wells, golf courses, roads, housing developments and the like) in endangered species habitat. But Hamilton gave

the green light to all of these projects, except one. By contrast, during the same period the Rocky Mountain Office of the Fish and Wildlife Service officially consulted on 586 planned projects and issued 100 objections or so-called jeopardy opinions. Hamilton has by far the weakest record of any of his colleagues on endangered species protection.

There's plenty of evidence to show that Hamilton routinely placed political considerations ahead of enforcing the wildlife protection laws. For example, in the agency's Vero Beach, Florida office Fish and Wildlife Service biologists wrote a joint letter in 2005 complaining that their supervisors had ordered them not to object to any project in endangered species habitat—no matter how ruinous.

Take the case of the highly endangered Florida panther. One of Hamilton's top lieutenants in Florida has been quoted as telling his subordinates that the big cat was a "zoo species" doomed to extinction and that to halt any developments projects in the panther's habitat would be a waste of time and political capital.

"Under Sam Hamilton, the Endangered Species Act has become a dead letter," says PEER's Executive Director Jeff Ruch, noting that the White House announcement on Hamilton touted his "innovative conservation" work. "Apparently, the word 'no' is not part of 'innovative' in Mr. Hamilton's lexicon. To end the cycle of Endangered Species Act lawsuits, the Fish and Wildlife Service needs a director who is willing to follow the law and actually implement the Act. Hamilton's record suggests that he will extend the policies of Bush era rather than bring needed change."

Obama and Salazar put the fate of the jaguar, grizzly and northern spotted owl in his compromised hands. Feel the chill?

Over at the Agriculture Department Obama made a similarly cynical pick when he chose former Iowa governor Tom Vilsak to head the agency that oversees the national forests. Vilsak resides to the right of Salazar and not just in the sitting arrangement at Cabinet meetings. He is a post-Harken Iowa Democrat, which means he's essentially a Republican who believes in evolution six days a week. (He leaves such Midwestern heresies at the door on Sundays.) Think Earl Butz—minus the racist sense of humor (as far as we know).

Vilsak is a creature of industrial agriculture, a brusque advocate for the corporate titans that have lain waste to the farm belt: Monsanto, Archer Daniels Midland and Cargill. As administrations come and go, these companies only tighten their stranglehold, poisoning the prairies, spreading their clones and frankencrops, sucking up the Oglalla aquifer, scalping topsoil and driving the small farmers under. It could have been different. Obama might have opted for change by selecting Wes Jackson of the Land Institute, food historian Michael Pollan or Roger Johnson, president of the National Farmers Union. Instead he tapped the old guard, a man with a test tube in one hand and Stihl chainsaw in the other.

Through a quirk of bureaucratic categorization, the Department of Agriculture is also in charge of the national forests. At 190 million acres, the national forests constitute the largest block of public lands and serve as the principal reservoir of biotic diversity and wilderness on the continent. They have also been under a near constant state of siege since the Reagan era: from clearcuts, mining operations, ORV morons, ski resorts and cattle and sheep grazing.

Since 1910, when public outrage erupted after President William Taft fired Gifford Pinchot for speaking out against the corrupt policies of Interior Secretary Richard Ballinger, the chief of the Forest Service had been treated as a civil service employee and, much like the director of the FBI and CIA, was considered immune from changes in presidential administrations. This all changed when Bill Clinton imperiously dismissed Dale Robertson as chief in 1994 and replaced him with Jack Ward Thomas, the former wildlife biologist who drafted Clinton's plan to resume logging in the ancient forests of the Pacific Northwest. Thomas's tenure at the agency proved disastrous for the environment. In eight years of Clinton time, the Forest Service cut six times as much timber as the agency did under the Reagan and Bush I administrations combined. The pace of logging set by Thomas continued unabated during the Bush the Younger's administration.

So Vilsak soon gave the boot to Gail Kimbell, Bush's compliant chief, and replaced her with a thirty-two-year veteran of the agency named Tom Tidwell. Those were thirty two of the darkest years in the Forest Service's long history, years darkened by a perpetual blizzard of sawdust. You will search Google in vain for any evidence that during the forest-banging years of the Bush administration, when Tidwell served as Regional Forester for the Northern Rockies, this man ever once stood up to Kimbell or her puppetmaster Mark Rey, who went from being the timber industry's top lobbyist to Bush's Undersecretary of Agriculture in charge of the national forests. No, Tidwell was no whistleblower. He was, in fact, a facilitator of forest destruction, eagerly implementing the Kimbell-Rey agenda to push clearcuts, mines, oil wells and roads into the heart of the big wild of Montana and Idaho.

Despite this dismal resumé, Tidwell's appointment received near unanimous plaudits, from timber companies, ORV user groups, mining firms and, yes, the Wilderness Society. Here's the assessment of Cliff Roady, director of the Montana Forest Products Association, a timber industry lobby outfit: "His appointment keeps things on a fairly steady course. He reported to Gail Kimbell, and they worked together really well. He's somebody we'd look forward to working with."

And here, singing harmony, were the tweets of Bob Eckey, a spokesman for the Wilderness Society, which some seasoned observers of environmental politics consider to be yet another timber industry lobby group: "Tidwell understands the American public's vision for a national forest has been changing."

During his tenure in Montana, Tidwell specialized in the art of coercive collaboration, a social manipulation technique that involves getting environmental groups to endorse destructive projects they would normally litigate to stop. Yet, when copiously lubricated with the magic words "collaboration" or "climate change" most environmentalists can be enticed to swallow even the most ghastly of clearcuts in the most ecologically sensitive sites, such as the Bitterroot Mountains in Montana to the fast-dwindling ponderosa pine forests of Oregon's Blue Mountains.

One of Tidwell's highest priorities is to turn the national forests into industrial biomass farms, all in the name of green energy. Under this destructive scheme, forests young and old alike will be clearcut, not for lumber, but as fuel to be burned in biomass power generators. Already officials in the big timber states of Oregon and Washington are crowing that they will soon be able to become the "Saudi Arabia" of biomass production. Did they run this past Smokey the Bear?

Of course Smokey, that global icon of wildfire suppression, and Tidwell found common ground on another ecologically dubious project: thinning and post-fire salvage logging. We've reached the point where old-fashioned timber sales are a thing of the past. Now every logging operation comes with an ecological justification—specious though they all certainly turn out to be.

The Alliance for the Wild Rockies, one of the few green outfits to consistently stand up against Democratic Party-sponsored depredations on the environment, sued Tidwell at least twenty times during his time as regional forester in Missoula. There's no record of Tidwell being sued even once by Boise-Cascade, Plum Creek Timber or the Noranda Gold Mining Company.

Yet by and large, the mainstream environmental movement muzzled itself while the Obama administration stocked the Interior Department with corporate lawyers, extraction-minded bureaucrats and Clinton-era retreads. This strategy of a self-imposed gag order only served to enable Salazar and Vilsak to pursue even more rapacious schemes without any fear of accountability.

The pattern of political conditioning has been honed to perfection. Every few weeks the Obama administration drops the Beltway Greens a few meaningless crumbs—such as the reinstitution of the Clinton Roadless Area rule—which they greedily gobble up one after the other until, like Hansel and Gretel with groupthink, they find themselves hopelessly lost in a vast maze of Obama-sanctioned clearcuts. After that, they won't even get a crumb.

On the environment, the transition between Bush and Obama has been disturbingly smooth when it should have been decisively abrupt.

The Wall Street White House

By ANDREW COCKBURN

Robert Hormats, Vice Chairman of Goldman Sachs, was installed as Under Secretary of Economics, Business, and Agricultural Affairs. This comes as one more, probably unnecessary reminder of the total control exercised by Wall Street over the Obama administration's economic and financial policy. True, Hormats is "a talker rather than a decider" according to one former White House official, but he will find plenty of old friends used to making decisions, almost all of them uniformly disastrous for the US and global economics.

Among the familiar Wall Street faces that Hormats will encounter in his new post will be that of Deputy Secretary of State Jacob Lew, lately Chief Financial Officer of Citigroup Alternative Investments Group, which lost $509 million in the first quarter of 2008 alone. On visits to the White House he is sure to bump into Michael Froman, who also tore a swath through the Citi balance sheet at the alternative investments shop (they specialized in "esoteric" investments such as private highways) but is now Obama's Deputy National Security Adviser for International Economic Affairs. If Froman is otherwise engaged, Hormats can interface with Froman's deputy, David Lipton, who was until recently running Citi's global country risk management effort.

Citigroup is also well represented at Treasury, in the form of Lewis Alexander, formerly the bank's chief economist and now Counselor to Treasury Secretary Timothy Geithner. Given the role played by all of the above in bankrupting us all, Alexander's 2007 verdict on the onset of the mortgage crash, "I think that's not going to spill more broadly into the economy and so I think we're going to have a normal kind of housing cycle through the middle of this year," can only have been a recommendation in the eyes of his current employer.

Alexander's function at Citi may have been merely to endorse the financial depredations of colleagues with economic blather, rather than exercise loss-making functions personally. Not so Deputy Treasury Secretary Neal Wolin, who has moved over to the number two job at the department from the Hartford Insurance Company, where he served as president and chief operating officer of the Property and Casualty Group. Hartford was one of the insurance companies that got suckered by the banks into backing their ruinous investments in real estate and other esoterica, but Wolin's Treasury has just handed Hartford $3.4 billion of our money in the form of TARP funds.

Hormats's agricultural responsibilities will of necessity bring him into frequent contact with the Chairman of the Commodity Futures Trading Commission, Gary Gensler—a former Goldman partner. As Assistant Secretary of Treasury in the Clinton Administration Gensler played a key role in greasing the skids for the notorious Commodity Futures Modernization

Act of 2000, which set the stage for the great credit default swaps scam that underpinned the recent bubble and subsequent collapse. News of the appointment did generate threats of obstruction in the Senate—any one of the senators could have blocked the appointment had they really wished to do so—but such threats proved predictably hollow. Had they been otherwise, Treasury Chief of Staff Mark Patterson could of course have lent the expertise he gained as Goldman's lobbyist to overcome the obstacle.

For sheer gall it would be hard to equal the appointment of Gensler, one of the engineers of this catastrophe, but the administration has managed it with the selection of Linda Robertson, formerly a key Enron lobbyist and intimately involved in pushing through the commodity futures act as chief flack for the Federal Reserve. Prior to joining the crooked energy-trading firm, Robertson was an important figure in the Clinton Treasury Department, latterly serving her friend Larry Summers and before him Robert Rubin during their terms as Treasury Secretaries.

Such connection to the key enablers of our bankrupt casino helps explain many of the other hires listed above. Michael Froman was Chief of Staff to Robert Rubin at Treasury before following Rubin to his reward at Citigroup. Most significantly, it was Froman who first introduced Rubin to his Harvard classmate Barack Obama. David Lipton also served in the Rubin Treasury, as deputy under secretary for international affairs. Neal Wolin, on the other hand, appears to have been more an acolyte of Summers, who cherished him as Treasury General Counsel from '99 to '01. Summers and Robertson were similarly close, and certainly he raised no objection to her fatal submissions on behalf of her paymasters at Enron.

Recent reports suggest that financial industry lobbying in Washington, at $104.7 million for the first three months of 2009, is 8 percent down on last year. But that is to be expected—why should Wall Street continue paying top dollar for a wholly owned subsidiary?

Andrew Cockburn writes about national security and related matters. His most recent book is Rumsfeld: His Rise, Fall, and Catastrophic Legacy. *He is the co-producer of* American Casino, *the feature documentary on the ongoing financial collapse.*

The Honduran Coup: A US Connection

By CONN HALLINAN

While the Obama Administration was careful to distance itself from the recent coup in Honduras—condemning the expulsion of President Manuel Zelaya to Costa Rica, revoking Honduran officials' visas, and shutting off aid—that doesn't mean influential Americans aren't involved, and that both sides of the aisle don't have some explaining to do.

The story most US readers are getting about the coup is that Zelaya—an ally of Venezuelan President Hugo Chavez—was deposed because he tried to change the constitution to keep himself in power.

That story is a massive distortion of the facts. All Zelaya was trying to do is to put a non-binding referendum on the ballot calling for a constitutional convention, a move that trade unions, indigenous groups and social activist organizations had long been lobbying for. The current constitution was written by the Honduran military in 1982 and the one term limit allows the brass hats to dominate the politics of the country. Since the convention would have been held in November, the same month as the upcoming presidential elections, there was no way that Zelaya could have remained in office in any case. The most he could have done was to run four years from now. And while Zelaya is indeed friendly with Chavez, he is at best a liberal reformer whose major accomplishment was raising the minimum wage. "What Zelaya has done has been little reforms," Rafael Alegria, a leader of Via Campesina told the Mexican daily *La Jornada*. "He isn't a socialist or a revolutionary, but these reforms, which didn't harm the oligarchy at all, have been enough for them to attack him furiously."

One of those "little reforms" was aimed at ensuring public control of the Honduran telecommunications industry and that may well have been the trip wire that triggered the coup.

The first hint that something was afoot was a suit brought by Venezuelan lawyer Robert Carmona-Borjas claiming that Zelaya was part of a bribery scheme involving the state-run telecommunication company, Hondutel.

Carmona-Borjas has a rap sheet that dates back to the April 2002 coup against Chavez. It was he who drew up the notorious "Carmona decrees," a series of draconian laws aimed at suspending the Venezuelan constitution and suppressing any resistance to the coup. As Chavez supporters poured into the streets and the plot unraveled, he fled to Washington DC.

There he took a post at George Washington University and brought Iran-Contra plotters Otto Reich and Elliott Abrams to teach his class on

"Political Management in Latin America." He also became vice-president of the right-wing Arcadia Foundation, which lobbies for free market policies.

Weeks before the June 28 Honduran coup, Carmona-Borjas barnstormed the country accusing Zelaya of collaborating with narco-traffickers.

Reich, a Cuban-American with ties to right-wing factions all over Latin America, and a former Assistant Secretary of State for Hemispheric Affairs under George W. Bush, has been accused by the Honduran Black Fraternal Organization of "undeniable involvement" in the coup.

This is hardly surprising. Reich's priors makes Carmona-Borjas look like a boy scout.

He was nailed by a 1987 Congressional investigation for using public funds to engage in propaganda during the Reagan Administration's war on Nicaragua. He is also a fierce advocate for Orlando Bosch and Luis Posada Carriles, both implicated in the bombing of a Cuban airliner in 1973 that killed all seventy three on board.

Reich is a ferocious critic of Zelaya and, in a recent piece in the *Weekly Standard*, urged the Obama Administration not to support "strongman" Zelaya because it "would put the United States clearly in the same camp as Cuba's Castro brothers, Venezuela's Chavez, and other regional delinquents."

Zelaya's return was unanimously supported by the UN General Assembly, the European Union, and the Organization of American States.

One of the charges that Reich levels at Zelaya is that the Honduran president is supposedly involved with bribes paid out by Hondutel. Zelaya is threatening to file a defamation suit over the accusation.

Reich's charges against Hondutel are hardly happenstance.

The Cuban-American, a former lobbyist for AT&T, is close to Arizona Senator John McCain and served as McCain's Latin American advisor during the Senator's run for the presidency. John McCain is Mr. telecommunications.

The Senator has deep ties with telecom giants AT&T, MCI and Qualcomm and, according to Nikolas Kozloff, author of *Hugo Chavez: Oil, Politics and the Challenge of the U.S.*, "has acted to protect and look out for the political interests of the telecoms on Capitol Hill."

AT&T is McCain's second largest donor, and the company also generously funds McCain's International Republican Institute (IRI), which has warred with Latin American regimes that have resisted telecommunications privatization. According to Kozloff, "President Zelaya was known to be a fierce critic of telecommunications privatization."

When Venezuelan coup leaders went to Washington a month before their failed effort to oust Chavez, IRI footed the bill. Reich, as then Secretary of State Condoleezza Rice's special envoy to the Western Hemisphere, met with some of those leaders.

In 2004, Reich founded his own lobbying agency and immersed himself in guns, rum, tobacco, and sweat. His clients include Lockheed Martin (the world's largest arms dealer), British American Tobacco and Bacardi. He is also vice-chairman of Worldwide Responsible Apparel Production, a clothing industry front aimed at derailing the anti-sweatshop movement.

Republicans in Congress have accused the Obama Administration of being "soft" on Zelaya, and protested the White House's support of the Honduran president by voting against administration nominees for the ambassador to Brazil and an assistant secretary of state.

But meddling in Honduras is a bi-partisan undertaking.

"If you want to understand who is the real power behind the [Honduran] coup, you need to find out who is paying Lanny Davis," says Robert White, former US ambassador to El Salvador and current president of the Center for International Policy.

Davis, best known as the lawyer who represented Bill Clinton during his impeachment trial, has been lobbying members of Congress and testifying before the House Foreign Affairs Committee in support of the coup.

According to Roberto Lovato, an associate editor at New American Media, Davis represents the Honduran chapter of CEAL, the Business Council of Latin America, which strongly backed the coup. Davis told Lovato, "I'm proud to represent businessmen who are committed to the rule of law."

But White says the coup had more to do with profits than law.

"Coups happen because very wealthy people want them and help to make them happen, people who are used to seeing the country as a money machine and suddenly see social legislation on behalf of the poor as a threat to their interests," says White. "The average wage of a worker in free trade zones is 77 cents per hour."

According to the World Bank, 66 percent of Hondurans live below the poverty line.

The US is also involved in the coup through a network of agencies that funnel money and training to anti-government groups. The National Endowment for Democracy (NED) and the US Agency for International Development (USAID) contribute to right-wing organizations that supported the coup, including the Peace and Democracy Movement and the Civil Democratic Union. Many of the officers that bundled Zelaya off to San Jose were trained at the Western Hemispheric Institute for Security Cooperation, the former "School of the Americas" that has seen torturers and coup leaders from all over Latin America pass through its doors. Reich served on the Institute's board.

The Obama Administration condemned the coup, but when Zelaya journeyed to the Honduran-Nicaragua border, US Secretary of State Hillary Clinton denounced him for being "provocative." It was a strange statement, since the State Department said nothing about a report by the Committee of Disappeared Detainees in Honduras charging 1,100 human rights violations by the coup regime, including detentions, assaults and murder.

Human rights violations by the coup government have been condemned by the Inter American Commission for Human Rights, the International Observer Mission, Human Rights Watch, Amnesty International, the Committee to Protect Journalists, and Reporters Without Borders.

Davis claims that the coup was a "legal" maneuver to preserve democracy. But that is a hard argument to make, given who some of the people behind it were. One of those is Fernando Joya, a former member of Battalion 316, a paramilitary death squad. Joya fled the country after being charged with kidnapping and torturing several students in the 1980s, but he has now resurfaced as a "special security advisor" to the coup makers. He recently gave a TV interview that favorably compared the 1973 Chilean coup to the June 28 Honduran coup.

According to Greg Grandin, a history professor at New York University, the coup makers also included the extremely right-wing Catholic organization Opus Dei, whose roots go back to the fascist regime of Spanish caudillo Francisco Franco.

In the old days when the US routinely overthrew governments that displeased it, the Marines would have gone in, as they did in Guatemala and Nicaragua, or the CIA would have engineered a coup by the local elites. No one has accused US intelligence of being involved in the Honduran coup, and American troops in the country are keeping a low profile. But the fingerprints of US institutions like the NED, USAID and School of the Americas—plus bipartisan lobbyists, powerful corporations, and dedicated Cold War warriors—are all over the June takeover.

Conn Hallinan can be reached at: ringoanne@sbcglobal.net.

Obama's Immigration Reforms: Neither Humane Nor Thoughtful

By WAJAHAT ALI

While attending the North American summit with leaders of Mexico and Canada, President Obama stated that no comprehensive immigration legislation would occur before 2010, thus predictably ensuring a commitment to the highly ineffective, unjust and draconian policies of the US immigration system that needlessly detains immigrants as scapegoats to appease unfounded national security concerns.

With the pressing financial crisis and health care reform dominating the President's attention, Obama pledges a sincere attempt to eventually overhaul the system allowing a "pathway to citizenship for millions of illegal immigrants" in a way that "avoids tensions with Mexico" while acknowledging the process "is going to be difficult."

Perhaps impossible might be more accurate considering President Bush's attempts at immigration reform, which were surprisingly progressive and pragmatic, failed twice. Even Senator John McCain was forced to renege his immigration policy to win paranoid voters terrified by an over exaggerated threat of the brown, illegal immigrant menace.

Individuals such as former Republican Congressman Tom Tancredo bartered fear mongering for votes, stating that illegal immigrants "need to be found before it is too late. They're coming here to kill you, and you, and me, and my grandchildren." CNN's Lou Dobbs, whose credibility is forever nullified by his advocacy of "The Birthers," routinely terrifies middle class America about the immigrant threat with specials such as "Exporting America," "Broken Borders," and "War on the Middle Class."

Similarly, the Democrats are culpable for feeding the hysteria by enacting the brutal Illegal Immigration Reform and Immigrant Responsibility Act (IIRIRA) of 1996 under President Clinton. IIRIRA requires mandatory detention of immigrants and lawful permanent residents with criminal convictions throughout their immigration proceeding, despite the fact that most of these individuals have minor offenses, such as drug possession, and are neither major safety threats nor flight risks.

As a result, the federal government now holds more than 32,000 detainees, which is nearly five times the number held in 1994. Nearly 19,000 of these detainees have no criminal records, over half do not have attorneys, and many have been detained for more than a year, despite the US Supreme Court ruling in *Zadvydas v. Davis* that ICE ("US Immigration Customs and Enforcement") has six months to release or deport immigrants after their case is decided.

The budget for detaining immigrants has nearly doubled costing taxpayers $1.7 billion. This statistic should factor into the next, right wing tirade when deciding whom to properly blame for burdening the economy and hurting the middle class.

Echoing the sentiments of most immigration experts, Kevin Johnson, Dean of UC Davis School of Law and author of *Opening the Floodgates: Why America Needs to Rethink Its Borders and Immigration Laws*, concludes the current system is "broken." Johnson told me the key question for President Obama is "how to come up with a legally enforceable system of detention in which there is checks and balances. The administration has refused to promulgate an enforceable rule or regulation [for immigration detention]."

In an attempt to repair the innumerable abuses, as well as ensure appropriate oversight and accountability, Obama's administration recently announced it will transform the current immigration detention system, inelegantly comprised of private prisons and local jails, into an oxymoronic "truly civil detention system." As an initial measure, ICE announced it will replace private contractors with federal employees for appropriate oversight of major detention centers and will stop holding children in Texas's private Corrections Corporation of America ("CCA") T. Don Hutto Residential Center.

The President of the Center, Damon Hininger, reacted to the announcement by concisely summarizing the overall result of this measure: "In some respects there may not have been much of a change."

One would assume the US government had learned about the dangers of outsourcing core public functions to private actors from various debacles in Iraq involving Blackwater and Halliburton. However, our tone-deaf reliance on the private sectors to perform public functions without an enforceable system of regulations has produced an abusive system depriving individuals of basic rights. As a result of the current immigration policy, overpopulated, remote detention centers house immigrants who are denied meaningful contact with their lawyers, access to legal resources to fight their case, proper medical care and contact with family members. Yet thankfully for the shareholders of CCA, the company expects a twenty-year contract with ICE to detain individuals in a new facility. In a hemorrhaging economy, they also fortuitously experienced a 5 percent revenue growth.

Immigrant detainees are not so lucky. Currently, most detainees are rarely afforded an opportunity for an individualized bond hearing, where a neutral judge can assess the constitutionality and necessity for their detention. As a result, they languish in remote detention centers with atrocious living standards. Furthermore, nearly 90 percent of detainees cannot afford an attorney due to extreme poverty. Thankfully, non-profit legal organizations such as The Florence Project of Arizona provide free legal services to individuals detained by ICE.

Despite the overwhelming evidence and recommendations of immigration reform advocates, John Morton, the head of ICE, pledged a commitment to large-scale detentions but added, "it needs to be done thoughtfully and humanely."

As an Attorney with experience in assisting detained immigrants, I cannot fathom how the current system of mandatory detention is remotely "humane or thoughtful." When I was a law student interning at the Immigration Clinic of UC Davis King Hall School of Law, we fought for a bond hearing and subsequent release of a sixty-year-old Mexican American grandfather detained for nearly three years on a simple meth possession. He existed in a hellish, legal purgatory. Exasperated at his nebulous legal status and languishing in a detention center, he begged us to force the government to simply make up their mind—either deport or release him.

Holly Cooper, head of the Immigration Law Clinic of The UC Davis School of Law, told me "the current system is such a train wreck that the Obama proposal will not stop the immediate crisis." She relayed a story from one of her favorite clients: "[Detained] Individuals are affected in ways that I can't describe in words. One of my clients said it was as if he was dead for the five years he was detained and has decided to deduct the five years of detention from his age."

Thankfully, a federal judge recently recognized this madness and ruled that two immigrants, who have been detained for twenty months and nine months respectively, were entitled to a hearing to determine if their constitutional rights were violated by unnecessarily prolonged detention.

Ultimately, the Obama administration must seriously commit to immigration reform that ensures ICE and DHS comply with sensible and fair regulations that afford individuals' rights that are currently detained by an inefficient and morally bankrupt system.

Wajahat Ali is a writer and attorney. He is the author of "The Domestic Crusaders," a landmark play about Muslim Americans.

The Wolf at Trout Creek

By JEFFREY ST. CLAIR

The bison are in rut at Alum Creek.

Two or three hundred of the shaggy beasts are crowded in the little valley. The bulls have left their normal bachelor groups and joined the big herds of cows and calves to parry each other for preferred mates. They are antsy, kicking up dust devils that swirl around them like brown mist.

I walk slowly up the creek to a group of five dark bison, three females and two males. One of the bulls looks ancient. His eyes are crusty, one of his black horns broken. He is large, but unsteady on his legs, which look too thin to support his bulk. He sucks breaths deeply and raggedly. His lower lip is extended and quivering as he approaches one of the young cows. He shakes his head, his tongue flicks repeatedly at the air, as if tasting the estrus.

As the old patriarch struggles to mount the cinnamon-colored female, a young bull rushes over, butts him in the side, nearly knocking him down. The young bull kicks at the ground, snorts aggressively. The old bull stands his ground for a moment, drool stringing from his mouth. Then finally he turns away from what will almost certainly be his last summer. He staggers downstream towards me, his head hung low, flies gathering at his eyes.

I am less than a mile from Yellowstone's main road through the Hayden Valley, an artery thickly clogged with vans, mobile homes and the leather-and-chrome swarms of weekend motorcycle ganglets. There is no one else here in the pathway of the great herds. Even the metallic drone of the machines has faded so that I can hear the heavy breath of the bison in their annual ceremony of sexual potency.

Even bison, the very icon of the park, aren't safe here in their last sanctuary. The shaggy bovines are victims of rancher panic and a gutless government. Like cattle and elk, bison can carry an infectious bacterium that leads to a disease called brucellosis which can, rarely, cause cows to abort fetuses. There's no evidence that Yellowstone bison have transmitted the disease to Montana cattle, grazing cheaply on public lands near the park. But as a preventive strike, all bison that wander outside the boundaries of the park in search of forage during the deep snows of winter are confined in bison concentration camps, tested and either killed on site or shipped to slaughter-houses.

Not to worry. Ted Turner is coming to the rescue. I read in the morning paper that Turner is offering to liberate the bison quarantined at Corwin Springs, ship them to his 113,000 acre Flying D Ranch south of Bozeman, fatten them on his vast rangeland grasses and serve them up for $18 a plate at his restaurants.

Suddenly, the old bull turns my direction, angry and frustrated. He snorts, paws at hard dirt and feigns a charge.

I retreat and stumble south across the slope of stubborn sagebrush, over a rounded ridge and down into the Trout Creek valley, leaving the bison to settle their mating preferences in peace.

I'm leaking a little blood. The day before I took a nasty plunge down the mossy face of an andesite cliff at a beautiful waterfall in the Absaroka Mountains, ripping the nail off my big toe.

Each time my foot snags a rock an electric jolt stabs up my left leg. I stop at the crest of the ridge, find a spot clear of bison pies, and sit down. I ease off my boot and bloody sock, untwist the cap from a metal flask of icy water and pour it over my swollen toe, already turning an ugly black.

Even in late summer, the valley of Trout Creek is lush and green with tall grasses in striking contrast to the sere landscape of the ridges and the broad plain of the Hayden Valley. The creek itself is an object lesson in meander, circling itself like a loosely coiled rope on its reluctant path to the Yellowstone River. Once acclaimed for its cutthroat trout, the creek has been invaded by brookies, rainbows and brown trout—though these genetic intrusions are viewed with indifference by the great blue heron that is posing statuesquely in the reeds, waiting to strike.

Fifty years ago, Trout Creek was an entirely different kind of place. This valley was a dump, literally, and as such it was then thick with grizzly bears. The bears would assemble in the early evening, after the dump trucks had unloaded the day's refuse from the migration of tourists to Fishing Bridge and Canyon and Tower Junction. Dozens of grizzlies would paw through the mounds of debris, becoming conditioned to the accidental kindness of an untrustworthy species.

The bears became concentrated at the dump sites and dependent on the food. This all came to a tragic end in 1968 when the Park Service decided to abruptly close the Trout Creek dump, despite warnings from bear biologists, Frank and John Craighead. Denied the easy pickings at the trash head that generations of bears had become habituated to, the Craigheads predicted that the grizzlies would begin wandering into campgrounds and developed sites in search of food. Such entanglements, the Craigheads warned, would prove fatal, mostly to the bears.

And so it came to pass. The dump-closure policy inaugurated a heinous decade of bear slaughter by the very agency charged with protecting the bruins. From 1968 to 1973, 190 grizzly bears in Yellowstone were killed by the Park Service, roughly a third of the known population. That's the official tally. The real number may have been twice that amount, since the Park Service destroyed most of the bear incident reports from that era. Many bears died from tranquilizer overdoses and dozens of others were air-dropped outside the park boundaries only to be killed by state game officials.

The situation for the great bear has scarcely improved over the last forty years. There are more insidious ways to kill, mostly driven by the government's continued lack of tolerance for the bear's expansive nature. New park developments have fragmented its range, while cars, trashy campers, gun-toting tourists and back-country poachers rack up a grim toll. And now the climate itself is conspiring against the grizzly by inexorably burning out one of the bear's main sources of seasonal protein, the whitebark pine.

Yellowstone is a closed system, a giant island. Genetic diversity is a real concern for Yellowstone's isolated population of bears. So is the possibility of new diseases in a changing climate. The death rate of Yellowstone grizzlies has been climbing the last two years. The future is bleak. So, naturally, as one of its parting shots, the Bush administration delisted the Yellowstone population from the Endangered Species Act, stripping the bear of its last legal leverage against the forces of extinction. To date, the Obama administration has shown not the slightest inclination to reverse this travesty.

During the very week I was hobbling around Yellowstone one of Montana's most famous grizzlies was found by a rancher, shot and killed on the Rocky Mountain Front near the small town of Augusta. He was a giant, non-confrontational bear who weighed more than 800 pounds and stood more than seven-and-a-half feet tall. He was beloved by grizzly watchers, who called him Maximus. His anonymous killer left his corpse to rot in a field of alfalfa in the August sun. The government exhibited only its routine apathy at this illegal and senseless slaying. Let us pray that the great bear's DNA is widely disseminated across the Northern Rockies and that his killer meets with an even more painful and pitiless end.

I catch a flash of white circling above me. Osprey? Swainson's hawk? I dig into my pack and extract my binoculars and am quickly distracted by a weird motion on the ridgeline across the valley. I glass the slope. Four legs are pawing frantically at the sky. It is a wolf, rolling vigorously on its back, coating its pelt in dirt, urine or shit. Something foul to us and irresistible to wild canids.

The wolf rolls over and shakes. Dust flies from his fur. He tilts his head, then rubs his neck and shoulders onto the ground. He shakes again, sits and scans the valley.

His coat is largely gray, but his chest is black streaked by a thin necklace of white fur. He presents the classic lean profile of the timber wolf. Perhaps he is a Yellowstone native. He was certainly born in the park. His neck is shackled by the tell-tale telemetry collar, a reminder that the wolves of Yellowstone are under constant surveillance by the federal wolf cops. He is a kind of cyber-wolf, on permanent parole, deprived of an essential element of wildness. The feds are charting nearly every step he takes. One false move, and he could, in the antiseptic language of the bureaucracy, be "removed," as in erased, as in terminated.

This wolf is two, maybe three years old. His coat is thick, dark and shiny. There is no sign of the corrosive mange that is ravaging many of the

Yellowstone packs, a disease, like distemper and the lethal parvo virus, vectoring into the park from domestic dogs.

It has been nearly fifteen years since thirty-one gray wolves were reintroduced into the park, under the Clinton administration's camera-ready program. With great fanfare, Bruce Babbitt hand-delivered the Canadian timber wolves to their holding pens inside the high caldera. Of course, it was an open secret—vigorously denied by the Interior Department—that wolves had already returned to Yellowstone on their own—if, that is, they'd ever really vanished from the park despite the government's ruthless eradication campaign that persisted for nearly a century.

These new wolves came with a fatal bureaucratic catch. Under Babbitt's elastic interpretation of the Endangered Species Act, the wolves of Yellowstone were magically decreed to be a "non-essential, experimental population." This sinister phrase means that the Yellowstone wolves were not to enjoy the full protections afforded to endangered species and could be harassed, drugged, transported or killed at the whim of federal wildlife bureaucrats. Deviously, this sanguinary rule was applied to all wolves in Yellowstone, even the natives.

The Yellowstone packs, both reintroduced and native, are doing well, but not well enough considering the lethal threats arrayed against them, even inside the supposedly sacrosanct perimeter of the park.

This young wolf might well be a member of the Canyon pack, a gregarious gang of four wolves frequently sighted at Mammoth Hot Springs on Yellowstone's northern fringe, where they dine liberally on the elk that hang around the Inn, cabins and Park Headquarters. This close-up view of predation-in-action agitated the tourists and when the tourists are upset, the Park Service responds with a vengeance. The federal wolf cops were dispatched to deal with the happy marauders. When the wolves began stalking the elk, Park Service biologists lobbed firecracker grenades at them and shot at the wolves with rubber bullets. Finally, the small pack left Mammoth for less hostile terrain, showing up this summer in the Hayden Valley, throbbing with elk and bison.

But the non-lethal warfare waged on the Canyon pack wolves came with a bloody price. The wolves lost their litter of pups, a troubling trend in Yellowstone these days. Pup mortality in Yellowstone is on the rise. Last year, on the northern range of the Park only eight pups survived. Several packs, including the Canyon and Leopold packs, produced no pups. Over the last two years, the wolf population inside the Park has dropped by 30 percent. Even so, the Bush administration decided to strip the wolf of its meager protections under the Endangered Species Act in Montana and Idaho, opening the door for wolf hunting seasons in both states. Then Judge Donald Molloy, a no-nonsense Vietnam vet, placed an injunction on the hunts and overturned the Bush administration delisting order.

Revoltingly, this spring, the Obama administration redrafted the Bush wolf-killing plan and again stripped the wolf of its protections under the Endangered Species Act. So now both Montana and Idaho are set to kill hundreds of wolves in state authorized hunts—unless Judge Molloy once again intervenes to halt the killing. Both states have brazenly threatened to defy the court if Judge Molloy rules in favor of the wolf. The putatively progressive governor of Montana, Brian Schweitzer, has been especially bellicose on the matter, vowing: "If some old judge says we can't hunt wolves, we'll take it back to another judge."

In Idaho, the state plans to allow 220 wolves to be killed in its annual hunt and more than 6,000 wolf gunners have bought tags for the opportunity to participate in the slaughter. Up near Fairfield, Idaho rancher vigilantes are taking matters into their own hands. Last week, six wolves from the Solider Mountain pack in the wilds of central Idaho were killed, probably from eating a carcass laced with poison. Don't expect justice for these wolves. Rex Rammell, a Republican candidate for governor of Idaho, has placed wolf eradication at the top of his agenda. He has also made repeated quips about getting a hunting tag for Obama. After catching some heat for this boast, Rammell sent out a clarifying Tweet: "Anyone who understands the law, knows I was just joking, because Idaho has no jurisdiction to issue hunting tags in Washington, D.C." Welcome to Idaho, where Sarah Palin got educated.

Across the valley, the wolf is standing rigid, his ears pricked by the bickering of a group of ravens below him on the far bank of Trout Creek. He moves slowly down the slope, stepping gingerly through the sagebrush. He stops at one of the looping meanders, wades into the water and swims downstream. He slides into the tall grass and then playfully leaps out, startling the ravens, who have been busy gleaning a bison carcass. Earlier in the morning a mother grizzly and two cubs had feasted here, I later learned from a Park biologist. Perhaps the Canyon wolves had made the kill, only to be driven away by a persuasive bear. Perhaps it was an old bull, killed during the rut.

The wolf raises his leg and pisses on the grass near the kill site. He sniffs the ground and paces around the remains. Then he rolls again, twisting his body violently in mud near the bison hide and bones. The ravens return, pestering and chiding the wolf. He dismisses their antics and grabs a bone in his mouth.

I lurch down the hillside for a better view, bang my aching foot on a shard of basalt and squeal, "Fuck!"

The wolf's ears stiffen again. He stares at me, bares his teeth, growls and sprints up and over the ridge, his mouth still clamped tightly on the prized bone, and down into the Alum valley, where he disappears into the dancing dust of mating bison.

Obama's Mistakes in
Health Care Reform

By VICENTE NAVARRO

Let me start by saying that I have never been a fan of Barack Obama. Early on, I warned many on the left that his slogan, "Yes, we can," could not be read as a commitment to the major change this country needs. Still, I actively supported him against John McCain and was very pleased when he became president—for many reasons, encompassing a broad range of feelings. One reason was that Obama is African-American, and the country needed to have a black president. Another was that his election seemed to signal the end of the Bush era. But, the most important reason was that I saw him as a decent man, surrounded by some good people who could promote change from the center and open up some possibilities for progress, giving the left a chance to influence the administration's policies.

Well, after just over seven months of the Obama White House, I have no reason to doubt that he is a decent man, but I am dismayed by the bad judgment he has shown in the choice of some of his staff and advisors. I really doubt that he is going to be able to make the changes we need. As I said, I never had great expectations about him and his policies, but even the lowest of my expectations have not been met.

Some among the many skeptics on the left might add, "What did you expect?" Well, at least I expected Obama to show the same degree of astuteness that he and his team had shown during the campaign. He seemed to be a brilliant strategist, and his election proves this. But my greatest disappointment is the strategies he is now following in his proposals for health care reform—they could not be worse. I am really concerned that the fiasco of this reform may make Obama a one-term president.

Error Number One

One of the two major objectives for health care reform, as emphasized by Obama, is the need to reduce medical care costs. The notion that "the economy cannot afford a medical care system so costly, with the annual increases of medical care running wild" has been repeated over and over—only the tone varies, depending on the audience. An element of this argument is Obama's emphasis on eliminating the federal deficit. He stresses that most of the government deficit is due to the outrageous growth in costs in federal health programs. Thus, a crucial part of the message he is transmitting is the health care reform objective of reducing costs.

This message, as it reaches the average citizen, seems like a threat to achieve cost reductions by cutting existing benefits. This perception is particularly accentuated among elderly people—which is not unreasonable, given that the president indicates that the funds needed to provide health benefits coverage to the 48 million currently uncovered will come partially from existing programs, such as Medicare, with savings supposedly achieved by increasing efficiency. To the average citizen (who has developed an enormous skepticism about the political process), this call for savings by increasing efficiency sounds like a code for cutting benefits. Not surprisingly, then, one sector of the population most skeptical about health care reform is seniors—the beneficiaries of Medicare. The comment that "government should keep its hands off my Medicare," as heard at some of the town hall meetings, is not as paradoxical or ridiculous as the liberal media paint it. It makes a lot of sense. An increasing number of elderly people feel that the uninsured are going to be insured at the expense of seniors' benefits.

Error Number Two

The second major objective of health care reform as presented by Obama is to provide health benefits coverage for the uncovered: the 48 million people who don't have any form of health benefits coverage. This is an important and urgently needed intervention. The US cannot claim to be a civilized nation and a defender of human rights around the world unless this major human and moral problem at home is resolved once and for all. But, however important, this is not the largest problem we have in the health care sector. The most widespread problem is not being uninsured but underinsured: the majority of people in the US—168 million, to be precise—are underinsured. And many (32 percent) are not even aware of this until they need their health insurance coverage. This undercoverage is an enormous human, social, and economic problem. Among people who are terminally ill, 42 percent worry about how they or their family will pay for medical care. And most of these people are insured—but their insurance does not cover all of their conditions and necessary interventions. Co-payments, deductibles, and other extra expenses—besides the insurance premiums—can amount to 10 percent or even higher proportion of disposable income.

During the presidential campaign, both Obama and Hillary Clinton, in discussing the need for health care reform, made frequent reference to heartbreaking stories—cases in which families and individuals suffer under our current system of medical care. But none of the proposals that the Obama administration is ready to support would address most of these cases. It will be an embarrassing and uncomfortable moment during the 2012 presidential campaign if someone asks candidate Obama about what has happened to some of the people whose stories he told in the 2008 campaign.

Error Number Three

Obama plans to cover the uninsured by increasing taxes on the rich (a very popular measure, as shown in all polls) and by transferring funds saved through increased efficiencies in existing programs, including Medicare (an unpopular measure, for the reasons I've mentioned). We see here the same problems we've seen with other programs targeted to specific, small sectors of the population, such as the poor. Programs that are not universal (i.e., do not benefit everyone) are intrinsically unpopular. This is why antipoverty programs are unpopular. People feel that they are paying, through taxation, for programs that do not benefit them. Compassion is not, and never has been, a successful motivation for public policy. Solidarity is. You support others with the understanding that they will support you when you need it most. The long history of social policy, in the US and elsewhere, shows that universality is a better way to get popular support for a program than means-testing for programs targeted to specific vulnerable groups. The limited popularity of the welfare state in the US is precisely due to the fact that most programs are not universal but means-tested. The history of social policy shows that the best way to resolve poverty is not by developing antipoverty programs, but by developing universal programs to which all people are entitled—for example, job and incomes programs. In the same way, the problem of noncoverage by health insurance will not be resolved without resolving the problem of undercoverage, because both result from the same failing: the absence of government power to ensure universal rights.

There is no health care system in the world (including the fashionable Swiss model) that provides universal health benefits coverage without the government intervening, using its muscle to control prices and practices. The various proposals being put forward by the Obama administration are simply tinkering with, not resolving, the problem. You can call this government role "single-payer" or whatever, but our experience in the US has already shown (what other countries have known and practiced for decades) that without government intervention, all the measures now being proposed by this administration will be handsome bailouts for the medical-insurance-pharmaceutical complex.

Error Number Four

I can understand that Obama does not want to advocate single-payer. But he has made a huge tactical mistake in excluding it as an option for study and consideration. He needs single-payer to be among the options under discussion. And he needs single-payer to make his own proposal "respectable." (Keep in mind how Martin Luther King became the civil rights figure promoted by the establishment because, in the background, there was a Malcolm X threatening the establishment.) This was a major mistake made by Bill Clinton in 1993. When Clinton gave up on single-payer, his own proposal became the "left" proposal (unbelievable as that may seem) and was dead on arrival in Congress. The historical function of the left in this country has been to make the center "respectable." If there is no left alternative, the

Obama proposals will become the "left" proposal, and this will severely limit whatever reform he will finally be able to get.

But there's another reason that Obama has erred in excluding single-payer. He has antagonized the left of his own party that supports single-payer, without which he cannot be reelected in 2012. He cannot win only with the left, of course, but he certainly cannot win without the mobilization of the left. His victory in 2008 is evidence of this. And today, the left is angry at him. It is a surprise to me, but Obama is going to pay the same price Clinton paid in 1994. Clinton antagonized the left by putting deficit reduction (under pressure from Wall Street) at the top of his policies and supporting NAFTA against the wishes of the AFL-CIO and the majority of Democrats. The Gingrich Republican Revolution of 1994 was due to a demobilization of the left. The Republicans got the same (I repeat the same) number of votes in the 1994 congressional election that they got in 1990 (the previous non-presidential election year). Large sectors of the grassroots of the Democratic Party that voted Democratic in 1990 stayed home in 1994. Something similar could happen in 2010 and in 2012. We could see a strong mobilization of the right and a very demoralized left. We are already seeing this. Why aren't those on the left out in force at the town hall meetings on health care reform? Because the option they want—single-payer—has already been excluded from the debate by a president they fought to get elected.

This is my concern. The alternative to Obama is Sarah Palin or someone like her. Palin has a lot of support among the people who mobilized to support John McCain. And the ridicule heaped on her by the liberal media (which is despised by large sectors of the working class of this country) helps her, or her like, enormously. I am afraid we may have, in the near future, friendly fascism. And I do not use the term lightly. I grew up under fascism, in Franco's Spain, and if nothing else, I recognize fascism when I see it. And we are seeing a growing fascism with a working-class base in the US. This is why we cannot afford to see Obama fail. But his staff and advisors are doing a remarkable job to achieve this. Ideologues such as chief-of-staff Rahm Emanuel (who, when a congressman, was the most highly funded by Wall Street) and his brother, Ezekiel Emanuel (who did indeed write that old people should have a lower priority for health care spending) are leading the country along a wrong path.

I don't doubt that President Obama, a decent man, wants to provide universal health care to all citizens of this country. But his judgment in developing his strategy to reach that goal is profoundly flawed, and, as mentioned above, it may cost him the presidency—an outcome that would be extremely negative for the country. He should have called for a major mobilization against the medical-industrial complex, to ensure that everyone has the same benefits that their representatives in Congress have, broadening and improving Medicare for all. The emphasis of his strategy should have been on improving health benefits coverage for everyone, including those who are currently uncovered. And to achieve this goal—which the majority of the population supports—he should have stressed the need for government to ensure that this extension of benefits to everyone will occur.

That he has not chosen this strategy touches on the essence of US democracy. The enormous power of the insurance and pharmaceutical industries corrupts the nature of our democracy and shapes the frontiers of what is possible in the US. Given this reality, it seems to me that the role of the left is to initiate a program of social political agitation and rebellion (I applaud the health professionals who disrupted the meetings of the Senate Finance Committee), following the tactics of the Civil Rights and anti-Vietnam War movements of the 1960s and 1970s. It is wrong to expect and hope that the Obama administration will change. Without pressure and agitation, not much will be done.

Vicente Navarro, M.D., Ph.D., professor of Health Policy at Johns Hopkins University and editor-in-chief of the International Journal of Health Services. *The opinions expressed here are those of the author and do not necessarily reflect the views of the institutions with which he is affiliated.*

The Afghan War Question

By FRANKLIN C. SPINNEY

In the opening lines of the oldest treatise on the conduct of war, Sun Tzu said that the question of war is vital to the state, and therefore, it is imperative to study it. This timeless advice has been ignored repeatedly by the US since the end of WWII. The inevitable result has been an insensible rise of war mongering, fueled by arrogance and ignorance, culminating in the chaotic spectacle now enveloping the Afghan war question in Washington.

The intellectual content of the debate over whether or how much to escalate our forces in Afghanistan, has degenerated into formless ranting by all sides. The content of this debate is not conditioned by a clear definition of military success. Nor is it conditioned by a definition of a desired political endstate. When asked how he would define victory, the State Department's special advisor on Afghanistan and Pakistan, Richard Holbrooke, arrogantly summed up the collective state of mind by saying pithily, "we will know it when we see it." With thinking like this, it should not be surprising that there can be no definition of an exit strategy or a timeline for ending a war we are admittedly losing, even though that war is now in its ninth year. By the way, Sun Tzu also advised to avoid protracted war, and the only protracted shooting war we ever won was the American Revolution, in which we were the insurgents.

Yet, in the middle of the worst domestic economic crisis since the 1930s, President Obama is on the verge of caving in to the irrational pressures for throwing more troops and money into the bottomless pit of Afghanistan. How did the Afghan escalation question degenerate into such a ridiculously chaotic state?

Its immediate antecedents are quite clear.

At the center of this debate is, or should be, the strategic plan submitted to President Obama in August by the theater commander General Stanley MacChrystal. That plan's centerpiece is to provide security for the Afghan people by accelerating the training and expansion of the Afghan Army and Police Forces (ANSF). To buy time for this expansion, MacChrystal said a surge in US forces of 40,000 is needed, an estimate, according to subsequent reports, that may have been expanded to as many as 80,000 troops, a number the US would not be able to field and sustain without a reinstitution of the draft. MacChrystal—or one his war mongering allies in the Pentagon or in the right wing of the Republican Party—immediately increased the beating of the war drums by leaking a carefully "redacted" version of his "secret" recommendations to the most obliging courtier of the permanent Washington apparat, Bob Woodward of the *Washington Post*. By not attempting to find and discipline those responsible for a blatantly insubordinate act aimed a pre-empting his decision-making prerogatives, President Obama, the constitutionally designated commander-in-chief, telegraphed pusillanimity to the proponents of escalation, and thus set the tone for subsequent events.

In the best of circumstances, building an effective military force from scratch takes a long time. History has shown repeatedly that, absent a well trained reserve force and a highly trained active duty officer and NCO corps, it is impossible to rapidly expand the active duty forces of any military organization without seriously degrading its recruiting and training standards. This is the case, even when one is expanding it from the base of a competent core force, which is certainly not the case in Afghanistan. Nevertheless, MacChrystal's plan was fatally flawed, because it contained no systematic evaluation outlining the strengths and weaknesses of the current state of the Afghan forces he wants to double in size over a very short period.

In normal circumstances, such a failure of analysis would have been a sloppy, irresponsible omission. In this particular case, the omission was made even more outrageous for at least two reasons: First, building a national army that puts loyalty to the state ahead of tribe, clan, and family in Afghanistan's ancient clan based vendetta culture would be, in the most ideal of circumstances, a highly dubious proposition, because its goal would go against the traditional perquisites implicit in an ancient, highly-evolved culture. At the very least, this challenge ought to have been subjected to the closest anthropological and historical analysis. Second, conditions are hardly ideal. Indeed, it is common knowledge that the current Afghan security forces are already riven by corruption, the conflicted loyalties of warlordism, drug trafficking and murderous criminality, not to mention the central fact that Afghanistan's Pashtun plurality, whose alienated hearts and minds are crucial to the success of any counterinsurgency strategy, is grossly underrepresented in the army and police forces.

In short, MacChrystal's cavalier portrayal of the Afghan National Security Forces at the center of his plan ought to have been a show stopper. Moreover, the fact that it was leaked by a politically motivated military officer or a civilian powerbroker to increase pressure on the President for its approval ought have resulted in visible discipline. But of course, the huge hole in MacChrystal's plan was ignored and is now forgotten. No one was hung for crass insubordination. So, it should not be surprising that the Afghan war question devolved into an evermore formless debate.

A recent AP report by Ben Feller and Anne Gearan introduces two interesting points that will add to the confusion.

Rather than lowering the boom and acting as if it was controlling the events it should be controlling, the White is now retaliating by leaking like a sieve. Unnamed officials now tell us that Obama senses (correctly) that he is being railroaded and, in secret diplomatic cables, Ambassador Eikenbury recently injected his objections to the pervasive corruption infecting the government of Hamid Karzai. Obama, reportedly, is using Eikenbury's objections as leverage to slow down deliberations and to justify his demand for a timetable laying out how long a continued US presence will be needed.

On the other hand, the report, in what is no doubt a trial balloon, says Obama is leaning toward a "compromise" position of authorizing an increase of 30,000 troops, including three Army brigades and an unspecified USMC contingent. Included in this "compromise" head count of 30,000, however, would be an authorization for the bloated overhead of a huge new headquarters housing 7,000 or more troops. Such a headquarters will no doubt necessitate a huge outlay in construction dollars to house it, a quantum increase in the thruput of logistics pipelines, and a large increase in the number of field grade and general officers to man it. Therefore, this approval also implies an approval for an increase in the size of and vested interests in an open-ended commitment.

President Obama has been accused of dithering by delaying his decision to escalate, but his politically costly purchase of time is not serving to bring clarity to the debate. He has allowed the huge hole in MacChrystal's incompetent plan to remain unaddressed, except perhaps obliquely by Ambassador Eikenbury, and to metastasize into a festering state of confusion. This confusion has opened the door to the displacement of rationality by emotion.

Not surprisingly, given the growing tolerance for irrationality in Versailles on the Potomac, the war mongering proponents of immediate escalation are becoming increasingly hysterical. If the mindless mutterings by the likes of David Brooks (*New York Times*) and Michael Gerson (*Washington Post*) are representative, the proponents of escalation have now reduced themselves to emulating the irrational exhortations made by Adolf Hitler, from the depths of his führer bunker cut off from reality, about victory being merely a question of willpower.

This kind of lunatic ranting should not be surprising, because as my good friend Werther recently explained, the triumph of the will over the intellect is an example of the Right Wing's historic preference for emotion over reason. This kind of ranting also sets the stage for a future stab in the back argument that blames Obama for losing what was in reality a colossal Bush screw up.

Of course, the histrionics of Brooks and Gerson do not come close to rivaling the emotive power of the torchlight Nuremberg parades immortalized by Leni Riefenstahl in her film classic, *The Triumph of the Will*. But the feebleness of their imitation makes it all the more pathetic when a man as intelligent as Barack Obama, a gifted speaker who has all the advantages of the bully pulpit together with the awesome status of commander-in-chief, lacks the moral courage to lift his nation out of their kind of darkness into light of reason.

Franklin C. Spinney is a former military analyst for the Pentagon.

Obama and Nuclear Power: Resurrecting a Failed Industry

By JOSHUA FRANK and JEFFREY ST. CLAIR

He may soon be called the nuclear industry's Golden Child. No president in the last three decades has put more taxpayer dollars behind atom power than Barack Obama. And there may be good reason why the president is salivating over the prospect of building new nuclear power plants around the country.

It was one of the most important issues of the 2008 presidential campaign. The perceived threat of global warming began to make even the most skeptical of politicians a bit nervous. Both the Democrats and Republicans proposed searching for more domestic oil supplies, promising to drill up and down the spine of the Rocky Mountains and even off the fragile coastlines of Florida and California. The future of the planet, they claimed, is more perilous than ever.

Al Gore made his impact.

Too bad the Gore effect is like a bad hangover: all headache and no buzz. The purported solution the Obama administration has heaved at the imminent warming crisis, nuclear technology, is just as hazardous as our current methods of energy procurement. Yet, Obama isn't the first Democrat in recent years to tout nuclear virtues.

Al Gore, who wrote of the potential green merits of nuclear power in his book *Earth in the Balance*, earned his stripes as a Congressman protecting the interests of two of the nuclear industry's most problematic enterprises, the TVA and the Oak Ridge Labs. And, of course, Bill Clinton backed the Entergy Corporation's outrageous plan to soak Arkansas ratepayers with the cost overruns on the company's Grand Gulf reactor, which provided power to electricity consumers in Louisiana.

The Clinton years indeed saw an all-out expansion of nuclear power around the globe. First came the deal to begin selling nuclear reactors to China, announced during Jiang Zemin's 1997 visit to Washington, even though Zemin brazenly vowed at the time not to abide by the so-called "full scope safeguards" spelled out in the International Atomic Energy Act.

The move was apparently made over the objections of Clinton's National Security Adviser Sandy Berger, who cited repeated exports by China of "dual use" technologies to Iran, Pakistan and Iraq. The CIA also weighed in against the deal, pointing out in a report to the president, "China was the single most important supplier of equipment and technology for weapons of mass destruction" worldwide. In a press conference on the deal, Mike McCurry said these nuclear reactors will be "a lot better for the planet than a bunch of dirty coal-fired plants" and will be "a great opportunity for American vendors"—that is, Westinghouse.

A day later, Clinton signed an agreement to begin selling nuclear technology to Brazil and Argentina for the first time since 1978, when Jimmy Carter canceled a previous deal after repeated violations of safety guidelines and nonproliferation agreements.

In a letter to Congress, Clinton vouched for the South American countries, saying they had made "a definitive break with earlier ambivalent nuclear policies." Deputy National Security Adviser Jim Steinberg justified the nuclear pact with Brazil and Argentina as "a partnership in developing clean and reliable energy supplies for the future." Steinberg noted that both countries had opposed binding limits on greenhouse emissions and that new nuclear plants would be one way "to take advantage of the fact that today we have technologies available for energy use which were not available at the time that the United States and other developed countries were going through their periods of development."

The atom lobby during the 1990s had a stranglehold on the Clinton administration and now they seem to have the same suffocating grip around the neck of Barack Obama.

In 2006 Obama took up the cause of Illinois residents who were angry with Exelon, the nation's largest nuclear power plant operator, for not having disclosed a leak at one of their nuclear plants in the state. Obama responded by quickly introducing a bill that would require nuclear facilities to immediately notify state and federal agencies of all leaks, large or small.

At first it seemed Obama was intent on making a decent change in the reporting protocol, even demonizing Exelon's inaction in the press. But Obama could only go so far, as Exelon executives, including Chairman John W. Rowe, who serves as a key lobbyist for the nuclear energy lobby, have long been campaign backers, raising hundreds of thousands of dollars dating back to Obama's days in the Illinois State Legislature.

Despite his initial push to advance the legislation, Obama's office eventually rewrote the bill, producing a version that was palatable to Exelon and the rest of the nuclear industry. "Senator Obama's staff was sending us copies of the bill to review, we could see it weakening with each successive draft," said Joe Cosgrove, a park district director in Will County, Illinois, where the nuclear leaks had polluted local ground water. "The teeth were just taken out of it."

Inevitably, the bill died a slow death in the Senate. And like an experienced political operative, Obama came out of the battle as a martyr for both sides of the cause. His constituents back in Illinois thought he fought a good fight, while industry insiders knew the Obama machine was worth investing in.

Obama's campaign wallet during the 2008 election, while rich with millions from small online donations, was also bulging in contributions given by employees of Exelon, his fifth largest bloc of campaign contributors. Two of Obama's largest campaign fundraisers include Frank M. Clark and John W. Rogers Jr., both top Exelon officials. Clark served as a "bundler" for

Obama for America, helping raise millions of dollars for the campaign. Even Obama's chief strategist in 2008, David Axelrod, has done consulting work for the company.

During a Senate Committee on Environment and Public Works hearing in 2005, Obama, who served on the committee, asserted that since Congress was debating the negative impact of CO_2 emissions "on the global ecosystem, it is reasonable—and realistic—for nuclear power to remain on the table for consideration." Shortly thereafter, *Nuclear Notes*, the industry's leading trade publication, praised the senator. "Back during his campaign for the U.S. Senate in 2004, [Obama] said that he rejected both liberal and conservative labels in favor of 'common sense solutions'. And when it comes to nuclear energy, it seems like the Senator is keeping an open mind."

Obama's Department of Energy committed a total of $8.33 billion in loan guarantees for the construction and operation of two new nuclear reactors at a plant in Georgia. It was the administration's first move to throw taxpayer dollars at new nuclear power operations.

"When the new nuclear reactors come on line, they will provide reliable, base-load electricity capable of serving about 550,000 residences or 1.4 million people," the Energy Department said in a press release.

Carol Browner, director of the White House Office of Energy and Climate Change Policy said, "[reactors are] just the first of what we hope will be many new nuclear projects."

As you go up the nuclear fuel chain, you have carbon dioxide emissions at every single step—from uranium mining, milling, enrichment, fuel fabrication and reactor construction to the transportation of the radioactive waste.

The nuclear lobby likes to compare its record to polluting coal-fired plants, rather than renewables such as solar, wind and geothermal. Even when compared to coal, atomic power fails the test if investments are made to increase the efficient use of the existing energy supply instead. One recent study by the Rocky Mountain Institute found that "even under the most optimistic cost projections for future nuclear electricity, efficiency is found to be 2.5 to 10 times more cost effective for CO_2-abatement. Thus, to the extent that investments in nuclear power divert funds away from efficiency, the pursuit of a nuclear response to global warming would effectively exacerbate the problem."

Clearly, Obama recognizes the inherent dangers of nuclear technology and knows of the disastrous failures that plagued Chernobyl, Mayak and Three Mile Island. Yet, despite his attempts to alert the public of future toxic nuclear leaks, Obama still considers nuclear power a viable alternative to coal-fired plants. The atom lobby must be glowing with pride.

The Novocaine Presidency

By KEVIN ALEXANDER GRAY

"It's like when you go to the dentist, and the man's going to take
your tooth. You're going to fight him when he starts pulling. So
he squirts some stuff in your jaw called novocaine, to make you
think they're not doing anything to you. So you sit there and
'cause you've got all of that novocaine in your jaw, you suffer
peacefully. Blood running all down your jaw, and you don't know
what's happening. 'Cause someone has taught you to suffer—
peacefully."—Malik Shabazz (Malcolm X), "Message to the
Grassroots" (1964).

There's a picture of Barack Obama next to one of Jesus in the front window
of the small, black art gallery that I drive past almost everyday. And I still
see someone wearing an Obama t-shirt maybe once a week, but sometimes
it's the same guy. If you're looking, you can a find a variety of shirts in just
about every corner store where I live. They're on the wall, next to the Bob
Marley, Tupac, Biggie Smalls and Al Pacino "Scarface" t-shirts. You can get
an Obama hat and a presidential calendar there too. There are still a few
Obama yard signs in the neighborhood, usually in a window. A few people
still have an Obama bumper sticker on their cars. Not as many as some might
think. Certainly not as many as the number of Confederate flags on vehicles
in this part of the country.

Racial solidarity is the mood that helped get Obama into the White
House. The traditional source of power and survival among blacks, it is also
the novocaine of the moment, a numbing agent as people suffer through
what, despite the more hopeful official forecasts, feels like a full-blown depression where I live. The pride is real, but so is the pain, and it's coming in
sharp stabs despite the shot. The novocaine is still working, just not so well,
and the result is a discomfiting confusion.

In late September I spoke at a "Black Male Summit" about eighty miles
northwest of Columbia in Rock Hill, South Carolina, which is famous in
civil rights' lore as the first stop in the Deep South for the Freedom Riders
testing the 1960 Supreme Court decision outlawing racial segregation in all
interstate public facilities. Rock Hill is where Student Nonviolent Coordinat-
ing Committee (SNCC) activist John Lewis and another man stepped off the
bus and were beaten by a white mob. The town is mentioned in Chuck Berry's
"Promised Land"—only the "poor boy" on the Greyhound is lucky as his bus
"bypassed Rock Hill" in the song. Things are still tough in the town just south
of Charlotte. Since February of 2008 the number of jobs here has fallen by
15 percent, and the average salary for people lucky enough to be employed is

about $28,000. In June of this year, Yvette Williams, a fifteen-year-old black girl, was shot and killed by two police officers after she robbed a grocery store. The two officers fired on Williams five times after she pointed a gun at them and refused to drop it, according to Rock Hill Police Chief John Gregory. He said he felt the police response was justified. A witness who lives across the street from where the shooting happened, told the local paper she was in bed when she heard shots and got up, looked out her window and saw the girl fall to the ground. She said she then saw an officer shoot again.

The theme I was asked to speak on in Rock Hill was "How do we restore dignity back to black communities?" My initial response was I didn't know we'd lost it. But I knew the idea was a nod to Obama's tough-love trick bag. "Post-racialism" is nonsense, but as an ideological concept it's real, with real political consequences. On the right, it is license for white blowhards to go on any racist tirade they like so long as they don't actually broadcast the word "nigger." In the black community it's alive wherever blacks argue among themselves as to whether they are individually or collectively responsible for the conditions they face, or if they're as criminal or immoral or lazy or violent or promiscuous or stupid as racists believe them to be. Sherman Porterfield, one of the organizers of the event, was quoted in the local paper, "Obama talked about it," this claimed loss of dignity; "he has challenged us. The question now is, are we up to the challenge? Our young people are dropping out of school in record numbers, and it's our fault. Nobody is shooting water hoses at us anymore. But we are allowing our young brothers to shoot each other. And that is not acceptable."

I've known Porterfield since the 1988 Jesse Jackson campaign when he was a car salesman and donated the campaign cars. I like him. As folks say, "his heart is in the right place." Still, I was surprised when he invited me to speak to his group. We've talked politics over the years. Our conversations haven't been discourteous, but we don't always see eye to eye. I've been reluctant to say whether I think Obama is good or bad for black people, but I've always been clear that skin color has never been a sufficient factor for winning my political support. I was antsy about the invite because I didn't want to be put on the hot seat. Race solidarity is a big stumbling block these days. Say the wrong thing and you're called a "hater." But I didn't go to bad-mouth Obama. I went to talk about a different kind of solidarity, one informed by an understanding of the structures that keep people down. I had forty five minutes to speak, followed by a panel consisting of a preacher, school administrator, police chief, two politicians and a government worker.

Before introducing me, Sherman briefly repeated what he said in the newspaper article. The people applauded when he said Obama's name. It wasn't long or raucous, but it governed how I managed my words. I opened with Malcolm's novocaine quote. I was careful. I tried to stay on the economic and social numbers and on how precarious a time it is for blacks. I talked about the unemployed, the dropout rate, and police violence, with the Williams' killing in mind.

The audience was open to what I had to say about the police having too much power. I mentioned how the share of public funds to the police-penal state has nearly doubled as a percentage of civilian government spending over the past fifty years and now stands at 15 percent of the latter and that we needed to de-militarize the police and end the drug war. I said that I understood why Obama backed off of the "police acted stupidly" in the Henry Louis Gates affair so as not to sidetrack his health insurance funding push. But I didn't yield on him being wrong for not supporting free speech or First Amendment rights and the right to be secure in one's home. I reminded the audience that while a disorderly charge is "minor" in that it's only a misdemeanor, many young black, brown and poor whites get their first taste of jail by misuse of the charge.

In the talk I had said that Obama siding with Sgt. James Crowley wasn't as egregious as his Justice Department going before the Supreme Court in May to argue against a twenty-three-year-old precedent for defendants' rights set by *Michigan v. Jackson*. The issue before the Court was whether a defendant who has already been appointed counsel may be interrogated by police without that counsel present. The Justice Department agreed with Justice Antonin Scalia that the *Michigan* restriction "serves no purpose," and the Court ruled by a 5–4 decision that such interrogation was not a violation of a defendant's Sixth Amendment right to counsel. Justice John Paul Stevens, who wrote the 1986 *Michigan* decision, spoke for the dissenters saying, "If a defendant is entitled to protection from police-initiated interrogation under the Sixth Amendment when he merely requests a lawyer, he is even more obviously entitled to such protection when he has secured a lawyer."

I addressed Porterfield's assertion that "our young people are dropping out of school in record numbers, and it's our fault." In South Carolina, according to the State Legislative Black Caucus, only three out of ten black males and four out of ten black females graduate from high school, but pick just about any state or locale, and the black and brown graduation rates are low and the dropout rates are high. So, people can believe either that most of their kids are stupid or that something's wrong with an educational system with such a high failure rate and so much flimflam around school reform.

In South Carolina, Democrat Robert Ford has made school reform his marquee issue in preparing to run for governor next year. This past year Ford offered a bill in the General Assembly that would make uttering profanity in public—whether in writing or orally—a felony and another bill that would require South Carolina cities and counties to give their workers a paid day off for Confederate Memorial Day or lose millions in state funds. Now he's pushing charter schools although it is unclear what his plan is or if he has one. Many believe he's in it for the money. He's allied with Al Sharpton who jumped aboard the corporate education reform gravy train after receiving a half million dollars last year for his National Action Network, reportedly brokered by New York City Schools Chancellor Joel Klein through a right-wing non-profit agency that promotes charter schools. I mentioned the president's friend and fellow Chicagoan, Secretary of Education Arne Duncan, who tried out his experiments in reform first on public school students in Chicago, where he was a CEO of Chicago Public Schools. Duncan militarized and corporatized the third largest school system in the nation, vastly expanded draconian student expulsions, instituted sweeping surveillance practices, advocated a growing police presence in the schools, arbitrarily shut down entire schools and fired entire school staffs. As a result Chicago's public schools are now being sued by black teachers for racial discrimination over the dismissal of hundreds of qualified black teachers, replaced with younger, cheaper, less experienced and mostly whiter ones. And, some suggest that his charter schools plan has led to a spike in violence. Yet the Obama administration is withholding federal education funds from states and school districts to force nationwide implementation of Duncan's charter school model.

The audience nodded approval when I warned them to be on the lookout for politicians who could make things worse by offering nothing but a flimsy promise of something better. They gave a start when I said I hoped Joe Wilson was right in calling Obama a liar after the president said that improvements in the health care system would not apply to undocumented immigrants. It was a church-going crowd so I quickly followed with the story of the Good Samaritan and said a Christian is bound to give aid or health care to the stranger or immigrant. They also nodded in agreement when I said that Jimmy Carter, an eighty-five-year-old white Southerner knew more about how white Southerners feel, think or believe than the son of a white woman from Kansas and a black man from Kenya who was raised in Hawai'i and Indonesia. And maybe many of them, raised in the South, in a state that honors the Confederate flag, did too.

When it was the panelists' turn, the youth jobs coordinator said he sent kids home even before he interviewed them if they exhibited behavior that he didn't like, such as talking in the waiting room or wearing saggy pants. They're probably the kids that need help the most, I thought, but he said he told them "to go home and ask your mother why you didn't get in the program." The school administrator favored Obama's charter school approach. The cop talked about "weed and seed," a 1980s-vintage federal program that aims to weed out the bad elements in a neighborhood via police power and community collaboration, although I'm still unsure what type of seeding comes after other than federal dollars. The politicians didn't have much to offer. The preacher had the last word. He was on the defensive about what the church was or wasn't doing in the community these days, and reiterated the need for black men "to be responsible."

I had concluded my rap, saying black politics was about more than just one person, whether that be the man on the street or the man in the White House. That blacks should treat Obama as they would any other person in power. And that it doesn't help them, or him, to stand down, back up or hush up. They had to give him some backbone.

Doubtless, most blacks never expected Obama to take racism and its material effects head on. I keep hearing, "We know he can't say everything that's on his mind," or "He's doing the best he can under the circumstances"—those "circumstances" being white people. That's usually followed by "if you can't say something good, don't say anything at all." I was talking about how subdued blacks seem to be with a friend who works in a university office where there are few other blacks. I had to listen hard as she whispered into the phone: "You know how they [whites] are. They think we can't do anything. To them there's always something wrong with us even when it's not evident or even there. So when they tear him [Obama] down, they are really tearing all of us down. So we got to stand behind the brother."

Many blacks, regardless of class, see themselves and their aspirations in Obama. The threats against his life only strengthen that support. Their enthusiasm may also reflect an optimism that the nation is on the way to becoming a less racist and fairer one. It seems that black middle class support is tied in with their societal role as control agents and their illusions of being part of what W.E.B. Dubois called "the talented tenth." The black bourgeoisie wants acceptance by whites and Obama represents this acceptance. For others, his "just not embarrassing black folk" is enough. So folk just cross their fingers in hopes that even though he may never openly express it, he understands what white entitlement and racism is all about.

At a conference in Atlanta of Sharpton's National Action Network this summer, John Silvanus Wilson, the executive director of the White House Initiative on Historically Black Colleges and Universities (HBCU), was urging his audience simply to believe. Obama has "top notch blacks" in his administration who "would do what they could" to help financially struggling black colleges, Wilson told the group, but people had to "chill out" and "give them time." He warned that schools ought not expect the government to be enthused about helping them "if their alumni weren't giving to the schools." That sounds reasonable if one ignores the reality that many former HBCU students are strapped for years after graduation paying back loans at a higher interest rate than the bank that received government bailout money have to pay back. Before ending his talk Wilson asked for "patience," urging the audience to "crush the haters" who would challenge the pace of the administration in addressing black concerns.

Yet that silence has allowed Obama to get away with not saying or doing anything that would appear to favor black interest, and doing things against their interest, like bailing out Wall Street fat cats while everyday people are cast adrift, and saying things to and about black people that a white person couldn't say without challenge or scorn, things he'd dare not say to any other racial or ethnic group in the US. As much as some people might like to believe the post-racial storyline of Obama, the side effect is that he becomes the substitute for real structural progress, and blacks are left to suck it up and either pretend racism isn't what it is or question their understanding of what it is.

All of this has put people in an awkward bind, knowing things aren't right but trying to justify their loyalty anyway. In the 1998 movie *Primary Colors*, based on the first presidential bid of Bill Clinton, campaign manager Henry Burton is confronted by his ex-girlfriend demanding to know why he was working for someone she considered to be just another unprincipled politician. Henry responds, "I can tell the difference between a man who believes what I believe and lies to get elected, and a man who just doesn't give a fuck. And I'll take the liar."

If only it were that simple.

For me, what is simple is that Obama hasn't had to offer much to get and keep black support, so he hasn't. And, he hasn't had to lie about it. At a June 23rd press conference, a black reporter asked Obama what he intended to do in the face of reports that the African-American unemployment rate will go to 20 percent or more by the end of this year. The reporter asked, "Why not target intervention now to stop the bloodletting in the black unemployment rate?" Obama offered trickle-down economics saying, "The best thing that I can do for the African-American community or the Latino community or the Asian community, whatever community, is to get the economy as a whole moving." It was as though the unemployed were not part of the "whole" that needs to get "moving."

Unemployment among blacks was high before Obama took office. For blacks in the sixteen to twenty four demographic it's been double-digit unemployment for decades. Nevertheless, in the time between George W. Bush's relocation back to Texas and Obama's move into the White House, the unemployment rates for the parents of many of those unemployed youth nearly doubled. As of September, the "official" Bureau of Labor Statistics data shows the overall black unemployment rate at 15.4 percent: 16.5 percent for adult men, 12.5 for adult women and 40.8 percent for teenagers. Some economists estimate that the actual overall rate is in the 27 to 30 percent range, with the "unofficial" teenage rate far surpassing the 50 percent mark. Perhaps, the only uptick in young black male employment in the last year has been in illicit drug sales. By any economic measure the black community is in a severe depression. African Americans make up about 13 percent of the population but represent 17 percent of the uninsured. Nearly 25 percent of blacks, or 9.4 million people, lived in poverty in the United States in 2008, compared with 8.6 percent of whites, or 17 million people. Of the 2.3 million people in jail or prison, half are black. Among black women ages thirty five to thirty nine, one in 100 is behind bars, compared with one in 355 for white women in the same age group. Yet no targeted youth or adult jobs program was part of the $787 billion stimulus package. The most that the jobless got out the stimulus deal was extension of unemployment benefits, if they hadn't already dropped off the rolls. At best, stimulus dollars forestalled some teachers being laid off and kept road crews working. If hiring more cops is a good thing, the bill did that as well. Yet, unless the parents of those unemployed young people were fortunate enough to have a public works job, many were facing foreclosure and other financial woes.

Obama is not the culprit for the crisis in black homeownership. There have been big problems for a very long time. According to the NAACP, before the current foreclosures wave, African Americans had a homeowners' rate of 47.2 percent, compared with 75.2 percent for whites. Between 2004 and 2007 the black home ownership rate declined by nearly two percentage points. According to the Home Mortgage Disclosure Act database, minorities got half the subprime loans (for home purchases and refinancings) handed out in the big years of 2004–07. Mortgage dollars (prime and subprime) for home purchases loaned to blacks went up 397 percent from 1999 to 2006, compared with 100 percent for whites. (It was a staggering 691 percent for Hispanics.) The housing market meltdown only speeded up the process of people losing the homes they had only a 50/50 chance of keeping within the first seven years anyway.

Adding to their woes, those targeted for subprime loans are "redlined" for high interest rates for just about every financial product that the law requires them to have, like home and auto insurance on the cars they purchased via "predatory," albeit "voluntary" consumer loans. Then, when they fall into foreclosure, the cost of everything goes up because of their diminishing Beacon score or worsening credit status. It's the ghetto adage: "The po' pay mo'." This is why 75 percent of homeowners in foreclosure end up losing their homes.

Homeownership advocates have pleaded for a federal foreclosures moratorium in a vocal way for three or four years. They were loud enough during the 2008 primaries for Hillary Clinton to make a moratorium part of her campaign platform to try to woo black voters away from Obama. Yet even as those voters rejected Clinton, there was no hint Obama would help black homeowners with credit problems associated with being in bankruptcy and/or foreclosure. He was deaf to those who got played by a tilted set of rules and were left with bad or worse credit, saying, "We will help those with good credit who played by the rules."

Upon entering office Obama declared, "I won't stop until all responsible homeowners can stay in their homes." He offered $75 billion in incentives to lenders to reduce loan payments for troubled borrowers with the "goal of preventing up to four million foreclosures," just as the Mortgage Bankers Association reported that, in the first three months of 2009, about 5.4 million mortgages were delinquent or in some stage of foreclosure and it was going to get worse. But the lenders didn't extend the money to people they still regarded as bad risks. Lower interest rates alone could not help struggling homeowners, who needed a meaningful "time out" to regroup financially and mentally from the stress of being on the bubble.

A few banks, Citigroup, JPMorgan Chase, Bank of America, Morgan Stanley and Wells Fargo, all initiated short-term foreclosure moratoriums and voluntary loan modifications prior to the White House plan. Some say they did it to blur notice of their prior lending practices while waiting to get their take of the $700 billion Troubled Asset Relief Program (TARP) money. Almost every bank mentioned is being sued either by investors or consumers over their behavior in the subprime-lending debacle and/or for discriminatory lending practices.

Now it appears that Obama's anti-foreclosure plan has had little meaningful effect on the homeowners' crisis, given the additional fuel of growing unemployment.

From March to June, a little more than 100,000 homeowners had been offered loan modifications, according to the Treasury Department. The lion's share of initial assistance went to homeowners at the high end of the income ladder. Meanwhile, tens of thousands of distressed moderate and low-income homeowners stood in line outside sporting arenas and civic centers across the country hoping to get what help they could from advocacy groups like the Neighborhood Assistance Corporation of America. NACA did a ten-city tour and estimated it helped 180,000 participants and "successfully renegotiated loan agreements for 1 out of 3 troubled mortgagers."

By the end of August 360,165 loans had been modified, but in July alone RealtyTrac reported 360,149 foreclosures, which means one month's foreclosures wiped away the cumulative gains since March.

Obama's $787 billion stimulus plan didn't much help homeowners in distress. Most local and state governments used the money to cover deficits in their operating budgets to include ongoing downtown development to shore up the local commercial market, highway projects, and sustaining ongoing gentrification projects, which is how many of the people struggling in subprime housing developments got there in the first place. The funds also allowed local government to suspend or reduce developers' taxes on repossessed houses or vacant properties in areas of overdevelopment. It bailed out the developers and the banks that loaned them the money to throw up all those subprime developments by giving local governments the funds to buy their foreclosed properties.

The city of Columbia used stimulus money to purchase more than "3,500 made in China or Korea tasers," since that is where they come from, for police and to hire more officers, ostensibly to ramp up their drug war and gang suppression activities. Around the time of the Gates controversy, a young man in an adjoining neighborhood who alleges that county police were "planting drugs" on folk stopped me on the street to describe how local sheriff's deputies swooped down en masse on an area of alleged drug activity with guns and cameras. They weren't there just to make arrests; they also took individual snapshots of people they didn't arrest. Whoever refused to be photographed was charged with disorderly conduct and arrested. He said he was arrested and was tased three times, yet he faced charges for assaulting an officer as he was twitching on the ground. "They tell us that we got nobody on our side to speak for us. And they're right," he said.

The Gates episode and the Obama Justice Department taking sides against the rights of the accused may be signs of things to come in the face of rising unemployment and folks losing their homes by the millions. It leaves those under the gun with fewer rights the law is bound to respect and little or no recourse to complain.

So as wealth, poverty, education and health disparities between blacks and whites grow wider, and as the number of black homeless, jobless and incarcerated increases, there is a host of questions blacks need to find answers to and act on. How do they pursue a political agenda, recognizing that Obama is not the "president of black America" and is unwilling to go to the mat for black Americans or any really progressive policies? What is the change they need, and who leads the fight? The Congressional Black Caucus and its individual members have very little stroke outside of their corporate-sponsored CBC weekend. Civil rights leaders and organizations have become slaves to Wall Street and corporate America or are old and out of touch. What does the community do about that, and about the black press, now reduced to offering "great man" coverage week after week with little, if any, critical assessment of what is or isn't being done by the Democratic president? When does it stop just being about Obama and solidarity for the sake of the symbolic?

It's a safe bet that despite it all, Obama would hold on to overwhelming black support when re-election time rolls around. Yet blacks cannot hope to progress if they continue to miss, endure, ignore and maybe even accept the institutional denial of their real life experiences and a very real retreat from defense of some basic civil rights for solidarity's sake. They can oppose the organized forces of white supremacy and the racist outlook validated by post-racialism, but they can't feel sorry for Obama; he volunteered.

Princeton University Professor Cornel West, speaking after another of Obama's "tough-love" speeches remarked, "I would rather be in a crack house than a White House that promotes neoimperial policies abroad and neoliberal policies at home." When asked to explain himself West said, "Because in a crack house, at least I'm in solidarity with folk who are sensitive to a pain. It's just that they have the wrong response to their pain. Instead of being in a crack house, they ought to be organizing. But they're dealing with their suffering. They're just dealing with it in the wrong way. The White House is escaping from the suffering."

It used to be that the black community operated on a certain ethos—that the system was rotten and needed changing—and that the idea that people were oppressed, killed, wronged because of their race or some other factor not of their control or making was wrong. At this point in time blacks can't worry about those freaking out because they are losing their sense of entitlement and privilege and it's all coming apart for them. Blacks must continue to take on empire, pull it apart and build something else. In a more everyday way, in order to survive without violence being inflicted among us and against us, we must build a community-based economy. And we can't back down on what we are trying to accomplish—a more civilized, humane and sustainable society. And if Obama is not part of the solution, he's part of the problem. Right now, he's the latter. And he better look out if the Novocaine wears off.

Obama's War for Oil
in Colombia

By DANIEL KOVALIK

This past summer, President Obama announced that he had signed an agreement with Colombia to grant the US military access to seven military bases in Colombia. As the UK's *Guardian* newspaper announced at the time, "[t] he proposed 10-year lease will give the US access to at least seven Colombian bases—three air force, two naval and two army—stretching from the Pacific to the Caribbean." And, these bases would accommodate up to 800 military and 600 civilian US contractors. As the *Guardian* explained, this announcement caused outrage in neighboring Latin American nations and "damaged Barack Obama's attempt to mend relations with the region."

This announcement also angered human and labor rights advocates in both the US and Colombia as the US was now solidifying a cozier military alliance with by far the worst labor and human rights abuser in the Western Hemisphere. The human rights nightmare in Colombia, fueled by billions of dollars of US military assistance, includes the forced internal displacement of nearly 4 million civilians—the second largest internally displaced population in the world (Sudan holding the number one position); the extraordinary killing of over 2,700 union members since 1986 (by far the greatest number in the world), with thirty five being killed in 2009 alone; and the extrajudicial killing of around 2,000 civilians by the Colombian military since President Uribe took office in 2002.

As for the extra-judicial killings by the Colombian military, these were carried out as part of the "false positive" scandal—a controversy involving the military murdering civilians and then dressing them up to look like guerillas in order to increase their body count numbers, thereby guaranteeing further US aid. That scandal deepened earlier this month when thirty one Colombian soldiers awaiting trial for their role in the killings were released from prison because of the Colombian government's failure to indict them in a timely fashion.

While the US has claimed for years that it is fighting a drug war in Colombia, though having to sheepishly admit year after year that its ostensible efforts have not yielded any decrease whatsoever in the amount of coca grown in Colombia or cocaine exported to the US, the real reason for the war has always been the control of Colombia's rich oil resources.

Indeed, at a Congressional hearing in 2000, entitled "Drugs and Social Policy in Colombia"—a hearing to debate the relative merits of Clinton's new Plan Colombia, pursuant to which the US. has sent billions of dollars of military assistance to Colombia—one of the key witnesses invited to testify in support of this policy was none other than Lawrence Meriage, the Vice-President of Occidental Petroleum. Not surprisingly, Mr. Meriage had nothing to say about drugs or social policy in Colombia, but a lot to say about the need for military assistance to protect his oil pipelines.

Now, according to a January 19, 2010 *Bloomberg* article, "The Export-Import Bank of the United States [a US government agency] announced Jan. 19 its approval of a $1 billion preliminary commitment to help finance the sale of goods and services from various U.S. exporters to Ecopetrol S.A., Colombia's national oil company." It should be noted that Ecopetrol is a business partner with L.A.-based Occidental Petroleum.

Citing an industry expert, the Bloomberg article goes on to explain that "Ecopetrol is being aggressive in exploration and production," and that, with the help of the financing from the Export-Import Bank, "Ecopetrol will almost double to 1 million barrels daily by 2015 as the company drills more wells in Colombia and neighboring South American nations."

As a November 12, 2009 press release from the human rights group Amazon Watch explained, Ecopetrol is currently engaged in oil exploration on the sacred land of the U'wa indigenous peoples and against their wishes. A spokesperson for the U'wa explained that, as is invariably the case, with Ecopetrol's exploration and drilling comes the Colombian military, as well as paramilitaries, to protect Ecopetrol's operations.

As Ecopetrol's own website indicates, it is also involved in oil exploration in Peru and Brazil. As for Peru, Survival International, a UK-based human rights group advocating for the rights of threatened indigenous tribes, warned last year that Ecopetrol's exploration of the Peruvian Amazon jungle threatens hitherto uncontacted indigenous tribes whose very existence will be jeopardized by these operations.

As Survival International explained, these uncontacted tribes are "exceedingly vulnerable to any contact with outsiders because of their lack of immunity to disease." Prior contacts between companies and uncontacted tribes have resulted in the mortality of 50 percent of the tribe.

Daniel Kovalik is a labor and human rights lawyer working in Pittsburgh, PA.

Blowback of the Drones

By GARY LEUPP

As of January 17, there had been ten drone attacks on Pakistan so far this year. There were forty-four in all of 2009. One attack in August killed Baitullah Mehsud, thirty-five-year-old leader of Tehreek-e Taliban Pakistan (TTP), a local group inspired by the Taliban of Afghanistan and conjured into being by the US bombing of both countries.

Now the main target is Mehsud's successor, Hakimullah Mehsud. If and when he is killed (along with some civilians, if precedent is followed), there will be another TTP leader, another main target for the drone strikes. And when he's killed, another. Although the Afghan Taliban has officially distanced itself from Al Qaeda, offering last month to provide a "legal guarantee" that it would not intervene in foreign countries after resuming power, this is precisely the cycle of violence Al Qaeda wishes to encourage throughout the Muslim world.

It is doing so successfully from the Swat Valley to southern Yemen and has infinite potential to spread the jihad elsewhere if the US continues to swallow the bait.

Every expert on Pakistan notes that the drone strikes on the country have outraged public opinion and damaged the president, Asif Ali Zardari. Zardari, responding to mass demonstrations and protests by the legislature and newspaper editors, has repeatedly stated that "the U.S. actions should remain on the Afghan side of the border" (that is to say, the US should respect Pakistani sovereignty and international law).

He told a delegation of US legislators, including Sen. John McCain, that "drone attacks on Pakistani territory undermined the national consensus" against Islamist militants. McCain responded, "The drone strikes are part of an overall set of tactics which make up the strategy for victory and they have been very effective." (That is to say: Our strategy for victory trumps your petty claim to national independence.)

Zardari told US special envoy for Pakistan and Afghanistan Richard Holbrooke that the drone strikes were "a cause of great concern" and urged a policy review by the Obama administration. Asked by the press how the strikes were affecting relations between the US and Pakistan, Holbrooke was both coy and condescending. "I am limited in what I can talk about on this subject, but sometimes policies … have costs and benefits," he said. In other words: Yes, our violation of Pakistan's sovereignty is infuriating its people, a potential downside, but on the bright side, that violation has resulted in some militants' deaths. The same logic as McCain.

Pakistani officials have been protesting the attacks for a long time. Speaking in parliament in November 2008, Prime Minister Yousuf Raza Gilani denounced the most recent attack, which had occurred at the Bannu district in the northwest. This was the first such attack outside the border tribal areas. "These attacks are adding to our problems," he declared. "They are intolerable and we do not support them." At that time Foreign Minister Shah Mehmood Qureshi summoned the US ambassador to once again protest US violations of Pakistan's sovereignty, and to declare that such attacks were not helping counter-terrorism efforts. During the same month the Pakistani Army held a training exercise in using surface-to-air missiles and anti-aircraft guns to shoot down drones. This was widely interpreted as a move to pressure the government to stand up to the US.

All this took place during November 2008, the month of Obama's election, during a year when the Bush administration executed seventeen drone attacks on Pakistan, reportedly killing 165 people. (There'd been seven between 2004 and 2007.) Perhaps Pakistanis hoped that there'd be a change under Obama.

Early on in his administration, we came to associate global cowboy bullying with George W. Bush. Widely perceived as simplistic in his thinking, he divided the complex world into two, announcing after 9-11 "You're either for us or against us," and demanding fealty as security against attack. Pakistan's leader Gen. Pervez Musharraf, an ally of the Taliban for his own geostrategic reasons, was ordered to sever ties with the organization and cooperate with the US "War on Terror" or "get bombed back to the Stone Age." The general obeyed, was paid well for his efforts, but also paid a political price. A poll taken in September 2007 showed him trailing Osama bin Laden in approval ratings in Pakistan, 46 to 38 percent.

Zardari, president since September 2008, represents a return to civilian rule and has a broader political base than Musharraf, who had seized power in a military coup in 1999. He's the husband of former president Benazir Bhutto, assassinated by terrorists during her presidential campaign in December 2007, and can count on the support of the Pakistan Peoples Party, the largest party in the country. But he too must comply with Washington's wishes, and Washington has not become less demanding or more respectful with the advent of Barack Hussein Obama.

Obama is in some ways (style, certainly) the antithesis of Bush. His smooth Cairo speech to the Muslim world in June 2009 was designed to counter the cowboy-outlaw image and portray the US as a respectful partner of Muslim nations, capable of self-reflection and self-criticism. He pointedly noted that the invasion of Iraq had been "a war of choice" (without however drawing the obvious conclusion that it was a war in violation of international law whose architects should be prosecuted). But the key passage in the dignified address was this one, which could have been penned by a Bush speechwriter:

> Over seven years ago, the United States pursued Al Qaeda and the Taliban with broad international support. We did not go by choice,

we went because of necessity. I am aware that some question or justify the events of 9/11. But let us be clear: Al Qaeda killed nearly 3,000 people on that day. The victims were innocent men, women and children from America and many other nations who had done nothing to harm anybody. And yet Al Qaeda chose to ruthlessly murder these people…. These are not opinions to be debated; these are facts to be dealt with.

Make no mistake: we do not want to keep our troops in Afghanistan…. We would gladly bring every single one of our troops home if we could be confident that there were not violent extremists in Afghanistan and Pakistan determined to kill as many Americans as they possibly can. But that is not yet the case.

Here the candidate of "change" (champion of a system that does not change) trotted out the same old tired myth that launched a thousand others in the period since: the notion that Al Qaeda = the Taliban. *That* is surely an "opinion to be debated," and if debated those conflating the two will be easily exposed as manipulative, fear-mongering deceivers. The US and its allies are not fighting those in Afghanistan who killed 3000 on 9/11 but Pashtun nationalists indignant that their country's been invaded and occupied. US intelligence quietly confirms that Al Qaeda has been driven from Afghanistan and any presence now is "minor." What the US faces now are new enemies that it multiplies each day through its behavior.

This is true in Pakistan too. Indeed, by its bombing of the Afghanistan-Pakistan border (the "Durand Line" legacy of British colonialism ignored by the Pashtuns who straddle it) the US played midwife to the birth of the Pakistani Taliban movement. US action has produced huge problems for the Pakistani state and its military, which officials show little understanding or empathy for.

From the point of view of the former, India occupying over half of Muslim Kashmir rather than their former Talib allies constitutes the primary threat to Pakistan's national security. But the real issue is not the legitimacy of Pakistan's claim to all of Kashmir or Indian counter-claims but the arrogance of a foreign power preaching to the Pakistanis where the real threats to themselves reside and demanding cooperation in confronting those threats. The Bush and Obama administrations have paid lip-service to the idea that "the Kashmir problem must be resolved," much as Obama has insisted, in words, that Israeli settlers must be withdrawn from the occupied West Bank, where they remain comfortably.

But then officials blithely suggest that giant India, with which the US has signed an agreement to sell nuclear reactors and equipment and is developing a military alliance (indeed urging it to become a "superpower" to challenge China and dominate the Indian Ocean), is no problem. Pakistan, they insist, ought to redeploy tens of thousands of troops from Kashmir to the Afghan border. The message remains the same as it was during the Bush administration: You're either for us or against us. Jump aboard our project; make our war your war and leave your other petty regional concerns (so difficult for Americans to understand) aside. And if with each missile we lob onto your sovereign territory without your permission and against your people's will we exacerbate the problem we've created, join with us in suffering the consequences.

Or rather, bear the great bulk of those consequences yourselves! Over 7000 civilians dead (according to one report, 90 percent of the 700 killed by drone strikes in 2009 were civilians).

Three thousand soldiers and police killed, over 13,000 militants (reportedly) killed, *three and a half million people displaced,* puritanical Islamism on the rise throughout the country. Even if the US absorbed the entire $35 billion price tag for the war, the socio-economic results have been disastrous. Hence as Zardari rather timidly understates it: "a cause of great concern." US attacks have indeed undermined any "national consensus" and instead produced deep fissures in Pakistani society (rather like the increasingly frequent drone attacks are doing in Yemen).

And the Obama administration, as Holbrooke's dismissive remarks make clear, just doesn't care. A very conventional president of an imperialist country with a savage history of wars against "communism" (i.e., to defend and expand capitalism), wars to expand empire, wars for control of resources and markets (which he defended in his Nobel Peace Prize speech as wars that "helped underwrite global security for more than six decades with the blood of our citizens and the strength of our arms") Obama weighs "costs and benefits" and calculates that the suffering of the Pakistani people and the stresses imposed on the Islamabad government are worth the occasional announcement that we slew one militant per ten or so "collateral" civilians. (Perhaps 100 civilians per Baitullah Mehsud-quality hit.)

Obama's much keener to fight the war in what his advisors call "Af-Pak" than was his bellicose predecessor. (Again: just twenty four drone attacks on Pakistan during the entire Bush administration, at least fifty four so far since Obama took office.) It's his war now, as key to his legacy as the health care reform bill. Reliant upon unmanned aerial vehicles and remote sensing to fire missiles at ground targets, it's a war without US casualties and thus no apparent immediate risk. But rest assured, the repeated, naked, callous violation of a proud, populous, nuclear-armed Muslim nation's sovereignty will produce some blowback over time.

You cannot deliberately cultivate hatred through your actions and expect it to just dry up and blow away. Human beings don't operate that way. They react. Until there's real change (not in the face on the system, but of the system itself) the cycle will continue.

Gary Leupp is Professor of History at Tufts University, and Adjunct Professor of Religion. He is the author of Servants, Shophands and Laborers in the Cities of Tokugawa Japan; Male Colors: The Construction of Homosexuality in Tokugawa Japan; *and* Interracial Intimacy in Japan: Western Men and Japanese Women, 1543–1900.

America the Pacified
By KATHY KELLY

If the US public looked long and hard into a mirror reflecting the civilian atrocities that have occurred in Afghanistan over the past ten months, we would see ourselves as people who have collaborated with and paid for war crimes committed against innocent civilians who meant us no harm.

Two reporters, Jerome Starkey (*The Times* UK), and David Lindorff, (*CounterPunch*), have persistently drawn attention to US war crimes committed in Afghanistan. Makers of the film *Rethinking Afghanistan* have steadily provided updates about the suffering endured by Afghan civilians. Here is a short list of atrocities that have occurred in the months since General McChrystal assumed his post in Afghanistan.

December 26th, 2009: US-led forces, (whether soldiers or "security contractors"—mercenaries—is still uncertain), raided a home in Kunar Province and pulled eight young men out of their beds, handcuffed them, and gunned them down execution-style. The Pentagon initially reported that the victims had been running a bomb factory, although distraught villagers were willing to swear that the victims, youngsters, aged eleven to eighteen, were just seven normal schoolboys and one shepherd boy. Following courageous reporting by Jerome Starkey, the US military carried out its own investigation and on February 24th, 2010, issued an apology, attesting the boys' innocence.

February 12, 2010: US and Afghan forces raided a home during a party and killed five people, including a local district attorney, a local police commander, two pregnant mothers and a teenaged girl engaged to be married. Neither Commander Dawood, shot in the doorway of his home while pleading for calm waving his badge, nor the teenaged Gulalai, died immediately, but the gunmen refused to allow relatives to take them to the hospital. Instead, they forced them to wait for hours barefoot in the winter cold outside.

Despite crowds of witnesses on the scene, the NATO report insisted that the two pregnant women at the party had been found bound and gagged, murdered by the male victims in an honor killing. A March 16, 2010 UN report, following on further reporting by Starkey, exposed the deception, to meager American press attention.

Two weeks later: February 21st, 2010: A three-car convoy of Afghans was traveling to the market in Kandahar with plans to proceed from there to a hospital in Kabul where some of the party could be taken for much-needed medical treatment. US forces saw Afghans travelling together and launched an air-to-ground attack on the first car. Women in the second car immediately jumped out waving their scarves, trying desperately to communicate that they were civilians. The US helicopter gunships continued firing on the now unshielded women. Twenty one people were killed and thirteen were wounded.

There was press attention for this atrocity, and US General Stanley McChrystal would issue a videotaped apology for his soldiers' tragic mistake. Broad consensus among the press accepted this as a gracious gesture, with no consequences for the helicopter crew ever demanded or announced.

Whether having that gunship in the country was a mistake—or a crime—was never raised as a question.

And who would want it raised? Set amidst the horrors of an ongoing eight-year war, how many Americans think twice about these atrocities, hearing them on the news?

So I'm baffled to learn that in Germany, a western, relatively comfortable country, citizens raised a sustained protest when their leaders misled them regarding an atrocity that cost many dozens of civilian lives in Afghanistan.

The air strike was conducted by US planes but called in by German forces. On September 4, 2009, Taliban fighters in Kunduz province had hijacked two trucks filled with petrol, but then gotten stuck in a quagmire where the trucks had sank. Locals, realizing that the trucks carried valuable fuel, had arrived in large numbers to siphon it off, but when a German officer at the nearest NATO station learned that over 100 people had assembled in an area under his supervision, he decided they must be insurgents and a threat to Germans under his command. At his call, a US fighter jet bombed the tankers, incinerating 142 people, dozens of them confirmable as civilians.

On September 6, 2009, Germany's Defense Minister at the time, Franz Josef Jung, held a press conference in which he defended the attack, playing down the presence of civilians. He wasn't aware that video footage from a US F15 fighter jet showed that most of the people present were unarmed civilians gathering to fill containers with fuel.

On November 27, 2009, after a steady outcry on the part of the German public, the Defense Minister was withdrawn from his post, (he is now a Labor Minister), and two German military officials, one of them Germany's top military commander Wolfgang Schneiderhan, were forced to resign.

I felt uneasy and sad when I realized that my first response to this story was a feeling of curiosity as to how the public of another country could manage to raise such a furor over deaths of people in faraway Afghanistan. How odd to have grown up wondering how anyone could ever have been an uninvolved bystander allowing Nazi atrocities to develop and to find myself, four decades later, puzzling over how German people or any country's citizenship could exercise so much control over their governance.

Today, in the US, attacks on civilians are frequently discussed in terms of the "war for hearts and minds."

Close to ten months ago, Defense Secretary Robert Gates told reporters at a June 12, 2009 press conference in Brussels that General Stanley McChrystal "would work to minimize Afghan civilian casualties, a source of growing public anger within Afghanistan."

"Every civilian casualty—however caused—is a defeat for us," Gates continued, "and a setback for the Afghan government."

On March 23rd, 2010, McChrystal was interviewed by the *Daily Telegraph*. "Your security comes from the people," he said. "You don't need to be secured away from the people. You need to be secured by the people. So as you win their support, it's in their interests to secure you,… This can mean patrolling without armored vehicles or even flak jackets. It means accepting greater short-term risk—and higher casualties—in the hope of winning a 'battle of perceptions and perspectives' that will result in longer-term security."

And on March 2nd, 2010, he told Gail McCabe "What we're trying to do now is to increase their confidence in us and their confidence in their government. But you can't do that through smoke and mirrors, you have to do that through real things you do—because they've been through thirty-one years of war now, they've seen so much, they're not going to be beguiled by a message."

We're obliged as Americans to ask ourselves whether we will be guided by a message such as McChrystal's or by evidence. Americans have not been through thirty-one years of war, and we have managed to see very little of the consequences of decades of warmaking in Afghanistan.

According to a March 3, 2010 Save the Children report, "The world is ignoring the daily deaths of more than 850 Afghan children from treatable diseases like diarrhea and pneumonia, focusing on fighting the insurgency rather than providing humanitarian aid." The report notes that a quarter of all children born in the country die before the age of five, while nearly 60 percent of children are malnourished and suffer physical or mental problems. The UN Human Development Index in 2009 says that Afghanistan is one of the poorest countries in the world, second only to Niger in sub-Saharan Africa.

The proposed US defense budget will cost the US public two billion dollars per day. President Obama's administration is seeking a $33 billion supplement to fund wars in Iraq and Afghanistan.

Most US people are aware of Taliban atrocities, and many may believe the US troops are in Afghanistan to protect Afghan villagers from Taliban human rights abuses. At least the mainstream news media in Germany and the UK will air stories of atrocities. The US people are disadvantaged inasmuch as the media and the Pentagon attempt to pacify us, winning our hearts and minds to bankroll ongoing warfare and troop escalation in Afghanistan. Yet it isn't very difficult to pacify US people. We're easily distracted from the war, and when we do note that an atrocity has happened, we seem more likely to respond with a shrug of dismay than with a sustained protest.

At the Winter Soldier hearings, future presidential hopeful John Kerry movingly asked Congress how it could ask a soldier "To be the last man to die for a mistake," while contemporary polls showed less prominent Americans far more willing to call the Vietnam war an evil—a crime, a sin—than "a mistake." The purpose of that war, as of Obama's favored war in Afghanistan, was to pacify dangerous populations—to make them peaceful, to win the battle of hearts and minds.

Afghan civilian deaths no longer occur at the rate seen in the war's first few months, in which the civilian toll of our September 11 attacks, pretext for the war then as it is now, was so rapidly exceeded.

But every week we hear—if we are listening very carefully to the news, if we are still reading that final paragraph on page A16—or if we are following the work of brave souls like Jerome Starkey—of tragic mistakes. We are used to tragic mistakes. Attacking a country militarily means planning for countless tragic mistakes.

Some of us still let ourselves believe that the war can do some good in Afghanistan, that our leaders' motives for escalating the war, however dominated by strategic economic concerns and geopolitical rivalries, still in some small part include the interests of the Afghan people.

There are others who know where this war will lead and know that our leaders know, and have simply become too fatigued, too drained of frightened tears by this long decade of nightmare, to hold those leaders accountable anymore for moral choices.

It's worthwhile to wonder, how did we become this pacified?

But far more important is our collective effort to approach the mirror, to stay in front of it, unflinching, and see the consequences of our mistaken acquiescence to the tragic mistakes of war, and then work, work hard, to correct our mistakes and nonviolently resist collaboration with war crimes.

Kathy Kelly co-coordinates Voices for Creative Nonviolence. She is the author of Other Lands Have Dreams *published by CounterPunch/AK Press.*

Kagan's Disturbing Record

By MARJORIE COHN

After President Obama nominated Elena Kagan for the Supreme Court, he made a statement that implied she would follow in the footsteps of Justice Thurgood Marshall, the civil rights giant and first black Supreme Court justice. Kagan served as a law clerk for Marshall shortly after she graduated from Harvard Law School. Specifically, Obama said that Marshall's "understanding of law, not as an intellectual exercise or words on a page, but as it affects the lives of ordinary people, has animated every step of Elena's career." Unfortunately, history does not support Obama's optimism that Kagan is a disciple of Marshall.

Kagan demonstrated while working as his law clerk that she disagreed with Marshall's jurisprudence. In 1988, the Supreme Court decided *Kadrmas v. Dickinson Public Schools*, a case about whether a school district could make a poor family pay for busing their child to the closest school, which was sixteen miles away. The five-justice majority held that the busing fee did not violate the Fourteenth Amendment's Equal Protection Clause. They rejected the proposition that education is a fundamental right which would subject the statute on which the school district relied to "strict scrutiny." The Court also declined to review the statute with "heightened scrutiny" even though it had different effects on the wealthy and the poor. Instead, the majority found a "rational basis" for the statute, that is, allocating limited governmental resources.

Marshall asked clerk Kagan to craft the first draft of a strong dissent in that case. But Kagan had a difficult time complying with Marshall's wishes and he returned several drafts to her for, in Kagan's words, "failing to express in a properly pungent tone—his understanding of the case." Ultimately, Marshall's dissent said, "The intent of our Fourteenth Amendment was to abolish caste legislation." He relied on *Plyler v. Doe*, in which the Court had upheld the right of the children of undocumented immigrants to receive free public education in the State of Texas. "As I have stated on prior occasions," Marshall wrote, "proper analysis of equal protection claims depends less on choosing the formal label under which the claim should be reviewed than upon identifying and carefully analyzing the real interests at stake." Kagan later complained that Marshall "allowed his personal experiences, and the knowledge of suffering and deprivation gained from those experiences to guide him."

Kagan evidently rejects these humanistic factors that guided Marshall's decision making and would follow a more traditional approach. This is a matter of concern for progressives, who worry about how the Supreme Court will deal with issues like a woman's right to choose, same sex marriage, "don't ask, don't tell," and the right of corporations to donate money to political campaigns without restraint. While Kagan has remained silent on many controversial issues, she has announced her belief that the Constitution provides no right to same-sex marriage. If the issue of marriage equality comes before the Court, Justice Kagan would almost certainly rule that denying same sex couples the right to marry does not violate equal protection.

There are other indications that should give progressives pause as well. During her solicitor general confirmation hearing, Kagan said, "The Constitution generally imposes limitations on government rather than establishes affirmative rights and thus has what might be thought of as a libertarian slant. I fully accept this traditional understanding." But the Constitution is full of affirmative rights—the right to a jury trial, the right to counsel, the right to assemble and petition the government, etc. Does Kagan not understand that decisions made by the Supreme Court give life and meaning to these fundamental rights? Is she willing to interpret those provisions in a way that will preserve individual liberties?

While Kagan generally thinks the Constitution serves to limit governmental power, she nevertheless buys into the Republican theory that the Executive Branch should be enhanced. In one of her few law review articles, Kagan advocated expansive executive power consistent with a formulation from the Reagan administration. This is reminiscent of the "unitary executive" theory that George W. Bush used to justify grabbing unbridled executive power in his "war on terror."

As solicitor general, Kagan asserted in a brief that the "state secrets privilege" is grounded in the Constitution. The Obama White House, like the Bush administration, is asserting this privilege to prevent people who the CIA sent to other countries to be tortured and people challenging Bush's secret spying program from litigating their cases in court.

Marjorie Cohn is a professor at Thomas Jefferson School of Law and immediate past president of the National Lawyers Guild. She is a member of the Bureau of the International Association of Democratic Lawyers. Her latest book is Rules of Disengagement.

Obama and the Nuclear Rocket

By KARL GROSSMAN

The Obama administration is seeking to renew the use of nuclear power in space. It is calling for revived production by the US of plutonium-238 for use in space devices—despite solar energy having become a substitute for plutonium power in space.

And the Obama administration appears to also want to revive the decades-old and long-discredited scheme of nuclear-powered rockets—despite strides made in new ways of propelling spacecraft. Last month, Japan launched what it called its "space yacht" which is now heading to Venus propelled by solar sails utilizing ionized particles emitted by the Sun. "Because of the frictionless environment, such a craft should be able to speed up until it is traveling many times faster than a conventional rocket-powered craft," wrote Agence France-Presse about this spacecraft launched May 21.

But the Obama administration would return to using nuclear power in space—despite its enormous dangers.

A cheerleader for this is the space industry publication *Space News.* "Going Nuclear" was the headline of its editorial on March 1 praising the administration for its space nuclear thrust. *Space News* declared that "for the second year in a row, the Obama administration is asking Congress for at least $30 million to begin a multiyear effort to restart domestic production of plutonium-238, the essential ingredient in long-lasting spacecraft batteries."

The *Space News* editorial also noted that "President Obama's NASA budget [for 2011] also includes support for nuclear thermal propulsion and nuclear electric propulsion research under a $650 million Exploration Technology and Demonstration funding line projected to triple by 2013."

Space News declared: "Nuclear propulsion research experienced a brief revival seven years ago when then-NASA administrator Sean O'Keefe established Project Prometheus to design reactor-powered spacecraft. Mr. O'Keefe's successor, Mike Griffin, wasted little time pulling the plug on NASA's nuclear ambitions."

Being referred to by *Space News* as "spacecraft batteries" are what are called radioisotope thermoelectric generators or RTGs, power systems using plutonium-238 to provide on-board electricity on various space devices including, originally, on satellites.

But this came to an end when in 1964 a US Navy navigational satellite with a SNAP-9A (SNAP for Systems Nuclear Auxiliary Power) RTG on board failed to achieve orbit and fell to the Earth, disintegrating upon hitting the atmosphere. The 2.1 pounds of plutonium fuel dispersed widely. A study by a group of European health and radiation protection agencies subsequently reported that "a worldwide soil sampling program carried out in

1970 showed SNAP-9A debris present at all continents and at all latitudes."
Long linking the SNAP-9A accident to an increase of lung cancer in people
on Earth was Dr. John Gofman, professor of medical physics at the University of California at Berkeley, who was involved in isolating plutonium for
the Manhattan Project.

The SNAP-9A accident caused NASA to turn to using solar photovoltaic
panels on satellites. All US satellites are now solar-powered.

But NASA persisted in using RTGs on space probes—claiming there
was no choice. This was a false claim. Although NASA, for instance, insisted—including in sworn court depositions—that it had no alternative but
to use RTGs on its Galileo mission to Jupiter launched in 1989, documents
I subsequently obtained through the Freedom of Information Act from
NASA included a study done by its Jet Propulsion Laboratory stating that
solar photovoltaic panels could have substituted for plutonium-fueled RTGs.

And right now, the Juno space probe—which will be getting its on board
electricity only from solar photovoltaic panels—is being readied by NASA
for a launch next year to Jupiter. It's to make thirty two orbits around Jupiter
and perform a variety of scientific missions.

In recent years facilities in the US that produce plutonium-238—
hotspots for worker contamination and environmental pollution—have been
closed and the US has been obtaining the radionuclide from Russia. Under the Obama 2011 budget, US production would be restarted. Last year,
Congress refused to go along with this Obama request.

As for rocket propulsion with atomic energy, building such rockets was a
major US undertaking fifty and sixty years ago, under a program called NER-
VA (for Nuclear Engine for Rocket Vehicle Application) followed by Projects
Pluto, Rover and Poodle. Billions of dollars were spent and ground-testing
done, but no nuclear rocket ever got off the ground. There were concerns over
a nuclear rocket blowing up on launch or crashing back to Earth. The effort
ended in 1972 but was revived in the 1980s under President Reagan's Star
Wars program. The "Timberwind" nuclear-powered rocket was developed
then to loft heavy Star Wars equipment into space and also for trips to Mars.
Most recently, Project Prometheus was to build nuclear-powered rockets,
begun by NASA in 2003, but ended in 2006, the cancellation referred to in
the *Space News* editorial.

Obama's choice to head NASA, Charles Bolden, favors nuclear-powered
rockets—but he acknowledges public resistance. In a recent presentation
before the Council on Foreign Relations, he opened the door to having a
nuclear-powered rocket launched conventionally and moving in space with
nuclear power.

Bolden, a former astronaut and US Marine Corps major general, spoke
in the May 24th address, of work by another ex-astronaut, Franklin Chang-
Diaz, on a nuclear-propelled rocket. "Chang-Diaz is developing what's called

a VASIMIR [Variable Specific Impulse Magnetoplasma Rocket] rocket," said Bolden. "It's an ion engine, very gentle impulse that just pushes you forever, constantly accelerating. And this, theoretically, is something that would enable us to go from Earth to Mars in a matter of some time significantly less than it takes us now."

But, he said, "most people … in the United States are never going to agree to allow nuclear rockets to launch things from Earth." Yet "once you get into space, you know, if we can convince people that we can contain it and not put masses of people in jeopardy, nuclear propulsion for in-space propulsion" would enable a faster trip to Mars. He said, "You don't want to have to take eight months to go from Earth orbit to Mars."

Having nuclear power systems only activated once up in space was a system followed by the Soviet Union—because of it having suffered many launch pad explosions. Still, the scheme wasn't accident-free. The worst Soviet space nuclear device accident involved its Cosmos 954 reconnaissance satellite. Its on-board nuclear reactor was only activated after launch when the reactor was in orbit. But then there was a malfunction causing Cosmos 954 to tumble out of control and hurtle back to Earth, breaking up and spreading hotly radioactive debris over 124,000 square miles of the Northwest Territories of Canada.

President Obama, in a speech on "Space Exploration in the 21st Century" given April 15 at NASA's Kennedy Space Center, didn't mention nuclear-powered rockets (not even those that would only be activated after launch). He did announce that "we will invest more than $3 billion to conduct research on an advanced heavy lift rocket—a vehicle to efficiently send into orbit the crew capsules, propulsion systems and large quantities of supplies needed to reach deep space. In developing this new vehicle, we will not only look at revising or modifying older models; we want to look at new designs, new materials, new technologies that will transform not just where we can go but what we can do when we get there. And we will finalize a rocket design no later than 2015 and then begin to build it."

"At the same time, after decades of neglect, we will increase investment—right away—in other groundbreaking technologies that will allow astronauts to reach space sooner and more often, to travel farther and faster," he said.

"How do we supply spacecraft with energy needed for these far-reaching journeys? These are questions that we can answer and will answer. And these are the questions whose answers no doubt will reap untold benefits right here on Earth."

"And by 2025," Obama said, "we expect new spacecraft designed for long journeys to allow us to begin the first-ever crewed missions beyond the Moon into deep space. So we'll start—we'll start by sending astronauts to an asteroid for the first time in history. By the mid-2030s, I believe we can send humans to orbit Mars."

"I want to repeat this," Obama asserted. "Critical to deep space exploration will be the development of breakthrough propulsion systems and other advanced technologies."

With Obama on the platform was Senator Bill Nelson of Florida—who he introduced at the start of his speech. In 1986, Nelson was a passenger on the space shuttle (before the 1986 Challenger disaster ended the shuttle passenger program) and he is a member of Senate Science and Transportation Committee. Although Obama was not specific on the kind of spacecraft he envisioned for trips to Mars, later that day on *Hardball With Chris Matthews* on MSNBC, Nelson was—and it was Chang-Diaz's nuclear rocket. "One of my crewmates," said Nelson, speaking of former astronaut Chang-Diaz who was with him on the 1986 shuttle flight, "is developing a plasma rocket that would take us to Mars in 39 days."

The object of Administrator Bolden and Senator Nelson's technical affections, Chang-Diaz, a Costa Rican-native, the first naturalized US citizen to become a US astronaut, founded the Ad Astra Rocket Company after retiring from NASA in 2005. He is its president and CEO. In an interview with Seed.com last year, he said the engine for his VASIMIR could work with solar power. The engine uses plasma gas heated by electric current to extremely high temperatures.

But larger versions are needed for space travel and they require nuclear power, said Chang-Diaz. "What we really need is nuclear power to generate electricity in space. If we don't develop it, we might as well quit, because we're not going to go very far. Nuclear power is central to any robust and realistic human exploration of space. People don't really talk about this at NASA. Everybody is still avoiding facing this because of widespread anti-nuclear sentiment."

"People have fears of nuclear power in space," continued Chang-Diaz, "but it's a fear that isn't really based on any organized and clear assessment of the true risks and costs."

Comments Bruce Gagnon, coordinator of the Global Network Against Weapons & Nuclear Power in Space: "Despite claims that 'new' and innovative technologies are under development at NASA, the story remains much the same—push nuclear power applications for future space missions. Obama is proving to be a major proponent of expansion of nuclear power—both here on Earth and in space. His 'trip to an asteroid and missions to Mars' plan appears to be about reviving the role of nuclear power in space. The nuclear industry must be cheering."

Karl Grossman, professor of journalism at the State University of New York/ College at Old Westbury, has focused on investigative reporting on energy and environmental issues for more than forty years. He is the host of the nationally-aired TV program Enviro Close-Up *(www.envirovideo.com) and the author of numerous books.*

Torturing the Rule of Law at Obama's Gitmo

By CHASE MADAR

President Obama may lack the nerve to stare down Liz Cheney or Bibi Netanyahu, but no one can deny that our commander-in-chief had the guts to take on a child soldier. In October of 2010 a military commission in Guantánamo convicted Omar Khadr, a Canadian national captured outside Kabul in 2002, when he was just fifteen-years-old. It was only the third complete Gitmo trial and the Obama administration's first, and there wasn't anything kinder and gentler about it.

But give Team Obama credit for breaking new ground: no nation had tried a child soldier for war crimes since World War II. (The decision to prosecute Khadr drew protests from UNICEF, headed by a former US national security adviser, as well as every major human-rights group.) But then many Americans are baffled by the idea of clemency for a youthful offender, let alone an accused terrorist. In a country where dozens of prisoners are serving life without parole for crimes committed when they were twelve or thirteen, and trying fifteen-year-old felons as adults is routine if not mandatory, the prosecution of Omar Khadr has never lacked its supporters.

The hopeless audacity doesn't stop there: charges against Khadr included "murder in violation of the rules of war," a newly minted war crime wholly novel to the history of armed conflict. Battlefield deaths do not usually result in murder trials for prisoners of war—certainly no American soldier captured in Vietnam or Nazi Germany was ever tried for the crime. But according to the Department of Defense, Omar Khadr was never a bona-fide POW but a non-uniformed, "unprivileged belligerent." The laws of war used to just call such people "savages," proof that in the past hundred years we have made great strides with our euphemisms.

Khadr was accused of throwing a hand grenade that killed a US serviceman, Sgt. First Class Christopher Speer, in a firefight between US forces and jihadis outside of Kabul in July, 2002. Khadr confessed to tossing the grenade from his hospital bed at Bagram prison while heavily sedated, his chest wounds barely closed. Over months, an extravagantly detailed confession was developed by a succession of interrogators, from the since convicted abuser of prisoners who first interviewed Khadr to a female military interrogator with an MA in anthropology who soothed him to good effect. Omar Khadr repudiated his confession after being transported to Guantánamo, and alleged in a lengthy affidavit that he suffered torture and abusive coercion at both prisons. Not many would deny that Khadr was tortured—one interrogator testified that he first laid eyes on the youth hooded and chained to the walls of his cell, standing with his shackled arms extended at head level. Nevertheless, commission judge Patrick Parrish concluded that none of this constituted torture or even the coercive treatment more broadly defined by the military tribunal guidelines. If the finding had been made under Bush and Cheney, it would have been noisome proof of their barbarity; under Obama both the media and the liberal-minded public have become far more blasé about torturing minors in the name of national security.

At the hopeful beginning of the Obama administration (was it only three years ago?) everyone except the Right's usual panic-merchants was sick of Guantánamo, and Obama promised its closure by the end of 2009. But that deadline has passed, in part because the president fumbled his chance to channel the prisoners into civilian federal courts. Instead of first getting buy-in for this politically delicate course of action from elected officials in New York, where trials would be held, Eric Holder unilaterally announced the proposal, to the seething irritation of Mayor Michael Bloomberg and Senator Chuck Schumer. Thus blindsided, New York officials who might have been able to build support and broker a deal for federal civilian trials were left looking like fools, and they refused to back the administration's plan. (This has not been the only example of Team Obama's surprisingly flatfooted political skills.)

Meanwhile, support for Guantánamo has crept back up and solidified among congressional Republicans and many Democrats as well, such that now Gitmo will surely remain open for years to come. Outrage is passé and the media are heartily sick of the story; the reporters I joined there in April of 2010 told me they had to beg their editors to be sent down to cover the Khadr hearings.

Anyone expecting to witness eye-popping tableaux of Rumsfeldian cruelty at Gitmo today will be disappointed. It's a military base like many others, except instead of the nearby base town with obligatory pawn shop, strip club, and Korean restaurant, you find an impermeable barrier sealing base dwellers and visitors inside. Overall, it's not a bad deployment: soldiers can at least get a beer off duty, the snorkeling is good, and the roads are free of IEDs. Given the paucity of lurid local color, scribblers who take the military flight—when I flew down, a leased Delta aircraft from Andrews Air Force Base—have been reduced to soliloquizing about the Gitmo McDonald's and the banality of evil amid the french fries.

The prison complex's population continues to trickle away—to a point. Over 600 prisoners have been let go, most by the Bush administration, and of the fifty one habeas petitions for release filed since the *Boumediene* decision in 2008, thirty seven have been granted. Were these really "the worst of the worst"? Hardly, and the WikiLeaks cables on Guantánamo show that this was known from the beginning. Still, the Obama administration has announced that it will continue to hold some forty five detainees indefinitely without charges, one of George W. Bush's most radical policies, now zeal-ously defended by a smoother, smarter team of Democratic lawyers. This is exactly the kind of lawlessness that Harold Koh, a human-rights icon, used to condemn from his bully pulpit as dean of Yale Law. Now, as legal adviser to the Department of State, he's tasked with justifying indefinite detention.

Team Obama's reaction has been to paper over this abyss with a layer of legality. There are new, improved rules for the military commissions, signed by the secretary of defense the night before Khadr's April 2010 hearings began (and still in place for the hearings that will resume in late 2011). Alas, they continue to fall short in core areas of juridical fairness. There is no right to a speedy trial, no pretrial investigation to weed out weak cases, and the defense's requests for witnesses must go through the prosecution. There is no credit for pretrial detention—now nearly a decade for many prisoners—and no right of equal access to witnesses and evidence. Freshly invented war crimes like "material support for terrorism," retroactively applied, violate the fundamental juridical principle of *nulla poena sine lege* (no crime without a prospective law).

The greatest flaw is structural: the interference of the "Convening Au-thority"—the politically appointed head of the commissions—into the pros-ecutions has been documented again and again. Brig. Gen. Thomas Hart-mann, former legal adviser to the Convening Authority, was so blatant in his attempts to secure convictions that he was banned from any involvement in three separate trials for his "undue command influence." One former chief prosecutor at Guantánamo has said that Hartmann pushed hard for the Khadr case because he thought it would be "sexy, the kind of case the public's going to get energized about." Such micromanaging did not endear Hartmann to his colleagues: former deputy prison camps commander at Guantánamo Brig. Gen. Gregory Zanetti testified in 2008 that Hartmann's conduct was "abusive, bullying and unprofessional ... pretty much across the board."

One might expect that a legal system thus rigged would greatly appeal to its prosecutors. Until now, one would be wrong. Half a dozen prosecutors have quit the commissions in disgust, most with blistering criticisms on their way out. Col. Morris Davis, former chief prosecutor of the commissions until Oc-tober 2007, said that constant political pressure made full, fair and open trials impossible: "What we are doing at Guantánamo is neither military nor justice."

No less scathing is Lt. Col. Darrel Vandeveld, formerly lead prosecutor in another commissions case against a child soldier—a case that collapsed midway through, in 2008, with the government dropping all charges. "It would be foolish to expect anything to come out of Guantánamo except de-cades of failure. There will be no justice there, and Obama has proved to be an almost unmitigated disaster," he told me on Memorial Day, 2010. After re-signing from the commissions as a matter of ethical principle, Vandeveld was punished with a mandatory psychiatric evaluation and gratuitous hearings into his fitness for remaining in the Army, even though at the time he had only months remaining in his term of service. Vandeveld, who has deployed to Iraq, Afghanistan, and Bosnia, doubts very much that any more prosecutors will resign after his highly visible reprimand. (Vandeveld, who has truly served his country as a military lawyer of iron principles, now runs the public defender office in Erie, PA.)

The new head of the prosecution team, Capt. John Murphy, told me proudly in May 2010 that morale has never been higher on his team. Half of the four lawyers looked young enough to have started law school long after 2001, and it is hard to imagine young attorneys quitting the commissions without established careers to fall back on. With no adult memories of the law or national security before 9/11 allegedly changed everything, the permanent state of emergency might seem to them blandly normal.

This may spell the end to a golden chapter in JAG history: throughout the sordid drama of Guantánamo, the few glimmers of governmental integrity have come from the JAG corps' dissent. They even earned the ultimate ethical accolade, the disapproval of John Yoo, who scolded the military lawyers for adhering to the rule of law in defiance of the "unitary executive authority" as embodied by torture buffs such as himself.

For its part, Team Obama's main innovation has been to ban troublesome journalists from the base, a move Bush never dared. On May 6, 2010, toward the end of this round of hearings, the Joint Task Force abruptly barred four of the most knowledgeable reporters from returning to Gitmo, accusing them of violating an order that the identity of Omar Khadr's primary interrogator be kept secret. It doesn't matter that "Interrogator Number One," convicted in a 2005 court martial for prisoner abuse at Bagram prison, had already been interviewed by one of these journalists two years ago and that his identity was available in the public record.

One of the banned journalists, Carol Rosenberg of McClatchy, was hounded in the summer of 2009 by a risible and quickly dismissed sexual harassment complaint made by then-Navy press officer Jeffrey Gordon. Rosenberg is the acknowledged dean of Gitmo journalists, and getting rid of her would have been a singularly effective way for the Department of Defense to regain some control over the sordid War Court narrative. Carol and the other journalists have since been reinstated after reaffirming their allegiance to the DoD's "ground rules" at Gitmo, but the government's warning shot has been heard.

The uproar over the banned journalists did successfully deflect attention from the prosecution's cozy arrangements with a convicted detainee abuser. Joshua Claus, or "interrogator number one" as he was called in the hearings, was court-martialed for detainee abuse in 2005, and pled guilty to maltreatment and assault on a taxi driver known only as Dilawar, who was beaten to death by his Bagram interrogators. (Dilawar's crime had been to drive his taxi near the detention centre at the wrong time.) Though Claus was not convicted of murder (no one was), he did admit to throttling Dilawar and forcing water down his throat, and he was the last interrogator seen with the prisoner before his death. Claus's pledge to cooperate with the Khadr prosecution team helped earn him a lenient sentence of only five months. Though called as a defense witness in the recent Khadr hearings, Claus had spent far more time conferring with the prosecution, and his well-prepared statements in the hearings evinced much rehearsal and preparation with them. The prosecution's warmly collegial relationship with a court-martialed detainee abuser: this is not the stuff for an Obama-era rehabilitation of Guantánamo's public image.

And that image remains pretty terrible, even if Camp X-Ray, the open-air cages that held orange jumpsuited detainees for four months in 2002, is now growing weeds. Camp Delta, the detention complex, is rather prosaic. Camp 5, for the least compliant prisoners, is a direct modular copy of a block from the federal prison in Terre Haute, Indiana; Camps 4 and 6, for the most compliant, of Lawanee Prison in Adrian, Michigan. Some detainees are able to take courses in Arabic, English, and art. And so what?

A prison doesn't have to be a Gothic nightmare to threaten the rule of law. As the ACLU's Ben Wizner puts it, "At this point, Guantánamo isn't a place anymore, it's a principle." A normal-looking prison that just happens to hold people indefinitely without charge is a far more insidious threat to the integrity of the legal system than Camp X-Ray ever was. For this reason, the ACLU does not see transporting the system to Thomson Correctional Facility in Illinois as progress, but rather as an insidious regression. (If this is the only alternative, libertarians, liberals and radicals ought to pray fervently that Obama does NOT make good on his promise to shut down Gitmo.)

Guantánamo, wherever it is located, runs the grave risk of normalization, a process already well underway. Over a few nights during the Khadr hearings, I read in my air-conditioned tent a law-review article by Prof. Adrian Vermeule, an up-and-comer at Harvard Law School. He proposes that legal black holes—the term was coined by a British law lord expressly for Guantánamo—are not only tolerable but necessary. Any attempt to fill them in with law would be "hopelessly utopian," "quixotic" even. "Our Schmittian Administrative Law," published in 2009 in the *Harvard Law Review*, draws heavily on the work of wannabe-Nazi jurist Carl Schmitt, lifelong opponent of the rule of law and liberal democracy. A figure of fascination among left-wing academics for the cold eye he cast on liberalism's sacred myths, Schmitt's ideas had always been held at a prophylactic distance.

No longer. Schmitt's ready-made conceptual lexicon for political emergencies, non-state combatants, and the need for strident executive authority has proven irresistible to ambitious intellectuals in the revolving door between federal government and the finer law schools. These tweedy immoralists urge us to relax our square-jawed commitment to the rule of law and embrace strong executive action. Surely the moralizing banalities of rule-of-law theorists are inadequate for the unique challenges of the post-9/11 global order, they tell us.

But as the events of the past decade plainly show, one would be on safer ground drawing the opposite conclusion about the rule of law's value—and effectiveness. Our government responded to 9/11 with numerous extraordinary measures contemptuous of ordinary legality, and virtually every one of them has been catastrophic in its consequences. From the illegal conquest of Iraq to rampant torture to mass warrantless wiretapping to the military commissions of Guantánamo, these policies have been exorbitantly costly in blood, money, and national prestige. Convicting a child soldier who was tortured in custody of a newly invented "crime" in a shambolic court is not going to solve anything. Has any part of our frenzied rejection of legal restraints improved national security one bit? Just how did any of these radical above-the-law measures help America, let alone the world?

Vermeule is correct to note that these black holes are likely to dilate rather than contract as an imperialist foreign policy strains our legal system, not only with the panic and fervor of war but with juridical conundrums of extraterritoriality, non-state belligerents, and geographically far-fetched definitions of self-defense. Already a new Guantánamo for indefinite detainees has opened up in Bagram, which will be much less accessible to media, nonprofit observers, and defense counsel.

Meanwhile, the rule of law will continue to suffer rough treatment at the hands of our best and brightest. The concept of the rule of law has been debunked in varying degrees by many insightful jurists, many of whose criticisms are not without merit. But to say the rule of law is a mythical ideal is quite different from dismissing it out of hand. All over the world where violent lawlessness is rife, people see the rule of law as far more than mere rhetorical window dressing. From Colombia to Egypt to Italy to Guantánamo's neighboring Cuba, citizens who risk their lives against the depredations of organized crime or authoritarian states routinely invoke the rule of law to give meaning to their acts of resistance. Yes, the rule of law may be an ideal—but it is not a folktale for chuckleheads.

Repairing the many legal black holes in America might start by shutting down Guantánamo (wherever it may be located) and radically rethinking our post-9/11 security policies. Indefinite detention in some nondescript prison with a few art classes doesn't make for splashy headlines, but it marks yet another serious injury to the rule of law as we would like to know it. The Obama administration has failed utterly to rethink, much less reform, the counterproductive emergency measures installed by George W. Bush, an opinion widely shared not just among civil libertarians but among former Bush-Cheney officials.

UPDATE: Khadr's conviction and sentence

In October 2010, Omar Khadr agreed to plea guilty to the five charges against him in exchange for a sentence of eight years not including time served; the deal further stipulates that after one year at Gitmo, Khadr may be allowed to return to Canada where he will be eligible for supervised release out of prison. Even so, the military tribunal's jury was allowed to deliver its own sentence: an amazing forty years. The widow of Khadr's purported victim reacted with unrestrained joy to the verdict and announced to the Gitmo press gaggle that this was the happiest day of her life, before quickly adding, "aside from my wedding day, of course." Even as Washington spends millions of USAID dollars in Afghanistan trying to erect a modern justice system, our own courts become ever more indistinguishable from tribal blood-feuds, whether in Gitmo or Georgia.

At this writing, Khadr is finishing his first year of his sentence, which has been spent in solitary confinement, a condition shared by tens of thousands of Americans in the everyday "normal" penal system on the mainland. (Khadr had been living among the relatively low-security inmate population at Gitmo, but as a convicted prisoner the authorities claimed to have no choice but to place him in solitary.) The solitary confinement of Khadr and of anyone else ought to be viewed as torture, given the well-documented permanent psychological damage it inflicts, but there has been negligible outcry. We will soon see whether the military authorities will keep their bargain and allow Omar Khadr to return to Canada where his long imprisonment, bracketed on both ends by legalized torture, will finally come to an end. Military commission trials are scheduled to resume at Guantanamo at the end of 2011.

Chase Madar is a lawyer in New York, and can be reached at chase.madar@ gmail.com. This is an updated version of reports that originally appeared in the August 2010 issue of The American Conservative *magazine and the August 2010 issue of* Le Monde diplomatique.

Eat, Pray, Be Disappointed
By PAUL KRASSNER

Dear President Obama,

It seems that the theme emanating from the White House is "Eat, Pray, Be Disappointed." And yet, whenever I do feel disappointed, I always realize that the alternative was John McCain, with Sarah Palin just one Halloween "Boo!" away from the presidency, and then I always feel a sense of relief.

Actually, you've kept one big campaign promise—to send more troops to Afghanistan—so I guess we can't fault you for that. In fact, according to Bob Woodward in *Obama's Wars*, all you want to do now is get *out* of Afghanistan. Well, why don't you just do what Osama bin Laden did; cross over to Pakistan. Since we bribe Pakistan to be our ally, you'd think they would never consider harboring bin Laden, though they reek with empathy when our outsourced drones drop those bombs.

Also, during the campaign you said you believe that the legality of same-sex marriage should be decided by the states, but that you personally think marriage should be between a man and a woman. Which is exactly the position that eventually led to the revocation of Carrie Prejean's Miss USA crown. And another thing. You promised to end the raids on medical marijuana dispensaries, but they haven't stopped.

[In 2009, Attorney General Eric Holder issued a memo ordering an end to federal raids of medical marijuana dispensaries. In March 2011, there were twenty eight such raids in a duration of twenty four hours.]

Here's how I understand Washington. America's puritanical political process serves as a buffer between the status quo and the force of evolution. For instance, in order to get Republican votes for the children's health care bill, Democrats agreed to fund $28 million to *their* abstinence-only program.

And, during your own campaign, you admitted, in the context of health care reform, that the multinational insurance conglomeration is so firmly entrenched that you would be unable to dispense with it. So there would have to be compromises. Now, what with the compromises made to help passage of Prop. 19, amnesty becomes the single-payer system of marijuana reform, and growing your own pot becomes the public option. Meanwhile, as long as any government can arbitrarily decide which drugs are legal and which drugs are illegal, then anyone serving time for a nonviolent drug offense is a political prisoner.

In his new book, Bob Woodward writes about Colin Powell's status as an adviser to you. Referring to his previous book, *Plan of Attack*, the *New York Times* then reported that "Secretary of State Colin Powell disputed Woodward's account.... He said that he had an excellent relationship with Vice President Dick Cheney, and that he did not recall referring to officials at the

Pentagon loyal to Cheney as the 'Gestapo office.'" Who among us would be unable to recall uttering such an epithet? Powell later apologized for it. He has also changed his mind about gays in the military. In my capacity as a stand-up satirist, I used to conduct an imaginary dialogue with Powell.

"General Powell, you're the first African-American to be head of the Joint Chiefs of Staff, and you come from the tradition of a military family. So you know that blacks were once segregated in the Army because the other soldiers might feel uncomfortable if blacks slept in the same barracks. And now that's what they say about gays, that other soldiers might feel uncomfortable about *gays* sleeping in the same barracks." "Well, you have to understand, we never *told* anybody we were black."

And, Mr. President, that was the forerunner of the same "Don't ask, don't tell" policy that you promised to rescind, only you haven't been acting like a Commander-in-Chief. All you have to do is sign such a directive. Those who serve in the military are trained to follow orders. If they can follow orders to kill fellow humans, they can certainly follow orders to treat openly gay service people with total equality.

Not only is the current guideline counterproductive, but also this display of trickle-down immorality must, on some level of consciousness, serve as a contributing factor to enabling the anti-gay bullying and torturing of innocent victims. I know, you don't want to take a chance that retracting the policy would interfere with your re-election. You've made the point that you don't want Mitt Romney to win in 2012 and turn around all the good things you've accomplished.

Incidentally, Romney had wanted to overturn *Roe vs. Wade*, yet, in 1994, when he was running for the Senate, he came out in *favor* of choice for women. However, freelance journalist Suzan Mazur revealed that he admitted to Mormon feminist Judith Dushku that "the Brethren" in Salt Lake City *told* him he could take a pro-choice position, and that in fact he probably *had* to in order to win in a liberal state like Massachusetts. Pandering trumps religious belief.

Meantime, since gays and lesbians have waited so long for basic fairness, they might as well just wait for the next election. If you win, then would you kindly do immediately what you believe is right, constitutionally and in your heart, and end this injustice? The ultimate irony is that gays in the military are fighting, being maimed and dying unnecessarily, supposedly to protect the freedom their own country is denying them.

Sincerely,
Paul Krassner

Postscript:

My letter was published on such blogsites as *Huffington Post, CounterPunch, Rag Blog, Free Press* and *Newsroom*. Among the responses that day, I received a message from a mother on Facebook: "I am trying to explain this to my twelve-year-old son, who wants to know why, if men and women don't share barracks in the military, why gay men and hetero men should share barracks, but then follows with 'They should all sleep in the same place.'"

That night, I received this e-mail from a seasoned journalist: "I know it's late, but I cannot wait to ask if this letter is a spoof, or you've actually sent it to Obama. If it's a spoof and you've not sent it to him, would you like to? I've got his fax number and he's got a great sense of humor. May I have your permission to send this to him?"

"Absolutely," I replied.

Two days later, to the dismay of Obama—who told a town hall meeting that he was restricted because the "Don't ask, don't tell" policy was written into law, adding, "This is not a situation where I can, by the stroke of a pen, end this policy"—he wanted Congress to repeal it after the November midterm election, but Federal Judge Virginia Phillips upset that timetable by issuing an immediate and permanent ban on what she considered to be unconstitutional. This ruling was not a spoof, though it was treated as one by an appeals court that set aside her injunction. In December 2010, Congress repealed the seventeen-year-old law.

Nor was it a spoof when Attorney General Holder—having been pressured by nine former DEA chiefs, plus the president of Mexico—warned that if Prop. 19 was passed, making California the first state to legalize pot, the federal government would not look the other way, as it has done with medical marijuana. Holder (who wouldn't prosecute the Bush administration for promulgating torture) explained:

> Let me state clearly that the Department of Justice strongly opposes Proposition 19. If passed, this legislation will greatly complicate federal drug enforcement efforts to the detriment of our citizens. We will vigorously enforce the [law] against those individuals and organizations that possess, manufacture or distribute marijuana for recreational use, even if such activities are permitted under state law.

In a truly free society, the distinction of whether marijuana is used for medical or recreational purposes would be as irrelevant an excuse for discrimination as whether the sexual preference of gays and lesbians is innate or a matter of choice.

Paul Krassner's latest book is an expanded edition of his autobiography, Confessions of a Raving, Unconfined Nut: Misadventures in the Counterculture

Let Them Eat Oil: The Bi-Partisan Path to the Gulf Catastrophe

By JEFFREY ST. CLAIR

The mood in the Alaska office of the Minerals Management Service (MMS) was festive. Word had just reached Anchorage that the president was preparing plans to expand offshore drilling in Alaska. John Goll, the service's regional director, summoned his top lieutenants to his office for a briefing of the joyous news. After confirming the rumors that had circulated all morning, Goll invited "all hands" in the office to join him for coffee and pastries. At the center of the table, the cheering staffers were greeted by a large cake, with "Drill Baby Drill" scrawled across it in chocolate icing.

The year was not 2004. The president was not George W. Bush. This scene took place in 2009, a few months into Barack Obama's first term as president.

As it turned out, Goll had several reasons to be upbeat. Not only had the new administration steamrolled its environmentalist allies and decided to move forward with new drilling operations along Alaska's fragile coastline, but Goll and his troubled agency had survived the presidential transition intact. Goll, who was appointed to the powerful post of Alaska regional director in 1997 during the Clinton administration's drive to escalate drilling on the North Slope, had come into his prime as a bureaucratic facilitator of big oil under George W. Bush.

As detailed in a Government Accountability Office investigation of the Alaska Office of the MMS under Goll's tenure, the relationship between the government regulators and the oil industry was incestuous. The report revealed an agency that approved nearly every drilling plan without restrictions, muzzled internal dissent and gagged agency scientists. Environmental reviews, when they were undertaken—which was rarely—were cursory and fast-tracked. The only obligation for the oil companies was: just drill. Drill where you want, how you want.

There's nothing to indicate that after Ken Salazar piously declared that he was going to weed out and reinvent the MMS as a fierce regulatory watchdog, Goll and his cronies did anything but chuckle.

Perhaps Goll knew more about the real Salazar than the mainstream environmental groups who had blindly lauded the man-in-the-hat's appointment as interior secretary. In the first year of the Obama administration, Salazar's Interior Department had put fifty three million acres of offshore oil reserves up for lease, far eclipsing the records set by the Bush administration. This staggering achievement probably came as no surprise to Goll and his oil industry cronies. When Salazar served in the US Senate, he publicly chided the Bush administration for the lethargic pace of its drilling operations in the Gulf of

Mexico. Peeved, Salazar co-sponsored the Gulf of Mexico Energy Security Act, which opened an additional eight million acres of the Gulf to new drilling.

In this optimistic spirit, Goll's office proceeded to swiftly and blithely approve one of the most contentious oil drilling plans of the last decade—a scheme by Shell Oil to sink exploratory wells in Beaufort and Chukchi Seas, crucial habitat for the endangered bowhead whale.

The drilling plan was hastily consecrated on the basis of a boilerplate environmental review despite the fact that even a minor oil spill in these remote Arctic seas would prove to be an uncontrollable ecological catastrophe. Indeed, under Goll's direction, the Alaska office of the MMS was so uninterested in environmental analysis that it had failed to even develop a handbook for writing environmental reviews as required by the Department of Interior. Why bother, when Shell Oil could be depended on to write its own environmental analysis? That's efficiency.

Goll wasn't the only Bush holdover at MMS to survive the Obama transition. There is the curious case of Chris C. Oynes. Oynes served for twelve years as the director of oil and gas leasing operations for the MMS in the Gulf of Mexico. Those were buxom years for the oil industry. During his tenure in the Louisiana regional office, Oynes approved nearly 1,000 new oil drilling permits, roughly a fifth of all the current drilling sites in the Gulf of Mexico. Few of these operations underwent even the most simplistic environmental reviews or on-site inspections. Instead, as detailed in a blistering report from the Interior Department's inspector general, under Oynes's watch the repeat offenders in the oil industry were allowed to police themselves, writing their own environmental analyses, safety inspections and compliance reports, often in pencil for MMS regulators to trace over in ink.

The inspector general concluded that the agency fostered a "culture of ethical failure." That may be putting it mildly. For Oynes and his colleagues, it wasn't about ethics but serving the interests of big oil. And he did that in a big way that meant billions for Gulf oil drillers.

Here's how it went down. In 1995, Congress, in collaboration with the Clinton administration, passed the Deep Water Royalty Relief Act, a bill meant to encourage oil companies like BP to begin the risky proposition of drilling for oil more than a mile beneath the surface of the Gulf. As an incentive to drill, the deepwater operators were exempted from paying royalties until the amount of oil produced hit certain price and production triggers. These triggers were supposed to be written into the lease contracts. For example, the price trigger was set at $28 per barrel. The companies were meant to pay royalties to MMS on all oil sold above this rate, which was substantially below the market price of crude in the late 1990s. But this language mysteriously disappeared from the contracts. One MMS staffer later told investigators with the inspector general's office that he had been instructed to remove the price trigger language from the leases.

The man who signed off on most of the 113 deepwater leases offered in 1998 and 1999 was the MMS's regional director at the time, Chris Oynes, who duly told investigators that he simply overlooked the missing language. But executives at Chevron, ever conscious of the bottom line, noticed the absence of price triggers and met with Oynes three times to discuss the matter. Apparently satisfied with the terms of the deal, Chevron plunged into the deepwater bonanza in the Gulf. For his part, Oynes said he had no recollection of these meetings.

A year later, officials at the Interior Department discovered the mistake. Panicky emails flew back and forth inside the agency. But instead of exposing the debacle and trying to rectify the problem, they covered it up for the next six years. The assistant director of MMS decided not to inform the head of the agency, and the sweetheart deal with deepwater drillers remained buried until 2006, when it was unearthed by Inspector General Earl Devaney, who called the affair "a jaw-dropping example of bureaucratic bungling."

Devaney put dozens of MMS officials under the microscope in an attempt to identify the official who ordered that the price triggers be removed from the deepwater leases. Oynes himself was made to take a polygraph test. But, in the end, Devaney found no smoking gun, largely because of the convenient death of one of the central players in the affair. Frustrated at every turn, the inspector general ended his investigation, appalled at the entire agency: "Simply stated, short of a crime, anything goes at the highest levels of the Department of Interior."

What Devaney termed a "blunder" ended up allowing the deepwater drillers to stiff the federal treasury out of an estimated $12 billion in royalty payments. Some might write this off as a monumental mistake. But at the MMS, these kinds of screwups always seem to end up bulging the pockets of the oil companies.

As for Oynes, he survived the royalty affair unscathed. He escaped indictment. He wasn't forced to resign. He wasn't even demoted. Instead, in 2007 Johnnie Burton, Bush's head of MMS, appointed Oynes assistant director of MMS in charge of offshore drilling. His charmed career continued a year later, when Ken Salazar, ignoring furious protests from environmentalists and former Interior Department staffers, decided to retain Oynes in that fatal post.

Oynes is the one constant figure in the Deepwater Horizon catastrophe. The project originated during his term in the Bush administration and was approved under his watch in the Obama administration. Despite the highly experimental nature of the drilling operation, the MMS's approval came without environmental review. It contained no special restrictions or impositions on BP's operating plan. Just like old times.

On May 16, however, after the explosion of the Deepwater Horizon rig and with a damaging new IG report on criminally lax safety inspections by the MMS at Gulf drilling sites during Oynes years as head of the Louisiana regional office looming, he quietly resigned his post.

As Oynes skulked from his office, with oil tides coating the marshes of coastal Louisiana in an indelible brown crude, he must have looked back on his thirty-year career with a sense of pride. Servicing big oil is precisely what MMS has always been about. The agency was created during the Reagan administration by James Watt as a bureaucratic handmaiden for the oil and gas industry. Oynes had done his job and done it well. As an MMS press release noted, "During his tenure in the Gulf of Mexico he conducted 30 lease sales and oversaw a 50 percent rise in oil production."

And that, after all, is the name of the game.

BP's Inside Game

By the morning of May 24, the tide had turned against President Barack Obama in the Gulf. Weeks of indecision at the White House and the Interior Department had shifted the balance of blame. BP was no longer seen as the lone culprit. Now, the Obama administration was viewed by many—including some senior members of their own party—as being fully culpable for the ongoing disaster off the coast of Louisiana. The political situation was so dire that Rahm Emanuel called an emergency meeting in the Oval Office to regroup. Huddling with Obama and Rahm that bleak morning were Homeland Security Secretary Janet Napolitano, Interior Secretary Ken Salazar, Coast Guard Commandant Thad Allen, climate czar Carol Browner and, most cynical of all, economic advisor Lawrence Summers, author of an infamous 1991 memo at World Bank calling "the economic logic behind dumping a load of toxic waste in the lowest wage country […] impeccable and we should face up to that."

The president was pissed. In a rare display of emotion, Obama ranted for twenty straight minutes. The target of his anger wasn't BP but the press. He fumed that he was being unfairly portrayed as being remote and indifferent to the mounting crisis in the Gulf. "Hell, this isn't our mess," Obama railed. The president expressed particular contempt for Louisianan James Carville, whose nightly barbs on CNN seemed to have found their mark. After two hours of debate, Obama's Gulf supposed dream team arrived at the dubious conclusion that the main problem was that there were simply too many public voices speaking for the administration. No one seemed to be in control. There were discordant accounts of the severity of the spill between the EPA and the Interior Department. Agencies were intruding on each other's terrain.

So, it was decided that the administration would speak with one voice, and that voice would be Thad Allen's, the portly Coast Guard Commandant who had been lauded in the press as a heroic figure in the aftermath of Katrina. It was the wrong lesson to draw after a month of false moves. The problem wasn't message control, but a profound bureaucratic lethargy that ceded almost absolute control over the response to the spill to BP. This fatal misstep came courtesy of yet more bad advice from Ken Salazar, who told Obama that under the terms of the Oil Pollution Act of 1990, passed in the wake of the wreck of the Exxon Valdez, BP was legally responsible for the cleanup of the Gulf.

Salazar's logic was perverse. He reasoned that, by giving free rein to BP under the cover of the Oil Pollution Control Act, the administration could keep its hands clean and blame any failures in the Gulf on the oil company. This strategy blew up in the face of the administration. It was all over once Rep. Ed Markey pressured BP into releasing the live video feeds from the remote-controlled submersibles, showing the brown geyser of crude erupting from the remains of the failed blowout preventer.

But then the administration was boxed into an untenable position. Instead of distancing itself from BP, the Obama team, thanks to Salazar, found itself shackled to the company. Two weeks after the blowout, a top Coast Guard official went so far as to praise "BP's professionalism" during a nationally televised press briefing.

It should have been different. Within hours of the explosion, the federal government should have seized control of both the well and the cleanup operations. The only responsibility that should have been left to BP was to sign checks for billions of dollars. The authority for such a takeover derives from an administrative rule called the National Contingency Plan, which calls for the federal government to take authority over hazardous waste releases and oil spills that pose "a substantial threat to the public health or welfare of the United States based on several factors, including the size and character of the discharge and its proximity to human populations and sensitive environments. In such cases, the On-Scene Coordinator is authorized to direct all federal, state, or private response and recovery actions. The OSC may enlist the support of other federal agencies or special teams."

The National Contingency Plan calls for the On-Site Coordinator "to direct all federal, state and private response activities at the site of discharge." The Plan, written in 1968, came in response to one of the world's first major oil spills and cleanup debacles. On March 18, 1967, the Liberian-flagged supertanker *Torrey Canyon*, taking a dangerous shortcut near Seven Stones reef, struck Pollard's Rock off the coast of Cornwall, gouging a deep hole into the holds of the ship. Over the course of the next few days, oil drained into the Atlantic. Then, on Easter the ship itself broke in two, releasing all 35 million gallons of crude oil, owned by, yes, British Petroleum into sea. The wreck plunged the government of Harold Wilson into crisis mode. The government allowed BP to pour millions of gallons of an unproven but toxic dispersant on dark-stained waters—the chemical had been manufactured by a subsidiary of the oil company. When that proved to have little effect, the Wilson government called upon the Royal Air Force to conduct a bombing raid on the

Torrey Canyon. The planes dropped forty two bombs in an effort to sink the ship and burn off the oil slick. The sea burned for two weeks, but the incendiary raids did little to staunch the oily tides. In the end, more than 120 miles of the Cornish Coast were coated in oil and the spill took a heavy toll on fish, birds and sea mammals. The crude spoiled beaches from Guernsey to Brittany.

In order to avoid a similar cleanup folly in the US, the National Contingency Plan called for a single agency to take swift control over big oil spills. That agency was the newly created EPA. But when Rahm Emanuel summoned the administration's oil response team to the strategy session in the Oval Office, he didn't send an invitation to Lisa Jackson, the spunky head of the Environmental Protection Agency. Why was Jackson missing? Because she had reportedly incurred the wrath of BP executives for pressing the company to curtail its controversial use of the toxic dispersant Corexit. Also noticeably absent from the Obama brain trust were two other officials who might have contributed a more realistic appraisal of the deteriorating situation in the Gulf: Jane Lubchenko, director of the National Oceanic and Atmospheric Administration NOAA, and Energy Secretary Stephen Chu, owner of the Nobel Prize, so often invoked by White House press secretary Robert Gibbs as a public assurance that the administration was on top of the situation. Each had been inexplicably exiled from Obama's inner circle.

It didn't help, of course, that in the early days of the disaster Obama's officials opted to downplay the severity of the oil gusher erupting out of the crumpled riser pipe 5,000 feet below the surface of the Gulf. In the first official remarks from the administration after the explosion of the Deepwater Horizon rig, Coast Guard rear admiral told the press that the spill was expected to be very minor, amounting to only the few thousands gallons of crude present in the mile-long pipe at the time of the accident. This false information flowed directly from BP. A few days later, after the incinerated rig had toppled and sank to the bottom of the Gulf, this specious number was revised upward to a total of no more than 1,000 gallons a day. So said Admiral Thad Allen, head of the Coast Guard and Incident Commander for the Gulf. Again, Allen had made this optimistic assessment based solely on information coming from BP. Two weeks later, the upper limit for the leak was raised to 5,000 barrels a day.

But NOAA knew better. In fact, in the hours after the spill, top NOAA officials gathered in Seattle for an emergency session that was streamed live on the agency's website. The video feed, which was later removed from the website, captured the agency's top scientists at work. Their initial survey of the scope of the spill proved prescient. One scientist warned that the agency needed "to be prepared for the spill of the decade." Another NOAA scientist charted out the worst-case scenario on a whiteboard: "Est. 64k–100k barrels a day." Right on the money, even though it took the Obama administration more than fifty days to admit that the oil was flowing at a rate of more than 14,000 barrels a day.

Of course, the administration could have simply subpoenaed BP's own records, as Congressman Ed Markey eventually did. On June 20, Markey released an internal memo from BP that estimated that as much as 100,000 barrels a day might be surging out of the broken wellhead. Far from fact-checking BP's information, some members of the Obama administration were acting as conduits for the company's lowballing. None played a more important role than Sylvia Baca, whose facility with moving seamlessly between the government and the corporations she was meant to regulate should had won her frequent flyer points for trips through the revolving door. Last summer, Ken Salazar appointed Baca to serve as assistant administrator for lands and minerals of the scandal-rife MMS. This powerful but shadowy post did not require Senate confirmation. Thus, Baca's previous career did not become the subject of public inquiry.

Salazar had plucked Baca right from the ranks of BP's executive suites, where, according to her CV, she served "as general manager for Social Investment Programs and Strategic Partnerships at BP America Inc. in Houston, and had held several senior management positions with the company since 2001, focusing on environmental initiatives, overseeing cooperative projects with private and public organizations, developing health, safety, and emergency response programs and working on climate change, biodiversity and sustainability objectives." Prior to joining BP, Baca spent six years at the right hand of Bruce Babbitt, serving as assistant secretary of the Interior for Lands and Minerals Management.

Baca's years in the Clinton administration proved very productive for the oil industry as a whole and her future employer in particular, a period when oil production on federal lands soared far above the levels of the first Bush administration. An internal Interior Department memo from April 2000 spelled out the achievement for Big Oil:

> We have supported efforts to increase oil and gas recovery in the deep waters of the Gulf of Mexico; we have conducted a number of extremely successful, environmentally sound offshore oil and gas lease sales; and we have opened a portion of the National Petroleum Reserve in Alaska to environmentally responsible oil and gas development, where an estimated 10 trillion cubic feet of recoverable gas resources lie in the northeast section of the reserve.

The memo goes on to highlight the feats in the Gulf of Mexico, which saw a tenfold increase in oil leasing during the Clinton years,

> From 1993 to 1999, 6,538 new leases were issued covering approximately 35 million acres of the Outer Continental Shelf.... Lease Sale 175 in the Central Gulf of Mexico, held on March 15, 2000, offered

4,203 blocks (22.29 million acres) for lease. The Interior Department received 469 bids on 344 blocks. There were 334 leases awarded.... More than 40 million acres of federal OCS blocks are currently under lease. Approximately 94 per of the existing OCS leases (7,900) are in the Gulf, and about 1,500 of these leases are producing.... Issued over 28,000 leases and approved over 15,000 permits to drill.... Implemented legislation changing the competitive lease term from five years to ten years, allowing lessees greater flexibility in exploration without endangering the lease.

Thus had the table been set for the depredations of the George W. Bush administration.

Mission accomplished, Baca settled into her high-paying gig as a BP executive. One of Baca's roles was to recruit Hollywood celebrities to help greenwash the oil giant as environmentally enlightened corporation, which was engaged in a mighty war against the evil forces of climate change. When Baca left BP to join the Obama administration, they weren't left in the lurch. As the curtains closed on the Bush administration, BP recruited one of the Interior Department's top guns to join its team. As the chief of staff for the MMS in the Gulf Region, James Grant had worked to make sure that deepwater leases moved forward with, as he put it in one memo, "few or no regulations or standards."

Having succeeded in this endeavor, BP enticed Grant to join their team as their "regulatory and environmental compliance manager" for the Gulf of Mexico, an assignment that included shepherding the Deepwater Horizon through the regulatory maze at MMS. Grant began lobbying his former colleagues in the Interior Department to open currently protected areas to oil leasing, particularly in the eastern Gulf of Mexico near the coast of Florida. Grant also warned the Obama administration, including his former corporate colleague Sylvia Baca, not to cave to demands by environmentalists for "policies that may establish exclusionary zones, disrupt MMS leasing or affect opportunities for economic growth." He needn't have worried.

* * *

It's clear that Sylvia Baca should never have been eligible to resume her job at the Interior Department. Obama had piously pledged to close the revolving door and bar corporate lobbyists from taking posts in agencies that regulated the activities of their former employers. Several environmental lobbyists were denied positions in the Interior Department and EPA under these supposedly ironclad ethics rules. However, Baca slipped through at the behest of Salazar who made a special appeal to Attorney General Eric Holder. Salazar told Holder that Baca was an "indispensable" member of his team, emphasizing her "detailed knowledge of Interior's land and energy responsibilities."

According to Deputy Interior Secretary David Hayes, Baca recused herself from all leasing decisions regarding BP. However, sources inside the Interior Department tell me that Baca played a key role in a procedural decision in the early days of the Obama administration that allowed the Deepwater Horizon project and Big Oil operations on federal lands to move forward with scant environmental review. The National Environmental Policy Act (NEPA) is a federal law passed during the glory days of environmental legislation, otherwise known as the Nixon administration. It requires a full-scale environmental impact statement (EIS) for any federal project that might pose a "significant impact on the quality of the human environment."

These EISs often run to more than a 1,000 pages in length and evaluate the possible ecological, social and economic consequences of the proposal, including worst-case scenarios. These documents are prepared by the permitting agency with consultation from the Fish and Wildlife Service and the EPA. But an administrative order during the second Bush administration ordered the Minerals Management Service to issue "categorical exclusions" from NEPA compliance to Big Oil projects in the Gulf and Alaska. In addition, the Bush administration allowed the oil companies to prepare their own safety and environmental plans, which would then be rubber-stamped by officials at MMS. From 2001 through 2008, more than 2,400 oil leases had been allowed to go forward in the Gulf without any serious environmental review.

When the Obama administration came into power, this policy was under furious legal and political assault by environmental groups. But Salazar was zealous that there would be no interruption in the pace of oil leasing in the Gulf. In fact, he wanted it speeded up. Restoring NEPA compliance to the oil industry, Salazar's enforcer, Baca warned, would slow down the approval process for leases by a year or more and, even worse, make the projects vulnerable to protracted litigation by environmentalists. She counseled that it would be better to stick with the Bush era rules. Salazar agreed.

So, it came to pass that on April 6, 2009, the Interior Department granted BP a categorical exemption for Lease 206, the Deepwater Horizon well. The BP exploration plan included a skimpy thirteen-page environmental review, which called the prospect of a major spill "unlikely." The company told the Interior Department that in the event of a spill "no mitigation measures other than those required by regulation and BP policy will be employed to avoid, diminish or eliminate potential impacts on environmental resources." The request was approved in a one-page letter that imposed no special restrictions on the oil company, warning only that BP "exercise caution while drilling due to indications of shallow gas."

Famous last words.

Obama's Sellout on Taxes

By MICHAEL HUDSON

I almost feel naïve for being so angry at President Obama's betrayal of his campaign promises regarding taxes. I had never harbored much hope that he actually intended to enact the reforms that his supporters expected—not after he appointed the most right-wing of the Clintonomics gang, Larry Summers, then Tim Geithner, Ben Bernanke and other Bush neoliberals.

But there is something so unfair and wrong that I could not prevent myself from waking up early Tuesday morning to think through the consequences of President Obama's sellout in the years to come. Contrary to his pretense of saving the economy, his action will intensify debt deflation and financial depression, paving the way for a long-term tax shift off wealth onto labor.

In achieving a giveaway that Democrats never would have let George Bush or other Republicans enact, Obama has laid himself open to the campaign slogan that brought down British Prime Minister Tony Blair: "You can't believe a word he says." He has lost support not only personally, but also—as the Republicans anticipate—for much of his party in 2012.

Yet Obama has only done what politicians do: He has delivered up his constituency to his campaign backers—the same Wall Street donors who back the Republicans. What's the point of having a constituency, after all, if you can't sell it?

The problem is that it's not going to stop here. Monday's deal to re-instate the Bush era tax cuts for two more years sets up a 1-2-3 punch. First, many former Democratic and independent voters will "vote with their backsides" and simply stay home (or perhaps be tempted by a third-party candidate), enabling the Republicans to come in and legislate the cuts in perpetuity in 2012—an estimated $4 trillion to the rich over time.

Second, Obama's Republican act (I hate to call it a compromise) "frees" income for the wealthiest classes to send abroad, to economies not yet wrecked by neoliberals. This paves the way for a foreign-exchange crisis. Such crises traditionally fall in the autumn—and as the 2012 election draws near, it will be attributed to "uncertainty" if voters do not throw the Democrats out. So to "save the dollar" the Republicans will propose to replace progressive income taxation with a uniform flat tax (the old Steve Forbes plan) falling on wage earners, not on wealth or on finance, insurance or real estate (FIRE sector) income. A VAT will be added as an excise tax to push up consumer prices.

Third, the tax giveaway includes a $120 billion reduction in Social Security contributions by labor—reducing the FICA wage withholding from 6.2 percent to 4.2 percent. Obama has ingeniously designed the plan to dovetail neatly into his Bowles-Simpson commission pressing to reduce Social

Security as a step toward its ultimate privatization and subsequent wipe-out grab by Wall Street. This cutback will accelerate the point at which the program moves into supposed "negative equity"—a calculation that ignores the option of restoring pension funding to the government's general budget, where it would be paid out of progressively levied income tax and hence borne mainly by the wealthy, not by lower-income wage earners as a "user fee."

So the game plan is not merely to free the income of the wealthiest class to "offshore" itself into assets denominated in harder currencies abroad. It is to scrap the progressive tax system altogether. The Democratic Congress is making only token handwringing protests against this plan, no doubt with an eye looking forward to the campaign contributors two years down the road.

Crises usually are orchestrated years in advance. Any economic recovery typically is shaped by the way in which its predecessor economy collapsed. Medieval Europe's emergence from the Dark Age, for example, was shaped by ancient Rome's debt crisis caused by its aggressive oligarchy. In a similar fashion, the coming epochal tax shift off finance and property onto labor will be introduced in response to the dollar's crisis, in much the way that we have seen Ireland and Greece tap their pension funds to bail out reckless bankers. In America as in Europe, the large "systemically important banks" that caused the crisis will be given enough money by the government—at the expense of labor ("taxpayers") to step in and "rescue" the bad debt overhang (i.e., toxic junk).

The tactics of this fiscal game sequence are so time-tested that there should not be much surprise. So President Obama's deal is not only financial and fiscal in scope, it is a political game changer. When Congressional Democrats sign on to this betrayal of their major election promise, they will be re-branding their claim to be the "non-Wall Street party."

Barack Obama was trained as a lawyer. I've rarely met a lawyer who understands economics. That's not their mind-set. They make deals to minimize the risk of surprises, often settling in the middle. That is legal pragmatism. When candidate Obama promised "change," I don't think he had any particular change in economic policy in mind. It was more a *modus operandi*. I suspect that he simply thought of the Presidency as being referee on "bringing people together." Probably this personality trait was formed as a teenager, in the kind of popularity contest that teenagers engage in student council elections. Obama's aim was to be accepted, even admired, by negotiating a compromise. He probably didn't care much about the content.

He did care about getting political campaign backing, of course, and the rules for this are clear enough in today's world. He was given a policy to plead, and a set of experts to plead his case. There are always enough Junk Economics advisors to work on politicians to try and convince them that "doing the right thing" means helping Wall Street. It is not a matter simply of believing that "What's good for Wall Street is good for the economy." To hear Tim Geithner and Ben Bernanke tell the story, the economy can't function without a "solvent" banking system—meaning that no bank is to lose money. All gamblers on the winning side (such as Goldman Sachs) are to be made whole in cases where they cannot collect from bad casino-capitalist gamblers on the losing side (such as A.I.G. and Lehman Brothers).

So should we say that Obama's plan really helps the economy simply because the stock market jumped sharply on Tuesday? Or are we dealing with a zero-sum game, where the predator's subsidy is at the cost of the host economy?

Contra Obama's pretense, cutting taxes for the rich will not spur recovery. The wealthiest 2 percent do not spend their income on consuming more. They invest it financially—mainly in bonds, establishing more debt claims on the economy. Giving creditors more money will deepen the economy's debt deflation, shrinking "the market's" ability to spend on goods and services. And part of the tax subsidy will be recycled into Congressional lobbying and campaign contributions to buy politicians who will promote even more pro-financial deregulatory policies and tax benefits. There still has been no prosecution of banking crime or other financial fraud by large institutions, for example. Nor is there any sign of Attorney General Holder initiating such prosecutions.

It is a travesty for Obama to trot out the long-term unemployed (who now get a year's extension of benefits) like widows and orphans used to be. It's not really "all for the poor." It's all for the rich. And it's not to promote stability and recovery. How stable can a global situation be where the richest nation does not tax its population, but creates new public debt to hand out to its bankers? Future taxpayers will spend generations paying off their heirs.

The "solution" to the coming financial crisis in the US may await the dollar's plunge as an opportunity for a financial Tonkin Gulf resolution. Such a crisis would help catalyze the tax system's radical change to a European-style "Steve Forbes" flat tax and VAT sales-excise tax falling almost entirely on employment. Big fish will eat little fish. More government giveaways will be made to the financial sector in a vain effort to keep bad debts afloat and banks "solvent." As in Ireland and Latvia, public debt will replace private debt, leaving little remaining for Social Security or indeed for much social spending.

The bottom line is that after the prolonged tax giveaway exacerbates the federal budget deficit—along with the balance-of-payments deficit—we can expect the next Republican or Democratic administration to step in and "save" the country from economic emergency by scaling back Social Security while turning its funding over, Pinochet-style, to Wall Street money managers to loot as they did in Chile. And one can forget rebuilding America's infrastructure. It is being sold off by debt-strapped cities and states to cover their budget shortfalls resulting from un-taxing real estate and from foreclosures.

Welcome to debt peonage. This is worse than what was meant by a double-dip recession. It will be with us much longer.

Michael Hudson is a former Wall Street economist. A Distinguished Research Professor at University of Missouri, Kansas City (UMKC), he is the author of many books, including Super Imperialism: The Economic Strategy of American Empire *(new ed., Pluto Press, 2002) and* Trade, Development and Foreign Debt: A History of Theories of Polarization v. Convergence in the World Economy.

Obama and Rendition: Exporting Torture

By STEVE HENDRICKS

Exactly two years have passed since President Obama banned the US from torturing captives—sort of. More precisely, he banned the US from torturing captives *directly*. He left intact the option of sending captives elsewhere to be tortured.

We know this because CIA Director Leon Panetta has assured us that extraordinary rendition—i.e., kidnapping someone and sending him to a Third World dungeon, where he will all but certainly be tortured—remains a tool in the president's toolbox. If the president has availed himself of this maul, as is likely, then he has made himself a criminal no less than his predecessor in the Oval Office did.

Their common crime is violating the UN Convention Against Torture, which Congress and President Clinton made law in 1994 (after years of stalling by Presidents Reagan and Bush the elder). The law says, "It shall be the policy of the United States not to expel, extradite, or otherwise effect the involuntary return of any person to a country in which there are substantial grounds for believing the person would be in danger of being subjected to torture."

Apologists of extraordinary rendition and torture have argued that our extraordinary enemy justifies extraordinary measures. But this is a canard the Convention Against Torture foresaw. "No exceptional circumstances whatsoever," the law reads, "whether a state of war or a threat of war, internal political instability, or any other public emergency may be invoked as a justification of torture or other cruel, inhuman or degrading treatment or punishment."

The punishment for breaking the law is a fine of unlimited amount and, if the torturer's victim survives, imprisonment for up to twenty years. If the victim dies, the penalty could be death. The Convention Against Torture obligates its signatories to prosecute torturers within their borders, but Obama needn't worry about a stay in the Florence Supermax anytime soon. Federal prosecutors serve at his pleasure, and any who indicted him would soon be looking for other work, not that any have shown an inclination to indict.

Foreign prosecutors, however, are not so constrained and could someday charge him under a doctrine known as universal jurisdiction. The doctrine holds that when an atrocity is (a) so grave as to constitute an assault on all peoples of the world and yet (b) goes unpunished in the country where it was committed, a prosecutor anywhere may indict and try the suspected perpetrator. The doctrine is legitimated by several international accords, including the Convention Against Torture, and by a growing body of other international and national law. It was under universal jurisdiction that Spanish magistrate

Baltasar Garzón issued his celebrated arrest warrant in 1998 for the murderous Chilean dictator Augustus Pinochet.

Is America's outsourcing of torture so momentous a crime as to permit prosecution under universal jurisdiction? Indeed it is, for systematic torture (including systematically outsourced torture) is viewed by international law as not merely a crime but a crime against humanity. At Nuremberg we prosecuted Nazis for similarly overseeing torture—and we executed some of the guilty.

For the moment, however, Obama is safe from prosecution abroad, because the most prevalent interpretation of universal jurisdiction holds that sitting officials are immune from prosecution. But the younger Bush and Clinton enjoy no such immunity. (Clinton isn't often spoken of as a criminal against humanity, but it was his White House that conceived of and ordered America's first extraordinary rendition—then ordered several dozen thereafter.) Will Bush and Clinton remain uncharged? Will Obama? Only time will tell. Pinochet, after all, was not prosecuted until two decades after he committed his crimes. But already we know that Spanish and Italian magistrates have gathered evidence against senior Bush officials, and perhaps even against Bush himself, for authorizing torture. Exhibit A in their indictments might be Bush's boasts of having been, as he might say, "the authorizer." Exhibit B might be the similar boasts of former Vice President Cheney.

Obama has refused to investigate Bush's crimes because, he says, he wants to look forward, not backward. While it is no doubt true that Obama views such investigations as backward-looking distractions, a fuller truth—one almost entirely overlooked by the media—is that were he to prosecute Bush, he would set a precedent for prosecuting himself and Clinton. There are as few Democrats who wish for his indictment as there are Republicans who wish for Bush and Cheney's—and that will be true for quite some time. Which is why if America's moral reckoning is to come sooner rather than later, it will probably come from the chambers of an Old World magistrate with a principled abhorrence of torturers-in-chief.

Steve Hendricks is the author of A Kidnapping in Milan: The CIA on Trial, *which chronicles the CIA's extraordinary rendition of an Egyptian cleric and the trial in Italy of the CIA kidnappers.*

The Murdered Women of Juarez
By LAURA CARLSEN

Marisela Escobedo's life changed forever in August 2008 when her sixteen-year-old daughter Rubi failed to come home. What was left of Rubi's body was found months later in a dump—thirty nine pieces of charred bone.

Rubi became one more macabre statistic in Ciudad Juarez's nearly two-decade history of femicide. The murder of young women, often raped and tortured, brought international infamy to the city long before it became the epicenter of the Calderon drug war and took on the added title of murder capital of the world.

But Rubi never became a statistic for her mother. Marisela knew that a former boyfriend, Sergio Barraza, had murdered her daughter. As authorities showed no interest in investigating the case, she began a one-woman crusade across two states to bring the murderer to justice. The Mexican magazine *Proceso* recently obtained the file on her case. Marisela's odyssey tracks a murderer, but it also tracks a system of sexism, corruption and impunity.

It's an odyssey that ends with Marisela—the mother—getting her brains blown out on December 16, 2010 as she continued to protest the lack of justice in her daughter's murder two years earlier.

Trail of Impunity

Marisela Escobedo eventually tracked down Barraza. She had him arrested and brought to trial, and finally saw a chance for the hard-sought justice that could at least allow her to move on with her life.

But in Ciudad Juarez, the term "justice" is a bad joke, especially if you're a woman. Despite the fact that Barraza confessed at the trial and led authorities to the body, three Chihuahua state judges released him. Marisela watched as the confessed assassin of her daughter left the courtroom absolved of all charges due to "lack of evidence."

As pressure from women's and human rights organizations mounted, a new trial was called and Barraza was condemned to fifty years in prison. But by that time, he was long gone and still has not been apprehended, despite Marisela's success in discovering his whereabouts and providing key information to police and prosecutors.

The story doesn't end there. Every day, Marisela fought for justice for her daughter and sought out the killer. She received multiple death threats. She responded saying, "If they're going to kill me, they should do it right in front of the government building so they feel ashamed."

And they did. Marisela took her demands for justice from the border to the state capital where a hit man approached her in broad daylight, chased her down, then shot her in the head.

A family's story had come full circle. By all accounts, Rubi's death came at the hands of an abusive boyfriend. Marisela's death, however, was caused by an abusive system that sought to protect itself from her determination to expose its injustice. The gunman's identity is unknown, but responsibility clearly lies with members of a state at best incapable of defending women and at worst culpable of complicity in killing them.

Gender Violence and Drug Violence

Ciudad Juarez in recent years has been described as a no-man's land, where legal institutions have lost control to the armed force of drug cartels. The femicides show us, though, that the causal chain is really the reverse.

Seventeen years ago, Ciudad Juarez began to register an alarming number of cases of women tortured, murdered or disappeared. Over the decades, national and international feminist organizations pressed the government for justice. The government in turn formed commissions that changed directors and initials with each new governor. They all shared one distinct feature: never getting anywhere on solving the crimes of gender violence, much less preventing them. Recommendations to the Mexican government piled up alongside the bodies: missions from the United Nations and the Organization of American States provided over 200 recommendations on protecting women's rights, with fifty for Ciudad Juarez alone.

Marisela's murder marked a year since the Inter-American Court of Human Rights issued a ruling calling the Mexican government negligent in the murders of young women. The ruling on the "Cotton Field" case—named after the lot where the bodies of three women were found on Nov. 21, 2001—includes a list of measures and reparations, most of which have been rejected or ignored.

Since the cases analyzed in the Court ruling, the drug war in Ciudad Juarez waged by the Mexican government with the support of the US Merida Initiative has led to a record number of homicides—15,273—in 2010 (with a total of 34,612 over the four years since Calderon launched the offensive). The strategy has focused on violently confronting drug cartels to interdict shipments and capture drug lords. It relies on the militarization of the city, which has brought more violence to the region than anyone imagined.

Ironically, President Felipe Calderon says the goals of the drug war are to increase public safety and strengthen legal institutions. But the history of gender crimes and government response reveals the fundamental flaws of the current counter-narcotics efforts and of a system that practically guarantees impunity through a combination of institutional corruption, sexism, racism, incompetence and indifference.

Given that background of institutionalized injustice, the drug war in Juarez short-circuited from the start. The logical sequence of investigation, arrest, prosecution and punishment simply does not exist in the absence of a functioning justice system. By destabilizing the drug cartels' cross-border business and setting off turf wars, the government unleashed a storm of drug-related violence that can't be dealt with by police and legal institutions because those institutions are dysfunctional. In the absence of supporting institutions or a coherent strategy, the resulting explosion from this direct confrontation with drug cartels could have been predicted. If the tragedy of the pink crosses erected in the desert to mark the unsolved cases of murdered women showed us anything, it was that the fundamental problem in Juarez traces back to the government itself. Until impunity ends, the region will continue to attract crime—common, organized, or just plain perverse.

In this environment, the femicides in Juarez have not only never been solved, they've risen dramatically—to nearly 300 in 2010—alongside overall homicide rates. The government's drug war has stimulated more gender violence instead of less. It shelters those who commit murder and other barbarities against women by making murder a normal part of daily life. It promotes an armed society where people too poor to move have no choice but to bunker down against all sides. Not only does Juarez shelter murderers, torturers, and rapists of women, it attracts them.

Women's vulnerability increases. For years, impunity gave free rein to women-killers who found women workers at the maquiladoras to be particularly easy targets for torture, acts of sadism, rape and murder and other acts possibly related to snuff films and international crime rings, all covered up by government officials. Lately women human rights defenders have become the targets. Shortly after Marisela's assassination, Susana Chavez was found murdered with her hand cut off. Chavez was a feminist poet who coined the phrase "Not One More Death!"—which became the slogan of the Juarez women's movement. Women activists feel as though open season has been declared on them.

Civil Society Responds

The only ray of light has come from the response of Mexican civil society. Following Marisela's murder, a former head of one of the government commissions, Alicia Duarte, wrote in an open letter to President Calderon:

> Three years ago, when I quit my post as Special Prosecutor for Attention to Crimes Related to Acts of Violence Against Women of the Attorney General's Office, I noted clearly that I did it out of the shame I felt for belonging to the corrupt system of justice of our country. Today that shame comes back and burns in my skin and conscience, so I must join in the indignation of all women in this country who, when they found out about the assassination of Marisela Escobedo Ortiz and the attacks on her family of the recent days, demand justice.

Women and men have demonstrated throughout the country to demand that Marisela's and Rubi's cases be solved, to call for an end to the impunity that protects murderers in hundreds of other cases, and to force the government to comply with recommendations to protect women and prevent more deaths. Their protests have united with a new nationwide citizens' movement called "No More Blood" to reject the current drug-war strategy. A tipping point has finally been reached.

Marisela's murder practically at the steps of the State Capitol symbolizes the relationship between gender violence in the private and the public spheres, between the lethal sexism of men who kill women and of governments who let them get away with it, between an out-of-control counter-narcotics war and the long-boiling situation of unpunished gender crimes.

No one in the Mexican government acknowledges these relationships. The same holds true for the US government. The last State Department report gave Mexico a pass on human rights to authorize more Merida Initiative support for the drug war. The current indignation over Marisela's murder and the new "No More Blood" campaign demonstrate that the Mexican public has had enough excuses for the violence it has been forced to live with.

Until both governments turn their sights to the hypocrisy of their legal systems and policies, the downward spiral of violence will only continue. To honor Marisela and all the others who have dared to defend human rights and justice in Mexico, it is time for civil society on both sides of the border to demand an end to bloodshed.

Laura Carlsen is director of the Americas Policy Program in Mexico City.

Obama's Puzzling Silence

By RALPH NADER

President Obama uses his bully pulpit to tout profit-seeking corporations, but he rarely uses it to promote nonprofits that deliver social justice at home and abroad.

When Mr. Obama went to India in November, for example, he was accompanied by corporate CEO's, and unabashedly promoted US exports and companies like Boeing and Harley-Davidson.

The president says he will go anywhere in the world to promote trade, presumably for the jobs that exports create. Fair enough, assuming fair-trade agreements.

But so far, he has rarely gone anywhere, even to places near the White House, to highlight the good works done by national advocacy and charitable groups seeking a fairer society. It is puzzling why Mr. Obama, who knows how to attract the news media to his cause, has left in the shadows the all-important "independent sector" (to use the language of President Johnson's health and education secretary John Gardner).

After all, nonprofits also employ millions of people and are a major pillar of the American community. These nonprofits are run by a cadre of workers who probably voted for Mr. Obama in far bigger numbers than they did for his opponent in the presidential election.

At critical points in history, civic values have prevailed over the demands of commerce—and children, workers, consumers and the environment have all benefited. For example, laws have been passed that abolished child labor, instituted fairer labor standards and safer workplaces, protected consumers from unfair business practices and product defects, and given ordinary people greater access to the courts to hold manufacturers of dangerous products accountable.

All these and other advances in justice could be stopped or eroded by undue influence of commerce over civic values—exemplified in recent decades by a corporate government delivering handouts, bailouts, bloated corporate military contracts, and an unprecedented level of subsidized inequality of wealth between the top 1 percent and the rest of the population.

By using his bully pulpit to emphasize the activities of budget-pressed nonprofits that every day serve the needs of Americans, he could inspire public-service workers, give them visibility, and attract the attention of younger generations to follow careers in public service.

As a lawyer, former teacher, and community organizer, Mr. Obama knows the critical role nonprofits play. In the past century, they led the way for civil rights, civil liberties, environmental and consumer protections, and the alleviation of poverty and illness. In the 19th century, they were in the forefront of demanding the abolition of slavery, women's right to vote, volunteer fire protection, and food and shelter for the poor.

Mr. Obama knows that nonprofits have been overwhelmed by the demands for their services during this Great Recession. Legal services for the poor, nonprofit day-care centers, and many other types of groups strain to keep up with people knocking on their doors for aid.

Yet, though he rhetorically urges more volunteerism, as all presidents do, in his travels around the country, he stops most often at factories and campaign fund-raising events patronized by the wealthy rather than at the regional Salvation Army and other organizations devising solutions to the problems facing America's most vulnerable people.

Other high-profile events show a similar contrast.

Mr. Obama visits military installations and military academies for major addresses. He has never spoken to any convocation of peace groups. Their numbers and activities would expand were he to do so.

During last year's debate on health insurance, Mr. Obama, who once preferred a single-payer system (full Medicare for all), invited the chief executives of Aetna and Pfizer—companies that would lose out in a single-payer system—to the White House half a dozen times. Not once did he meet with his erstwhile friend back in Chicago, Dr. Quentin Young, a longtime leader of the single-payer movement. What's more, Mr. Obama errs when he promotes companies as the sole creators of jobs—given how much nonprofits do to lay the groundwork for industries that will eventually create many jobs, such as solar energy and the preservation of aging structures.

It's time for Mr. Obama to leave the promotion of for-profits to the secretary of commerce and introduce organizations that truly make a difference on the presidential stage. He could start by showing a willingness to give a speech at a special gathering of national citizen groups, representing millions of Americans, as President-elect Jimmy Carter did in 1976. Many advocacy groups don't have their own conventions, but they would visit Washington to hear from the president.

Nonprofit groups should have higher expectations from Mr. Obama. They must urge him to shift his presidential attentions and priorities and remind him of what both community and organizing mean for the civil society in America.

Ralph Nader is the founder of the Center for Study of Responsive Law, in Washington.

Inside Obamanomics
By ISMAEL HOSSEIN-ZADEH

President Reagan did not make any bones about his intention to reverse the New Deal economics when he set out to promote the neoliberal economics. Likewise, President George W. Bush did not conceal his agenda of aggressive, unilateral militarism abroad and curtailment of civil liberties at home.

There is a major similarity and a key difference between these two presidents, on the one hand, and President Obama, on the other. The similarity lies in the fact that, like his predecessor, President Obama faithfully, and indeed vigorously, carries out both the neoliberal and militaristic policies he inherited.

The difference is that while Reagan and Bush were, more or less, truthful to their constituents, President Obama is not: while catering to the powerful interests vested in finance and military capitals, he pretends to be an agent of "change" and a source of "hope" for the masses.

There has been a wide-ranging consensus that the excessive financial/economic deregulations that started in the late 1970s and early 1980s played a critical role in both the financial bubble that imploded in 2007–2008 and the continuing persistence of the chronic recession, especially in the labor and housing markets.

Prior to his recent u-turn on the regulation-deregulation issue, President Obama shared this near unanimous view of the destructive role of the excessive deregulation of the past several decades and, indeed, strongly supported the need to bolster regulation: "It's time to get serious about regulatory oversight," Mr. Obama argued as the Democratic nominee for President; and again, "…this crisis has reminded us that without a watchful eye, the market can spin out of control," as he stated in his inaugural speech.

Expressions of such pro-regulation sentiments were part of his earlier promises of "hope" and "change" in a new direction. Back then, that is, before showing his neoliberal hand, the majority of the American people believed him—the middle, lower-middle, poor and working people who were tired of three decades of steady losses of economic security were desperately willing to believe a charismatic leader who peddled hope and change in their favor.

Recently, however, the president seems to have had a change of heart, or perhaps an epiphany, regarding the regulation-deregulation debate: he now argues that protracted recession and persistent high levels of unemployment are not due to excessive deregulation but to overregulation! Accordingly, he issued an executive order on 18 January 2011 that requires a comprehensive review of all existing government regulations. On the same day, the president wrote an op-ed piece for the *Wall Street Journal* in which he argued that the executive order was necessary in order "to remove outdated regulations that stifle job creation and make our economy less competitive." The president further argued that "Sometimes, those [regulatory] rules have gotten out of balance, placing unreasonable burdens on business—burdens that have stifled innovation and have had a chilling effect on growth and jobs.... As the executive order I am signing makes clear, we are seeking more affordable, less intrusive means to achieve the same ends—giving careful consideration to benefits and costs."

Stripped from its Orwellian language, this "cost-benefit" approach to health, safety and environmental standards is clearly the familiar neoliberal rhetoric that is designed to help big business and their lobbies that have been working feverishly to stifle the widespread pro-regulation voices that have grown louder since the 2007–08 financial melt-down.

Indeed, the president's recent agenda of further deregulation has already born fruits for big business. The *Wall Street Journal* reported on 20 January 2011:

> A day after President Barack Obama ordered the government to get rid of burdensome rules, two federal agencies backed down from proposals that had drawn jeers from businesses.... The Labor Department said it was withdrawing a proposal on noise in the workplace that could have forced manufacturers to install noise-reducing equipment. And the Food and Drug Administration retreated from plans to tighten rules on medical-device approvals, postponing a proposal that would have given the FDA power to order additional post-market studies of devices.... Industry leaders praised the moves, while consumer advocates expressed disappointment.... 'This is a very positive step forward,' said Bill Hawkins, chief executive of medical-devices heavyweight Medtronic Inc.

How is the president's sharp turnaround on the regulation-deregulation debate to be explained? What "outdated deregulation" is he talking about? How could deregulation, which is widely believed to have been the problem, also be the solution? Why this sudden u-turn?

The change in the president's view from the need for regulation to that of further deregulation can be explained on a number of planes.

On a narrow, personal and (perhaps) simplistic level, it can be argued that the president's about-face on the issue of deregulation should not really be surprising; the turnaround represents quintessential Obama: spineless and/or unscrupulous, if you are a critic of the president; pragmatic and/or complex, if you are an apologist or defender of him.

There are also, of course, re-election considerations here. And here it seems that the president's team is pinning his chances for re-election on big business and big media; confident that once he is able to win their hearts and minds, they will, in turn, be able to manipulate the public to vote for him—just as they did in the 2008 election.

On a deeper (but still personal) level, that is, on a philosophical or ideological level, it can be argued that the president has always been a neoliberal thinker, albeit a stealth neoliberal, who is coming out of the closet, so to speak, carefully and gradually. Evidence of his being ideologically more a partisan of neoliberal than New Deal economics is overwhelming.

It is necessary to point out that although the stealth neoliberal president has been taking baby steps out of the closet, he would always stay by the entrance: as long as there is no popular anger or pressure against his neoliberal policies, he would stay on the outside; at the first signs of a threatening pressure from the grassroots, however, he would crawl back inside the closet, and begin preaching populism or uttering ineffectual, benign corporate-bashing rhetoric. This is his mission and his political forte—a master demagogue. And this is why the politico-economic establishment promoted him to presidency as they found him the most serviceable presidential candidate. None of his presidential rivals could have served the tycoons of the finance world and the kings of Wall Street as well as he has.

On a more fundamental level, President Obama's reversal of his view from the need for rigorous regulation to the need for further deregulation, and his economic policies in general, show that while the politics and personalities of a president ought not be ignored, presidential economic policies cannot be explained by purely personality issues such as a failure of nerve, conviction, or ideas. The more crucial determinants of national economic policies are often submerged: the balance of social forces and the dominant economic interests that shape such policies from behind the scene. Stabilization, restructuring or regulatory policies are often subtle products of the outcome of the class struggle.

Thus, when the balance of social forces is tilted in favor of the rich and powerful, crisis-management economic policies would be crafted at the expense of the working people and other grassroots. In other words, as long as the costly consequences of the brutal neoliberal restructuring policies (in terms of job losses, economic insecurity, and environmental degradation) are tolerated, business and government leaders, Republican or Democrat, would not hesitate to put into effect draconian measures to restore conditions of capitalist profitability at the expense of the impoverishment of the public. On the other hand, when crisis periods give rise to severe resistance from the people to cuts in social spending, such crisis-management policy measures could also benefit the public. A comparison/contrast of policy responses to major economic crises in the US clearly supports this point. Economic historians have identified four major economic crises in the past 150 years or so: The First Great Depression (1873–97), The Second Great Depression (1929–37), the long recession of 1973–83 (also known as the stagflation of the 1970s), and the current long recession that started in 2007–08.

Since there was no compelling grassroots pressure in response to either the First Great Depression of 1873–97 or the long recession of the 1970s, crisis management policies in both instances were decisively of the neoliberal, supply-side type: suppression of trade unions and curtailment of wages and benefits; promotion of mergers, concentrated industries and big business; extensive deregulations and generous corporate welfare plans; in short, huge transfers of income from labor to capital. Likewise, a glaring lack of grassroots resistance in the face of the current long recession has allowed the ruling kleptocracy (both in the US and beyond) to adopt similarly brutal austerity policies that are gradually reviving financial/corporate profitability at the expense of the poor and working people.

By contrast, in response to the Great Depression of the 1930s workers and other popular forces achieved employment and income security as a result of a sustained pressure from "below."

The contrast between these two entirely different types of restructuring strategies shows that, as Mark Vorpahl, a union steward, recently put it, "Working people and the unemployed cannot rely on the politicians to get the change we need. We can only rely on our own collective strength. That is, we need to organize and mobilize as a united, massive, powerful force that cannot be ignored by those more intent to do Wall Street's bidding." Only the threat of revolution can force people-friendly reform on the ruling kleptocracy.

Ismael Hossein-zadeh, author of The Political Economy of U.S. Militarism *(Palgrave-Macmillan 2007), teaches economics at Drake University, Des Moines, Iowa.*

The US as Israel's Enabler in the Middle East

By KATHLEEN CHRISTISON

About ten days ago I had a particularly interesting discussion about Israel and its relationship to US policy in the Middle East and to the events swirling there now, in Egypt and throughout the Arab world. My interlocutor is one of the most astute commentators, particularly on US policy, in the alternative media, but he made it clear that, to his mind, Israel does not play a role of any notable relevance to what the United States is doing in the region.

I would say that he has a bit of a blind spot about Israel—a not uncommon phenomenon among progressive thinkers. But perhaps the current turmoil in the region will ultimately open his eyes and those of others who minimize Israel's centrality to US policy. Recent events unfolding in Egypt and surrounding WikiLeaks-released State Department cables and al-Jazeera-released Palestinian papers dealing with Palestinian-Israeli talks are demonstrating graphically, as no other series of events probably ever has, that the United States does what it does in the Middle East in great measure because of Israel—to protect and safeguard Israel from Arab neighbors who object to its treatment of its Palestinian subjects, from Muslims with similar grievances, from criticism of Israel's military exploits against neighboring states, from the ire of other states still threatened by Israel, from governments in the region that challenge Israel's nuclear monopoly or attempt to develop their own arsenals to defend against Israel.

It is instructive to remember that Egypt is important to the United States almost entirely because it signed a peace treaty with Israel in 1979 and helps guarantee Israel's security, guarding its western border, helping its military assaults on other Arab countries, closing the tunnels into Gaza through which Hamas smuggles some weapons and the Gazan population obtains food and other essentials, undermining Hamas's rule in Gaza. The United States also regards Egypt as an important cog in the machine of its "war on terror" and its war on Islamic radicalism, a collaboration also closely linked to Israel's security interests.

Egypt is obviously important in the region in its own right. Its size and strategic location guarantee that it will always have considerable influence in Middle East politics, and it has long been the heart of Arab culture, even without US help. The last three weeks of the Egyptian people's struggle for democracy have further enhanced its importance, capturing the imagination of people around the world (with the exception of many, perhaps the majority, in Israel and among the curmudgeonly right in the United States, including Israel's US supporters).

But the fundamental reality is that the United States would not have the close military, political, and economic relationship it has had with Egypt for the last thirty-plus years were it not for the fact that Egypt is friendly with Israel and the fact that, in the words of Middle East expert Rashid Khalidi, Egypt has always acquiesced "in Israel's regional hegemony." The $1.5 billion annually in military aid, and the $28 billion in economic and development assistance across the last thirty five years would not have been given had not Mubarak's predecessor Anwar Sadat virtually begged for and then finally signed a peace treaty with Israel that removed Egypt, the largest Arab military force, as a threat to Israel, abandoning the Palestinians and the other Arab parties to their own devices. With Egypt out of the picture and indeed often assisting, Israel has been free to launch military assaults on several of its neighbors, including Lebanon twice and Gaza and the West Bank repeatedly, and free to expand settlements, absorb Palestinian territory, and severely oppress Palestinians without fear of retaliation or even significant disagreement from any Arab army.

Israeli commentator Aluf Benn has pointed out furthermore that, with Mubarak in office, Israel could always feel safe about its western flank if it were to attack Iran, but now Israel will not dare attack when it can no longer rely on Egypt's "tacit agreement to its actions." Whoever replaces Mubarak would, by this reasoning, be too concerned about popular rage if he were to collaborate with Israel. "Without Mubarak, there is no Israeli attack on Iran."

For Israel and therefore for the United States, the US investment of billions in Egypt over the years has been well worth the cost. The loss of the "stability" that Egypt provided—meaning Israel's loss of certainty that it remained the secure regional dominant power—has been a huge game-changer for Israeli and US strategic calculations.

Before the Egyptian-Israeli peace treaty, the United States never considered that Egypt was quite the strategic asset that it became when it surrendered its military capability in the interests of Israel. The same can be said about the US's relations with several other Arab states. Its involvement in Lebanon over the years—including its effort to remove Syrian forces from Lebanon—has been almost entirely linked to Israel's interests there. The fallout from Israel's 1982 invasion of Lebanon still reverberates: in response to the invasion, the United States sent a contingent of Marines, which became involved in direct fighting with Lebanese factions, leading in turn to a devastating bombing of Marine headquarters that killed 241 US personnel in 1983; Hezbollah, representing a besieged Shiite population in southern Lebanon, arose as a direct result of Israel's invasion; the spate of kidnappings of US personnel by Hezbollah throughout the 1980s grew out of hostility to the US because of its support for Israel; Israel withdrew from a two-decade-long occupation of southern Lebanon in 2000, leaving behind a strengthened Hezbollah; continued conflict along the border led to Israel's brutal assault on Lebanon in the summer of 2006, which failed to defeat the Islamic organization or undermine its popularity; and as a result, the United States has for years pursued efforts to undermine Hezbollah and, essentially, to maintain Lebanon as an Israeli sinecure.

Jordan has been a minor US ally for decades, but its conclusion of a peace treaty with Israel in 1994 enhanced its standing in US eyes and gained the small state on Israel's eastern border additional US military and economic aid. The State Department's official profile of Jordan relates the US rationale for its good relationship with Jordan more or less directly to Israel, although without ever mentioning Israel: "U.S. policy seeks to reinforce Jordan's commitment to peace, stability, and moderation. The peace process and Jordan's opposition to terrorism parallel and indirectly assist wider US interests. Accordingly, through economic and military assistance and through close political cooperation, the United States has helped Jordan maintain its stability and prosperity." The allusions to "reinforcing" Jordan's commitment to "peace, stability, and moderation" and to maintaining Jordan's "stability and prosperity" are obvious references to helping keep the area, and particularly Israel's border, quiet. Just as clearly, "indirectly assist[ing] wider U.S. interests" refers to the US commitment to Israel's security interests. "Moderation" in State Department jargon is a code word for a pro-Israeli stance; "stability" is code for a secure environment that benefits Israel primarily.

It is safe to say that neither Lebanon nor Jordan would be at all as important to the United States if it were not considered necessary to keep each of these bordering countries in a stable, quiescent state for Israel's security. The same situation does not apply in Saudi Arabia, where the US has vital oil interests quite apart from Israel's concerns. But at the same time, it is the case that the US has managed to tame any Saudi impulse to speak out on behalf of the Palestinians, or any other Arabs under Israeli siege, and align the Saudis at least implicitly on the Israeli side of most issues, whether this is the 2006 attack on Lebanon or the 2008–2009 assault on Gaza or the supposed threat from Iran. The day when the Saudis were angry enough with United States over its support for Israel to impose an oil embargo, as occurred in 1973, is long over.

The recent WikiLeaks releases of State Department cables and particularly al-Jazeera's release of a raft of Palestinian documents dealing with negotiations over the last decade also demonstrate with striking clarity how hard the United States works, and has always worked, to help Israel in the Palestinian-Israeli negotiating process. US support for Israel has never been a secret, becoming less and less so in recent years, but the leaked documents provide the most dramatic picture yet of the US's total disdain for all Palestinian negotiating demands and its complete helplessness in the face of Israeli refusal to make concessions. It is striking to note from these papers that the US role as "Israel's lawyer"—a description coined by Aaron David Miller after his involvement in negotiations during the Clinton era—is the same whether the administration is Bill Clinton's or George W. Bush's or Barack Obama's. Israel's interests and demands always prevail.

Beyond the Arab world, US policy on Iran is dictated more or less totally by Israel. The pressure to attack Iran—either a US attack or US support for an Israeli attack—that has been brought to bear for most of the eight years since the start of the war on Iraq, has come entirely from Israel and its supporters in the United States. This pressure is quite open and impossible to deny the way Israel's pressure for the attack on Iraq has been. If the United States ever does become involved in a military assault on Iran either directly or through backing up Israel, this will be because Israel wanted it; if there is no attack, this will most likely be, as Aluf Benn surmises, because Israel got cold feet in the aftermath of the Egyptian revolution.

Israel, and the desire to ensure its regional hegemony, also played a substantial role in leading the United States into war in Iraq, although this view is a harder sell and a much more controversial position among progressives and conservatives alike than is anything else about US-Israel-Arab relationships.

My progressive interlocutor, for instance—who has strongly opposed the US adventure in Iraq, equally strongly opposes any possibility of an attack on Iran, and was undoubtedly uncomfortable with US vacillation about pressing for Mubarak's departure—disagreed totally with my suggestion that Israel and its neocon supporters were a factor in getting the United States into the Iraq war. Early in our discussion, he talked at length about the neocons, their erstwhile think tank, the Project for a New American Century (PNAC), and the overriding neocon-PNAC interest in advancing US global hegemony, and he made the point that when George W. Bush came to power, an entire think tank was moved into the administration. But, despite this recognition of neocon objectives and the success they enjoyed in advancing them, he would not agree that PNAC and the neocons were as much interested in advancing Israel's regional hegemony as they were in furthering US imperialism.

When, on the other hand, I observed that not only had Bush moved a think tank into the administration, he had also effectively moved the Israel lobby, or its then most active wing, into the highest rungs of his administration's policymaking councils, my friend readily agreed: oh, of course, he asserted quite vigorously, they—meaning the neocons—"are all Likudniks." There is some kind of disconnect here, which he seemed not to notice: although, on the one hand, he acknowledged the neocons' very close connection to Israel, he does not on the other hand agree that the neocons did anything in a policy sense for Israel. As if they had checked their pro-Israel sympathies at the doors of the White House and the Pentagon when they officially became policymakers. As if they had discarded their own long history of pro-Israel advocacy and the policy guidance that many of them had long been giving to Israeli leaders—guidance that included an actual advisory written for the Israeli government in 1996 to move against Iraq.

It has been clear to most analysts for years, even decades, that the United States favors Israel, but this reality has never been revealed so explicitly until recent events laid the relationship bare, and laid bare the fact that Israel is at the center of virtually every move the United States makes in the region. There has long been a taboo on talking about these realities, a taboo that has tied the tongues of people like my interlocutor. People do not mention Israel because they might be called anti-Semitic, they might be attacked as "singling out" Israel for criticism; the media fail to discuss Israel and what it does around the Middle East and, most directly, to the Palestinians who live under its rule because this might provoke angry letters to the editor and cancelled subscriptions by Israel supporters. Congressmen will not endanger campaign funds by talking honestly about Israel. And so Israel is taken off everyone's radar screen. Progressives may "mention Israel in passing," as my friend told me, but they do no more. Ultimately, because no one talks about it, everyone stops even thinking about Israel as the prime mover behind so many US policies and actions in the Middle East.

It is time we began noticing. Everyone in the Middle East already notices, as the Egyptian revolution has just made clear. And probably everyone throughout the world also notices. We should begin listening to the world's people, not to their leaders, who tell us what they think we want to hear.

Kathleen Christison is a former CIA political analyst and the author of several books on the Palestinian situation, including Palestine in Pieces, *co-authored with her late husband Bill Christison.*

Obama the Deregulationist

By ANDREW LEVINE

"Ask Not What Capitalism Can Do For You; Ask What You Can Do For Capitalists." That was the gist of Barack Obama's "State of the Union" address. It is useful to state his point in a Kennedyesque way since it might otherwise be lost amidst all the soporific invocations of "moderation" and "centrism." There was more going on in that speech than the absence of substance. Obama used the occasion to reveal more plainly than ever before what his underlying political philosophy is. It is not what is widely supposed. Obama is a libertarian, and therefore not, according to the most pertinent sense of the term in our political discourse today, a liberal.

Gone are the days when Obama's vacuities functioned like Rorschach tests, empty vessels upon which the gullible could project their dreams. Gone too is the illusion that Obama is a wily progressive, faking right the better to steer the ship of state leftward. And does anyone still think that it was "f...ing retard" advisors that made milquetoast out of his health care and financial reforms or that kept his foreign policy, along with almost everything else, glued to the track George Bush set? By now only the willfully blind can deny that our current president is as dedicated a steward of ruling class interests as his predecessor was. The difference is that he is more capable—who wouldn't be?—and that, as a Democrat, he is better placed for bringing capitalism's victims along.

Unlike a Republican or a Blue Dog Democrat, Obama is not just a toady; and, unlike a true Clintonite, there's more to his governance than crass opportunism. It is plain too that there is more going on with him than just a pathological need, never requited, to work with, rather than against, the most pernicious elements of our political class. Obama holds convictions that conventional liberals do not share, libertarian convictions. Let me explain.

Partisans of order, tradition, family and faith—in other words, men (with women in tow) of conservative dispositions have always been with us; we have always had a political right, opposed to the enlightened ideals of our revolutionary founders and of many, probably most, Americans since. But, outside barely assimilated Catholic circles, genuine philosophical conservatism has always been rare on our shores. This is mainly a consequence of America's colonial past. Already in the throes of capitalist development, seventeenth and eighteenth century Protestant England was problematic territory for conservative political philosophy, and it was in that milieu that what Americans now call "conservatism" took shape.

This is why our self-described conservatives seldom appeal to the (purported) depravity of human nature, and seldom defend established institutions on the grounds that they are necessary for saving ourselves from its free expression. The most important strain of conservative political philosophy in the Western tradition takes sin (human imperfection) seriously. It has been largely a continental European phenomenon; and usually, it is theologically driven. But this strain of political philosophy was not unknown in the British Isles, and it can take on a secular guise. Indeed, its most philosophically astute exponent was an Englishman, Thomas Hobbes (1588–1679), who was widely believed to be an atheist.

There is another kind of conservative philosophy that focuses more on the nature of governance than on human nature, and that is more characteristically British and more unequivocally secular. Michael Oakeshott (1901–1990) captured its nature well by emphasizing conservatism's incompatibility with what he called "rationalism" in politics. Strictly speaking, rationalism is a philosophical position pertaining to the forms and limits of human knowledge. Rationalists hold that knowledge is possible thanks to "innate ideas," as they once were called—mental structures that are, as it were, hard wired into our minds. Rationalism is standardly contrasted with empiricism, though their differences are not as clear as is widely assumed. Empiricists maintain that knowledge comes entirely from sense perception, though in practice they too ascribe an indispensable role to mental activity; while rationalists, conceding the obvious, acknowledge that knowledge of "the external world" must derive in part from sense experience. Nevertheless, the standard understanding does track a difference real enough to underlie distinct philosophical traditions.

Perhaps the best-known rationalist philosopher was René Descartes (1596–1650). As every Philosophy 101 student is taught, Descartes sought to overthrow received beliefs (about what is real) and to reconstruct knowledge claims, including those based on sense perception, on rationally defensible foundations.

An analogy with revolutionary politics, the bugbear of conservatives in the modern era, is plain. Revolutionaries seek to overthrow the old order and then, as the song goes, "to build a new world on the ashes of the old." In contrast, empiricists, being disinclined to put faith in human reason (outside mathematical and logical contexts), are generally accepting of received understandings; in this respect, they are like conservatives. It is telling that the British empiricist tradition was long held to have conservative implications. [This was the view, not only of Bishop Berkeley (1685–1753), one of empiricism's most important and politically conservative exponents, but of V. I. Lenin (1870–1924) as well.]

As Oakeshott maintained, empiricism is of a piece with the core idea of the English common law tradition—that cases should be decided not on the basis of rationally compelling first principles, but in accord with what precedent prescribes. The idea is that there is a collective wisdom inherent in the way problems were addressed in the past, and that the best course of action is to build on it slowly and carefully, avoiding the reckless bravado rationalists in politics and philosophy exude.

Oakeshott's conservatism is arguably more congenial to American sensibilities than is the more venerable continental variety, but it assumes an aristocracy trained from birth to govern. How else, after all, could the craft of wise governance be learned? This is why even this strain of conservative philosophy never quite took hold on the American scene. Thanks to the revolutionary origins of our republic, we have never been encumbered with the rigid class divisions that afflicted our colonizer.

However, in Britain and later in America, conservative modes of thought ran up against an emerging capitalist order that is massively destructive of tradition, order, family and established forms of faith—a point epitomized by the observation registered in *The Communist Manifesto* that, under capitalism, "all that is solid melts into air."

In these circumstances, even in aristocratic Britain (though to a lesser degree), the conservative dispositions that define the political right bended to accommodate pro-market, pro-capitalist ideas, to the detriment of robust conservative political philosophies. The result was never entirely coherent, but there was nevertheless a point of contact with genuine conservatisms: the idea that the most urgent political imperative is to defend the status quo, whatever it is, or, what comes to the same thing, to defend the power of those who benefit most from it. In an already partially democratized Great Britain where, after the revolution in France, calls for liberty, equality and fraternity were in the air, this meant opposition to the "moral economy" of traditional British society and support for what was increasingly supplanting it, untrammeled market relations. It meant subordinating other moral concerns to a (tendentious) conception of justice that supports the inviolability of (private) property rights.

In the US, we call contemporary exponents of this early nineteenth century ideology "libertarians" or "classical liberals." Their philosophy comes in many flavors, not all of them despicable; and although being libertarian is a way of being on the right, libertarians need not oppose liberty, equality and fraternity, though most of them do.

For many decades, important segments of the American right have attached themselves to libertarianism's more noxious strains. A case in point was the Republican rejoinder Congressman Paul Ryan delivered in response to Obama's State of the Union address. Billed as an intellectual leader, Ryan, like many of his fellow Republicans and Tea Partiers, considers himself a follower of a virulently libertarian but enormously popular pseudo-philosopher, Ayn Rand (1905–1982). His remarks reeked of her views. Michele Bachmann's Tea Party rejoinder, though cut from the same cloth, was even less coherent than Ryan's. Bachmann is someone whose thinking might actually be improved by a study of Ayn Rand's work.

Libertarians love private property and markets the way the faithful love God, and they think that, like God, "free" (capitalist) markets are perfectly good. Philosophically minded believers have arguments that purport to show that God exists. These arguments can be interesting, but they are profoundly flawed in ways that have been evident for centuries. Still they persist. Libertarian ideology, though many times defeated by events on the ground, persists too; and its "theologians" also have interesting arguments. Those arguments are not flawed. However, they apply only in highly stylized and unrealizable conditions. Therefore their bearing on real world market arrangements in capitalist societies is, for all practical purposes, nil.

Still, there is no denying that markets can work well (efficiently) in many circumstances, mainly because they simplify the information processing tasks that undid their main twentieth century competitor, central planning. But even before this became evident across the political spectrum, many on the left had already made peace with market arrangements. This was especially the case on the right of the left, in social democratic and liberal circles; in other words, within political formations that sometimes assumed the burdens of governance in capitalist states. In these quarters, markets were accepted for want of suitable alternatives. But they were not loved, and no one considered them or their consequences for the societies in which they operate unequivocal blessings.

American liberalism of the New Deal and Great Society variety stood as far to the right as one could and still be on the left. Thus our liberals accepted the capitalist order, but they hardly loved markets the way the benighted love God; they accepted them *faute de mieux*. They therefore did not oppose welfare state measures that advance the public good apart from or in opposition to market arrangements. They welcomed them.

Not Obama. To be sure, there were times in the first two years of his administration when exigent circumstances caused the difference to fade from view; times when one could suppose, without undue strain, that Obama fell, say, in the Ted Kennedy mold. Apparently, Kennedy himself thought so, and so did other dinosaurs left over from the pre-Clinton Democratic Party. But Obama and the old-line liberals held different ideologies, even if their policy prescriptions sometimes overlapped.

No doubt, Obama favors a more democratic and egalitarian conception of justice than the average libertarian; and he is surely not opposed, as most libertarians are, to the values implicit in the call for "liberty, equality and fraternity." He is not a man of the right but rather, as he and his defenders proclaim, of the center—in the ideal or notional sense of that term, according to which a centrist stands between genuine progressives and genuine conservatives (and can go either way depending on the balance of political forces). But he is a libertarian, not a liberal, even so—because unlike the liberals in whose ranks conventional wisdom casts him, he is an enthusiastic, not a reluctant, free marketeer.

According to some of his defenders, Obama is a "pragmatist," a non-ideological politician, unencumbered by principles (though that implication of what pundits call "pragmatism" is, for obvious reasons, seldom stressed). But even allowing that this is a possible position—in other words, that one can be an adroit tactician without being guided by any ideologically-driven strategy—the description plainly does not apply to Obama. As much as any bona fide (right-wing) libertarian, he is guided by the idea that market arrangements, left undisturbed, lead, as if by an invisible hand, to the best of all possible worlds.

Thus his politics is more like, say, Charles Murray's than Ted Kennedy's; philosophically, if not at a policy level, it is of a piece with the so-called new libertarian thinking that emerged in the 1980s when, having vanquished social democrats and liberals politically, the right still had to consolidate its victory ideologically. New libertarianism was the answer. The old libertarian view, made new again by benighted Tea Partiers, was that justice requires that people be "free" to endure the vicissitudes of capitalist markets. Old libertarians decry state assistance on the grounds that doing good is bad inasmuch as people deserve their market-generated due, and therefore insist that the state do nothing to enhance equality or social solidarity. New libertarian thinking was kinder and gentler; it held that efforts to improve the condition of the badly off through non-market means were laudable but wrong-headed because, in one way or another (for example, by creating a "culture of poverty"), they make outcomes worse. The new libertarians did not directly take on the progressive ideals the left advanced; if anything, they supported them. What they claimed is that the way to achieve those goals, the only effective way, is to let markets do their beneficent work. To this day, that thought remains the public face of the libertarian "lamestream."

Obama's faith in markets resembles theirs. If his policy prescriptions appear more like Kennedy's than, say, Rand Paul's, it is only because he has a more realistic view than Paul or other self-identified libertarians of what states must do to help markets achieve their wondrous effects. As a matter of principled conviction, Obama agrees with the libertarian right that they should do as little as possible. He differs from Tea Partiers and other Republicans only on empirical grounds—because he has a more sensible view than they do of what, in real world conditions, as little as possible involves.

Realizing that Obama is a libertarian explains a great deal: why, for instance, in the debate over "Obamacare," the "public option" was dispensable window-dressing, while the "private option" was never in question. It explains Obama's readiness to let Wall Street call the shots, and his attack on business regulations. It explains why Obama is so eager to get the most shameless corporate types into his administration, and why, on matters of war and trade and other issues of immediate concern to capitalists, he can't do enough for them—to the detriment of his core constituencies. These are not just political maneuvers or expressions of unrequited bipartisan yearning, and neither are they concessions to ineluctable constraints. They are misguided but principled positions that actually make conventional liberalism look good.

And it explains Obama's "bipartisan" endeavors too. To conclude as I began, with yet another familiar trope, just as "a house divided against itself cannot stand," neither can a Reagan-besotted executive committee of the entire ruling class.

Andrew Levine is a Senior Scholar at the Institute for Policy Studies, the author most recently of The American Ideology *(Routledge) and* Political Keywords *(Blackwell), as well as of many other books and articles in political philosophy. He was a Professor (philosophy) at the University of Wisconsin-Madison and a Research Professor (philosophy) at the University of Maryland-College Park.*

Monsanto's Minions: The White House, Congress, and the Mass Media

By RONNIE CUMMINS

The US is rapidly devolving into what can only be described as a Monsanto Nation. Despite Barack Obama (and Hillary Clinton's) campaign operatives in 2008 publicly stating that Obama supported mandatory labels for GMOs, we haven't heard a word from the White House on this topic since Inauguration Day. Michele Obama broke ground for an organic garden at the White House in early 2009, but after protests from the pesticide and biotech industry, the forbidden "O" (Organic) word was dropped from White House PR. Since day one, the Obama Administration has mouthed biotech propaganda, claiming, with no scientific justification whatsoever, that biotech crops can feed the world and enable farmers to increase production in the new era of climate change and extreme weather.

Like Obama's campaign promises to end the wars in Iraq and Afghanistan; like his promises to bring out-of-control banksters and oil companies under control; like his promises to drastically reduce greenhouse gas pollution and create millions of green jobs; Obama has not come though on his 2008 campaign promise to label GMOs. His unilateral approval of Monsanto's genetically engineered alfalfa, overruling the federal courts, scientists, and the organic community, offers the final proof: don't hold your breath for this man to do anything that might offend Monsanto or Corporate America.

Obama's Administration, like the Bush and Clinton Administrations before it, has become a literal "revolving door" for Monsanto operatives. President Obama stated on the campaign trail in 2007–2008 that agribusiness cannot be trusted with the regulatory powers of government.

But, starting with his choice for USDA Secretary, the pro-biotech former governor of Iowa, Tom Vilsack, President Obama has let Monsanto and the biotech industry know they'll have plenty of friends and supporters within his administration. President Obama has taken his team of food and farming leaders directly from the biotech companies and their lobbying, research, and philanthropic arms:

Michael Taylor, former Monsanto Vice President, is now the FDA Deputy Commissioner for Foods. Roger Beachy, former director of the Monsanto-funded Danforth Plant Science Center, is now the director of the USDA National Institute of Food and Agriculture. Islam Siddiqui, Vice President of the Monsanto and Dupont-funded pesticide-promoting lobbying group, CropLife, is now the Agriculture Negotiator for the US Trade Representative. Rajiv Shah, former agricultural-development director for the pro-biotech Gates Foundation (a frequent Monsanto partner), served as Obama's USDA Under-Secretary for Research Education and Economics and Chief Scientist and is now head of USAID. Elena Kagan, who, as President Obama's Solicitor General, took Monsanto's side against organic farmers in the Roundup Ready alfalfa case, is now on the Supreme Court. Ramona Romero, corporate counsel to DuPont, has been nominated by President Obama to serve as General Counsel for the USDA.

Of course, America's indentured Congress is no better than the White House when it comes to promoting sane and sustainable public policy. According to Food and Water Watch, Monsanto and the biotech industry have spent more than half a billion dollars ($547 million) lobbying Congress since 1999. Big Biotech's lobby expenditures have accelerated since Obama's election in 2008. In 2009 alone Monsanto and the biotech lobby spent $71 million. Last year Monsanto's minions included over a dozen lobbying firms, as well as their own in-house lobbyists.

America's bought-and-sold mass media have likewise joined the ranks of Monsanto's minions. Do a Google search on a topic like citizens' rights to know whether our food has been genetically engineered or not, or on the hazards of GMOs and their companion pesticide Roundup, and you'll find very little in the mass media. However, do a Google search on the supposed benefits of Monsanto's GMOs, and you'll find more articles in the daily press than you would ever want to read.

Although Congressman Dennis Kucinich (D-Ohio) recently introduced a bill in Congress calling for mandatory labeling and safety testing for GMOs, don't hold your breath for Congress to take a stand for truth-in-labeling and consumers' right to know what's in their food. In a decade of Congressional lobbying, the OCA has never seen more than twenty four out of 435 Congressional Representatives co-sponsor one of Kucinich's GMO labeling bills. Especially since the 2010 Supreme Court decision in the outrageous "Citizen's United" case gave big corporations like Monsanto the right to spend unlimited amounts of money (and remain anonymous, as they do so) to buy elections, our chances of passing federal GMO labeling laws against the wishes of Monsanto and Food Inc. are all but non-existent. Keep in mind that one of the decisive Supreme Court swing votes in the "Citizen's United' case was cast by the infamous Justice Clarence Thomas, former General Counsel for Monsanto.

To maneuver around Monsanto's minions in Washington we need to shift our focus and go local. We've got to concentrate our forces where our leverage and power lie, in the marketplace, at the retail level; pressuring retail food stores to voluntarily label their products; while on the legislative front we must organize a broad coalition to pass mandatory GMO (and CAFO) labeling laws, at the city, county, and state levels. And while we're doing this we need to join forces with the growing national movement to get corporate money out of politics and the media and to take away the fictitious "corporate personhood" (i.e. the legal right of corporations to have all the rights of human citizens, without the responsibility, obligations, and liability of real persons) of Monsanto and the corporate elite.

Monsanto's Minions: Frankenfarmers in the Fields

The unfortunate bottom line is that most of the North American farmers who have planted Monsanto's Roundup-resistant or Bt-spliced crops (soybeans, corn, cotton, canola, sugar beets, or alfalfa) are either brain-washed, intimidated (Monsanto has often contaminated non-GMO farmers crops and then threatened to sue them for "intellectual property violations" if they didn't sign a contract to buy GMO seeds and sign a confidentiality contract to never talk to the media), or ethically challenged. These "commodity farmers," who receive billions of dollars a year in taxpayer subsidies to plant their Frankencrops and spray their toxic chemicals and fertilizers, don't seem to give a damn about the human health hazards of chemical, energy and GMO-intensive agriculture; the cruelty, disease and filth of Factory Farms or CAFOs; or the damage they are causing to the soil, water and climate. Likewise, they have expressed little or no concern over the fact that they are polluting the land and the crops of organic and non-GMO farmers.

Unfortunately, these Frankenfarmers, Monsanto's minions, have now been allowed to plant GMO crops on 150 million acres, approximately one-third of all US cropland. With GE alfalfa they'll be planting millions of acres more.

The time has come to move beyond polite debate with America's frankenfarmers, and their powerful front groups such as the American Farm Bureau, the Biotechnology Industry Organization, and the Grocery Manufacturers Association. "Coexistence" is a joke when you are dealing with indentured minions whose only ethical guideline is making money. When I asked a French organic farmer a few years ago what he thought about the idea of coexistence with GE crops and farmers, he laughed. "If my neighbor dared to plant Monsanto's GM crops, I'd hop on my tractor and plow them up." Thousands of European farmers and organic activists have indeed uprooted test plots of GMOs over the past decade. Unfortunately if you get caught destroying frankencrops in the US, you'll likely be branded a terrorist and sent to prison.

Apart from direct action, it's time to start suing, not just Monsanto and the other biotech bullies, but the Frankenfarmers themselves. Attorneys have pointed out to me that the legal precedent of "Toxic Trespass" is firmly established in American case law. If a farmer carelessly or deliberately sprays pesticides or herbicides on his or her property, and this toxic chemical strays or "trespasses" and causes damage to a neighbor's property, the injured party can sue the "toxic trespasser" and collect significant damages. It's time for America's organic and non-GMO farmers to get off their knees and fight, both in the courts and in the court of public opinion. The Biotech Empire of Monsanto, Dow, Dupont, Bayer, BASF and Syngenta will collapse if its frankenfarmers are threatened with billions of dollars in toxic trespass damages.

In just one year, Monsanto has moved from being Forbes's "Company of the Year" to the worst stock of the year. The biotech bully of St. Louis has become one of the most hated corporations on Earth.

The biotech bullies and the Farm Bureau have joined hands with the Obama Administration to force controversial frankencrops like alfalfa onto the market. But as African-American revolutionary Huey Newton pointed out in the late 1960s, "The Power of the People is greater than the Man's technology."

Ronnie Cummins is director of the Organic Consumers Association.

The Torture of Bradley Manning

By MEDEA BENJAMIN and CHARLES DAVIS

Bradley Manning is accused of humiliating the political establishment by revealing the complicity of top US officials in carrying out and covering up war crimes. In return for his act of conscience, the US government is holding him in abusive solitary confinement, humiliating him and trying to keep him behind bars for life.

The lesson is clear, and soldiers take note: You're better off committing a war crime than exposing one.

An Army intelligence officer stationed in Kuwait, the twenty-three-year-old Manning, outraged at what he saw, allegedly leaked tens of thousands of State Department cables to the whistle-blowing website WikiLeaks. These cables show US officials covering up everything from US tax dollars funding child rape in Afghanistan to illegal, unauthorized bombings in Yemen. Manning is also accused of leaking video evidence of US pilots gunning down more than a dozen Iraqis in Baghdad, including two journalists for Reuters, and then killing a father of two who stopped to help them. The father's two young children were also severely wounded.

"Well, it's their fault for bringing kids into a battle," a not-terribly-remorseful US pilot can be heard remarking in the July 2007 "Collateral Murder" video.

None of the soldiers who carried out that war crime have been punished, nor have any of the high-ranking officials who authorized it. Indeed, committing war crimes is more likely to get a solider a medal than a prison term. And authorizing them? Well, that'll get you a book deal and a six-digit speaking fee. Just ask George W. Bush or Dick Cheney, Donald Rumsfeld or Condoleezza Rice. Or the inexplicably "respectable" Colin Powell.

In fact, the record indicates Manning would be far better off today—possibly on the lecture circuit rather than in solitary confinement—if he'd killed those men in Baghdad himself.

Hyperbole? Consider what happened to the US soldiers who, over a period of hours—not minutes—went house to house in the Iraqi town of Haditha and executed twenty four men, women and children in retaliation for a roadside bombing.

"I watched them shoot my grandfather, first in the chest and then in the head," said one of the two surviving eyewitnesses to the massacre, nine-year-old Eman Waleed. "Then they killed my granny." Almost five years later, not one of the men involved in the incident is behind bars. And despite an Army investigation revealing that statements made by the chain of command "suggest that Iraqi civilian lives are not as important as U.S. lives," with the murder of brown-skinned innocents considered "just the cost of doing business," none of their superiors are behind bars either.

Now consider the treatment of Bradley Manning. On March 1, the military charged Manning with twenty two additional offenses—on top of the original charges of improperly leaking classified information, disobeying an order and general misconduct. One of the new charges, "aiding the enemy," is punishable by death. That means Manning faces the prospect of being executed or spending his life in prison for exposing the ugly truth about the US empire.

Meanwhile, the Obama administration has decided to make Manning's pre-trial existence as torturous as possible, holding him in solitary confinement twenty three hours a day since his arrest ten months ago—treatment that the group Psychologists for Social Responsibility notes is, "at the very least, a form of cruel, unusual and inhumane treatment in violation of U.S. law."

In addition to the horror of long-term solitary confinement, Manning is barred from exercising in his cell and is denied bed sheets and a pillow. And every five minutes, he must respond in the affirmative when asked by a guard if he's "okay."

Presumably he lies.

And it gets worse. On his blog, Manning's military lawyer, Lt. Col. David Coombs, reveals that his client is now being stripped of his clothing at night, left naked under careful surveillance for seven hours. When the 5:00 am wake-up call comes, he's then "forced to stand naked at the front of the cell."

If you point out that the emperor has no clothes, it seems the empire will make sure you have none either.

Officials at the Quantico Marine Base where Manning is being held claim the move is "not punitive" but rather a "precautionary measure" intended to prevent him from harming himself. Do they really think Manning is going to strangle himself with his underwear—and that he could do so while under twenty-four-hour surveillance?

"Is this Quantico or Abu Ghraib?" asked Rep. Dennis Kucinich in a press release. Good question, congressman. Like the men imprisoned in former President Bush's Iraqi torture chamber, Manning is being abused and humiliated despite having not so much as been tried in a military tribunal, much less convicted of an actual crime.

So much for the constitutional lawyer who ran as the candidate of hope and change.

Remember back when Obama campaigned against such Bush-league torture tactics? Recall when candidate Obama said "government whistleblowers are part of a healthy democracy and must be protected from reprisal"? It appears his opposition to torture and support for whistleblowers was only so much rhetoric. And then he took office.

Indeed, despite the grand promises and soaring rhetoric, Obama's treatment of Manning is starkly reminiscent of none other than Richard Nixon. Like Obama—who has prosecuted more whistleblowers than any president in history—Nixon had no sympathy for "snitches," and no interest in the American public learning the truth about their government. And he likewise argued that Daniel Ellsberg, the leaker of the Pentagon Papers, had given "aid and comfort to the enemy" for revealing the facts about the war in Vietnam.

But there's a difference: Richard Nixon never had the heroic whistle-blower of his day thrown in solitary confinement and tortured. If only the same could be said for Barack Obama.

Medea Benjamin is cofounder of Global Exchange and
CODEPINK: Women for Peace.
Charles Davis is an independent journalist.

Winding Down Obama
By LINH DINH

Occupying Iraq, the US spends about $300 million a day. For Afghanistan, it's $200 million. These numbers are approximations because the Pentagon doesn't really know how much it has spent on anything, or how many it has killed in its several wars, big and small. It doesn't really care, I don't think. Imagine a team of alcoholics parked permanently at the bar, downing pints and shots with an open tab into infinity, or until the Second Coming, at least. In 2001, Donald Rumsfeld admitted that $2.3 trillion were unaccounted for. He blamed it on sloppy bookkeeping. It must be hard to keep track of so many digits.

As firemen and cops are being fired across America, as teachers are being told they must accept austerity measures—the country is broke, after all—as public radio and television, with their supposed liberal bias, lay on the chopping block, as more homeless sprawl and tent cities spring up, as casinos, a sure sign of desperation, mushroom—the US has entered another costly war without any fanfare or discussion whatsoever. Obama didn't have to persuade anybody, no sending a Secretary of State to make a fool of herself in front of the United Nations' General Assembly, no congressional vote, which, last time I checked, was supposed to be a Constitutional requirement, no media blitz. No lies even. He simply ordered more than a hundred Tomahawk missiles, so far, to rain down on Libya, with many more to come. In any case, this it not even a war, but merely a "kinetic military action," according to an Obama aide. Such straight faced butchery of language, even as one butchers real people, shows that the United States has entered a deep psychotic state. Upon winning the Nobel Peace Prize, Obama himself declared, "I am living testimony to the moral force of non-violence."

If this is Obama pacified, I hate to see him riled up, but of course he doesn't get riled up. Suave, articulate and personable, Obama is proving to be just as deadly as Bush, but clearly more cynical. A loyal tool of the establishment, Obama has dampened protest from American liberals. Though they know he has betrayed them, they're reluctant to show appropriate outrage because, not that long ago, they have cheered and wept for him so openly. The day after Obama won, Rebecca Solnit burbled in *The Nation*, "Citizenship is a passionate joy at times, and this is one of those times. You can feel it. Tuesday the world changed. It was a great day."

The President of the United States is a traveling salesman for the military industrial complex. In 2010, Obama came to India to visit the Mumbai home of Gandhi, a hero of his, someone he would most like to dine with, very touching, before announcing a mega arms deal of GE fighter jet engines and Boeing military transport planes. Now, as he bombs Libya, Obama tries to sell F-18 fighter planes to Brazil. According to an aide, "President Obama underscored that the F-18 is the best plane on offer" as he made a "strong pitch" to Brazilian President Dilma Rousseff.

The President of the United States is also a spokesman for murderers and crooks. He doesn't rule, but obeys. His main job is to deceive the masses as he serves his enablers. He can say anything at any time, and means none of it. The President of the United States is the world's most visible actor, in short. Campaigning in 2007, Obama said, "If American workers are being denied their right to organize and collectively bargain when I'm in the White House, I'll put on a comfortable pair of shoes myself. I'll walk on that picket line with you as president of the United States." Quite a performance. This year, as Wisconsin teachers fight to retain their right to collectively bargain, Obama has said absolutely nothing. One would have to be a fool to think he would join them.

Offshoring began under Clinton, and has continued unabated. Under the banner of free trade, the only goal of globalism is to couple capital with the cheapest labor available. Since organized workers are anathema to the bosses, American companies have moved their factories to totalitarian countries where workers have few rights, where they cannot be unionized. The idea is to roll back the clock to the earliest days of industrialism, where workers toiled all day long for next to nothing. In February, a bill was even introduced in Missouri to eliminate child labor laws. It seeks, in part, to get rid of "the prohibition on employment of children under age fourteen. Restrictions on the number of hours and restrictions on when a child may work during the day are also removed." Don't laugh. This may be a sign of things to come.

As for work that can't be outsourced, foreign workers are allowed or even invited in. US borders are not porous out of charity or ineptness, but because this benefits American businesses. During the recent housing bubble, builders employed countless Mexican workers, and every stateside restaurant these days seems to be staffed by Mexican busboys, cooks and dishwashers. Chinese engineering students can stay after graduating from American schools, and Indian doctors and nurses are given special visas. There are certain jobs, however, that can't easily be staffed by aliens, such as teachers, for example. If Albanians could be imported to teach English and American History to American kids, it would have happened already. The latest attack in this relentless war against American workers is the announcement that Mexican truckers will soon be allowed to drive into the US. Though ignored by the mainstream media, this calamity won't just put tens of thousands of American truck drivers out of work, but also many American dock workers. Containers can be shipped to Mexico, then trucked into the US by cheaper Mexican drivers.

Again, American borders are porous by design, just as other countries' borders are routinely violated by the US. There is a huge difference, however:

when Americans enter another country illegally, it's never to empty foreigners' bedpans or to wash their dishes, but usually to kill them.

As Obama fizzles out, as he loses legitimacy, the power brokers will come up with other figureheads and slogans for American liberals and conservatives to become passionate about. These candidates will jabber, jab and insult each other. As in professional wrestling, the battle will appear fierce. Barack, meanwhile, can look forward to a lucrative memoir and six-figure speaking fees. Even that man of malapropisms and snafus, the much despised Bush, is getting $150,000 each time he opens his mouth these days.

Linh Dinh is the author of two books of stories and five of poetry, and the recently published novel, Love Like Hate. *He's tracking our deteriorating socialscape through his frequently updated photo blog,* State of the Union.

Sexual Politics in the Age of Obama

By DAVID ROSEN

The clock is ticking down on Barack Obama's first term as president and, sadly, other than health care reform (which is significant) he has little to show for three-plus grueling years. A stagnant economy, a stuttering war machine and a savage reactionary right have paralyzed his presidency. To recover, Obama, and America, needs a miracle.

A growing number of Americans who brought him and other Democrats victory in 2008 feel deeply dispirited. What they will do in terms of the 2012 election is an open question.

Many of Obama's 2008 supporters feel betrayed, having drunk deeply from the "hope" cool-aid only to awaken to a deeply disturbing reality; they share a wicked hangover that little the candidate promised has come to fruition. Others share this profound disappointment, having invested much in the electoral process to only realize that power and wealth really determine government policy. A growing number of those who believed in America's "great black hope" feel betrayed by how the Obama administration and Congressional Democrats are failing to deal with the structural crisis redefining 21st century America.

The 2008 election was a repudiation of the Bush-era tyranny—the policies of robber baron greed, imperialist interventions and Christian (im)morality. Obama's campaign made voters aware that something was deeply wrong with the economy and the distribution of social wealth. A vast number of Americans sensed—unconsciously knew—that finance capital and the super-rich control the Capitol and caused the great recession.

Equally critical, many voters shared Obama's unstated recognition that while Muslim fanatics perpetrated the attacks of 9/11, their actions were facilitated by a failure of the US national intelligence racket. Most morally disturbing: No one was held accountable. So hypocritical was the coverup that the head of the failure, CIA director George Tenet, received an award for excellence. Making matters worse, a growing number of Americans, on the left and right, believe that this failure was used to legitimize the fraudulent, never-ending war on an undefined global enemy—"terrorism."

The refusal by the Obama administrations and Congressional Democrats to push their 2008 electoral success to a victorious repudiation of Bush-era policies created the opportunity for the Tea Party counter-revolution. Popular rage against ruling-class tyranny was left to dissipate. Capitalist schemers like Alan Greenspan were not forced to publicly recant and accept responsibility for their failed policies; corporatist conspirators like Countrywide's

Angelo Mozilo were not prosecuted for their roles in the economy's melt-down. Global war mongers like Donald Rumsfeld were not indicted; and mercenaries like Blackwater's Erik Prince have never been charged.

The failure by Obama and the Democratic leadership to transform a popular call for "hope" into a sustained movement for "change" created the opening for the Tea Party. This failure facilitated the Democratic rout in the 2010 midterm elections. It enabled finance capital and the super-rich to re-gain control over most elected officials and walk away with their proverbial pockets full of the loot plundered from the great recession. Equally troubling, the 2008 elections enshrined the 9/11 intelligence failures as mere oversights, legitimizing America's current policy of never-ending war.

Nevertheless, the Bush-era culture wars have taken a backseat in the face of the nation's overwhelming economic crisis and imperialist quagmire. While abortion rights and gay marriage (newly branded as "marriage equali-ty") remain at the top of the Christian right's anti-sex agenda, a host of other issues that dominated Bush-era cultural politics have faded from the debate. Foremost among these "secondary" issues are teen abstinence, religion in the classroom, obscenity standards, commercial sex and sex offenders. What happened to them?

For many, the "hope" that Obama represents, no matter how compro-mised, remains far more appealing then the prospects of yet another Republi-can reactionary like George Bush in the White House. Others recognize that not voting is worse than a no vote, so they will likely hold their proverbial noses and cast their votes for the best of the two evils, hoping it matters. Still others are more pragmatic, accepting the fact that the outcome of the 2012 election may well determine the future makeup of the Supreme Court, which seems to be going over the reactionary cliff. And then there are those who don't want to return to the culture wars of old and will cast their lot with Obama and the toothless Democrats.

* * *

A vicious class war has replaced the culture wars of the Bush era. While the rich get richer, the standard of living for most working Americans is in decline. For most Americans, wages are stagnate, unemployment lines are growing, personal debt is escalating, home foreclosures are mounting and those without health insurance are increasing in number. Against this de-pressing environment, America's sexual culture is also suffering.

The shift in national political and ideological priorities does not mean that the culture wars have ended. In a reincarnation of the 1920s' temperance campaign, rightwing Christians continue the never-ending battle to impose their repressive values on all Americans. Two minor examples are illustrative: the CEO of Curves fitness centers, Gary Heavin, donates millions to anti-abortion groups; and the founders of the fast-food chain Chick-fil-A, the

Cathy family, who are devout Baptists, believe in "the Biblical definition of marriage" and support faith-based groups opposed to same-sex relationships. Moralist crusaders are out there big time.

Abortion and gay marriage remain the most contested issues in the battle over morality. Obama has taken a strong stand in support of civil liberties for homosexual Americans, but has failed to aggressively contest rightwing reactionaries over a woman's right to choose to terminate her pregnancy. Its unclear why Obama, along with Congressional Democrats, have chosen such a compromised strategy. Some argue that it represents the good-old patriarchy of male power. Others believe that Obama sees a corollary between his parents marriage in 1961, before the Supreme Court's 1967 *Loving v. Virginia* decision legalizing interracial marriage, and the plight of homosexuals.

In the wake of New York State's June 2011 legalization of "marriage equality," Obama played his characteristic compromiser's wink-and-a-nod game. He has steadfastly supported civil unions for gay people as a state's rights issue; at convenient times, like fundraisers, he feigns support for gay marriage but holds back outright endorsement.

Nevertheless, Obama has taken unprecedented actions to end discrimination against homosexual women and men. Foremost, the administration ended Don't Ask/Don't Tell (DA/DT) within the US military. This is no minor accomplishment. In sympathy with the growing gay-rights movement of the early '90s, Bill Clinton supported the full integration of the US armed services, but under staunch Christian anti-gay pressure he capitulated and signed the DA/DT Act in 1993.

Second, the administration has determined that the Defense of Marriage Act (DoMA) is unconstitutional and is no longer having the Dept. of Justice enforce it. This has caused a firestorm among Christian conservatives who have charged Obama with not upholding a law of the land. (In July 2011, the Senate began debate over repealing the Act.)

Obama's decision has provided the basis for a series of actions extending federal benefits to federal employees, their families and others. These include sick and funeral leave, long-term care insurance, travel and relocation assistance, child care subsidies and certain retirement benefits.

The Human Rights Campaign identifies the following actions by various agencies to suggest the scope of change resulting from ending DoMA enforcement:

• The State Department extended numerous benefits to the same-sex partners of Foreign Service officers.

• The Department of Housing and Urban Development proposed regulations recognizing LGBT families for federal housing programs.

• The Department of Health and Human Services (HHS) ended its ban on HIV-positive visitors and immigrants.

• HHS issued regulations requiring all hospitals receiving Medicaid and Medicare funds to prohibit discrimination in visitation against LGBT people.

• HHS extended abstinence-only-until-marriage sex education funded programs to LGBT youth, thus undercutting the stigma many non-conforming young people experience.

In addition and as a direct repudiation of DoMA, federal deportation criteria was changed to recognize same-sex marriages, effecting an estimated 56,000 couples. Other changes included permitting same-sex adoption, joint same-sex bankruptcy petitions and support for same-sex foster care.

If gay rights is the major bright light in the Obama administration sex or cultural policies, its efforts relating to female reproductive health have been half-hearted and helped fuel the ongoing Christian conservative anti-sex campaign. The battle over female reproductive freedom involves a broad array of concerns, the three most contentious being abortion, family planning and sex education; a second tier of related issues include sexual violence toward women, sex trafficking and commercial sex.

In 2007, when he was a Senator, Obama cosponsored the Freedom of Choice Act (S. 1173) that would reaffirm *Roe* as a fundamental right. He then stated: "Throughout my career, I've been a consistent and strong supporter of reproductive justice, and have consistently had a 100% pro-choice rating with Planned Parenthood and NARAL Pro-Choice America."

Unfortunately, at a news conference in April 2008 marking his first 100 days in office, the new president declared: "Now, the Freedom of Choice Act is not my highest legislative priority." And added:

"I believe that women should have the right to choose, but I think that the most important thing we can do to tamp down some of the anger surrounding this issue is to focus on those areas that we can agree on. And that's where I'm going to focus."

To "tamp down" anger he took on the battle for national health care while abortion rights, along with immigration reform, climate change and labor rights, fell by the wayside. Even worse, to sell his health care program, Obama and the Democrats bartered away a woman's right to choose. The Stupak amendment adopted in the House bars private health insurance plans from covering elective abortion.

While *Roe* remains the law of the land, a woman's right to choose continues to erode. The abortion battle has shifted from the Congress to state legislatures. Across the country, especially in what are known as red states, the Christian right has moved aggressively to further tighten restrictions on "legal" abortions.

Antiabortion crusaders have used issues like "big" government, mounting state debt and immigration fears to wage campaigns against women considering an abortion. Their tactics have included forcing women to undergo an ultrasound visualization of the fetus, banning abortion coverage in the state employees' health plan, requiring the women to receive dubious antiabortion counseling and restricting public funding of abortion under the new health insurance exchanges.

In addition, antiabortion activists are employing provocative public media campaigns. Two are emblematic: billboards in Georgia targeting African-Americans identified black babies as an "endangered species" and slick posters on the New York City subways stated "abortion changes you" to push a more sophisticated antiabortion message. Going further, they have set up fictitious "abortion counseling" centers that do not provide medical advice but push an antiabortion message.

According to the Guttmacher Institute, since Obama was elected there has been a noticeable upswing in the number of bills introduced at state legislations to regulate abortion and related reproductive health services. It estimates that in 2010 370 bills regulating abortion were introduced compared to the 350 in each of the previous five years; during the 1990s, the annual average was 250 bills.

The two dirtiest words in the Christian right's vocabulary are: Planned Parenthood. Aligned with its effort to further restrict or end a woman's right to choose an abortion, the right seeks to strangle Planned Parenthood. It wants to end Planned Parenthood, ability to provide family planning and other services through ever-more cohesive state-based regulations.

At the federal level, Title X of the Public Health Service Act is the sole program devoted to family planning. In Obama's FY 2012 budget, he proposed a modest funding increase; unfortunately, Tea Party Republicans are seeking to slash Title X funding, some attempting to eliminate it entirely.

Title X funds subsidize family planning centers throughout the country. One-quarter of all poor women who obtain contraceptive services do so at centers receiving Title X funding. Guttmacher estimates that such direct client services helped women and couples avoid 973,000 unintended pregnancies, which would have resulted in 433,000 unplanned births and 406,000 abortions. Without these services, unintended pregnancies and abortions would be 33 percent higher.

Equally critical, 17 percent of poor women who obtain a Pap test or pelvic exam and 20 percent who obtain help for a sexually transmitted infection do so at these clinics. One can only suspect that class and race factors play as strong a role as issues of concern as "big" government and the debt in the Christian right's war against Planned Parenthood and family planning.

The Obama administration has, gratefully, abandoned the Bush-era abstinence-only crusade. Abstinence-only education contributed to unwanted pregnancies, oftentimes leading to unwanted abortions. Research findings during the Bush presidency showed an upswing in pregnancy among teen girls, indicating that the abstinence-only policy did not work. The 2008 election saga featuring the pregnancy of Sarah Palin's daughter, Bristol, revealed just how flawed the policy was.

Obama once insisted: "As President, I will improve access to affordable health care and work to ensure that our teens are getting the information and services they need to stay safe and healthy." This is one promise he has kept.

In his FY 2010 budget, Obama eliminated funding for two cornerstones of the Bush know-nothing policy, the Community-Based Abstinence Education and the mandatory Title V Abstinence Education program. The Obama administration committed $164 million for a new teen pregnancy prevention initiative targeted to encourage programs through state agencies, nonprofit organizations, school districts and universities. It also backed what it identified as "evidence-based programs" of sex ed and authorized $50 million in new mandatory teen pregnancy prevention grants.

Forcible rape of women is slowly declining. Two decades ago, however, it was a different story. According to Justice Department data, reported rapes of women "by force" jumped significantly between 1980 and 1990, from 63,599 to 85,541, and has remained relatively constant since, around 84,000 annually.

However, the country's population increases over time. Thus, it's necessary to analyze not only the number of forcible rapes, but also rape as a rate relative to the female population. Assessed in these terms, rape has witnessed a significant decline over the last two decades. The rate of rape peaked in 1990 at 80.5 rapes per 100,000 women and has steadily declined until in 2007 (the last year of available data) it was at 59.1. That's a 26 percent decline.

Obama's Department of Education has taken up this issue in a campaign against what some identify as an epidemic, on-campus sexual assault and rape of female students. Secretary of Education Arne Duncan announced this new effort: "Every school would like to believe it is immune from sexual violence, but the facts suggest otherwise." The DoE has reinterpreted Title IX legislation that bars sex discrimination in schools (and which has been effective promoting female sports) to cover on-campus sexual violence.

The Obama administration has run into a conservative buzzsaw over the issue of sex trafficking. The wrath of the right was brought down on Obama because he had the temerity to modify a Bush-era policy involving sex—sex occurring overseas. Bush policies barred US international aid organizations from working with groups that assisted prostitutes or other sex workers. Obama's policy affronted moral zealots because it allowed "affiliated entities" (e.g., a separate part of an organization receiving federal funds) to receive federal support assisting sex workers through HIV/AIDS prevention programs, the PEPFAR program (see below).

Some alarmists have declared that the US is facing a sex trafficking "epidemic." Artfully, they do not define "epidemic." While any case of trafficking is terrible, especially for the victim, compared to the 84,000 forcible rapes and the 56,000 new HIV/AIDS infections reported annually, one has to wonder whether such a misuse of language makes a bad situation worse.

Between January 1, 2008, and June 30, 2010, a cumulative total of 2,515 suspected incidents of human trafficking were reported in the US. This is the finding of the only comprehensive study of domestic sex trafficking, the federal taskforce on Human Trafficking Reporting System (HTRS).

Four-fifths (82%) of reported incidents of trafficking involved sex trafficking, including more than 1,200 incidents with allegations of adult sex trafficking and more than 1,000 incidents involved the exploitation of a child. Four-fifths (83%) of victims in confirmed sex trafficking incidents were identified as US citizens, of which 40 percent were black and 20 percent white.

Nearly half of all reports involved allegations of adult prostitution (48%) and 40 percent involved prostitution of a child or child sexual exploitation. The report includes a classification called "sexualized labor" that covers exotic dancing and unlicensed massage parlors, which accounts for 6 percent of the reported incidents.

Sadly underreported, between 2003 and 2010, the FBI rescued 886 child victims of sex traffickers and secured 510 convictions.

President Obama must have met one or more commercial sex workers during his days organizing on the streets of Chicago's South Side: He surely knows something about the reality of American urban life.

In hard times, many women and girls (along with some young men and boys) feel they have little but their bodies (and the attendant fantasy) to sell. As most rules regarding prostitution are covered by state and local regulations, nothing will likely change in terms of the arrest of hookers, whether down-market streetwalkers, massage-parlor workers, gentlemen's club lap-dancers or Craigslist courtesans.

(The Mann Act, officially known as the White-Slave Traffic Act and first passed by Congress in 1910 to prohibition interstate transportation of women for commercial sex, has fallen into disfavor. Its greatest casualty, Jack Johnson, the first black world boxing champion, was arrested, convicted and imprisoned in 1920. Many wondered why former New York Governor Eliot Spitzer did not face similar federal charges?)

The Obama administration has made one small advance over previous administrations regarding commercial sex workers. It accepted the Universal Periodic Review (UPR), Recommendation 86, from a report by the United Nations Human Rights Council Working Group. This obscure act is important because the US will now consider the vulnerability of LGBT people and sex workers in terms of human rights abuses and violence, and ensure that sex workers have access to appropriate services. Welcome to the world of small steps.

The US is engaged in a two-front war, one domestic, the other international, against HIV/AIDS, and other sexually-transmitted diseases. In the US, an estimated 1.1 million people live with HIV/AIDS. The principle modes of transmission involve: unprotected male-to-male anal sexual intercourse; injection drug use; unprotected heterosexual sexual intercourse; and other means like contaminated medical syringes.

Nearly half (500,000) of those infected in the US are African-Americans. A recent study by the Black AIDS Institute, "Deciding Moment: The State of AIDS in Black America," notes: "Every year, 56,000 Americans become infected with HIV. Nearly one out of two newly infected people are Black."

In July 2010, the Obama administration introduced the National HIV/AIDS Strategy, the nation's first comprehensive AIDS plan. It is organized around three core goals: to reduce new HIV infections, to increase access to care and improving health outcomes for people living with HIV and to reduce HIV-related disparities and health inequities.

The US spends $19 billion annually on domestic HIV/AIDS prevention, care and research. Last year, the US Dept. of Health and Human Services allocated $30 million in a major initiative to develop better HIV/AIDS prevention methods. The announcement was met with a ho-hum shrug by AIDS activists. Michael Weinstein of the AIDS Healthcare Foundation expressed the widely shared assessment: "This will be another report that will gather dust on the shelves of the Library of Congress."

Depressingly, any new federal effort will likely have only a marginal impact on the continuing spread of HIV/AIDS within the African-American community. African-Americans have been disproportionately affected by HIV/AIDS since the epidemic's beginning and this disparity has only deepened over time.

In his 2003 State of the Union address, President Bush declared: 'I ask the Congress to commit $15 billion over the next five years, to turn the tide against AIDS in the most afflicted nations of Africa and the Caribbean." The centerpiece of this campaign was the President's Emergency Plan for AIDS Relief (PEPFAR).

PEPFAR is intended for the care, treatment and prevention of HIV/AIDS in developing countries. In '08, Congress passed legislation reauthorizing the program and allocated $50 billion for the next five years. Unfortunately, it became *the quintessential example of what happens when Christian conservatives take control of a key program of American foreign policy.*

While the Obama administration has dropped the "anti-prostitution pledge" that restricted PEPFAR support for sex workers, it has taken a needlessly cautious approach with the program. It has shifted the PEPFAR strategy from one of fighting AIDS to a disease-prevention approach targeting pneumonia, diarrhea, malaria and fatal birth complications as well as AIDS. In addition, it reduced the targeted treatment goal of those on antiretroviral drugs. According to an analysis in the *New York Times*, "the program has put 2.4 million on the drugs since 2004, or almost 500,000 a year on average. Adding only 1.6 million over the next five years means adding only 320,000 each year." One step forward, two steps back.

Anticipated budget cuts will likely reduce support for a wide range of health-related programs. Likely across-the-board cuts will impact PEPFAR and other medical and scientific efforts. These cuts may well be less draconian than attacks on funding for family planning and reproductive health services. Stay tuned.

Four politically related sex and/or cultural issues that played an important role mobilizing the Bush's Christian base have faded from the media spotlight during Obama's first term—sex scandals, obscenity (including "sexting"), sex offenders and religion in the classroom.

Sex scandals involving politicians have played a disruptive, if secondary, role in recent elections. The scandals preceding the 2008 election involving Democrats John Edwards and Eliot Spitzer as well as Republicans Larry Craig and David Vitter captured front-page headlines, but played only a minor role in the election outcome. As the old political truism goes, "It's the economy, stupid."

A series of recent scandals involving former Congressmen Anthony Weiner (D-NY), Chris Lee (R-NY) and Mark Souder (R-IN) point to a new, more pro-active agenda adopted by both major parties. When a scandal erupts, the parties are imposing a "zero tolerance" policy, moving quickly and decisively to force the sinner to resign, pushing him from the media spotlight.

With all the hanky-panky, under-the-table payoffs, in-kind favors and unreported contributions that pass for business-as-usual in Washington, a sex scandal can occur at any time. A zero tolerance policy may work with low-level Congressmen, but whether it is enforceable with those further up the foodchain remains to be seen as evident in the cases of recent Republican senators John Ensign, Craig and Vitter.

Since Obama took office, issues involving public morals or "decency," most often framed in terms of pornography or obscenity, have been absent from the political debate. The alleged flood of child pornography on the Internet that so preoccupied Bush-era moralists has essentially disappeared; federal courts have determined it to be a non-issue. Similarly, the FCC's $500,000 fine against CBS for violating "decency" standards due to its over-the-air broadcast of Janet Jackson's exposed nipple during the 2004 SuperBowl halftime show was thrown out. The Supreme Court's June 2011 ruling blocking California's attempt to censor young people playing violent videogames further extends First Amendment protections.

A parallel issue involving the limits of free speech and young people involves the popular practice of "sexting," the sending and/or receiving personal sexual images over one's mobile phone or wireless device. Many young people are being arrested and prosecuted for all manner of illicit depictions associated with today's new form of personal expression, whether via mobile devices or shared on social networking sites. The fault lines of acceptable flirting, let alone pornography, are being tested. In time, this issue will get to the federal courts and we will see how far First Amendment protections go.

If one TV show reflected the mood of the Bush era it was the popular NBC Dateline series, "To Catch a Predator." Each week the show's producers lured a would-be adult male sex "offender"—a truly pathetic guy—to a fictitious rendezvous with an allegedly underage girl for sex. In this modern-day morality play, the offender was exposed, confesses his sins on camera and is taken off for prosecution by a local police officer. It was inauspiciously canceled in December '08.

In August 2009, Phillip Garrido, a registered sex offender, and his wife, Nancy Garrido, were arrested for the kidnapping, imprisonment and rape of Jaycee Lee Dugard. As everyone surely knows by now, Dugard was kidnapped when only eleven years old and held for 18 years, giving birth to two children that Garrido forcibly fathered. As could be expected, the NBC show would have offered little insight into the perpetrator's psychosis or the state's failed probation system that facilitated the scandalous crime.

The Obama administration, like Bush's, has no coherent policy with regard to sex offenders. He is following the "throw-away-the-key" policy favored by many states. In 2009, Chief Justice John Roberts granted an Obama Justice Department request to block the release of up to seventy seven sex offenders who had completed their federal prison sentences but were still being held under indefinite incarceration for being perceived as "sexually dangerous." In 2010, the Supreme Court upheld the government's right to detain an individual under civil commitment laws if the person is considered likely to commit more violent sexual crimes if released from custody.

Obama has done little to meaningfully address the issue. He has gone along with conventional proposals to tighten sex-offender registries and urged the private sector to create a trusted-identity system to boost consumer security in cyberspace, especially for kids and teens.

It's time for the American judicial and medical systems to address not only the real threat posed by (mostly male) sex offenders, but also to develop a rational and nonpunitive means of dealing with such offenders. Otherwise, we will end up with yet another population, like many held in Guantánamo, lost in a growing American gulag.

The year 2009 marked the 150th anniversary of the publication of Charles Darwin's "On the Origin of the Species." Obama's first term has been marked by the noticeable absence of battles over intellectual design or creationism and religion in the classroom. In the face of the profound economic and social crisis the nation confronts, the Christian right's moralistic hokum seems out of place. However, if the Tea Party further captures the Republican Party, and one of its ideological stalwarts runs for Vice President, these issues will likely reappear but in a far more virulent form. A warning to the wise.

The elections of 2012 will be pivotal in next phase of American history. Will the forces of finance capital (and the military-intelligence state) increase control over American society or will its drive for the fundamental reordering of social wealth (and, therefore, the "American dream") be halted? The era of the New Deal stuttered under the weight of the Great Society; a reordering of social relations took place during the period from Nixon through Clinton; the Bush-Obama legacy may well be the *coup de grâce* to the New Deal democracy.

Sexual and cultural history relate to the larger economic and political developments as a glove to a hand. In the face of the new austerity economy and the war over social wealth intensifies, expect sexual freedom to suffer. The fight to preserve a secular, progressive and humane sexuality is the fight for the freedom of all Americans. One can only hope that if Obama wins a second term, sexual health and pleasure, including the right to an abortion, will be at the center of his agenda. Surely, if the Republicans wins, it won't be.

David Rosen is author of Sex Scandal America: Politics & the Ritual of Public Shaming.

What Has Bin Laden's Killing Wrought?

By RAY McGOVERN

As America's morbid celebrations over the killing of Osama bin Laden begin to fade, we are left with a new landscape of risks—and opportunities—created by his slaying at the hands of a US Special Forces team at a compound in Abbottabad, Pakistan.

The range of those future prospects could be found in a single-day's edition of the *Washington Post*. On the hopeful side, a front-page article reported that the Obama administration was following up bin Laden's death with accelerated peace talks in Afghanistan.

On a darker note, a *Post* editorial hailed bin Laden's slaying as a model for "targeting" Libya's Muammar Qaddafi and his sons. So, while there is the possibility that the US might finally begin to wind down a near-decade-long war in Afghanistan, there is the countervailing prospect of the United States consolidating an official policy of assassination and violence as the way to impose Washington's will on the Muslim world.

If the *Post*'s neoconservative editors get their way and the US military is officially transformed into a roving assassination squad—a global "Murder, Inc."—it may turn out that future historians will view this as bin Laden's final victory.

Having already helped create the climate for George W. Bush's administration to overturn longstanding American principles—regarding civil liberties, aggressive war and torture—bin Laden could go to his watery grave with the satisfaction of officially branding the United States as a nation of assassins.

If assassination becomes the preferred calling card of US foreign policy, it is also a safe bet that the lines at Al Qaeda recruiting stations will grow longer, rather than shrink, and that more rounds of retaliatory violence will follow.

However, if Rajiv Chandrasekaran's speculation in the *Post*'s news article is closer to the mark—that bin Laden's death may clear the way for negotiations with the Taliban and a peace settlement in Afghanistan—then something truly positive might be salvaged from this grisly episode. Not only might the 100,000 US troops in Afghanistan start coming home in significant numbers in July, but the US might finally begin to repair its badly stained reputation as a "beacon" of liberty and the rule of law.

Targeted Killings

The circumstances surrounding the targeted killing of bin Laden remind us how far the US has strayed from its principles.

Though clearly bin Laden represented an extreme case—as the leader of an international terrorist organization that has slaughtered thousands of innocent people—his killing was not unique. Over the past decade, US Special Forces and sniper teams have been authorized to kill significant numbers of suspected militants on sight.

For instance, in 2007, a case surfaced regarding two US Special Forces soldiers who took part in the execution of an Afghan man who was a suspected leader of an insurgent group. Special Forces Capt. Dave Staffel and Sgt. Troy Anderson were leading a team of Afghan soldiers when an informant told them where the suspected insurgent leader was hiding. The US-led contingent found a man believed to be Nawab Buntangyar walking outside his compound near the village of Hasan Kheyl.

While the Americans kept their distance out of fear the suspect might be wearing a suicide vest, the man was questioned about his name and the Americans checked his description against a list from the Combined Joint Special Operations Task Force Afghanistan, known as "the kill-or-capture list."

Concluding that the man was Nawab Buntangyar, Staffel gave the order to shoot, and Anderson—from a distance of about 100 yards away—fired a bullet through the man's head, killing him instantly.

The soldiers viewed the killing as "a textbook example of a classified mission completed in accordance with the American rules of engagement," the *New York Times* reported. "The men said such rules allowed them to kill Buntangyar, whom the American military had designated a terrorist cell leader, once they positively identified him."

Staffel's civilian lawyer Mark Waple said the Army's Criminal Investigation Command concluded that the shooting was "justifiable homicide," but a two-star general in Afghanistan instigated a murder charge against the two men. That case, however, foundered over accusations that the charge was improperly filed.

According to evidence in a court martial at Fort Bragg, the earlier Army investigation cleared the two soldiers because they had been operating under rules of engagement that empowered them to kill individuals who have been designated "enemy combatants," even if the targets were unarmed and presented no visible threat.

In September 2007, a US military judge dismissed all charges against the two soldiers, ruling it was conceivable that the detained Afghan was wearing a suicide explosive belt, though there was no evidence that he was. In other words, the killing of Osama bin Laden was within well-established "rules of engagement" started under President Bush and continued by President Barack Obama.

Obama's proud announcement that "a small team of Americans" had killed bin Laden reflected not an anomalous action but a pattern of behavior, made distinctive only by the prominence of the target. "At my direction,"

Obama said, "a small team of Americans carried out the operation with extraordinary courage and capability.… After a firefight, they killed Osama bin Laden and took custody of his body."

Revised Accounts

On Monday, John Brennan, Obama's special assistant on terrorism, claimed that bin Laden either had a gun or was reaching for a gun when he was shot, but the White House on Tuesday amended that statement to say that bin Laden was unarmed when killed.

Further US revisions of the official story followed on Wednesday, as US officials acknowledged that the "firefight" in Abbottabad was extremely one-sided. They told the *New York Times* that only one of bin Laden's "couriers," Abu Ahmed al-Kuwaiti, fired at the US team from a nearby guesthouse before he and a woman with him were slain.

After the US troops entered the main building housing bin Laden, they assumed people they encountered might be armed, the US officials said.

According to this account, a second "courier" was killed inside the house as he was believed to be preparing to fire. One of bin Laden's sons who reportedly lunged toward the attackers was killed, too.

Upon reaching the third-floor room where bin Laden was, the US team spotted him within reach of an AK-47 and a Makarov pistol, the US officials said. The commandos then shot and killed him and wounded a woman, apparently one of his wives.

It is, of course, difficult to second-guess the split-second decisions of commandos on a dangerous nighttime mission as to whether there was a reasonable prospect of taking bin Laden alive or whether he did constitute a lethal threat. But their rules of engagement clearly were to shoot first and ask questions later.

As CIA Director Leon Panetta explained in TV interviews, the commandos were authorized to kill bin Laden on sight, although they were prepared to accept his surrender if there was no sign of resistance. Put differently, the orders were to "kill or capture" rather than "capture or kill." And the "kill" option appeared to be the favored choice.

Obama himself suggested that priority in his Sunday address, disclosing that at the start of his presidency, he ordered Panetta "to make the killing or capture of bin Laden the top priority of our war against Al Qaeda, even as we continued our broader efforts to disrupt, dismantle, and defeat his network." Obama, a former professor of constitutional law, has come a long way in accepting the frame of reference created by his predecessor who smirked at the niceties of international law and whose White House counsel Alberto Gonzales mocked the Geneva Conventions as "quaint" and "obsolete."

Dangers Ahead

As details of the bin Laden raid—and then the corrected details—spill out over the next several days, it is hard to predict the reaction in the Muslim world, and particularly in nuclear-armed Pakistan, where the targeted killing took place. Extremists of all stripes may be given extra incentive to upend governments that acquiesce to American violations of their sovereignty. There are also heightened dangers of anti-US terrorist attacks.

In Pakistan, where US drone strikes against Taliban and Al Qaeda militants, have been a major bone of contention, the bin Laden assault has already increased the turbulence in US-Pakistani relations.

According to both governments, Obama chose not to inform President Asif Ali Zardari until the nighttime raid was finished, apparently fearing that Pakistani authorities might tip off the bin Laden compound. Only after the fact did Obama reach Zardari by telephone to let him know what had just gone down.

The Pakistani government responded with a stern official statement of the obvious, that the "unilateral" attack had violated Pakistan's "sovereignty." But there was embarrassment, too, that the world's most hunted terrorist had been found living in a million-dollar compound just down the road from Pakistan's top military academia and a military base.

That fact set—and the history of Pakistan's chief intelligence agency, the ISI, playing double games regarding Islamic extremism—were factors in Obama's decision to go it alone, Panetta suggested in an interview with *Time* magazine. "It was decided that any effort to work with the Pakistanis could jeopardize the mission," the CIA director said. "They might alert the targets."

Still, the impression of the US running roughshod over the Pakistani government will make it more difficult for senior Pakistani military and government officials to cooperate—or even pretend to cooperate—with the US war across the border in Afghanistan. Zardari is already in a peck of trouble. His very position as president is in jeopardy.

That means Zardari will be under still more pressure to demonstrate his independence of Washington at a time when Pakistanis perceive they have been subjected to a string of indignities, even preceding the high-profile controversy over the bin Laden raid.

Whether or not the Pakistani military decides to allow President Zardari to remain in office, many Pakistanis are likely to react strongly against the US at a time when bilateral relations are already at their nadir. Since Sunday, many US officials have harshly criticized Pakistan for harboring bin Laden, with some suggesting major cuts in aid, which has totaled about $20 billion over the past decade.

For its part, Pakistan can retaliate by blocking the resupply of US and NATO forces along roads to the Khyber Pass and into Afghanistan. This extremely long logistics line may well prove the Achilles heel of the entire US war effort. No one knows this better than the Pakistanis who have already shown themselves ready to use the leverage afforded by NATO's dependence on the difficult supply line.

Ignoring Other Options

In favoring killing over capture, it also appears that the US passed up the prospects of questioning bin Laden about Al Qaeda in favor of killing him, all the better to avoid the messy legal complications of how to proceed against him. Yet, there are commonly accepted legal ways to capture and bring such people to a court of law—yes, even violent "bad guys" like Osama bin Laden. It is difficult—especially given the complexities with Pakistani authorities and the risks involved in grabbing a dangerous target—but it can be done.

That bin Laden might have had extremely valuable information to impart to interrogators is a no-brainer. But some of that information also might have been embarrassing to important elements of the US government, especially considering his longstanding relationship with the CIA going back to the 1980s and the anti-Soviet war in Afghanistan.

Much as some prominent US officials breathed a sigh of relief when Iraq's deposed dictator Saddam Hussein was hanged in 2006—avoiding a thorough investigation that might have exposed unwelcome secrets dating back to the 1980s—some operatives from the same period probably are glad that bin Laden's secrets are now buried at sea.

Yet, despite the future risks for the US and the Muslim world—and the fact that the US assault was a fairly clear violation of international law—the killing of bin Laden paradoxically does offer a possible route back from the institutionalization of American lawlessness.

Since bin Laden and his actions on 9/11 created the shock that allowed the Bush administration to lead the US into the "dark side" of "enhanced interrogations," "preemptive wars" and a wholesale assault on civil liberties, it could follow that the death of bin Laden will permit a retracing of those steps. The first step in that journey would be a serious attempt to negotiate a political settlement in Afghanistan and the withdrawal of American and NATO troops. If enough public pressure is brought to bear, there could even be a full-scale reassessment of US priorities focusing on what economists call "opportunity costs."

Only with strong grassroots pressure, including nonviolent civil disobedience when appropriate, will there be any real hope that the demon of "terrorism" periodically resurrected by the politicians can be exorcised. That, in turn, could bring an early end to the squandering of $2 billion a week into the stalemate in Afghanistan; the allocation of those resources to job creation and educational opportunity for tens of millions of Americans; and stanching the alarming erosion of the liberties the Constitution was carefully crafted to guarantee and the President solemnly sworn to enforce.

Ray McGovern was an Army officer and CIA analyst for almost thirty years. He now serves on the Steering Group of Veteran Intelligence Professionals for Sanity. He is a contributor to Imperial Crusades: Iraq, Afghanistan and Yugoslavia, *edited by Alexander Cockburn and Jeffrey St. Clair (Verso).*

Much Ado About Nothing: Obama's Big Immigration Speech

By ALVARO HUERTA

President Obama's recent immigrant speech in El Paso, Texas, amounted to "much ado about nothing" for Latinos.

Instead of sympathetic words for immigrants in a re-election campaign-style format, we need for Obama to make immigration reform a top priority in lieu of pandering to a growing Latino electorate.

Presidents, throughout US history, employ catchy phrases to identify their administration's policy priorities. We have, for example, President Lyndon B. Johnson's "War on Poverty," President Ronald Reagan's "War on Drugs" and, how can we forget, President George W. Bush's "War on Terror."

In this tradition, we need for President Obama to wage the "War on Xenophobia" campaign as a key part of his presidency.

Just like his predecessors, Obama's "War on Xenophobia" campaign or humane immigration reform should include concrete plans of action, lobbying efforts with Congress, executive orders, legislative bills, allocated funding, Blue Ribbon Commissions and the necessary political capital investment to ensure victory.

Obama should push for a humane immigration reform policy to counter the Republican's state-by-state xenophobia strategy. In doing so, Obama needs to be consistent.

While hectoring Republicans on the plight of undocumented immigrants and asking the GOP to acknowledge those who come to this country to "earn a living and provide for their families," Obama has outpaced Bush in terms of actual deportations. This not only includes immigrants with major and minor criminal records, including those wrongfully convicted, but also honest, hard working individuals who obey the laws, purchase goods and contribute more to the economy than they receive in return.

Where's the humanity that Obama talks about when a US-born child comes home only to learn that her Mexican immigrant mother was deported? Where's the justice that Obama talks about when 11 million undocumented workers toil in low-paying jobs that most Americans reject and benefit from in the form of cheap goods and services?

While Latinos represent more than 50 million individuals of the total US population, neither Obama nor the next Republican presidential candidate can afford to take this ethnic group for granted, especially since Latinos generally favor a humane immigration policy over the existing unjust and broken system. Take, for example, the DREAM Act—a bill aimed at helping qualified undocumented students and those who serve in the military with a pathway towards citizenship. While Obama supports this bill, he hasn't done enough to get the needed Republican votes.

If Obama truly supports Latinos in general and immigrants in particular, why didn't he invest the necessary political capital late last year in Congress before the Republicans killed the DREAM Act? Why didn't Obama play hardball with the Republicans, demanding the GOP's support for the bill, when they wanted to extend the Bush taxes for the rich?

Given that the Republicans prioritized the tax cuts for the rich over any other policy issue, including high unemployment rates and rising housing foreclosures, Obama had the perfect opportunity to get this bill passed. Instead, it died in Congress, like the dreams of countless immigrant students and those serving in the military.

If Obama isn't willing to risk his political capital, especially now with favorable poll numbers after the killing of Osama bin Laden, what makes the more than 50 million Latinos in this country think that Obama will pass a humane immigration reform bill anytime soon?

Alvaro Huerta is a Ph.D. Candidate in the Dept. of City & Regional Planning (UC Berkeley) and a Visiting Scholar at the Chicano Studies Research Center (UCLA).

The Obama Administration and Iran

By SASAN FAYAZMANESH

Since the 1979 Revolution in Iran and the end of a symbiotic relationship between the US and the Shah, successive American administrations have tried to contain Iran by various means, particularly sanctions and military threats. This includes the Obama Administration. Even though President Barack Obama came to office promising engaging Iran, in reality his administration has followed the policy of "tough diplomacy," which has included, among other hostile acts, imposing "crippling sanctions" against Iran. Indeed, a close look at the Obama Administration's policy toward Iran reveals a continuity between its policy and what was pursued by the administration of George W. Bush. Before looking at the policy of "tough diplomacy," however, a brief history of the containment of Iran is in order.

Containing Iran originally began during the Carter Administration with the so-called hostage crisis and the freezing of Iranian assets in 1979. But soon after it morphed into the policy of dual containment of Iran and Iraq, as the Carter Administration gave Saddam Hussein the green light to invade Iran. It was hoped that the war between Iran and Iraq would lead to the resolution of the hostage crisis and the overthrow of the Iranian government. But the US also hoped that down the line there would be a regime change in Iraq. This was evident in the fact that while the US was helping the Iraqi government, the Israelis were selling arms to Iran with the full knowledge of the US. Indeed, the Carter Administration itself was considering the possibility of providing Iran with military spare parts.

The dual containment policy became more overt and intense under the Reagan Administration. While the US blatantly supported Saddam Hussein in the war and even went as far as engaging Iran at the behest of Hussein, at the same time it took measures to assure that Hussein was not victorious either. Giving false information to both sides and selling arms to Iran, mostly with the help of the Israelis in the "Iran-Contra scandal," were examples of this double role that the Reagan Administration played in the Iran-Iraq war. After the war, the US and Israel concentrated primarily on containing Iraq.

Following the US invasion of Iraq in 1990–91, and the temporary containment of Saddam Hussein, once again, Iran became the main target of containment by means of sanctions. During the Clinton Administration the Israeli lobby groups, especially the American Israel Public Affairs Committee (AIPAC) and its affiliate the Washington Institute for Near East Policy (WINEP), became the main architects of US foreign policy toward Iran and underwriters of sanctions. Actually, it was in this period that Martin Indyk, the former head of WINEP and subsequently the national security advisor to President Clinton, claimed to have devised the policy of dual containment of Iran and Iraq. Indyk, along with other theoreticians of the Israeli lobby groups, formulated three sins of Iran as the main reasons for containing it: Iran's support for international terrorism, opposition to the Israeli-Palestinian peace process, and pursuit of weapons of mass destruction.

The containment of Iran, as well as Iraq, became more intensified with the election of George W. Bush and the takeover of the Middle East policy making process by the neoconservatives. Individuals affiliated with the Israeli lobby groups, such as Paul Wolfowitz, Richard Perle (both on the Board of Advisors of WINEP) and David Wurmser, became instrumental in turning the policy of dual containment into the policy of "dual rollback." Iraq was targeted for invasion in the hope of splitting its Shia from Iran. Thereafter, it was hoped, it would become easier to contain Iran by means of more severe unilateral and multilateral sanctions and, if necessary, military actions by the US, Israel or both. Israeli leaders, however, were more interested in targeting Iran rather than Iraq. But they ultimately settled for the neoconservative policy, hoping that after Iraq they could push Iran to the top of the US's "to do list," to use Ariel Sharon's words (*The Times*, November 5, 2002). Similar to the case of Iraq, the US and Israel used the allegation that Iran is developing weapons of mass destruction as the main reason to impose more severe sanctions and to prepare the ground for an eventual military operation.

The opportunity arose when in 2002 the Mujahedin-e-Khalq-e-Iran, an Iranian exile group working closely with the US and Israel, claimed that Iran is constructing an illegal uranium enrichment facility and a heavy water production plant. Following these claims, a case was made for reporting Iran to the UN Security Council and imposing sanctions. In July of 2006 the Security Council Resolution 1696 was passed, demanding that Iran suspend all enrichment-related and reprocessing activities. Iran did not halt its enrichment and the Security Council Resolution 1737, the first UN sanctions resolution against Iran, was enacted in December of 2006. This was the crown jewel of the US-Israeli policy of containment of Iran, the result of years of effort to pass multilateral sanctions against Iran. Subsequently, the Bush Administration managed to pass two additional sets of sanctions against Iran in the Security Council, Resolutions 1747 in March of 2007, and 1803 in March of 2008. Toward the end of the second term of the Bush Administration, there was a push for a fourth set of UN sanctions against Iran. Israel was also pushing the US to wage an attack on Iran's nuclear facilities. Yet, the Bush Administration was running out of time as the 2008 presidential election was approaching. Containment of Iran was left to the next administration.

Given the history of containment policy, it was not difficult to predict prior to the 2008 presidential election that regardless of the outcome, the US foreign policy toward Iran will be determined largely by Israel and its various lobby groups in the US, especially AIPAC and WINEP. Indeed, it was easy to foresee that if Obama became president, Dennis Ross, Obama's closest advisor on Iran and the former director of WINEP, will play a leading role in determining the policy. Based on Ross's writings and WINEP's publications, one could expect that Obama would pursue a "tough" or "aggressive diplomacy" with Iran. The diplomacy, as Ross and WINEP had formulated, was intended to give an ultimatum to Iran in some face to face meetings, telling Iran to either accept the US-Israeli demands or face aggression, including, ultimately, a naval blockade and military actions. The meetings were also intended to create the illusion of engaging Iran and, in so doing, gaining international support for aggressive actions.

Once Obama came to office Dennis Ross became special advisor to the Secretary of State for the "Gulf and Southwest Asia," then special assistant to President Obama and his senior director for the "Central Region." Thus, once more, an individual associated with WINEP became the main architect of Iran policy and in that capacity continued, with some modifications, the same policy that had been pursued by the Bush Administration.

It should, of course, be noted that beside Ross there have been other Iran policy makers in the Obama Administration close to Israel and its lobby groups. One such person, who left office in 2011, is Stuart A. Levey, the former Under Secretary for Terrorism and Financial Intelligence. Levey, a left-over from the Bush Administration, managed to carry on a crusade against Iran by formulating and implementing financial sanctions against Iran. Nevertheless, for the most part the Obama Administration policy toward Iran has proceeded along Ross's policy of "tough" or "aggressive diplomacy." How the policy has been implemented so far is briefly discussed below.

As mentioned earlier, one of the main aims of the policy of "tough diplomacy" was to create the impression that the US is trying its best to engage Iran. This was tried soon after President Obama took office. For example, Obama's message of March 21, 2009, on the occasion of the Persian New Year, was intended to create such an impression. To the uninitiated the message appeared to be conciliatory. But to those familiar with the history of the US-Iran relations, the message contained nothing that was essentially new and, indeed, accused Iran of some of the same charges that the Israeli lobby had concocted since the 1990s. Actually, a few days later Obama showed how little the US policy had changed when in his trip to Prague he spoke about a "real threat" posed by Iran to its "neighbors and our allies" and advocated the same missile defense system proposed by the Bush Administration.

By summer of 2009, while numerous unilateral sanctions were being renewed, passed or contemplated, the Obama Administration was working hard to pass the fourth multilateral, United Nations Security Council sanctions resolution against Iran. In order to get the Russian vote in the Security Council, in July of 2009 Obama offered the Russians a quid pro quo: in exchange for a deal on the expiring 1991 Strategic Arms Reduction Treaty and postponing the US deployment of an anti-missile system in Europe, Russia would agree to impose harsher sanctions against Iran. Later, the Obama Administration sweetened the deal by promising to drop the deployment of an anti-missile system in Europe altogether.

On October 1, 2009, Iran held a meeting with five permanent members of the Security Council and Germany, commonly referred to as P5+1. This, and three other meetings—one on October 19, 2009, and two others in December of 2010 and January of 2011—were the only formal "engagements" that Iran had with the Obama Administration. The first two meetings centered mainly on the swap of Iran's low enriched uranium for higher enriched uranium intended to be used by a reactor in Tehran that produces isotopes for medical purposes. The swap deal was viewed by many, both inside and outside of Iran, as a ploy by the US to get enriched uranium out of Iran and then give Iran an ultimatum to stop any further enrichment or face the fourth round of UN sanctions. Even some US officials described the deal as a clever ploy.

Under massive pressure at home, President Ahmadinejad's government, who had originally agreed to the swap, tried to modify the deal. Yet, the Obama Administration rejected any modification and began the final push for the fourth round of UN sanctions. By this time many US officials, including Secretary Clinton, were admitting openly that the Obama Administration's policy had been, throughout, not just an "engagement policy" but a "two-track policy" and that it was now time for the "pressure track." This was, indeed, similar to the "carrot and stick policy" of the Bush Administration, which was always no more than offering Iran a stick.

What stood between Iran and a new Security Council resolution, however, was China, which was opposed to additional UN sanctions. The Obama Administration therefore twisted China's arm, cajoled them and even threatened them financially, to go along with the new set of sanctions. By mid March 2010 China's resistance to slow down the US-Israeli push had weakened, and toward the end of March China joined the P4+1 to discuss the US proposal for the fourth round of UN sanctions. Now, the only stumbling block in getting a near unanimous vote in the Security Council was the presence of three non-permanent members on the Security Council, Turkey, Brazil and Lebanon, who opposed the sanctions despite massive pressure by the US to make them go along.

On May 17, 2010, Brazil and Turkey struck a deal with Iran for swapping enriched uranium, almost the same deal that had been offered by the P5+1 to Iran in October of 2009. The only difference between this so-called tripartite agreement and the US proposed swap deal was that Iran would send the low enriched uranium to Turkey rather than Russia, as it had been initially proposed. The Obama Administration rejected the tripartite agreement, making it clear that the original swap deal proposed was a ploy and that the ultimate intention of the US had been, all along, to use the deal to impose, in the language of Benjamin Netanyahu and Hillary Clinton, "crippling sanctions" against Iran.

On June 9, 2010, Resolution 1929, the fourth UN sanctions resolution against Iran was passed by the Security Council, with Brazil and Turkey voting "no" and Lebanon abstaining. This was, of course, the same resolution that the Bush Administration was unable to pass due to time running out. The passage of the resolution officially ended the "tough diplomacy" phase of the Obama Administration's Iran policy. After this multilateral sanction the US and EU intensified their unilateral sanctions, despite Russia's protest that the measures were exceeding the parameters agreed upon and reflected in the UN Security Council resolution.

With the Obama Administration giving the green light, the US Congress passed, on June 24, 2010, one of the most severe unilateral sanctions acts against Iran, the Comprehensive Iran Sanctions, Accountability, and Divestment Act (CISAD). The act had been in the pipeline for some time, but had been held back until the passage of the UN Resolution 1929. CISAD, which was signed by President Obama on July 1, 2010, strengthened the harshest sanctions act passed during the Clinton era, the Iran-Libya Sanctions Act.

After CISAD much of the new sanctions against Iran were enacted by the State and Treasury Departments, particularly under the leadership of Stuart Levey and his successor, David Cohen. In addition, there were once again repeated talk of possible military attacks on Iran by Israel, the US or both. This was not the usual talk by the Israelis, neoconservatives or media pundits, but threats made by some high officials in the Obama Administration, such as the Chairman of the Joint Chiefs of Staff Mike Mullen who stated on NBC's *Meet The Press* on August 1, 2010, that "military actions have been on the table and remain on the table." The push for attacking Iran intensified in late October and early November of 2010 as more Israeli and American officials and media pundits appealed to President Obama.

The combination of continuous threats and increasing sanctions affected the Iranian economy. In fall of 2010 the value of Iran's currency wildly fluctuated. The fluctuation was clearly a manifestation of uncertainty, speculation and fear that were caused by the cumulative effect of sanctions. The sanctions were also exacerbating the rate of inflation in Iran and reducing the rate of growth of the economy. For example, while the rate of growth in Iran's real GDP in 2007 was 7.8 percent, the rate for 2010, according to the April 2011 report of the International Monetary Fund, was only 1.0 percent. The same report forecasted the rate of growth in Iran's real GDP for 2011 to be 0 percent.

The Obama Administration appeared to be fully aware of the toll that the sanctions were taking on the Iranian economy and adopted a wait-and-see attitude, despite the pressure exerted on it to engage in military adventures against Iran. It also appears that the current administration found various forms of sabotage, such as the introduction of the Stuxnet computer worm in the Iranian nuclear facilities, assassinations of Iranian nuclear scientists and agitation by separatist movements in Iran, quite useful in containing Iran. The issue of human rights violations in Iran also became a convenient tool in the hands of the Obama Administration to mount verbal attacks against Iran.

By the end of 2010 the US policy toward Iran was back on the same track that it had been for over thirty years, a blatant containment policy. In other words, the policy of "tough diplomacy" had no more "diplomacy" left in it; it was simply a tough policy. The last two meetings between Iran and P5+1, on December 6, 2010, and January 21, 2011, were therefore devoid of any substance and merely provided a forum for the two sides to express their grievances.

With the advent of the so-called Arab Spring and the preoccupation of the US, Europe and Israel with the revolutionary upheavals in the Middle East, there was less news in the popular US media about Iran and the need to contain it. Indeed, to the extent that the Arab Spring challenged some aspects of the old order in the Middle East and created uncertainty about the future of this order, the pressure on Iran slightly subsided. Yet, as this essay is being concluded in summer of 2011, the containment policy continues and more and more sanctions are being devised, particularly by the US Department of Treasury. The push by Israel, its lobby groups and supporters in the US Congress, to intensify sanctions and threaten Iran militarily also continues. In addition, there is increasing pressure on Iran by the International Atomic Energy Agency (IAEA) to accept the US demands. Under IAEA's new director, Yukiya Amano—who was the preferred candidate of the West to replace Mohamed ElBaradei as the General Director of IAEA in 2010— Iran has faced harsh and confrontational reports about its nuclear activities.

In sum, the Obama Administration's policy of "tough diplomacy" has so far mostly followed the script written by individuals associated with Israel and its lobby groups. The policy is similar to those pursued by the neoconservatives under the previous administration. But while the "carrot and stick policy" of the Bush Administration was implemented in a brutish and dim-witted way, the Obama Administration's "two-track policy" has been carried out in a more refined and sophisticated way. Whether this policy will succeed to contain Iran, particularly by means of military confrontations at some point, remains to be seen. Much depends on such unforeseeable factors as the outcome of the Arab Spring, internal political dynamics in Iran and Iran's ability to develop its economy and military forces despite the crippling sanctions imposed upon it.

Sasan Fayazmanesh is Professor Emeritus of Economics at California State University, Fresno.

Obama's Nuclear Weapon Surge

By DARWIN BOND-GRAHAM

As with many aspects of the Obama presidency, expectations for drastic changes in nuclear weapons policy were high among liberals and the left. Many wanted to believe that a program, however modest, of scaling back the military-industrial complex was commencing. Obama stoked these impressions on the campaign trail and in the earliest days of his presidency, with rhetoric such as "a world without nuclear weapons is profoundly in America's interest and the world's interest. It is our responsibility to make the commitment, and to do the hard work to make this vision a reality."

Obama's first term will go down in history, however, as containing one of the single largest spending increases on nuclear weapons ever. His administration has worked vigorously to commit the nation to a multi-hundred-billion-dollar reinvestment in nuclear weapons, mapped out over the next three-plus decades.

At the center of Obama's ambitious nuclear agenda is the expansion of the US nuclear weapons complex via a multibillion-dollar construction program. Also, at the center of Obama's nuclear agenda is a commitment of tens of billions of dollars to designing and building the next generation of nuclear submarines, ballistic missiles, and heavy bombers. Stockpiled nuclear warheads will receive billions more in refurbishment and new components. All of this is now underway. Completion dates for various pieces of this puzzle span the next half-century. Finally, Obama's nuclear policies have been designed to leave the door open to new weapons at some future date.

Only one aspect of Obama's presidency deviates significantly from his predecessor's. Rather than projecting an unambiguously belligerent US foreign policy resting openly upon the nuclear arsenal, Obama has promoted an agenda that my colleagues and I have defined elsewhere as anti-nuclear imperialism.

And again, as with many aspects of the Obama presidency, liberals and even many anti-nuclear activists have failed to see the president's policy agenda for what it is. Instead of focusing on the reality of the Obama nuclear weapons surge, and instead of acknowledging the true pro-nuclear weapons goals of the administration, as they have been outlined in budget and planning documents (which exist in stark contrast against Obama's vacuous public pronunciations), many continue to dwell on his idealistic rhetoric.

Ironically, the only thing that seems capable of slowing the Obama administration's enormous investments in nuclear weapons is the budget crisis, and the desire of some Republicans in the House of Representatives to cut nuke spending. But even here, the administration and Republicans in the Senate have managed, through several rounds of negotiations, to politically insulate nuclear weapons spending from much of the austerity now stripping social spending and even some military programs.

Bringing Hope to the Nuclear Weapons Complex—A Brief Historical Reprise

To understand just how profoundly important the Obama administration has been in advancing the legitimacy of and funding commitments for nuclear weapons, a short and recent history of US nuclear policy is in order.

With the end of the Cold War in 1991, the institutions responsible for designing and building nuclear arms—a complex of labs, factories, test sites and dumping grounds, known as the "nuclear weapons complex," located in New Mexico, Tennessee, California, Nevada, Missouri, and South Carolina—underwent a succession of compounding crises. It began with the sudden loss of the "Evil Empire" that till then gave nuclear weapons, and those who built them, a sense of necessity, legitimacy, even valor.

The first President Bush actually oversaw a large disarmament program and defunding of nuclear weapons. Nukes truly receded in importance in US foreign policy. An important measure of this was the declining budget for nuclear weapons in the early 1990s.

The nuclear weapons complex, however, organized and lobbied for its interests to promote new missions for nuclear weapons. A slew of books and white papers poured out about the importance of nukes in a post-Cold War world, to guard against tyrants like Saddam Hussein, or to hedge against the emergence of new superpowers, or even to protect civilization against shadowy "terrorists." None of this ideological work stuck. The trend was toward disarmament by default, for no new all-encompassing justification for a multibillion-dollar nuclear weapons program was being articulated. Butter was beating guns in the budget debates. The two nuclear weapons labs, Los Alamos and Livermore, eyed each other with more than just the traditional competitive contempt; now they feared one of them would be closed, and they jockeyed for the position of the "best" nuke lab. It was a moment of weakness for the nuclear complex that could have been turned into an opportunity for anti-war and pro-democracy forces.

It was during the Clinton administration that the nuclear weapons complex staged a comeback by creating the Stockpile Stewardship and Management Program (SSM). The latter, which was dreamed up as a means of pumping billions of dollars into the weapons complex over more than a decade, constituted an actual increase in spending on nuclear weapons, even though they seemed more useless than ever. SSM came about largely because of the Clinton administration's counterproductive obsession with ratifying the Comprehensive Test Ban Treaty (CTBT). The CTBT would have barred the US and nearly all other nations from detonating nuclear weapons, thus halting the primary means by which new weapons can be designed, or the necessary step by which non-nuclear states can obtain nukes.

The nuclear weapons complex and its allies in the Pentagon, Congress and industry seized on the CTBT negotiations, using this treaty's ratification process to make obscure, pseudoscientific claims about how difficult it would be for the nation to "safely maintain" the "nuclear deterrent" without the ritual of full-blown nuke shots. An end to testing, they claimed, would require huge funding increases to build complex virtual testing facilities to use in lieu of nuclear shots under the desert. Even though Clinton approved SSM, setting in motion a decade of trough-feeding for the nuclear complex, the CTBT was never ratified by the Senate. Republicans balked. In a sort of de facto adherence to the treaty, the US hasn't vaporized the soil under the Nevada Test Site since, but as Obama, and the liberal imperialists he has installed in the State Department will claim, the unratified CTBT reduces America's moral and legal authority to challenge other nations with active nuclear-development programs.

Regardless, the clear winner of the CTBT debate was the nuclear weapons complex. It lost nothing it had not already given up under the first Bush (who, as I noted above, instituted the test moratorium). Some of the decline was temporarily staved off, the crisis of legitimacy paused, money flowed. The bomb at the heart of American empire was ticking again.

Fast-forward ten years. In the early 2000s, the nuclear weapons complex was coasting under the SSM program, burning billions each year on experiments meant to further refine nuclear weapons. The labs had even managed to sneakily design new weapons like the B61-11 bomb. However, even with large guaranteed funding streams (perhaps because of these), the weapons complex sank into scandal after scandal—rampant mismanagement and incompetence at the most senior levels; missing computers and memory chips with top secret data; a Chinese spy who turned out not to be one; a massive fire that almost burned through toxic and radioactive waste dumps; embezzled money; projects with skyrocketing prices, unknown completion dates, and dubious missions; innumerable accidents and safety lapses.

The root problem remained. The entire nuclear enterprise still lacked legitimacy and a sense of mission. Morale plummeted further. The brain centers of the weapons complex at Los Alamos and Lawrence Livermore national laboratories knew that the solution would require something that was supposedly not possible without the ability to conduct full-scale nuclear tests: a completely new weapon design starting with new manufactured plutonium pits.

The George W. Bush White House attempted to address this root problem by initiating a complete rebuild and repurposing of the nuclear weapons complex. At the center of this surge was a new nuclear weapon, at first called the Robust Nuclear Earth Penetrator, and later the Reliable Replacement Warhead (RRW). The RRW was intended to replace a large portion of the existing stockpile. To design it, and build thousands, would require flexing every muscle in the nuclear weapons complex. Therefore, Bush proposed building new labs and factories in Los Alamos, NM., Livermore, CA., Oak Ridge, TN., the Nevada Test Site, and Kansas City, MO. The centerpiece of it all would have been a "Modern Pit Facility," where the core plutonium component of the RRW would be milled.

As with many lofty but difficult to achieve ideas proposed by Bush (like the mission to Mars), the planned new surge came to naught. Just enough Democrats and some Republican members of the House obstructed the RRW, defunded the "Modern Pit Facility" and voted against huge increases in nuclear weapons spending. Anti-nuclear groups mobilized the larger anti-war movement vigorously against these proposals, creating political rewards for the Congress's nuclear skeptics. And perhaps most importantly, the Bush White House's own incompetence prevented these atomic dreams from advancing. The entire second term of Bush II was a period of modestly declining budgets for the nuclear weapons complex, and little to no advancement on any construction projects or weapons system development.

Obama has achieved what Bush could not. His reinvestments in nuclear weapons are not just a matter of dollar amounts. When put in the context of the mismanagement and declining morale of the past two decades, Obama is literally saving the nuclear weapons complex, reinvigorating it with legitimacy, and outflanking any who would dare to elevate a debate over military vs. social investments.

His pro-nuclear policies begin with his anti-nuclear rhetoric. Obama's famous Prague speech of April 2009 primed the international community to accept the image of a restrained US state, one promoting an ambitious vision of global nuclear disarmament, in splendid contrast to rogue states and shadowy atomic terrorists. Perhaps just as important, Obama's paeans to nuclear abolition were contrasted against the grandiose, more honest ambitions of his predecessor in the Oval Office. Obama's anti-nuclear rhetoric has subsequently been used to justify a harder line against Iran, North Korea, and other states that are said to have active nuclear weapons programs. Obama's anti-nuclear rhetoric has also disarmed most potential critics within the US, especially the liberal arms control and anti-nuclear organizations that have opposed—under past presidential administrations, especially the most recent—increased nuclear spending.

Obama's transition into the White House helped set the stage. His proclivity to keep Bush administration appointees in many posts overseeing the US nuclear weapons complex ensured that pro-nuclear voices would be firmly entrenched. While he appointed a new secretary of energy, he retained Bush's National Nuclear Security Administration (NNSA) Administrator Tom D'Agostino, a hawkish bureaucrat dedicated to increasing US nuclear weapons funding. Additionally, Obama retained Defense Secretary Robert Gates and many senior civilian Pentagon officials tasked with nuclear policy. Both Gates and D'Agostino were determined to restart the stalled nuclear modernization program that, to their frustration, withered through Bush's second term. Given a relatively free hand, they were able to bring in fresh blood where needed and prepare a more realistic, long-term investment in the nuclear weapons complex.

Showing much deference to this NNSA-Pentagon center of gravity, the Obama administration (mostly through Defense Secretary Gates' office) worked on an important policy statement, the Nuclear Posture Review. It was repeatedly delayed, in part because White House and State Department officials were trying to magically graft together otherwise mutually exclusive policies. They sought language to balance the anti-nuclear rhetoric, necessary for an aggressive foreign policy under the pretext of nonproliferation, and language that would simultaneously symbolize a continued, even boosted commitment to nuclear weapons. This was achieved in the document released in April of 2010, which succeeded in being many different things to many different readers.

In reading the NPR, those who would normally mount strong opposition to such an enormous program of nuclear armament (a rough sketch of which was in the NPR, with more detailed blueprints forthcoming) somehow only retained passages that warbled about Obama's desire to "seek a world free of nuclear weapons." The NPR did not offer any substantive policies that would advance this goal, nor even any that would truly de-emphasize the role of nuclear weapons in US foreign policy. The only offering along these lines included in the NPR involved the conditions under which the US would use nuclear weapons. To quote the administration, "the United States will not use or threaten to use nuclear weapons against non-nuclear weapons states that are party to the [Non-Proliferation Treaty] and in compliance with their nuclear non-proliferation obligations."

This convoluted assurance not to nuke some nations was widely reported to be a significant shift in US nuclear policy, even though it was not, and even though the NPR itself contradicted this exact statement only paragraphs later, e.g., "the United States reserves the right to make any adjustment in the assurance that may be warranted…," and, "the United States is therefore not prepared at the present time to adopt a universal policy that deterring nuclear attack is the sole purpose of nuclear weapons."

If liberals largely didn't see through these smokescreens and palliatives, the nuclear weapons complex, its powerful corporate contractors, and the military certainly could. When all the fluff about a nuke-free world was removed, the loud, clear, and road-mapped message contained in the NPR was that the administration was ready to ramp up spending on nuclear weapons programs and build the infrastructure and future weapons systems that would be comparable in scale and purpose to the nuclear wish list proposed eight years earlier by Bush.

To demonstrate the administration's sensitivity and responsiveness to the needs of the weapons complex and its corporate contractors, the NPR also acknowledged the crisis that has been brewing for over two decades: "Today's nuclear complex, however, has fallen into neglect […] Over the last decade, our human capital base has been underfunded and underdeveloped. Our national security laboratories have found it increasingly difficult to attract and retain the best and brightest scientists and engineers of today. Morale has declined with the lack of broad, national consensus."

Although the claim of being "underfunded" was absurd fantasy—due to the fact that the nuclear weapons complex was funded at levels matching Cold War highs throughout most of the Clinton and Bush II administrations—the recognition that the complex is in dire trouble due to lack of morale and defined mission was correct.

To solve these problems, and secure nukes forever, the NPR promised "recapitalization of the nuclear infrastructure through fully funding the NNSA." Finally, in coded language meant to leave the door open to new weapons designs (another RRW) in the future, something earlier in the NPR the administration claimed it would not seek, the NPR concludes, "some modest capacity will be put in place to surge production in the event of significant geopolitical 'surprise.'"

Coinciding with the release of the NPR was the signing of the New START treaty between the US and Russia, also in April of 2010. Like the NPR, New START was hailed by liberals and many anti-nuclear groups as a path-breaking disarmament treaty, an important "first step" toward Obama's vision of a nuclear weapons-free world. For Obama and his liberal imperialist cohort (which includes some senior Republicans and elder statesmen like George Shultz and Henry Kissinger), the treaty is the cornerstone of their anti-nuclear imperialist foreign policy.

It would, however, become a millstone when Obama's political advisers, and then the mainstreams of the anti-war and anti-nuclear movements, came to believe that ratification of New START would provide an important political "win" for the president, significantly boosting the Democrats in the midterm elections and helping Obama remain strong into 2012, all guided by the assumption that a Republican in the White House, or significant Republican control of the Congress, would advance a nuclear weapons surge. On a strategic basis then, the opponents of the nuclear surge proposed by Bush eight years earlier had checked out of reality. Worse than becoming insignificant, they became a pro-nuclear weapons lobbying force by pushing so hard for New START ratification.

Like the NPR, the actual legal and policy direction of New START has virtually nothing to do with restraint, or concrete disarmament steps. Instead, New START would serve as an "arms affirmation treaty."

On balance, the nominal reductions in nuclear weapons required by New START are insignificant when compared to the multibillion-dollar nuclear (and strategic non-nuclear) weapons programs committed to in the treaty's text (non-nuclear programs include "Prompt Global Strike" and "Missile Defense"). On paper, New START limits the US and Russia to a total deployed strategic arsenal of 1,550 warheads on 700 platforms each—platforms being the bombers and missiles that can launch these weapons. In a talking point that would gain universal circulation in the media, Obama lied and said this would amount to a 30 percent cut in nuclear weapons.

However, when the treaty's text was finally released and closely analyzed by independent experts, the consensus was that New START does not actually require much, if any, disarmament. Two highly respected arms-control analysts summed this up by noting that New START "doesn't actually reduce the number of warheads," and that, in fact, "the treaty does not require destruction of a single nuclear warhead and actually permits the United States and Russia to deploy almost the same number of strategic warheads that were permitted by the 2002 Moscow Treaty."

Even though New START was old wine, it set in motion the negotiations by which Obama and a cabal of Senate Republicans would haggle over the question of how much they would increase spending to achieve the goal of a revitalized nuclear weapons complex. Throughout these negotiations, one camp, led by Republican Senator Jon Kyl of Arizona, advocated a realistic set of budget projections and demanded immediate and binding commitments for funding at a level of at least $80 billion over ten years. Obama's team, led by Vice President Biden and Senator Kerry, advocated a more flexible and slightly smaller increase in nuke funding to achieve virtually the same goals.

The details of the Obama administration's nuclear investments, as they were forged through the New START debate in late 2010, are contained in two key documents released during the treaty's limbo.

First is the very detailed Stockpile Stewardship and Management Plan of 2011, the summary of which was made public in May. Obama's SSM Plan calls for spending several billion each year over the next decade and a half to provide what are called "life extensions" (LEP) for different model nuclear warheads and bombs in the arsenal. For example, the Obama administration is committed to ramping up the LEP for the B61 gravity bomb, and has spent more than $200 million in 2011 on this single program alone. By 2016, upward of $450 million will be spent, extending the "life" of this bomb design. The program is not expected to taper off and end until 2022, the result being hundreds of B61 nuclear bombs ready, after billions lavished upon them, to sit in bunkers and hangers for another few decades.

More importantly (because it's more expensive and will drive programs like the LEPs), the SSM Plan addresses the nuclear weapons complex's ambitious construction wish list that includes no less than seventeen "major infrastructure milestones." At the top of the pile are the Chemistry and Metallurgy Research Replacement Nuclear Facility (CMRR) and the Uranium Processing Facility (UPF), at Los Alamos Laboratory in New Mexico and Y-12 in Tennessee respectively. These two nuclear weapons component factories are projected to cost $5.8 billion and $6.5 billion. The CMRR, it should be pointed out, will fulfill virtually the same function as the Modern Pit Facility proposed by Bush.

In all, the SSM Plan is punctuated throughout with descriptions of "ramping up" (used six times), "increasing" (used fourteen times), and "committing" (used seventeen times) money for nuclear weapons programs. The administration's commitment to new nuclear weapons production facilities is described as a "capabilities-based" program, meaning essentially that the point is to build bomb factories capable of rolling out small and large orders, of old and possibly new designs—everything but the kitchen sink.

The second key Obama administration nuclear plan, of more importance to the deal forged during New START ratification, is the Section 1251 Report, named after the section of law in the 2010 Defense Authorization Act that required it be written. Like the SSM Plan, the Section 1251 Report is packed with commitments to increase spending on nuclear weapons through "life extension programs," new and refurbished bomb factories, and also new weapons systems like subs, ICBMs, and bombers. At twelve pages in length, the Section 1251 Report's update, completed in November of 2010, is the most succinct and honest summary of the Obama administration's nuclear policy goals. To quote straight from the horse's mouth:

> From FY 2005 to FY 2010 [Bush's second term], a downward trend in the budget for Weapons Activities at the National Nuclear Security Administration resulted in a loss of purchasing power of approximately 20 percent. As part of the 2010 Nuclear Posture Review, the administration made a commitment to modernize America's nuclear arsenal and the complex that sustains it.... To begin this effort, the president requested a nearly 10 percent increase for Weapons Activities in the FY 2011 budget.... Altogether, the president plans to request $41.6 billion for FY 2012–2016.

Add to this another $30 billion promised for development of a new nuclear-armed sub, $26 million per year for Air Force studies to decide when, and at what price, to refurbish or build new ICBMs, and another $1.7 billion, between 2011 and 2015, to contemplate a new long-range nuclear-armed bomber (which will be comparable in cost to the subs), and you will begin to get a sense of how committed the Obama administration is to nuclear armament.

Locked In?

The most remarkable thing about the Obama administration's nuclear surge is how it is uniquely insulated from the austerity program now gutting most other discretionary federal accounts.

Obama's team has made numerous pledges to fund the increasingly expensive capital program for the nuclear weapons complex, a program that, as of this writing, still has no final cost estimate. As the largest projects like the CMRR and UPF grow, the entire program will swell by many billions of dollars. Once the Pentagon begins in earnest its replacement of the existing fleet of nuclear-armed subs and other weapons systems, costs will multiply and inflate.

The commitment to fund all of this was made repeatedly during the New START ratification debate in such a publicly conspicuous way that any reduction in funds or program limitations would create an uproar that could significantly harm the Obama administration. Republicans sought more than just Obama's word. They sought a binding commitment. For example, the Senate briefly considered measures such as forward funding.

In its ratification resolution for New START, the Senate noted that its approval of the treaty was dependent on the progress of the Obama nuclear surge: "If appropriations are enacted that fail to meet the resource requirements set forth in the president's 10-year plan," the Senate warned, "or, if at any time more resources are required than estimated in the president's 10-year plan, the president shall submit to Congress, within 60 days of such enactment or the identification of the requirement for such additional resources, as appropriate, a report detailing … how the president proposes to remedy the resource shortfall," and furthermore requiring proposals for increased funds. The resolution stated unequivocally that "the United States is committed to accomplishing the modernization and replacement of its strategic nuclear delivery vehicles."

Ultimately, the nuclear surge that is well underway has no legally binding, ironclad commitment. It has the commitment of the Obama administration and the US Senate, a pact composed during the entire process surrounding New START. Key Democratic senators and representatives, in whose districts the nuclear weapons complex facilities are located, are strongly backing the plan and pulling a majority of Democrats along with them. The Tea Party Republicans in the House are a wild card, however. The fiscal situation of the US could derail the nuclear surge if revenues fall beneath some unknown threshold, making further cuts to social programs a cause of political instability, therefore requiring a slowdown or jettisoning of the surge, in parts or entirely.

Missing from this calculus today, and absent through Obama's first term, largely because of the Democratic president's own efforts to neutralize them, are the rank and file of the Democratic Party, and the same anti-nuclear and anti-war groups that so effectively exposed Bush's plans and derailed the nuclear surge back then. The result is a Left seemingly incapable of turning the dire fiscal situation and austerity assault into an opportunity to force a debate over nukes and war vs. jobs and social programs.

Darwin Bond-Graham is a sociologist who splits his time between New Orleans, Albuquerque, and Navarro, CA.

Friends Without Benefits: Obama and Organized Labor

By DAVID MACARAY

The President of the United States isn't King; he doesn't wield absolute power. Still, despite the obvious limitations of the job, he does have access to one unique and tantalizing resource. He—and he alone—has the bully pulpit. The media can second-guess him, the public can criticize, Wall Street can threaten, the military brass can smirk, and the Congress can play its little games, but no one has the power to shut him up.

Not only can no one shut him up, but when the President of the United States goes on national television, everybody tends to listen. Arguably, a prime-time presidential address, particularly one presented eloquently and compellingly (and repeated often), has the power to alter the national consciousness.

Which, given labor's long friendship with the Democratic Party and Obama's acknowledged brilliance as a speaker, is why his first term in office has been so disappointing. The tame and reluctant *President* Obama (as opposed to the bold, wildly idealistic *Candidate* Obama) has never used the bully pulpit to lobby for what is, undeniably, the country's heart and soul, not to mention its largest voting bloc: working people.

The man who said, "Politics didn't lead me to working folks; working folks led me to politics," has never gone on TV and declared his support for labor, and has never suggested publicly that the reason the economy is struggling is because, with barely 12 percent of the workforce earning a union wage, there aren't enough consumers out there who can afford to buy goods and services. As far as organized labor is concerned, Obama has been a washout.

Take Employee Free Choice Act (EFCA), for instance. This legislation would have given workers the right to join a union without having to navigate the treacherous waters of management hate campaigns or long, drawn-out NLRB elections. With EFCA they could join simply by signing cards ("card check"). If a majority said they wished to belong to a union, presto!—they were union members—which is more or less how they do it in Europe and Canada. Only in America is joining a union nearly as complicated as becoming a citizen.

In addition to the simple majority vote there were two other important provisions included in EFCA. One increased the penalties for management personnel found guilty of discriminating against employees engaged in union activism, and the other stipulated that if agreement on a contract couldn't be reached within 120 days, binding arbitration would set the terms.

What most people don't realize is that even after a successful union certification drive, things don't automatically proceed smoothly. Even after a union wins the right to represent the workers, many companies refuse to take "yes" for an answer. Seeking to sabotage the collective bargaining process, management does everything it can to avoid reaching agreement on a contract.

Some inaugural bargains have been known to limp along for as long as a year or more, with no resolution. It's management's hope that these stalling tactics will spook or frustrate the members to the point where they reconsider their union vote, and request to decertify. Odd as that sounds, it does happen. A newly formed union membership can be very skittish. The 120-day deadline would prevent that.

Of course, the Republican Party, the US Chamber of Commerce and the National Association of Manufacturers went berserk at the prospect of EFCA becoming the law of the land. Allowing working people more access to labor unions was by itself scary enough, but giving an outside agency— a federal arbitrator, no less—the authority to set the actual terms of the contract? That was terrifying.

In fact, the prospect was so frightening, corporate America closed ranks, went on a rampage and spent tens of millions of dollars lobbying against it … just as labor spent millions lobbying in favor of it. And with the money collected, the positions defined, the lines drawn, and both sides fully mobilized, the "Battle for the EFCA" officially began.

In classical times, according to legend, when Cicero finished speaking, people would nod appreciatively and say, "How well he spoke." But when Pericles finished speaking, the men would shout, "Let us march!" Such is the power of the spoken word. So, given Obama's extraordinary skills as an orator, what did he say to inspire the public? What was the theme of his rousing speech? Alas, there was no speech. He barely spoke.

While he did acknowledge support of EFCA, he did it flatly, mechanically, sounding more like an actuary than a champion of a cause. Instead of going on national television and presenting the EFCA inspirationally, introducing it as a monument to worker empowerment, Obama laid an egg. He handed the baton to chief of staff Rahm Emanuel, and told him to run with it.

And from the moment Emanuel got involved it became politics as usual. Not only did Emanuel spin his wheels, but by immediately offering concessions he revealed the White House's lack of commitment. Predictably, with Obama conspicuously silent and no one to lead the charge, the legislation, even in its watered-down form, died a natural death. By the time Senator Feinstein (D-CA) got around to announcing that she had changed her mind and wouldn't be voting for it, the bill was already dead.

Organized labor was furious. The EFCA was viewed by many as the most important labor initiative since the Taft-Hartley Act. If Obama had only done what he promised—had he set the national agenda and made EFCA part of the public debate—the legislation could have grown legs; it could very well have passed. Instead, Obama's actions made it clear that EFCA mattered little to him, that he was merely going through the motions, largely to placate labor. (Sorry, boys … at least we tried.)

The same indifference was evident in the president's shocking non-response to the attacks on America's public school teachers being made by anti-union forces and free-market fundamentalists. Although virtually every study ever conducted by reputable educational professionals has shown that the defects plaguing our school system *are not* the fault of the teachers, Obama chose to leave the teachers twisting slowly in the wind.

To his utter shame, Obama never once contradicted these slanderous, trumped-up accusations—which he could have refuted simply by citing the relevant statistics. Instead, Obama sought to curry favor with Republicans and free-market Independents by appointing the anti-union, platitude-spouting bureaucrat Arne Duncan (a former Chicago crony) Secretary of Education.

The only "studies" that blame teachers are the phony ones sponsored by Republican business groups whose goal is to replace public schools with private charters. Because there's money to be made, these entrepreneurs want to privatize everything. They want to profitize the world—with private police forces, private armies, private schools, beaches, toll roads, national parks, pay-as-you-go libraries, you name it. Were it not for the outrage it would create among evangelicals, they would privatize the churches, franchise them like multiplex theaters, and charge admission.

Accordingly, their first order of business was to demonize organized labor. They did this by claiming our schools were failing because so many "bad teachers" were being protected by teachers' unions. And without anyone in authority to step up and publicly refute those accusations—with the President of the United States unwilling to set the record straight—these lies morphed into sound-bites, and the sound-bites became part of the conventional wisdom.

Yet if anyone had taken two minutes to examine the statistics, they would have found that non-union teachers across the country get fired *at about the same rate* as union teachers. It's a fact. Also, they would have found that many of the states with a preponderance of union teachers (Oregon, Wisconsin, South Dakota, Connecticut, Vermont, Washington, Wisconsin, Minnesota, Maine, et al) happen to have excellent public schools, some of the finest in the country.

Oregon and Washington's public school teachers are 100 percent unionized. Wisconsin and Connecticut's are 98 percent unionized. Etc. In other words, the knock against public school teachers and the unions that represent them was all part of a well-planned, well-choreographed smear campaign.

But by chickening out, Obama allowed those smears to work. By refusing to defend public schools against these subversive accusations, he contributed to what we see today as an assault not only on teachers, but on all our public sector unions. If *President* Obama had been even half the friend to labor that *Candidate* Obama was, America's unions wouldn't be in the defensive position they are today.

The EFCA and school teachers are merely two disappointments. There have been others.

Candidate Obama acknowledged the problem of striker replacements. Heeding Supreme Court Justice Brandeis' observation ("Labor cannot, on any terms, surrender the right to strike"), he agreed that being permanently replaced while on strike was tantamount to *not having the right to strike*. Although striker replacement legislation would likely not have passed, it would have been a worthwhile salvo to fire across the bow because it would have captured the public's attention and redirected the debate. *President* Obama said nothing.

Another salvo across the bow should have been a spirited defense of the auto industry bailout. While Obama did eventually endorse the $18 billion loan package, he did so reluctantly, grimly, like a man with a gun to his head. Moreover, he allowed Senator Richard Shelby (R-Ala) to go on national TV and sanctimoniously rail against the United Auto Workers (UAW), blaming the union for the industry's problems.

Instead of coming to the defense of the UAW and revealing Shelby for the self-serving hypocrite he was, Obama backed away. In truth, Shelby and every other Southern politician wanted Detroit to fail—they *needed* Detroit to fail—so that the auto industry would continue to shift its operations to non-union Dixie. They were (and are) salivating at the prospect of the South becoming the new Detroit.

Another bully pulpit speech that should have been given was an exposé of what passes for so-called "fair trade." It goes without saying that the president has an obligation to protect American workers—not only because they're the country's largest constituency, but because fair play should count for something. Obama needed to go on national TV and clarify some economic realities.

He needed to inform the public that foreign governments routinely (and illegally) subsidize their industries in order to gain a foothold in the US market. It began with Japanese cars. He needed to tell the American public that it's time we stopped pretending we're engaged in anything resembling "free trade" or "fair competition," and time we stopped blaming American workers for our predicament. But Obama would never dare say anything so incendiary.

In trying to account for Obama's stunning betrayal of labor, we're more or less stuck with two explanations, neither of which gives us any pleasure. One is that Obama is way more conservative and establishment-minded than he made himself out to be, that he is, in fact, a closet aristocrat and union-hater. While that explanation is not wholly implausible, it's unconvincing.

The other explanation is that Obama is simply a political lightweight, a dilettante. This one makes more sense. While Obama is probably pro-labor *in principle*, he is, *in practice*, a mollifier, an eminently cautious, calculating politician who's unwilling to rock the boat and who, in truth, is a bit of an intellectual coward.

In my *CounterPunch* interview with Robert Reich (President Clinton's Secretary of Labor), he said, referring to the EFCA, "Once again, the leaders of organized labor got hoodwinked. It happened in the Clinton administration. It happened under Carter. Labor leaders support a Democratic candidate for president, and then are disappointed and surprised when he doesn't come through."

Because Obama believes America's labor unions have no place to reside except the Democratic Party, he condescends to them. He condescends to labor the same way and for the same reasons the Kennedy White House condescended to the civil rights movement. The message: If you think the Democrats aren't doing enough for you, try your luck with the Republicans.

David Macaray, a Los Angeles playwright and author of It's Never Been Easy: Essays on Modern Labor, *was a former labor union rep.*

War Colleges
By HENRY GIROUX

While there is an ongoing discussion about the increasing corporatization of higher education—extending from the attempted buying of faculty positions by right wing billionaires such as the Koch brothers to the increasing casualization of faculty labor and the commodification of knowledge, what is often left out of this analysis is the intrusion of the military into higher education.

The culture of organized violence is one of the most powerful forces shaping American society, extending deeply into every aspect of American life. There can be little doubt that America has become a permanent warfare state.

Not only is it waging a war in three countries, but its investment in military power is nearly as much as all of the military budgets of every other country in the world combined. The Stockholm International Peace Research Institute states that "The USA's military spending accounted for 43 percent of the world total in 2009, followed by China with 6.6 percent; France with 4.3 percent, and the UK with 3.8 percent."

The conflicts in Iraq and Afghanistan have cost Americans a staggering $1 trillion to date, second only in inflation-adjusted dollars to the $4 trillion price tag for World War II.

Pentagon spending for 2011 will be more than $700 billion. To make matters worse, as Tom Englehardt points out, "We dominate the global arms trade, monopolizing almost 70% of the arms business in 2008, with Italy coming in a vanishingly distant second. We put more money into the funding of war, our armed forces, and the weaponry of war than the next 25 countries combined (and that's without even including Iraq and Afghan war costs)."

Moreover, the US maintains a massive ring of military bases and global presence around the world, occupying "over 560 bases and other sites" and deploying over 300,000 troops abroad, "even as our country finds itself incapable of paying for basic services."

In spite of how much military expenditures drain desperately needed funds from social programs, the military budget is rarely debated in Congress or made a serious object of discussion among the public. Not only does the US squander its resources and human lives on foreign wars, we ignore facing "the realities and costs of war" at home.

As a central element of domestic and US foreign policy, the social costs of such wars are rarely subject to debate and largely endorsed by a pliant and conformist media. NBC *Nightly News*, for example, provides unproblematic representations of war narratives almost nightly, reducing such narratives to human interest stories while simultaneously depoliticizing the meaning and purpose of war and organized state violence. War is now normalized even as the US becomes more militarized, moving closer to being a national security state at home and an imperial/policing power abroad. One consequence of the increasing militarization of American society can be seen in changes that have taken place in public and higher education.

Schools have become the testing grounds for new modes of security and military-style authority, treating students as if they were largely detainees subject to a range of egregious disciplinary practices ranging from repressive zero tolerance policies to the criminalization of what is often considered trivial infractions such as dress code violations. The war at home is most obvious in the ways in which young people marginalized by class and color are now seen largely as disposable populations, whose behaviors are largely governed through a youth crime complex. In fact, in cities such as Chicago, military academies have become the institutions of choice in dealing with students marginalized by race and class. School for many young people has become simply a pipeline into the criminal justice and correctional system. In fact, a few years ago two judges in Luzerne County, in Northeastern Pennsylvania accepted over $2.6 million in kickbacks for sentencing hundreds of kids to a for-profit, privately owned juvenile detention center.

Since the tragic events of 9/11, state-sanctioned violence and the formative culture that makes it possible has increasingly made its way into higher education. While there is a long history of higher education taking on research funds and projects that serve the military-industrial complex, such projects were often hidden from public view. When they did become public, they were often the object of student protests and opposition, especially during the 1960s. What is new today is that more research projects in higher education than ever before are being funded by various branches of the military, but either no one is paying attention or no one seems to care about such projects.

Ethical and political considerations about the role of the university in a democratic society have given way to a hyper-pragmatism couched in the language of austerity and largely driven by a decrease in state funding for higher education and the dire lack of jobs for many graduates. It is also driven by a market-centered ethos that celebrates a militant form of individualism, a survivalist ethic, a crass emphasis on materialism, and an utter disregard for the responsibility of others. As research funds dry up for programs aimed at addressing crucial social problems, new opportunities open up with the glut of military funding aimed at creating more sophisticated weapons, surveillance technologies, and modes of knowledge that connect anthropological concerns with winning wars.

Military modes of education largely driven by the demands of war and organized violence are investing heavily in pedagogical practices that train students in various intelligence operations. Programs such as the Pat Roberts Intelligence Scholars Program and the Intelligence Community Scholarship Programs disregard the principles of academic freedom and recruit students to serve in a number of intelligence agencies, such as the CIA, that have a long history of using torture, illegal assassinations, murder, running illegal prisons, and on occasion committing domestic atrocities—such as spying on Juan Cole, a prominent academic and critic of the Iraq War. The increasingly intensified and expansive symbiosis between the military-industrial complex and academia is also on full display in the creation of the "Minerva Consortium," ironically named after the goddess of wisdom, whose purpose is to fund various universities to "carry out social sciences research relevant to national security."

As David Price has brilliantly documented, the CIA and other intelligence agencies "today sneak unidentified students with undisclosed links to intelligence agencies into university classrooms. A new generation of so-called flagship programs have quietly taken root on campuses, and, with each new flagship, our universities are transformed into vessels of the militarized state."

The Pentagon's desire to turn universities into militarized knowledge factories producing knowledge, research and personnel in the interest of the Homeland (In)Security State should be of special concern for intellectuals, artists, academics and others who believe that the university should oppose such interests and alignments. Connecting universities with any one of the fifteen US security and intelligence agencies replaces the ideal of educating students to be critical citizens with the notion of students as potential spies and citizen soldiers. Pedagogy, in this instance, becomes militarized.

At the very least, the emergence of the Minerva Consortium, the Pat Roberts Intelligence Scholars Program, and the Human Terrain System raises a larger set of concerns about the ongoing militarization of higher education in the US. Disciplines such as anthropology, political science, psychology and sociology are being tapped as resources to enhance new technologies and practices of violence. As a result of the increasing number of programs, university students no longer graduate with the aim of serving the common good. Instead, they end up in villages in Iraq and Afghanistan working as informers for the military, bringing their scholarship to bear on winning the "hearts and minds" of foreign populations for whom democracy becomes synonymous with war, torture and foreign occupation. Misled and miseducated psychologists and physicians assist in state sanctioned torture methods in order to keep detainees alive so they can continue to be tortured.

There is more at stake here than the corruption of academic fields, faculties and the overall ideal of the university as a democratic public sphere. There is the total transformation of the state from a liberal social one into a punishing state. The machinery of death is more than a technology; it is also driven by a formative culture that creates the knowledge, values and practices that enable human beings to work in the service of violence and death. When the military increasingly becomes a model for shaping the most basic institutions of society—institutions ranging from public schools and industry to higher education—the ideals of democracy become a faint memory and American society plunges into barbarism on all fronts.

Further evidence of the increasing militarization of American society can be found in the dominant media, popular culture, fashion and official politics. Violent video games, largely catering to young people, bring in billions of dollars in profits for Wal-Mart and the video game industry, while at the same time legitimating a culture of cruelty and violence. Soldier dolls such as G.I. Joe look tame compared to the current batch of video games that often appear to be modeled after slasher films on steroids. True to the increasing logic of privatization, private companies now offer military services for hire, treating their products as any other commodity for sale.

In a post-9/11 world, with its all encompassing celebration of war and state violence, the discourse and values of militarization both permeate the social order and increasingly produce a shift from a welfare state to a militarized and punishing society. Militarization suggests more than simply a militaristic ideal—with its celebration of war as the truest measure of the health of the nation and the soldier-warrior as the most noble expression of the merging of masculinity and unquestioning patriotism—but an intensification and expansion of the underlying values, practices, ideologies, social relations and cultural representations associated with military culture.

The values of militarization are no longer restricted to foreign policy ventures; the ideals of war in a post-9/11 world have become normalized, serving as a powerful educational force that shapes our lives, memories and daily experiences. The military has become a way of life producing modes of education, goods, jobs, communication and institutions that transcend traditional understandings of the geography, territory and place of the military in American society. Military values, social relations, and practices now bleed into every aspect of American life. What is distinctive about the militarization of the social order is that war becomes a source of pride rather than alarm, while organized violence is elevated to a place of national honor, recycled endlessly through a screen culture that bathes in blood, death and war porn. As democratic idealism is replaced by the combined forces of the military-industrial complex, civil liberties are gradually eroded along with the formative culture in which the dictates of militarization can be challenged. Wars abroad also further accentuate the failure to address serious problems at home. As Andrew Bacevich points out, "Fixing Iraq or Afghanistan ends up taking precedent over fixing Cleveland and Detroit."

Cities rot, unemployment spreads, bridges collapse, veterans are refused adequate medical care, youth lack jobs and hope and yet the permanent warfare state squanders over a trillion dollars waging wars in Iraq and Afghanistan. As Kevin Baker points out, "We now substitute military solutions for almost everything, including international alliances, diplomacy, effective intelligence agencies, democratic institutions—even national security.... The logic is inexorable."

A primitive tribalism now grips society as our democratic institutions and public spheres become inseparable from the military.

Nowhere is this more evident than in the ongoing symbiosis between military power and values and higher education. As higher education is weakened through an ongoing assault by right wing ideologues, corporate power and the forces of militarization, the very idea of the university as a site of critical thinking, public service and socially responsible research is in danger of disappearing. This is especially true as the national security state, the Pentagon, and corporate power set their sites on restructuring higher education at a time when it is vulnerable because of a loss of revenue and a growing public disdain towards critical thinking, faculty autonomy and the public mission of the university. Higher education has been targeted because when it aligns its modes of governance, knowledge production and view of learning with the forces of organized capital and the mechanisms of violence and disposability, it makes a belief in militarized and commodified knowledge a fact of everyday life. Imposing new forms of discipline, affective investments, modes of knowledge and values conducive to a public willing to substitute training for education, a militarized and corporatized mode of pedagogy removes ethical considerations from the social and human costs produced by the market and the permanent warfare state. More specifically, higher education in this instance makes possible a belief in militarized and instrumental knowledge as a fact of life while legitimating those social processes "in which civil society organizes itself for the production of violence."

Millions of students pass through the halls of higher education in the US. It is crucial that they be educated in ways that enable them to recognize the poisonous forces of corporatization and militarization, and their effects throughout American society. Particularly important is to understand how these effects threaten "democratic government at home just as they menace the independence and sovereignty of other countries."

Both students and the larger public must be alerted to the ways in which the Military-Industrial-Academic Complex has restructured higher education so as to dismantle it as a place in which to think critically, imagine otherwise and engage in modes of knowledge production and research that address pressing social problems and encourage students to participate in public debate and civic engagement.

But there is more at stake here than educating students to be alert to the dangers of militarization and the way in which it is redefining the very mission of higher education. Critics such as David Price, the late Chalmers Johnson, Sheldon Wolin and Andrew Bacevich have convincingly argued that if the US is to avoid degenerating into a military dictatorship, a grass-roots movement will have to occupy center stage in opposing militarization, government secrecy and imperial power, while reclaiming the basic principles of democracy.

This means rejecting the established political parties; forming alternative, democratic, anti-militarization movements, and developing the groundwork for long-term organizations, new solidarities and social movements to resist the growing ties among higher education, the armed forces, intelligence agencies and the war industries—ties that play a crucial role in reproducing militarized knowledge.

If higher education is to come to grips with the multilayered pathologies produced by militarization, it will have to rethink both the space of the university as a democratic public sphere and the global spaces and public spheres in which intellectuals, educators, students, artists, labor unions and other social actors and movements can form transnational alliances to oppose the death-dealing ideology of militarization and its effects on the world. These effects include violence, pollution, massive poverty, racism, the arms trade, growth of privatized armies, civil conflict, child slavery and the ongoing wars in Iraq and Afghanistan.

As the Obama regime embraces the policies of the Military-Industrial-Academic complex with unbridled fervor, it is time for educators and students to take a stand and develop global organizations that can be mobilized in the effort to supplant a culture of war with a culture of peace whose elemental principles must be grounded in relations of economic, political, cultural and social justice and the desire to sustain human life.

The degree to which higher education is being handed over to the values of corporate and military power is alarming. At a time when democratic social relations, workers, students and everything that can be termed public is under attack, it is crucial that higher education be viewed as a central site in the effort to keep alive institutions and a formative culture capable of educating students to struggle for democracy and against the technologies and machineries of death that appear to have a stranglehold on American society. Power is never sutured, never complete in its attempt to eliminate struggle, collective resistance and hope. We need a new language, formative culture and range of public spheres to reclaim power in the interests of democratic struggles.

There is both a theoretical and a political issue at stake here. Progressives and others on the left need to grasp the centrality of pedagogy to any viable understanding of politics. The struggle over ideas, values, identities, new modes of solidarity, economic equality and democratic social relations will not guarantee change, but it is certainly a precondition for making politics meaningful in order to lead to social transformation. Pedagogy raises the question of what it means for the American public to understand militarism, neoliberalism and other anti-democratic forces in ways that undo their self-evident and commonsense appeals. I think Michael Berube is right on target in arguing that one failure of the left has been its inability to tell a compelling story, to provide narratives that disrupt conventional and official modes of ideology. Other factors might include a focus on single issue movements, a politics of purity and an obsession with the language of critique to the exclusion of a discourse of hope and possibility.

Conservatives and neoliberals, by contrast, are no strangers to cultural politics. All one has to do is look at the proliferation of their think tanks, foundations, churches and a variety of other institutions designed to educate their own cadre and overrun the media and government with their anti-public intellectuals. Actually, all one has to do in this case is to go back and read the Powell Memo produced in the early 1970s to get a glimpse of how prescient conservatives were about the importance of cultural politics. Of course, C. Wright Mills, Ellen Willis and number of other theorists took seriously the nature of public pedagogy and cultural politics, but their voices were rarely heeded. While progressives clearly cannot match the deep pockets of the right, they can certainly put more efforts into developing public spheres in which they nurture intellectuals and educate generations of young people both in and out of the university. The fight for justice and democracy is taking place all over the globe with a new intensity. And while there are enclaves of resistance in the US now emerging in the face of an unapologetic attack on every vestige of democracy, we need to reclaim moral indignation, the power of collective agency, and the willingness to engage in civil disobedience. The left has been too timid in its reluctance to develop a public pedagogy that is critical, thoughtful, incisive and courageous. It needs to take the moral high ground away from the right and fight with all of the tools at its disposal in order to create a new and critical formative democratic culture and set of public spheres.

The left must move away from the abyss of compromise and stake out alternative visions around health care, education, national priorities, the environment, civil rights, foreign policy, employment, national security, the social state and the dismantling of the permanent warfare state. Put differently, progressives need to appropriate new strategies and build wide ranging alliances by giving credence to the tools and methods necessary to create critical modes of consciousness, literacy and meaning. This suggests a deeper understanding is needed of the merging of the political and the pedagogical—a more complex rendering of the dangers of militarization and the limits of state power, and a critical mapping of the emergence of the symbiosis between the military and corporate state and what it means to dismantle this pernicious register of power. We also need an understanding of what conditions are necessary to develop those formative cultures that enable people to translate private considerations into public issues along with a determined collective effort to wrench the old and new media away from the control of mega corporations and the pervasive discourse of celebrity and privatization. Public and higher education along with what C. Wright Mills called the cultural apparatus must be reclaimed as crucial pedagogical tools to fight the new militarism and culture of death that increasingly produce what the late Gil Scott Heron called "Winter in America."

Henry A. Giroux holds the Global TV Network chair in English and Cultural Studies at McMaster University in Canada. His most recent books include: Take Back Higher Education *(co-authored with Susan Searls Giroux, 2006),* The University in Chains: Confronting the Military-Industrial-Academic Complex *(2007),* Against the Terror of Neoliberalism: Politics Beyond the Age of Greed *(2008) and* Twilight of the Social: Resurgent Publics in the Age of Disposability *(2012).*

Politics as the Earth Burns: Obama and the Climate Crisis

By BRIAN TOKAR

Environmentalists across the US were energized and some were thrilled when one of Barack Obama's first public acts as president-elect was to offer a videotaped message of hope to a large international conference on climate issues. After eight years of a White House dominated by the politics of climate denial, Obama's message profoundly renewed many activists' belief that a new era was upon us.

"Once I take office, you can be sure that the United States will once again engage vigorously in these negotiations and help lead the world toward a new era of global cooperation on climate change," Obama told the 700 delegates meeting in Los Angeles in mid-November of 2008. "The science is beyond dispute, and the facts are clear," Obama continued, pledging a commitment to meaningful reductions in emissions of greenhouse gases and the implementation of a market-oriented "cap-and-trade" system to implement those reductions.

Within two short but heady years, activists' hopes had been thoroughly dashed. By the summer of 2010, months before the Republicans took control of the House, climate legislation was off the table in Congress following the demise of at least four different proposals. At the United Nations, the US continued to play a largely obstructive role in international climate negotiations, with Obama and Hillary Clinton co-leading the effort in Copenhagen in 2009 to replace the Kyoto Protocol's mandated emissions reductions with an unenforceable system of voluntary national pledges. The administration's top climate negotiator, Todd Stern, continues to blame developing countries for the lack of progress toward negotiated emissions cuts, and has publicly questioned whether the UN is even the appropriate forum for addressing global warming.

On one hand, no single individual can be blamed for such an utter failure of politics and diplomacy. Many in Congress, including key Democrats, are thoroughly beholden to fossil fuel interests, and several countries—notably China, Australia, and several European powers—helped construct diplomatic roadblocks in Copenhagen. Domestically, mainstream environmental organizations united in support of a series of fatally flawed proposals, while only a handful of smaller national groups joined with grassroots activists in questioning the highly compromised terms of the debate. Obama's actions do, however, fit the pattern he has repeated around so many other issues: failure to defend progressive principles, rapid capitulation to corporate interests and a chronic unwillingness to articulate a principled challenge to right wing political agendas. In this instance, not only Obama's political future, but the future of life on earth may be at stake.

According to *New Yorker* correspondent Ryan Lizza's "inside" account of the climate debate in Washington, the Obama administration initially put health care reform and climate legislation on an equal footing, planning to wait and see which set of proposals moved forward fastest. By June of 2009, progress on a climate bill seemed to be on track, as a bill authored by Reps. Waxman and Markey (of California and Massachusetts, respectively) passed the House, seemingly vindicating the administration's approach. However the fundamental problems with the Waxman-Markey bill quickly became apparent to critical observers. Its basic approach had been mapped out months earlier by a nefarious alliance of mainstream environmentalists and polluting corporations known as the Climate Action Partnership (US-CAP), which had urged Congress to focus on long-range rather than immediate goals, establish a market for trading greenhouse gas emissions among companies, freely distribute the majority of emissions allowances to polluting industries, and create a system of "offsets" that help companies defer pollution reductions well into the future.

The creation of a market to trade carbon dioxide and other greenhouse gases among corporations—the scheme that came to be known as "cap-and-trade"—was first proposed during the administration of the elder President George Bush as a "business-friendly" alternative to regulation and energy taxes. Aiming to prove their environmental credentials after the disastrous presidency of Ronald Reagan, the Bush administration established a trading mechanism to nominally reduce the sulfur dioxide pollution that is responsible for acid rain, and environmental officials such as the Environmental Defense Fund's Daniel Dudek quickly suggested that the program could be a "scale model" for globally trading greenhouse gas emissions.

Al Gore endorsed the idea in his 1992 book, *Earth in the Balance*, and received credit for "saving" the troubled UN climate talks in Kyoto in 1997 when he suggested that the US would sign on to a Kyoto Protocol if emissions cuts were implemented through a similar market-centered process. The Clinton/Gore administration, of course, never pushed to ratify Kyoto, but the rest of the world has had to live with the consequences of Gore's intervention, aptly described by *Guardian* columnist George Monbiot as "an exuberant market in fake emissions cuts."

Critical environmental groups such as Friends of the Earth and the Center for Biological Diversity, along with grassroots networks like Rising Tide and Climate SOS, quickly raised questions about the Waxman-Markey bill, citing its dependence on the flagrant corporate loopholes known as carbon offsets, billions of dollars in "special interest favors," as described by the *New York Times*, and perhaps most egregious of all, its prohibition of any further action against greenhouse gases by the EPA. By the time the debate moved to the Senate, the giveaways to the fossil fuel, coal and nuclear industries were too much even for some believers in environmental "consensus" and market-based carbon trading. Still, Senate Republicans boycotted the first committee hearing that was convened to address a proposal by Senators Kerry and Boxer, and Kerry shifted his focus toward crafting a "bipartisan" compromise, in collaboration with Joe Lieberman, the "independent" war hawk from Connecticut and Republican Lindsey Graham of South Carolina. One of the first public announcements of this unlikely collaboration was a *New York Times* opinion piece in which Kerry and Graham called for streamlining regulation of nuclear power and expanding offshore oil drilling. Kerry stated publicly that the EPA's authority to regulate greenhouse gases would be leveraged as a bargaining chip to help gain Republican support for his bill.

Defying all expectations that these giveaways could help rally corporate support for a climate bill, Obama went ahead and offered up many of the Kerry team's bargaining chips before either Senate bill came up for debate. Obama's budget proposal in early 2010 included nearly $55 billion in new loan guarantees for the nuclear industry. In late March, he offered a nationwide expansion of offshore oil drilling, a plan that was withdrawn only after BP's massive oil spill in the Gulf of Mexico. According to Ryan Lizza of the *New Yorker*, there was no coordination with Senate staffers around these proposals; instead, "Obama had now given away what the senators were planning to trade." The Obama White House also apparently sabotaged a pending deal with the oil companies to streamline their purchases of emissions permits; a White House staffer's leak to Fox News turned the deal into political poison for Graham by echoing Republican talking points that cast carbon credits as equivalent to a gas tax. Another bipartisan effort, led by Senators Cantwell (D-WA) and Snowe (R-ME) was praised by some environmentalists as closer to a real carbon tax, but ultimately proved to be too little too late.

Obama's approach to the international climate negotiations proved even more discouraging. Prominent environmental groups, particularly Greenpeace, had pinned their hopes on his personal participation in the Copenhagen summit and succeeded in making the largely irrelevant question of whether Obama would go to Copenhagen into the main media story and a primary focus for activists. In July of 2009, eleven Greenpeace climbers scaled Mount Rushmore to hang a giant banner featuring a portrait of Obama and the message, "America Honors Leaders, Not Politicians. Stop Global Warming." Soon, the media became distracted by the manufactured scandal stemming from the stolen emails from the Climate Research Unit in the UK and various officials began to proclaim the advantages of a non-binding "political" or "operational" agreement as an alternative to extending the binding reductions in greenhouse gas emissions that were built into the Kyoto Protocol. For the first time, European Union representatives began to echo the US refusal to make future commitments to reduce greenhouse gas pollution under the Kyoto framework, a switch that Naomi Klein credited to Obama's diplomacy and commitment to "multilateralism."

The alternative, non-binding approach to pollution reductions that Obama and Clinton brought to Copenhagen was laid out in detail in a little noticed article in the journal *Foreign Affairs* published several months before the UN conference. "The odds of signing a comprehensive treaty in December are vanishingly small," wrote Council on Foreign Relations (CFR) fellow Michael Levi, at a time when most of the world was still bracing for a deal. Levi articulated the outlines of the approach that the US would bring to Copenhagen: that legally binding emissions cuts should be replaced by a patchwork of country-specific pledges with the modest, and fundamentally inadequate, goal of halving world emissions of carbon dioxide by 2050. To avoid "excessive blame" for a diplomatic failure in Copenhagen, Levi suggested that the conference be reframed as similar to the beginning of a round of arms control or world trade talks, processes which invariably take many years to complete. "This 'Copenhagen Round,'" he argued, mirroring the typical World Trade Organization language, "would be much more like an extended trade negotiation than like a typical environmental treaty process."

As over 100,000 people took to the streets of Copenhagen, demanding a real agreement in line with the emerging principles of climate justice, the US brokered a deal with the fastest-developing countries (the so-called BASIC bloc: Brazil, South Africa, India and China) that largely echoed the Obama administration's and CFR's proposals. While mainstream media in the North tended to blame China for the lack of a stronger agreement in Copenhagen, the convergence of Chinese and US interests is clearly manifest in the Copenhagen Accord's transparent lack of substance. Nothing in the Accord would be binding on governments or corporations, and everything was voluntary, only to be assessed informally after five years.

When German climate scientists set out to evaluate the consequences of various countries' commitments under this regime, they concluded that it could likely result in a medium-term 6.5 percent *increase* in greenhouse gases relative to the 1990 baseline previously established in Kyoto corresponding to a devastating global average temperature increase of at least 5 degrees Celsius (9 degrees Fahrenheit). In unusually descriptive language for generally staid pages of the scientific journal *Nature*, the German group decried the lack of short-term emission-reduction goals as equivalent to "racing towards a cliff and hoping to stop just before it." Subsequent pronouncements by US climate negotiator Todd Stern and other administration officials suggested little likelihood of any further progress at the 2011 climate conference in Durban, South Africa, the last one before the Kyoto Protocol's initial commitment period was scheduled to expire.

Since the collapse of domestic climate legislation and the diplomatic debacle in Copenhagen, the Obama administration's efforts on climate have been rather minimal. The EPA's efforts to regulate greenhouse gas emissions, as mandated by the Supreme Court in 2007, have been delayed under pressure from Congressional Republicans, as have controls on mountaintop removal coal mining in Appalachia and several other scheduled anti-pollution measures. The support for energy efficiency improvements in the 2010 economic stimulus bill proved to be rather modest. One area where the administration has made some progress is in raising automobile fuel efficiency standards, a process that had been stalled since 1990. In early 2011 the administration raised the required average fuel economy of the US fleet to 35.5 miles per gallon by 2016 and, a few months later, to 54.5 mpg by 2025. These measures, however, fall short of proposals for more than 60 mpg that were actively under discussion, and feature an intricate system of credits, allowances and exemptions that give carmakers extra points for electric and "flex-fuel" (mainly ethanol-burning) vehicles and even for more efficient air conditioners, together with much lower standards for "light trucks," including most SUVs. Additionally, Obama thoroughly failed in his attempt to force cuts in the most egregious fossil fuel subsidies as part of his debt ceiling deal with congressional Republicans in the summer of 2011.

On the symbolic front, Obama stepped up his visits to sites of weather-related disasters in the Southeast, not wanting to echo George W. Bush's tepid response to Katrina. His appearances at various wind and solar energy manufacturing sites occasionally made the news, even as China began to dramatically outpace the US in renewable energy. But references to climate change and the urgency of preventing further disruptions of the earth's climate system were no longer to be found among Obama's prescribed talking points.

Meanwhile, the immediate effects of global climate chaos have spread from relatively isolated, vulnerable places on earth to affecting huge populations, both in the global South and the industrialized world. Massive flooding in Pakistan and wildfires in Russia were in the headlines in 2010; a year later wildfires in Arizona spread clouds of smoke across the US, a summer-long heat-wave scorched the Midwest, and record floods and tornadoes devastated places throughout the East. The Horn of Africa may be facing its worst-ever drought, turning perhaps hundreds of thousands of people into climate refugees. Still, surveys suggest that only about 40 percent of the US population is concerned about climate change, and about the same number accept the myth that scientists still disagree about its causes.

"When Obama took office, he appointed some of the country's most knowledgeable climate scientists to his Administration," reports the acclaimed climate writer Elizabeth Kolbert, "and it seemed for a time as if he might take his responsibility to lead on this issue seriously. That hope has faded."[1] While some of the blame clearly lies with the right-wing extremists who hijacked

---

1   Elizabeth Kolbert, "Storms Brewing," *New Yorker* June 13, 2011.

Congress in 2011—and with corporate-funded Beltway environmentalists who prefer to coast along with the Capitol's prevailing winds—the climate crisis remains one of the pivotal issues where Obama's tepid response, and his subservience to corporate interests, have only made things worse.

Brian Tokar's latest books are Toward Climate Justice *(New Compass Press) and* Agriculture and Food in Crisis *(co-edited with Fred Magdoff, Monthly Review Press). He is the director of the Vermont-based Institute for Social Ecology, and a lecturer in Environmental Studies at the University of Vermont.*

Obama's Attack on Social Security and Medicare

By DAVE LINDORFF

When Barack Obama was running for president, back in 2008, he was pretty definite about his seemingly progressive position on Social Security. While he conceded the arguable point that Social Security faced a crisis several decades hence, he also claimed, both on the stump and in debate with candidate Hillary Clinton, that he was opposed to benefit cuts and to privatization. He also insisted at that time that the answer was to raise the cap on income subject to Social Security taxation, and he declared himself opposed to the idea of putting some "commission" in charge of coming up with a "solution."

What a difference getting elected makes, especially when you get elected with the help of truckloads of money from Wall Street financial interests.

No sooner had Obama moved into the White House, than he changed his tune and began suggesting, in what has proved over the next two and a half years of his presidency to be his "negotiation" style, which is to give away 90 percent of the ground before you start to negotiate, that he was open to discussing benefit cuts. He also did a 180-degree turn and announced that he would appoint a deficit-reduction commission to come up with recommendations. When he appointed that commission, he announced in advance that he would be "agnostic" toward any recommended changes, including cuts to Social Security, thus telegraphing in advance, in case the commission members needed encouragement, that he was ready to undermine this key New Deal legacy.

Medicare was tossed into the same hopper. In fact, in the case of Medicare it got worse. Obama had campaigned for office claiming that he would fix the nation's disastrous health care system, which for decades now has featured the highest costs and the highest rate of cost inflation, as well as some of the poorest health statistics (life expectancy, infant mortality, etc.) in the developed world, all the while leaving some 40 percent of the population uninsured and without access to basic care. There was an easy fix to all these problems right in front of him—one which the majority of Americans, and the overwhelming percentage of those who had voted for Obama in November 2008, have consistently told pollsters they favored: extending Medicare to cover everyone, instead of just those sixty five and older.

Medicare, while it is hardly perfect, and has been weakened by Congressional restrictions on its ability to negotiate volume discounts for drugs and pharmaceutical products, and by privatization schemes that give huge subsidies to private insurers like Aetna and Humana that compete with Medicare, has nonetheless demonstrated for years that it can deliver quality care far more cheaply to everyone eligible for it than can private insurers. It has an admin-istrative overhead of just 4 percent, compared to over 20 percent for private insurers, and doesn't operate by trying to deny care, as private insurers do.

It is undeniable that if Medicare were simply expanded to cover all Americans, the result would be immediate and massive savings to both the general public and employers, and even for taxpayers, since it would elimi-nate the need for hundreds of billions of dollars currently spent annually on veterans' medical care, on Medicaid care for the poor, on subsidies and reim-bursements to hospitals for so-called "charity care," and most importantly, on the hidden subsidies for such charity care. These are hidden in the inflated fees charged by hospitals and doctors to insured patients and in the inflated premiums that their insurers charge to cover those inflated fees.

Yet when President Obama assembled a session with health care indus-try representatives at the White House to help him develop a health care reform plan, he deliberately excluded advocates of the idea of Medicare for all, or what has been called "single-payer," or alternately the Canadian-style health system, even barring representatives from the doctors' organization Physicians for a National Health Plan (PNHP). The fix was in. Obamacare was to be a plan constructed around the needs and interests of the health insurance industry, not around the needs of the people of the country.

Worse yet, Medicare, which is tasked with financing care of the sickest and most costly portion of the population—the disabled and the elderly—was left holding that bag, and even suffered cuts to help finance the additional costs embedded in Obamacare. Not surprisingly, having left Medicare out in the cold, the White House now is talking about cutting what is clearly one of the country's most successful federal programs—one that even had Tea Party activists defending it during the health care debates, with their oxymoronic signs saying: "Keep your government hands off my Medicare!"

For four decades Canada has been successfully operating a health care system (called Medicare!), which, exactly like the US Medicare program, is based upon private physicians, free doctor and hospital choice for patients, and which like Medicare in the US remains hugely popular among Canadi-ans and among Canadian businesses, and which covers everyone, at a cost of just over half, in terms of percent of GDP, of what the US spends on health care. How can it be that the White House, when it was developing its health reform plan, never even invited any of the Canadian system's administrators and advocates down to Washington to explain how they do it north of the border? Obama even lied about its relevance, at one point back in 2009, dur-ing an address to a joint session of Congress. He conceded that a single-payer system like Canada's might work well in some countries, but then said, "Since healthcare represents one-sixth of our economy, I believe it makes more sense to build on what works and fix what doesn't, rather than try to build an entirely new system from scratch."

Of course, he was dissembling. It wouldn't be "from scratch," since we already have a "Canadian-style" system in place for our elderly. It's called Medicare, and people love it.

The obvious and unavoidable answer is that this president has no interest in finding, or even in hearing about, the obvious solution to the nation's crisis in health care, which is now costing over 17 percent of GDP, when it costs just 10 percent of GDP in Canada, 12 percent of GDP in France, 11 percent of GDP in Germany, 8 percent of GDP in Japan and the UK and 9 percent of GDP in Italy. He is interested in finding a solution that will ingratiate him with the insurance industry, the pharmaceutical industry, and the AMA—the most retrograde, greedy and self-aggrandizing group of doctors you could find—all big contributors to his 2008 campaign.

And so we had the Deficit-Reduction Commission, which was headed by two known enemies of Social Security and Medicare, Erskine Bowles and former Wyoming Sen. Alan Simpson (who famously said, while serving as co-chair of the commission, that Social Security was "a milk cow with 310 million tits"). This commission, quite predictably, came out with "rescue" proposals that featured raising the retirement age for Social Security, reducing the benefits for future retirees, and "adjusting" the methodology for accounting for inflation in setting benefit payments for current and future retirees (a downward adjustment of course)—a sneaky and invisible way of slowly diminishing the benefits paid over time. And on Medicare, we had the wacky and thoroughly inhumane proposal to raise the age of eligibility from the current sixty five to sixty seven. After all, if employers continue to lay people off at sixty five, as they certainly will, and as people leave their jobs, often not because they want to but because they are no longer physically capable of doing them (think truck and bus drivers whose vision is failing, or manual laborers whose backs, legs or hearts are giving out), what are these retirees to do when they lose their employer-provided health insurance and their incomes, and yet still have to wait two years to get access to medical care through Medicare? (The idea is not even good for business, since the likelihood is that workers, knowing they would be on their own after retiring, would push forward any needed major medical procedures, such as a disk repair or a hip replacement, getting it done on the company plan before they lose it.)

Actually, it is at the other end, among the so called old "old," where all the costs are to be found. The oldest 10 percent of Medicare recipients are responsible for about 90 percent of the entire Medicare budget. People in their late '60s tend not to need all that much care, relatively speaking. In fact, lowering the age of Medicare eligibility would add incrementally less to the program's cost on a per-person basis as you move down in age from sixty to fifty to forty to thirty. It is only when you get to young children, and to women of child-bearing age, that per-person care costs start to rise again. If Obama really wanted to cut Medicare's costs significantly, then instead of making people aged sixty five to sixty seven ineligible, he should make those over ninety ineligible. Obviously this would be viewed by the public as heartless, so he can't do it, and is hoping that raising the entry age to the program will somehow prove more acceptable. Yet the rationale of axing one age group from access to the program is the same. Unmentioned of course, is the harsh reality that raising the age of eligibility for Medicare, besides meaning some people will just go untreated for medical conditions like heart problems, cancer and diabetes, simply shifts most of the costs of care of those people onto the states' struggling Medicaid programs, and onto the children of those who have been forced to wait for their Medicare.

But logic, economics and humane public policy are clearly not considerations in this White House, any more than they were in the Bush/Cheney White House that preceded it. The political calculus is all about pleasing the business interest groups that have the money to give to a re-election campaign. And that would be primarily the insurance industry in the case of Medicare, and the Wall Street gang in the case of Social Security.

The saga of the wholly artificial debt-ceiling "crisis" and of the alleged "crisis" of the nation's ballooning national deficit, were both just part of a Washington Kabuki theater set-piece in the long campaign by corporate interests to undermine and ultimately destroy Social Security and Medicare.

In truth, the debt ceiling has always been a contrivance for cutting popular social program spending. No other nation even has a debt ceiling. Their legislative bodies just pass budgets and their treasuries just make their principal and interest payments on any debt, as required to maintain a sovereign debt rating. Meanwhile, while it is true that this nation's overall debt has risen dramatically since 2000, the reason has nothing to do with either Medicare or Social Security, which have, all through the past decade, been taking in more money than they pay out. The debt has risen for several key reasons, none of which is being addressed by either President Obama or the two political parties in Congress.

The first of these is military spending, which annually consumes more than half of all tax revenues collected by the Treasury. The six wars that the nation is currently engaged in are being fought on borrowed funds, because the government war-mongers, knowing the unpopularity of these bloody adventures, has been afraid to ask the taxpayers to pay for them directly. One way they have borrowed to cover those enormous expenses is by quietly borrowing from the Social Security and Medicare Trust Funds—the monthly tax which workers pay out of each paycheck, matched by their employers, and which now total $2 trillion, but which are required by law to be invested fully in Treasury Bonds, meaning they are lent to the federal government.

Get it? The White House and Congress, for decades, have been collecting our FICA and Medicare taxes, and then taking that money to fund their wars, giving the two Trust Funds Treasury Bills, in exchange for which they have promised to pay interest. But now they are turning around and complaining that that interest money is a "burden" on the taxpayer, and that it has to be reduced.

That's why the Congressional Budget Office, in its 2011 report on the Social Security Trust Fund, claimed that it was running a $45 billion "deficit" this year for the first time. It was a report that allowed Obama and the gang in Congress that is gunning for Social Security and Medicare, to declare a crisis and to call for cuts in benefits. But the truth is, between the FICA taxes paid into Social Security by current workers, and the interest payments paid by the government, the fund was actually running a surplus of $2.6 trillion surplus.

Actually, the deception on the part of the CBO staff was even greater. In 2010, the White House got Congress to agree to "grant" workers a temporary one-year reprieve of 2 percent of the 7 percent normally paid out of every check into the Social Security Trust Fund. The idea was supposed to be that this would work like a 2 percent tax cut which would then put more money in the hands of consumers who would then go out and buy stuff and stimulate the economy. But in an act of staggering betrayal, these same politicians turned around and are now claiming that the $85 billion that the government paid into the Trust Fund to cover the missing employee tax payments meant the system was in deficit, and thus benefits needed to be cut. That is, the extra money they said they were "giving" workers as a tax "cut" would actually be coming out of their retirement benefit payments later, and would also be used as a justification for attacking the Social Security system.

It really doesn't get more obscene than this.

The other reason for the nation's huge deficit increase over the decade is the ongoing Bush tax cuts for the wealthy and for corporations, which could have been killed easily by an Obama veto, since they expired in 2010. But Obama has chosen to allow them to continue. Oh, he complains about them, but he had all the power he needed to end them. With only a narrow majority in the House and with Democrats in charge of the Senate, Republicans could never have managed an override, even with the votes of some conservative Democrats.

There is no question but that the Social Security System, which has been piling up surpluses since 1981 to cover the coming tsunami of the Baby Boomers into retirement, is going to come up short without some additional revenue—reportedly in 2037. People are living longer than anticipated, which should be seen as a good thing, not a crisis. But President Obama knows this is not a crisis. As he used to say, back when he was a candidate, it's a problem that can be easily solved if addressed now, by simply eliminating the cap on income subject to Social Security taxation—a cap that currently exempts all income above $106,000! In fact, the US is at the low end of developed nations in terms of the percent of retirement income provided by public pension, with the average American only having Social Security cover some 40 percent of their retirement expenses. That percentage could be easily raised, and more of our low-income elders who have no other resources, could be lifted out of abject poverty, if Congress and the President agreed to a stock transfer tax dedicated to Social Security, and if Social Security taxation, currently only applied to wages and the Schedule C profits of small businesses, were applied to investment income, or what the IRS calls, with no sense of irony, "unearned" income.

There are easy solutions for the financial problems facing both Medicare and Social Security. But both are political problems, not actuarial ones, as Obama and the lobbyist-owned members of the two parties in Congress are trying to have us believe.

Despite a constant barrage of misleading news reports on both issues, polls show that a majority of Americans instinctually get it, and know that the solutions are 1) an expansion of Medicare to cover all Americans, and 2) an increase in taxes on the rich to fully fund Social Security. It is an indictment of the American political system that despite this clear public preference, President Obama and the elected representatives and senators in the Congress, are not even discussing either approach.

Dave Lindorff is the author of Killing Time *and* The Case for the Impeachment of George W. Bush. *He edits the blog This Can't Be Happening.*

Obama's Assault on Civil Liberties: Twenty Examples

By BILL QUIGLEY

The Obama administration has affirmed, continued and expanded almost all of the draconian domestic civil liberties intrusions pioneered under the Bush administration. Here are twenty examples of serious assaults on the domestic rights to freedom of speech, freedom of assembly, freedom of association, the right to privacy, the right to a fair trial, freedom of religion and freedom of conscience that have occurred since the Obama administration has assumed power. Consider these and then decide if there is any fundamental difference between the Bush presidency and the Obama presidency in the area of domestic civil liberties.

1. Patriot Act. On May 27, 2011, President Obama, over widespread bipartisan objections, approved a Congressional four-year extension of controversial parts of the Patriot Act that were set to expire. In March of 2010, Obama signed a similar extension of the Patriot Act for one year. These provisions allow the government, with permission from a special secret court, to seize records without the owner's knowledge, conduct secret surveillance of suspicious people who have no known ties to terrorist groups and to obtain secret roving wiretaps on people.

2. Criminalization of dissent and militarization of the police. Anyone who has gone to a peace or justice protest in recent years has seen it—local police have been turned into SWAT teams, and SWAT teams into heavily armored military. Officer Friendly or even Officer Unfriendly has given way to police uniformed like soldiers with SWAT shields, shin guards, heavy vests, military helmets, visors, and vastly increased firepower. Protest police sport ninja turtle-like outfits and are accompanied by helicopters, special tanks, and even sound blasting vehicles first used in Iraq. Wireless fingerprint scanners first used by troops in Iraq are now being utilized by local police departments to check motorists. Facial recognition software introduced in war zones is now being used in Arizona and other jurisdictions. Drones just like the ones used in Kosovo, Iraq and Afghanistan are being used along the Mexican and Canadian borders. These activities continue to expand under the Obama administration.

3. Wiretaps. Wiretaps for oral, electronic or wire communications, approved by federal and state courts, are at an all-time high. Wiretaps in year 2010 were up 34 percent from 2009, according to the Administrative Office of the US Courts.

4. Criminalization of speech. Muslims in the US have been targeted by Obama's Department of Justice for inflammatory things they said or

published on the internet. First Amendment protection of freedom of speech, most recently stated in a 1969 Supreme Court decision, *Brandenberg v Ohio*, says the government cannot punish inflammatory speech, even if it advocates violence unless it is likely to incite or produce such action. A Pakistani resident legally living in the US was indicted by the DOJ in September 2011 for uploading a video on YouTube. The DOJ said the video was supportive of terrorists even though nothing on the video called for violence. In July 2011, the DOJ indicted a former Penn State student for going onto websites and suggesting targets and for providing a link to an explosives course already posted on the internet.

5. Domestic government spying on Muslim communities. In activities that offend freedom of religion, freedom of speech and several other laws, the NYPD and the CIA have partnered to conduct intelligence operations against Muslim communities in New York and elsewhere. The CIA, which is prohibited from spying on Americans, works with the police on "human mapping," commonly known as racial and religious profiling to spy on the Muslim community. Under the Obama administration, the Associated Press reported in August 2011, informants known as "mosque crawlers," monitor sermons, bookstores and cafes.

6. Top secret America. In July 2010, the *Washington Post* released "Top Secret America," a series of articles detailing the results of a two year investigation into the rapidly expanding world of homeland security, intelligence and counter-terrorism. It found 1,271 government organizations and 1,931 private companies work on counterterrorism, homeland security and intelligence at about 10,000 locations across the US. Every single day, the National Security Agency intercepts and stores more than 1.7 billion emails, phone calls and other types of communications. The FBI has a secret database named Guardian that contains reports of suspicious activities filed from federal, state and local law enforcement. According to the *Washington Post* Guardian contained 161,948 files as of December 2009. From that database there have been 103 full investigations and at least five arrests the FBI reported. The Obama administration has done nothing to cut back on the secrecy.

7. Other domestic spying. There are at least seventy two fusion centers across the US which collect local domestic police information and merge it into multi-jurisdictional intelligence centers, according to a recent report by the ACLU. These centers share information from federal, state and local law enforcement and some private companies to secretly spy on Americans. These all continue to grow and flourish under the Obama administration.

8. Abusive FBI intelligence operations. The Electronic Frontier Foundation documented thousands of violations of the law by FBI intelligence operations from 2001 to 2008 and estimate that there are over 4000 such violations each year. President Obama issued an executive order to strengthen the Intelligence Oversight Board, an agency that is supposed to make sure

the FBI, the CIA and other spy agencies are following the law. No other changes have been noticed.

9. WikiLeaks. The publication of US diplomatic cables by WikiLeaks and then by mainstream news outlets sparked condemnation by Obama administration officials who said the publication of accurate government documents was nothing less than an attack on the US. The Attorney General announced a criminal investigation and promised "this is not saber rattling." Government officials warned State Department employees not to download the publicly available documents. A State Department official and Colombia officials warned students that discussing WikiLeaks or linking documents to social networking sites could jeopardize their chances of getting a government job, a position that lasted several days until reversed by other Colombia officials. At the time this was written, the Obama administration continued to try to find ways to prosecute the publishers of WikiLeaks.

10. Censorship of books by the CIA. In 2011, the CIA demanded extensive cuts from a memoir by former FBI agent Ali H. Soufan, in part because it made the agency look bad. Soufan's book detailed the use of torture methods on captured prisoners and mistakes that led to 9/11. Similarly, a 2011 book on interrogation methods by former CIA agent Glenn Carle was subjected to extensive black outs. The CIA under the Obama administration continues its push for censorship.

11. Blocking publication of photos of US soldiers abusing prisoners. In May 2009, President Obama reversed his position of three weeks earlier and refused to release photos of US soldiers abusing prisoners. In April 2009, the US Department of Defense told a federal court that it would release the photos. The photos were part of nearly 200 criminal investigations into abuses by soldiers.

12. Technological spying. The Bay Area Transit System, in August 2011, hearing of rumors to protest against fatal shootings by their police, shut down cell service in four stations. Western companies sell email surveillance software to repressive regimes in China, Libya and Syria to use against protestors and human rights activists. Surveillance cameras monitor residents in high crime areas, street corners and other governmental buildings. Police department computers ask for and receive daily lists from utility companies with addresses and names of every home address in their area. Computers in police cars scan every license plate of every car they drive by. The Obama administration has made no serious effort to cut back these new technologies of spying on citizens.

13. Use of "State Secrets" to shield government and others from review. When the Bush government was caught hiring private planes from a Boeing subsidiary to transport people for torture to other countries, the Bush administration successfully asked the federal trial court to dismiss a case by detainees tortured because having a trial would disclose "state secrets" and

threaten national security. When President Obama was elected, the state secrets defense was reaffirmed in arguments before a federal appeals court. It continues to be a mainstay of the Obama administration effort to cloak their actions and the actions of the Bush administration in secrecy.

In another case, it became clear in 2005 that the Bush FBI was avoiding the Fourth Amendment requirement to seek judicial warrants to get telephone and internet records by going directly to the phone companies and asking for the records. The government and the companies, among other methods of surveillance, set up secret rooms where phone and internet traffic could be monitored. In 2008, the government granted the companies amnesty for violating the privacy rights of their customers. Customers sued anyway. But the Obama administration successfully argued to the district court, among other defenses, that disclosure would expose state secrets and should be dismissed. The case is now on appeal.

14. Material support. The Obama administration successfully asked the US Supreme Court not to apply the First Amendment and to allow the government to criminalize humanitarian aid and legal activities of people providing advice or support to foreign organizations which are listed by the government as terrorist organizations. The material support law can now be read to penalize people who provide humanitarian aid or human rights advocacy. The Obama administration Solicitor General argued to the court "when you help Hezbollah build homes, you are also helping Hezbollah build bombs." The Court agreed with the Obama argument that national security trumps free speech in these circumstances.

15. Chicago anti-war grand jury investigation. In September 2010, FBI agents raided the homes of seven peace activists in Chicago, Minneapolis and Grand Rapids seizing computers, cell phones, passports, and records. More than 20 anti-war activists were issued federal grand jury subpoenas and more were questioned across the country. Some of those targeted were members of local labor unions, others members of organizations like the Arab American Action Network, the Colombia Action Network, the Twin Cities Anti-War Campaign and the Freedom Road Socialist Organization. Many were active internationally and visited resistance groups in Colombia and Palestine. Subpoenas directed people to bring anything related to trips to Colombia, Palestine, Jordan, Syria, Israel or the Middle East. In 2011, the home of a Los Angeles activist was raided and he was questioned about his connections with the September 2010 activists. All of these investigations are directed by the Obama administration.

16. Punishing whistleblowers. The Obama administration has prosecuted five whistleblowers under the Espionage Act, more than all the other administrations in history put together. They charged a National Security Agency advisor with ten felonies under the Espionage Act for telling the press that government eavesdroppers were wasting hundreds of millions of dollars on

misguided and failed projects. After their case collapsed, the government, which was chastised by the federal judge as engaging in unconscionable conduct allowed him to plead to a misdemeanor and walk. The administration has also prosecuted former members of the CIA, the State Department, and the FBI. They even tried to subpoena a journalist and one of the lawyers for the whistleblowers.

17. Bradley Manning. Army private Bradley Manning is accused of leaking thousands of government documents to WikiLeaks. These documents expose untold numbers of lies by US government officials, wrongful killings of civilians, policies to ignore torture in Iraq, information about who is held at Guantanamo, cover ups of drone strikes and abuse of children and much more damaging information about US malfeasance. Though Daniel Ellsberg and other whistleblowers say Bradley is an American hero, the US government has jailed him and is threatening him with charges of espionage which may be punished by the death penalty. For months Manning was held in solitary confinement and forced by guards to sleep naked. When asked about how Manning was being held, President Obama personally defended the conditions of his confinement saying he had been assured they were appropriate and meeting our basic standards.

19. Solitary confinement. At least 20,000 people are in solitary confinement in US jails and prisons, some estimate several times that many. Despite the fact that federal, state and local prisons and jails do not report actual numbers, academic research estimates tens of thousands are kept in cells for twenty three to twenty four hours a day in supermax units and prisons, in lockdown, in security housing units, in "the hole," and in special management units or administrative segregation. Human Rights Watch reports that one-third to one-half of the prisoners in solitary are likely mentally ill. In May 2006, the UN Committee on Torture concluded that the United States should "review the regimen imposed on detainees in supermax prisons, in particular, the practice of prolonged isolation." The Obama administration has taken no steps to cut back on the use of solitary confinement in federal, state or local jails and prisons.

20. Special administrative measures. Special Administrative Measures (SAMS) are extra harsh conditions of confinement imposed on prisoners (including pre-trial detainees) by the Attorney General. The US Bureau of Prisons imposes restrictions such as segregation and isolation from all other prisoners, and limitation or denial of contact with the outside world such as: no visitors except attorneys, no contact with news media, no use of phone, no correspondence, no contact with family, no communication with guards and twenty four hour video surveillance and monitoring. The DoJ admitted in 2009 that several dozen prisoners, including several pre-trial detainees, mostly Muslims, were kept incommunicado under SAMS. If anything, the use of SAMS has increased under the Obama administration.

These twenty concrete examples document a sustained assault on domestic civil liberties in the United States under the Obama administration. Rhetoric aside, how different has Obama been from Bush in this area?

Bill Quigley is a human rights lawyer and law professor at Loyola University New Orleans. He also serves as Associate Legal Director of the Center for Constitutional Rights.

The Top Ten Myths in the War Against Libya

By MAXIMILIAN C. FORTE

Since Colonel Qaddafi has lost his military hold in the war against NATO and the insurgents/rebels/new regime, numerous talking heads have taken to celebrating this war as a "success." They believe this is a "victory of the Libyan people" and that we should all be celebrating. Others proclaim victory for the "responsibility to protect," for "humanitarian interventionism," and condemn the "anti-imperialist left." Some of those who claim to be "revolutionaries," or believe they support the "Arab revolution," somehow find it possible to sideline NATO's role in the war, instead extolling the democratic virtues of the insurgents, glorifying their martyrdom, and magnifying their role until everything else is pushed from view.

I wish to dissent from this circle of acclamation, and remind readers of the role of ideologically-motivated fabrications of "truth" that were used to justify, enable, enhance and motivate the war against Libya—and to emphasize how damaging the practical effects of those myths have been to Libyans, and to all those who favored peaceful, non-militarist solutions.

These top ten myths are some of the most repeated claims, by the insurgents, and/or by NATO, European leaders, the Obama administration, the mainstream media, and even the so-called "International Criminal Court"—the main actors speaking in the war against Libya. In turn, we look at some of the reasons why these claims are better seen as imperial folklore, as the myths that supported the broadest of all myths that this war is a "humanitarian intervention," one designed to "protect civilians." Again, the importance of these myths lies in their wide reproduction, with little question, and to deadly effect. In addition, they threaten to severely distort the ideals of human rights and their future invocation, as well aiding in the continued militarization of Western culture and society.

1. Genocide.

Just a few days after the street protests began, on February 21, the very quick to defect Libyan deputy permanent representative to the UN, Ibrahim Dabbashi, stated: "We are expecting a real genocide in Tripoli. The airplanes are still bringing mercenaries to the airports." This is excellent: a myth that is composed of myths. With that statement he linked three key myths together—the role of *airports* (hence the need for that gateway drug of military intervention: the no-fly zone), the role of "*mercenaries*" (meaning, simply, black people), and the threat of "*genocide*" (geared toward the language of the UN's doctrine of the Responsibility to Protect).

As ham-fisted and wholly unsubstantiated as the assertion was, he was clever in cobbling together three ugly myths, one of them grounded in racist discourse and practice that endures to the present, with newer atrocities reported against black Libyan and African migrants on a daily basis. He was not alone in making these assertions. Among others like him, Soliman Bouchuiguir, president of the Libyan League for Human Rights, told Reuters on March 14 that if Qaddafi's forces reached Benghazi, "there will be a real bloodbath, a massacre like we saw in Rwanda." That's not the only time we would be deliberately reminded of Rwanda. Here was Lt. Gen Roméo Dallaire, the much-worshipped Canadian force commander of the UN peacekeeping mission for Rwanda in 1994, currently an appointed senator in the Canadian Parliament and co-director of the Will to Intervene project at Concordia University. Dallaire, in a precipitous sprint to judgment, not only made repeated references to Rwanda when trying to explain Libya, he spoke of Qaddafi as "employing genocidal threats to 'cleanse Libya house by house.'" This is one instance where selective attention to Qaddafi's rhetorical excess was taken all too seriously, when on other occasions the powers that be are instead quick to dismiss it: US State Department spokesman, Mark Toner waved away Qaddafi's alleged threats against Europe by saying that Qaddafi is "someone who's given to overblown rhetoric."

How very calm, by contrast, and how very convenient—because on February 23, President Obama declared that he had instructed his administration to come up with a "full range of options" to take against Qaddafi.

But "genocide" has a well established international legal definition, as seen repeatedly in the UN's 1948 Convention on the Prevention and Punishment of the Crime of Genocide, where genocide involves the persecution of "a national, ethnical, racial or religious group." Not all violence is "genocidal." Internecine violence is not genocide. Genocide is neither just "lots of violence" nor violence against undifferentiated civilians. What both Dabbashi, Dallaire and others failed to do was to identify the persecuted national, ethnic, racial or religious group, and how it differed in those terms from those allegedly committing the genocide. *They really ought to know better* (and they do), one as a UN ambassador and the other as a much exalted expert and lecturer on genocide. This suggests that myth-making was either deliberate, or founded on prejudice.

What foreign military intervention did do, however, was to enable the actual genocidal violence that has been routinely sidelined until only very recently: the horrific violence against African migrants and black Libyans, singled out solely on the basis of their skin color. That has proceeded without impediment, without apology, and until recently, without much notice. Indeed, the media even collaborates, rapid to assert without evidence that any captured or dead black man must be a "mercenary." This is the genocide that the white, Western world, and those who dominate the "conversation" about Libya, have missed (and not by accident).

2. Qaddafi is "bombing his own people."

We must remember that one of the initial reasons in rushing to impose a no-fly zone was to prevent Qaddafi from using his air force to bomb "his own people"—a distinct phrasing that echoes what was tried and tested in the demonization of Saddam Hussein in Iraq. On February 21, when the first alarmist "warnings" about "genocide" were being made by the Libyan opposition, both Al Jazeera and the BBC claimed that Qaddafi had deployed his air force against protesters—as the BBC reported: "Witnesses say warplanes have fired on protesters in the city." Yet, on March 1, in a Pentagon press conference, when asked: "Do you see any evidence that he [Qaddafi] actually has fired on his own people from the air? There were reports of it, but do you have independent confirmation? If so, to what extent?" US Secretary of Defense Robert Gates replied, "We've seen the press reports, but we have no confirmation of that." Backing him up was Admiral Mullen: "That's correct. We've seen no confirmation whatsoever."

In fact, claims that Qaddafi also used helicopters against unarmed protesters are totally unfounded, a pure fabrication based on fake claims. This is important since it was Qaddafi's domination of Libyan air space that foreign interventionists wanted to nullify, and therefore myths of atrocities perpetrated from the air took on added value as providing an entry point for foreign military intervention that went far beyond any mandate to "protect civilians."

David Kirpatrick of the *New York Times*, as early as March 21 confirmed that, "the rebels feel no loyalty to the truth in shaping their propaganda, claiming nonexistent battlefield victories, asserting they were still fighting in a key city days after it fell to Qaddafi forces, and making vastly inflated claims of his barbaric behavior." The "vastly inflated claims" are what became part of the imperial folklore surrounding events in Libya, that suited Western intervention. Rarely did the Benghazi-based journalistic crowd question or contradict their hosts.

3. Save Benghazi.

This is being written as the Libyan opposition forces march on Sirte and Sabha, the two last remaining strongholds of the Qaddafi government, with ominous warnings to the population that they must surrender, or else. Apparently, Benghazi became somewhat of a "holy city" in the international discourse dominated by leaders of the European Union and NATO. Benghazi was the one city on earth that could not be touched. It was like sacred ground. *Tripoli? Sirte? Sabha?* Those can be sacrificed, as we all look on, without a hint of protest from any of the powers that be—this, even as we get the first reports of how the opposition has slaughtered people in Tripoli. Let's turn to the Benghazi myth.

"If we waited one more day," Barack Obama said in his March 28 address, "Benghazi, a city nearly the size of Charlotte, could suffer a massacre that would have reverberated across the region and stained the conscience of the world." In a joint letter, Obama with UK Prime Minister David Cameron and French President Nicolas Sarkozy asserted: "By responding immediately, our countries halted the advance of Qaddafi's forces. The bloodbath that he had promised to inflict on the citizens of the besieged city of Benghazi has been prevented. Tens of thousands of lives have been protected." Not only did French jets bomb a retreating column, what we saw was a very short column that included trucks and ambulances, and that clearly could have neither destroyed nor occupied Benghazi.

Other than Qaddafi's "overblown rhetoric," which the US was quick to dismiss when it suited its purposes, there is to date still no evidence furnished that shows Benghazi would have witnessed the loss of "tens of thousands" of lives as proclaimed by Obama, Cameron and Sarkozy. This was best explained by Professor Alan J. Kuperman in "False pretense for war in Libya?":

> The best evidence that Khadafy did not plan genocide in Benghazi is that he did not perpetrate it in the other cities he had recaptured either fully or partially—including Zawiya, Misurata, and Ajdabiya, which together have a population greater than Benghazi.... Khadafy's acts were a far cry from Rwanda, Darfur, Congo, Bosnia, and other killing fields.... Despite ubiquitous cellphones equipped with cameras and video, there is no graphic evidence of deliberate massacre.... Nor did Khadafy ever threaten civilian massacre in Benghazi, as Obama alleged. The 'no mercy' warning, of March 17, targeted rebels only, as reported by the *New York Times*, which noted that Libya's leader promised amnesty for those 'who throw their weapons away'. Khadafy even offered the rebels an escape route and open border to Egypt, to avoid a fight 'to the bitter end'.

In a bitter irony, what evidence there is of massacres, committed by both sides, is now to be found in Tripoli in recent days, months after NATO imposed its "life-saving" military measures. Revenge killings are daily being reported with greater frequency, including the wholesale slaughter of black Libyans and African migrants by rebel forces. Another sad irony: in Benghazi, which the insurgents have held for months now, well after Qaddafi forces were repulsed, not even that has prevented violence: revenge killings have been reported there too—more under #6 below.

4. African Mercenaries.

Patrick Cockburn summarized the functional utility of the myth of the "African mercenary" and the context in which it arose: "Since February, the insurgents, often supported by foreign powers, claimed that the battle was between Qaddafi and his family on the one side and the Libyan people on the other. Their explanation for the large pro-Qaddafi forces was that they were all mercenaries, mostly from black Africa, whose only motive was money." As he notes, black prisoners were put on display for the media (which is a violation of the Geneva Convention), but Amnesty International later found that all the prisoners had supposedly been released since none of them were fighters, but rather were undocumented workers from Mali, Chad and west Africa. The myth was useful for the opposition to insist that this was a war between "Qaddafi and the Libyan people," as if he had no domestic support at all—an absolute and colossal fabrication such that one would think only little children could believe a story so fantastic. The myth is also useful for cementing the intended rupture between "the new Libya" and Pan-Africanism, realigning Libya with Europe and the "modern world" which some of the opposition so explicitly crave.

The "African mercenary" myth, as put into deadly, racist practice, is a fact that paradoxically has been both documented and ignored. Months ago I provided an extensive review of the role of the mainstream media, led by Al Jazeera, as well as the seeding of social media, in creating the African mercenary myth. Among the departures from the norm of vilifying Sub-Saharan Africans and black Libyans that instead documented the abuse of these civilians, were the *Los Angeles Times* and Human Rights Watch—which found no evidence of any mercenaries at all in eastern Libya (totally contradicting the claims presented as truth by *Al Arabiya* and *The Telegraph*, among others such as *Time* and *The Guardian*). In an extremely rare departure from the propaganda about the black mercenary threat that Al Jazeera and its journalists helped to actively disseminate, Al Jazeera produced a single report focusing on the robbing, killing and abduction of black residents in eastern Libya (now that CBS, Channel 4, and others are noting the racism, Al Jazeera is trying to ambiguously show some interest). Finally, there is some increased recognition of these facts of media collaboration in the racist vilification of the insurgents' civilian victims—see FAIR: "*NYT* Points Out 'Racist Overtones' in Libyan Disinformation It Helped Spread".

The racist targeting and killing of black Libyans and Sub-Saharan Africans continues to the present. Patrick Cockburn and Kim Sengupta speak of the recently discovered mass of "rotting bodies of 30 men, almost all black and many handcuffed, slaughtered as they lay on stretchers and even in an ambulance in central Tripoli." Even while showing us video of hundreds of bodies in the Abu Salim hospital, the BBC dares not remark on the fact that most of those are clearly black people, and even wonders about who might have killed them. This is not a question for the anti-Qaddafi forces interviewed by Sengupta: "'Come and see. These are blacks, Africans, hired by Qaddafi, mercenaries,' shouted Ahmed Bin Sabri, lifting the tent flap to show the body of one dead patient, his grey T-shirt stained dark red with blood, the saline pipe running into his arm black with flies.

Why had an injured man receiving treatment been executed?" Recent reports reveal the insurgents engaging in ethnic cleansing against black Libyans in Tawergha, the insurgents calling themselves "the brigade for purging slaves, black skin," vowing that in the "new Libya" black people from Tawergha would be barred from health care and schooling in nearby Misrata, from which black Libyans had already been expelled by the insurgents. Currently, Human Rights Watch has reported: "Dark-skinned Libyans and sub-Saharan Africans face particular risks because rebel forces and other armed groups have often considered them pro-Gadhafi mercenaries from other African countries. We've seen violent attacks and killings of these people in areas where the National Transitional Council took control." Amnesty International has also just reported on the disproportionate detention of black Africans in rebel-controlled Az-Zawiya, as well as the targeting of unarmed, migrant farm workers. Reports continue to mount as this is being written, with other human rights groups finding evidence of the insurgents targeting Sub-Saharan African migrant workers. As the chair of the African Union, Jean Ping, recently stated: "NTC seems to confuse black people with mercenaries. All blacks are mercenaries. If you do that, it means (that the) one-third of the population of Libya, which is black, is also mercenaries. They are killing people, normal workers, mistreating them."

The "African mercenary" myth continues to be one of the most vicious of all the myths, and the most racist. Even in recent days, newspapers such as the *Boston Globe* uncritically and unquestioningly show photographs of black victims or black detainees with the immediate assertion that they must be mercenaries, despite the absence of any evidence. Instead we are usually provided with casual assertions that Qaddafi is "known to have" recruited Africans from other nations in the past, without even bothering to find out if those shown in the photos are black *Libyans*.

The lynching of both black Libyans and Sub-Saharan African migrant workers has been continuous, and has neither received any expression of even nominal concern by the US and NATO members, nor has it aroused the interest of the so-called "International Criminal Court." There is as little chance of there being any justice for the victims as there is of anyone putting a stop to these heinous crimes that clearly constitute a case of ethnic cleansing. The media, only now, is becoming more conscious of the need to cover these crimes, having glossed them over for months.

5. Viagra-fueled Mass Rape.

The reported crimes and human rights violations of the Qaddafi regime are awful enough as they are that one has to wonder why anyone would need to invent stories, such as that of Qaddafi's troops, with erections powered by

Viagra, going on a rape spree. Perhaps it was peddled because it's the kind of story that "captures the imagination of traumatized publics." This story was taken so seriously that some people started writing to Pfizer to get it to stop selling Viagra to Libya, since its product was allegedly being used as a weapon of war. People who otherwise should know better, set out to deliberately misinform the international public.

The Viagra story was first disseminated by Al Jazeera, in collaboration with its rebel partners, favoured by the Qatari regime that funds Al Jazeera. It was then redistributed by almost all other major Western news media.

Luis Moreno-Ocampo, Chief Prosecutor of the International Criminal Court, appeared before the world media to say that there was "evidence" that Qaddafi distributed Viagra to his troops in order "to enhance the possibility to rape" and that Qaddafi ordered the rape of hundreds of women. Moreno-Ocampo insisted: "We are getting information that Qaddafi himself decided to rape" and that "we have information that there was a policy to rape in Libya those who were against the government." He also exclaimed that Viagra is "like a machete," and that "Viagra is a tool of massive rape."

In a startling declaration to the UN Security Council, US Ambassador Susan Rice also asserted that Qaddafi was supplying his troops with Viagra to encourage mass rape. She offered no evidence whatsoever to back up her claim. Indeed, US military and intelligence sources flatly contradicted Rice, telling NBC News that "there is no evidence that Libyan military forces are being given Viagra and engaging in systematic rape against women in rebel areas." Rice is a liberal interventionist who was one of those to persuade Obama to intervene in Libya. She utilized this myth because it helped her make the case at the UN that there was no "moral equivalence" between Qaddafi's human rights abuses and those of the insurgents.

US Secretary of State Hillary Clinton also declared that "Gadhafi's security forces and other groups in the region are trying to divide the people by using violence against women and rape as tools of war, and the United States condemns this in the strongest possible terms." She added that she was "deeply concerned" by these reports of "wide-scale rape." (She has, thus far, said nothing at all about the rebels' racist lynchings.)

By June 10, Cherif Bassiouni, who is leading a UN rights inquiry into the situation in Libya, suggested that the Viagra and mass rape claim was part of a "massive hysteria." Indeed, both sides in the war have made the same allegations against each other. Bassiouni also told the press of a case of "a woman who claimed to have sent out 70,000 questionnaires and received 60,000 responses, of which 259 reported sexual abuse."

However, his teams asked for those questionnaires, they never received them—"But she's going around the world telling everybody about it ... so now she got that information to Ocampo and Ocampo is convinced that here we have a potential 259 women who have responded to the fact that they have been sexually abused," Bassiouni said. He also pointed out that it "did not appear to be credible that the woman was able to send out 70,000 questionnaires in March when the postal service was not functioning." In fact, Bassiouni's team "uncovered only four alleged cases" of rape and sexual abuse: "Can we draw a conclusion that there is a systematic policy of rape? In my opinion we can't." In addition to the UN, Amnesty International's Donatella Rovera said in an interview with the French daily *Libération*, that Amnesty had "not found cases of rape.... Not only have we not met any victims, but we have not even met any persons who have met victims. As for the boxes of Viagra that Qaddafi is supposed to have had distributed, they were found intact near tanks that were completely burnt out."

However, this did not stop some news manufacturers from trying to maintain the rape claims, in modified form. The BBC went on to add another layer just a few days after Bassiouni humiliated the ICC and the media: the BBC now claimed that rape victims in Libya faced "honour killings." This is news to the few Libyans I know, who never heard of honor killings in their country. The scholarly literature on Libya turns up little or nothing on this phenomenon in Libya. The honor killings myth serves a useful purpose for keeping the mass rape claim on life support: it suggests that women would not come forward and give evidence, out of shame.

Also just a few days after Bassiouni spoke, Libyan insurgents, in collaboration with CNN, made a last-ditch effort to save the rape allegations: they presented a cell phone with a rape video on it, claiming it belonged to a government soldier. The men shown in the video are in civilian clothes. There is no evidence of Viagra. There is no date on the video and we have no idea who recorded it or where. Those presenting the cell phone claimed that many other videos existed, but they were conveniently being destroyed to preserve the "honor" of the victims.

6. Responsibility to Protect (R2P).

Having asserted, wrongly as we saw, that Libya faced impending "genocide" at the hands of Qaddafi's forces, it became easier for Western powers to invoke the UN's 2005 doctrine of the Responsibility to Protect. Meanwhile, it is not at all clear that by the time the UN Security Council passed Resolution 1973 that the violence in Libya had even reached the levels seen in Egypt, Syria and Yemen. The most common refrain used against critics of the selectivity of this supposed "humanitarian interventionism" is that just because the West cannot intervene *everywhere* does not mean it should not intervene in Libya. Maybe ... but that still does not explain why Libya was the chosen target. This is a critical point because some of the earliest critiques of R2P voiced at the UN raised the issue of selectivity, of who gets to decide, and why some crises where civilians are targeted (say, Gaza) are essentially ignored, while others receive maximum concern, and whether R2P served as the new fig leaf for hegemonic geopolitics.

The myth at work here is that foreign military intervention was guided by humanitarian concerns. To make the myth work, one has to willfully ignore at least three key realities. One thus has to ignore the new scramble for Africa, where Chinese interests are seen as competing with the West for access to resources and political influence, something that AFRICOM is meant to challenge. Qaddafi challenged AFRICOM's intent to establish military bases in Africa.

AFRICOM has since become directly involved in the Libya intervention and specifically "Operation Odyssey Dawn." Horace Campbell argued that "U.S. involvement in the Libyan bombing is being turned into a public relations ploy for AFRICOM" and an "opportunity to give AFRICOM credibility under the facade of the Libyan intervention." In addition, Qaddafi's power and influence on the continent had also been increasing, through aid, investment, and a range of projects designed to lessen African dependency on the West and to challenge Western multilateral institutions by building African unity—rendering him a rival to US interests. Secondly, one has to ignore not just the anxiety of Western oil interests over Qaddafi's "resource nationalism" (threatening to take back what oil companies had gained), an anxiety now clearly manifest in the European corporate rush into Libya to scoop up the spoils of victory—but one has to also ignore the apprehension over what Qaddafi was doing with those oil revenues in supporting greater African economic independence, and for historically backing national liberation movements that challenged Western hegemony. Thirdly, one has to also ignore the fear in Washington that the US was losing a grip on the course of the so-called "Arab revolution." How one can stack up these realities, and match them against ambiguous and partial "humanitarian" concerns, and then conclude that, *yes, human rights is what mattered most*, seems entirely implausible and unconvincing—especially with the atrocious track record of NATO and US human rights violations in Afghanistan, Iraq, and before that Kosovo and Serbia. The humanitarian angle is simply neither credible nor even minimally logical.

If R2P is seen as founded on moral hypocrisy and contradiction—now definitively revealed—it will become much harder in the future to cry wolf again and expect to get a respectful hearing. This is especially the case since little in the way of diplomacy and peaceful negotiation preceded the military intervention—while Obama is accused by some of having been slow to react, this was if anything a rush to war, on a pace that dramatically surpassed Bush's invasion of Iraq. Not only do we know from the African Union about how its efforts to establish a peaceful transition were impeded, but Dennis Kucinich also reveals that he received reports that a peaceful settlement was at hand, only to be "scuttled by State Department officials." These are absolutely critical violations of the R2P doctrine, showing how those ideals could instead be used for a practice that involved a hasty march to war, and war aimed at regime change (which is itself a violation of international law).

That R2P served as a justifying myth that often achieved the opposite of its stated aims, is no longer a surprise. I am not even speaking here of the role of Qatar and the United Arab Emirates in bombing Libya and aiding the insurgents—even as they backed Saudi military intervention to crush the pro-democracy protests in Bahrain, nor of the ugly pall cast on an intervention led by the likes of unchallenged abusers of human rights who have committed war crimes with impunity in Kosovo, Iraq and Afghanistan. I am taking a narrower approach—such as the documented cases where NATO not only willfully failed to protect civilians in Libya, but it even deliberately and knowingly targeted them in a manner that constitutes terrorism by most official definitions used by Western governments.

NATO admitted to deliberately targeting Libya's state television, killing three civilian reporters, in a move condemned by international journalist federations as a direct violation of a 2006 Security Council resolution banning attacks on journalists. A US Apache helicopter—in a repeat of the infamous killings shown in the Collateral Murder video—gunned down civilians in the central square of Zawiya, killing the brother of the information minister among others. Taking a fairly liberal notion of what constitutes "command and control facilities," NATO targeted a civilian residential space resulting in the deaths of some of Qaddafi's family members, including three grandchildren. As if to protect the myth of "protecting civilians" and the unconscionable contradiction of a "war for human rights," the major news media often kept silent about civilian deaths caused by NATO bombardments. R2P has been invisible when it comes to civilians targeted by NATO.

In terms of the failure to protect civilians, in a manner that is actually an international criminal offense, we have the numerous reports of NATO ships ignoring the distress calls of refugee boats in the Mediterranean that were fleeing Libya. In May, 61 African refugees died on a single vessel, despite making contact with vessels belonging to NATO member states. In a repeat of the situation, dozens died in early August on another vessel. In fact, on NATO's watch, at least 1,500 refugees fleeing Libya have died at sea since the war began. They were mostly Sub-Saharan Africans, and they died in multiples of the death toll suffered by Benghazi during the protests. R2P was utterly absent for these people.

NATO has developed a peculiar terminological twist for Libya, designed to absolve the rebels of any role in perpetrating crimes against civilians, and abdicating its so-called responsibility to protect. Throughout the war, spokespersons for NATO and for the US and European governments consistently portrayed all of the actions of Qaddafi's forces as "threatening civilians," even when engaged in either defensive actions, or combat against armed opponents. For example, this week the NATO spokesperson, Roland

Lavoie, "appeared to struggle to explain how NATO strikes were protecting civilians at this stage in the conflict. Asked about NATO's assertion that it hit twenty two armed vehicles near Sirte on Monday, he was unable to say how the vehicles were threatening civilians, or whether they were in motion or parked."

By protecting the rebels, in the same breath as they spoke of protecting civilians, it is clear that NATO intended for us to see Qaddafi's armed opponents as mere civilians. Interestingly, in Afghanistan, where NATO and the US fund, train and arm the Karzai regime in attacking "his own people" (like they do in Pakistan), the armed opponents are consistently labeled "terrorists" or "insurgents"—even if the majority of them are civilians who have never served in any official standing army. They are insurgents in Afghanistan, and their deaths at the hands of NATO are listed separately from the tallies for civilian casualties. By some magic, in Libya, they are all "civilians." In response to the announcement of the UN Security Council voting for military intervention, a volunteer translator for Western reporters in Tripoli made this key observation: "Civilians holding guns, and you want to protect them? It's a joke. We are the civilians. What about us?"

NATO has provided a shield for the insurgents in Libya to victimize unarmed civilians in areas they came to occupy. There was no hint of any "responsibility to protect" in these cases. NATO assisted the rebels in starving Tripoli of supplies, subjecting its civilian population to a siege that deprived them of water, food, medicine, and fuel. When Qaddafi was accused of doing this to Misrata, the international media were quick to cite this as a war crime. Save Misrata, kill Tripoli—whatever you want to label such "logic," *humanitarian* is not an acceptable option. Leaving aside the documented crimes by the insurgents against black Libyans and African migrant workers, the insurgents were also found by Human Rights Watch to have engaged in "looting, arson, and abuse of civilians in [four] recently captured towns in western Libya." In Benghazi, which the insurgents have held for months now, revenge killings have been reported by the *New York Times* as late as this May, and by Amnesty International in late June and faulted the insurgents' National Transitional Council. The responsibility to protect? It now sounds like something deserving wild mockery.

7. Qaddafi—the Demon.

Depending on your perspective, either Qaddafi is a heroic revolutionary, and thus the demonization by the West is extreme, or Qaddafi is a really bad man, in which case the demonization is unnecessary and absurd. The myth here is that the history of Qaddafi's power was marked only by atrocity—he is thoroughly evil, without any redeeming qualities, and anyone accused of being a "Qaddafi supporter" should somehow feel more ashamed than those who openly support NATO.

This is binary absolutism at its worst—virtually no one made allowance for the possibility that some might neither support Qaddafi, the insurgents, nor NATO. Everyone was to be forced into one of those camps, no exceptions allowed. What resulted was a phony debate, dominated by fanatics of one side or another. Missed in the discussion, recognition of the obvious: however much Qaddafi had been "in bed" with the West over the past decade, his forces were now fighting against a NATO-driven takeover of his country.

The other result was the impoverishment of historical consciousness, and the degradation of more complex appreciations of the full breadth of the Qaddafi record. This would help explain why some would not rush to condemn and disown the man (without having to resort to crude and infantile caricaturing of their motivations).

While even Glenn Greenwald feels the need to dutifully insert, "No decent human being would possibly harbor any sympathy for Gadaffi," I have known decent human beings in Nicaragua, Trinidad, Dominica and among the Mohawks in Montreal who very much appreciate Qaddafi's support—not to mention his support for various national liberation movements, including the struggle against apartheid in South Africa. Qaddafi's regime has many faces: some are seen by his domestic opponents, others are seen by recipients of his aid, and others were smiled at by the likes of Silvio Berlusconi, Nicolas Sarkozy, Condoleeza Rice, Hillary Clinton and Barack Obama. There are many faces, and they are all simultaneously *real*. Some refuse to "disown" Qaddafi, to "apologize" for his friendship towards them, no matter how distasteful, indecent and embarrassing other "progressives" may find him. That needs to be respected, instead of this now fashionable bullying and gang banging that reduces a range of positions to one juvenile accusation: "you support a dictator." Ironically, we support many dictators, with our very own tax dollars, and we routinely offer no apologies for this fact.

Speaking of the breadth of Qaddafi's record, that ought to resist simplistic, revisionist reduction, some might care to note that *even now*, the US State Department's webpage on Libya still points to a Library of Congress Country Study on Libya that features some of the Qaddafi government's many social welfare achievements over the years in the areas of medical care, public housing, and education. In addition, Libyans have the highest literacy rate in Africa and Libya is the only continental African nation to rank "high" in the UNDP's Human Development Index. Even the BBC recognized these achievements:

> Women in Libya are free to work and to dress as they like, subject to family constraints. Life expectancy is in the seventies. And per capita income—while not as high as could be expected given Libya's

oil wealth and relatively small population of 6.5m—is estimated at $12,000 (£9,000), according to the World Bank. Illiteracy has been almost wiped out, as has homelessness—a chronic problem in the pre-Qaddafi era, where corrugated iron shacks dotted many urban centres around the country.

So if one supports health care, does that mean one supports dictatorship? And if "the dictator" funds public housing and subsidizes incomes, do we simply erase those facts from our memory?

8. Freedom Fighters—the Angels.

The complement to the demonization of Qaddafi was the angelization of the "rebels." My aim here is not to counter the myth by way of inversion, and demonizing all of Qaddafi's opponents, who have many serious and legitimate grievances, and in large numbers have clearly had more than they can bear. I am instead interested in how "we," in the North Atlantic part of the equation, construct *them* in ways that suit *our* intervention.

One standard way, repeated in different ways across a range of media and by US government spokespersons, can be seen in this *New York Times* depiction of the rebels as "secular-minded professionals—lawyers, academics, businesspeople—who talk about democracy, transparency, human rights and the rule of law." The listing of professions familiar to the American middle class which respects them, is meant to inspire a shared sense of identification between readers and the Libyan opposition, especially when we recall that it is on the Qaddafi side where the forces of darkness dwell: the main "professions" we find are torturer, terrorist, and African mercenary.

For many weeks it was almost impossible to get reporters embedded with the rebel National Transitional Council in Benghazi to even begin to provide a description of who constituted the anti-Qaddafi movement, if it was one organization or many groups, what their agendas were, and so forth. The subtle leitmotif in the reports was one that cast the rebellion as entirely spontaneous and indigenous—which may be true, in part, and it may also be an oversimplification. Among the reports that significantly complicated the picture were those that discussed the CIA ties to the insurgents; others highlighted the role of the National Endowment for Democracy, the International Republican Institute, the National Democratic Institute, and USAID, which have been active in Libya since 2005; those that detailed the role of various expatriate groups; and, reports of the active role of "radical Islamist" militias embedded within the overall insurgency, with some pointing to Al Qaeda connections.

Some feel a definite need for being on the side of "the good guys," especially as neither Iraq nor Afghanistan offer any such sense of righteous vindication. Americans want the world to see them as doing good, as being not only indispensable, but also irreproachable. They could wish for nothing better than being seen as atoning for their sins in Iraq and Afghanistan. This is a special moment, where the bad guy can safely be the other once again. A world that is safe for America is a world that is unsafe for evil. Marching band, baton twirlers, Anderson Cooper and confetti—we get it.

9. Victory for the Libyan People.

To say that the current turn in Libya represents a victory by the Libyan people in charting their own destiny is, at best, an oversimplification that masks the range of interests involved since the beginning in shaping and determining the course of events on the ground, and that ignores the fact that for much of the war Qaddafi was able to rely on a solid base of popular support. As early as February 25, a mere week after the start of the first street protests, Nicolas Sarkozy had already determined that Qaddafi "must go." By February 28, David Cameron began working on a proposal for a no-fly zone—these statements and decisions were made without any attempt at dialogue and diplomacy. By March 30, the *New York Times* reported that for "several weeks" CIA operatives had been working inside Libya, which would mean they were there from mid-February, that is, when the protests began—they were then joined inside Libya by "dozens of British special forces and MI6 intelligence officers."

The *NYT* also reported in the same article that "several weeks" before (again, around mid-February), President Obama "signed a secret finding authorizing the CIA to provide arms and other support to Libyan rebels," with that "other support" entailing a range of possible "covert actions." USAID had already deployed a team to Libya by early March. At the end of March, Obama publicly stated that the objective was to depose Qaddafi. In terribly suspicious wording, "a senior U.S. official said the administration had hoped that the Libyan uprising would evolve 'organically,' like those in Tunisia and Egypt, without need for foreign intervention"—which sounds like exactly the kind of statement one makes when something begins in a fashion that is not "organic" and when comparing events in Libya as marked by a potential legitimacy deficit when compared to those of Tunisia and Egypt. Yet on March 14 the NTC's Abdel Hafeez Goga asserted, "We are capable of controlling all of Libya, but only after the no-fly zone is imposed"—which is still not the case even six months later.

In recent days it has also been revealed that what the rebel leadership swore it would oppose—"foreign boots on the ground"—is in fact a reality confirmed by NATO: "Special forces troops from Britain, France, Jordan and Qatar on the ground in Libya have stepped up operations in Tripoli and other cities in recent days to help rebel forces as they conducted their final advance on the Gadhafi regime." This, and other summaries, are only scratching the surface of the range of external support provided to the rebels. The myth here is that of the nationalist, self-sufficient rebel, fueled entirely by popular support.

At the moment, war supporters are proclaiming the intervention a "success." It should be noted that there was another case where an air campaign, deployed to support local armed militia on the ground, aided by US covert military operatives, also succeeded in deposing another regime and even much more quickly. That case was Afghanistan. Success.

10. Defeat for "the Left."

As if reenacting the pattern of articles condemning "the left" that came out in the wake of the Iran election protests in 2009 (see as examples Hamid Dabashi and Slavoj Žižek), the war in Libya once again seemed to have presented an opportunity to target the left, as if this was topmost on the agenda—as if "the left" was *the* problem to be addressed. Here we see articles, in various states of intellectual and political disrepair, by Juan Cole (see some of the rebuttals: "The case of Professor Juan Cole," "An open letter to Professor Juan Cole: A reply to a slander," "Professor Cole 'answers' WSWS on Libya: An admission of intellectual and political bankruptcy"), Gilbert Achcar (and this especially), Immanuel Wallerstein, and Helena Sheehan who seemingly arrived at some of her most critical conclusions at the airport at the end of her very first visit to Tripoli.

There seems to be some confusion over roles and identities. There is no homogeneous left, nor ideological agreement among anti-imperialists (which includes conservatives and libertarians, among anarchists and Marxists). Nor was the "anti-imperialist left" in any position to either do real harm on the ground, as is the case of the *actual protagonists*. There was little chance of the anti-interventionists in influencing foreign policy, which took shape in Washington before any of the serious critiques against intervention were published. These points suggest that at least some of the critiques are moved by concerns that go beyond Libya, and that even have very little to do with Libya ultimately. The most common accusation is that the anti-imperialist left is somehow coddling a dictator. The argument is that this is based on a flawed analysis—in criticizing the position of Hugo Chávez, Wallerstein says Chávez's analysis is deeply flawed, and offers this among the criticisms: "The second point missed by Hugo Chavez's analysis is that there is not going to be any significant military involvement of the western world in Libya" (yes, read it again).

Indeed, many of the counterarguments deployed against the anti-interventionist left echo or wholly reproduce the top myths that were dismantled above, that get their geopolitical analysis almost entirely wrong, and that pursue politics focused in part on personality and events of the day. This also shows us the deep poverty of politics premised primarily on simplistic and one-sided ideas of "human rights" and "protection" (see Richard Falk's critique), and the success of the new military humanism in siphoning off the energies of the left. And a question persists: if those opposed to intervention were faulted for providing a moral shield for "dictatorship" (as if imperialism was not itself a global dictatorship), what about those humanitarians who have backed the rise of xenophobic and racist militants who by so many accounts engage in ethnic cleansing? Does it mean that the pro-interventionist crowd is racist? Do they even object to the racism? So far, I have heard only silence from those quarters.

The agenda in brow-beating the anti-imperialist straw man masks an effort to curb dissent against an unnecessary war that has prolonged and widened human suffering; advanced the cause of war corporatists, transnational firms and neoliberals; destroyed the legitimacy of multilateral institutions that were once openly committed to peace in international relations; violated international law and human rights; witnessed the rise of racist violence; empowered the imperial state to justify its continued expansion; violated domestic laws; and reduced the discourse of humanitarianism to a clutch of simplistic slogans, reactionary impulses and formulaic policies that privilege war as a first option. *Really, the left is the problem here?*

Maximilian Forte is an associate professor in the Department of Sociology and Anthropology at Concordia University in Montreal, Canada. His website can be found at http://openanthropology.org/ as can his previous articles on Libya and other facets of imperialism.

War and Debt

By MICHAEL HUDSON

To begin with the most obvious question: If governments run up their debt in the process of carrying out programs that Congress already approved, why would Congress have yet another option to stop the government from following through on these authorized expenditures, by refusing to raise the debt ceiling?

The answer is obvious when one looks at why this fail-safe check was introduced in almost every country of the world. Throughout modern history, war has been the major cause of a rising national debt. Most governments operate in fiscal balance during peacetime, financing their spending and investment by levying taxes and charging user fees. War emergencies push this balance into deficit—sometimes for defensive wars, sometimes for aggression.

In Europe, parliamentary checks on government spending were designed to prevent ambitious rulers from waging war. This was Adam Smith's great argument against public debts, and his urging that wars be financed on a pay-as-you-go basis. He wrote that if people felt the economic impact of war immediately—rather than postponing it by borrowing—they would be less likely to support military adventurism.

This obviously was not the Tea Party position, nor that of the Republicans. What is so remarkable about the August 2 debt ceiling crisis in the US is its seeming dissociation with war spending. To be sure, over a third ($350 billion) of the $917 billion cutback in current spending is assigned to the Pentagon. But that simply slows the remarkable escalation rate that has taken place from Iraq to Afghanistan to Libya.

What is even more remarkable is that last month, Democrat Dennis Kucinich and Republican Ron Paul sought to make President Obama obey the conditions of the War Powers Act and get Congressional approval for his war in Libya, as required when warfare goes on for more than three months. This attempt to apply the rule of law to the Imperial Presidency was unsuccessful. Obama claimed that bombing a country was not war. It was only war if a country's soldiers were being killed. Bombing of Libya was done from the air, at long distance, and perhaps also by drones. So is a bloodless war really a war—bloodless on the aggressor's side, that is?

Here was precisely the situation for which the debt ceiling rule was introduced in 1917. President Wilson had taken the US into the Great War, breaking his election campaign promise not to do so. Isolationists in the US sought to limit America's commitment, by imposing Congressional oversight and approval of raising the debt ceiling. This safeguard obviously was intended to be used against unscheduled spending that occurred without Congressional approval.

The present rise in US Treasury debt results from two forms of warfare. First is the overtly military oil war in the Near East, from Iraq to Afghanistan ("Pipelinistan") to oil-rich Libya. These adventures will end up costing between $3 and $5 trillion. Second, and even more expensive, is the more covert yet more costly economic war of Wall Street against the rest of the economy, demanding that losses by banks and financial institutions be passed onto the government balance sheet ("taxpayers"). The bailouts and "free lunch" for Wall Street—by no coincidence, Congress's number one political campaign contributor—cost $13 trillion.

It seems remarkable that Obama's major focus on the debt ceiling is to warn that Social Security funding must be cut back, along with that of Medicare and other social programs. He went so far as to say that despite the fact that FICA wage set-asides have been invested in Treasury securities for over half a century, the government might not send out checks this week.

A radical double standard is at work for democracies. Wall Street investors certainly had no such worry. In fact, interest rates on long-term Treasury bonds actually have gone down over the past month, and especially over the last week. So institutional debt holders obviously expected to get paid. Only the Social Security savers were to be stiffed—or was Obama simply trying to threaten them, so as to depict himself as a hero coming in to save their Social Security by negotiating a Grand Bargain?

Wall Street had it right. There was no real crisis. Authorization to raise the public debt ceiling is not a proper occasion to discuss long-term tax policy. Since 1962—just as the Vietnam War was starting to escalate—it has been raised seventy four times. This averages out to about once every eight months. It is like going to a Notary Public—just to make sure that the President is not doing something wrong. Mr. Obama could have asked for a limited vote just on this, without riders. Never before have riders such as this been attached. And even more remarkably, there was no attempt to impose a rider restricting the Obama Administration from spending any more funds on Libya, without getting an official Congressional declaration of war.

Obama could have invoked the 14th Amendment to pay. He could have taken the proposal made by Scott Fullwiler and other UMKC economists for the Treasury to issue a few $1 trillion coins and pay the Fed for Treasury securities, to retire. But Mr. Obama steered right into the debate, turning it into a discussion of how to cut back Social Security and Medicare in the emerging US class war, rather than overextending the Oil War to North Africa.

The first great victory for the financial sector in America's domestic class war was the Bush "temporary" tax cuts on the wealthy. This aggression was not undone in order to restore budget balance. No temporary tax cuts were revoked, no loopholes closed. The burden of balancing the budget was pushed even further onto the Democratic Party's own base: urban labor, racial and ethnic minorities, the Eastern and Western seaboards. Yet the Democrats split 95/95 on the vote to raise the debt ceiling by slashing social spending on their major voting constituency.

Voting constituency, but not campaign contributors. That looks like the key to how the debt crisis has unfolded. Although leading Democrats such as Maxine Walters Waters, Dennis Kucinich, Henry Waxman, Barney Frank, Edolphus Towns, Charles Rangel and Jerrold Nadler opposed it (and on the Republican side, Ron Paul, Michele Bachmann and Ben Quayle), much of the principled opposition has come from traditional Republicans. Reagan's Assistant Treasury Secretary Paul Craig Roberts accused the deal as being too right-wing and favoring the wealthy to a degree threatening to bring on depression.

The essence of classical free market economics was to restrict executive power—in an epoch when war-making power was the major abuse of national interests. Just as the lower house of bicameral legislatures had taken over the power to commit nations to permanent national debt—rather than royal debts that died with the kings, as were the norm before the 16th century—so parliaments asserted their rights to block warfare.

But now that finance is the new form of warfare—domestically, not externally—where is the power to constrain Treasury and Federal Reserve power to commit taxpayers to bail out financial interests at the top of the economic pyramid? The Fed and other central banks claim that their political "independence" is a "hallmark of democracy." It seems to be rather a transition to financial oligarchy. And now that finance has joined with the oil industry, major monopolies and privatizers of the public domain, the need for some kind of Congressional oversight is as necessary as was parliamentary power over military spending in times past.

No discussion of this basic principle was voiced in the debt-ceiling debate. Even critics who voted (ostensibly) reluctantly (so as to provide plausible deniability to what no doubt will be their later condemnations of the deal when election time comes around) acted as if they were saving the economy. The reality is that there is now little hope of rebuilding infrastructure as the president promised. Cutbacks in federal revenue sharing will hit cities and states hard, forcing them to sell off yet more land, roads and other assets in the public domain to cover their budget deficit as the US economy sinks further into depression. Congress has just added fiscal deflation to debt deflation, slowing employment even further.

How indeed will they explain all this in the November 2012 elections?

Michael Hudson is a former Wall Street economist. A Distinguished Research Professor at University of Missouri, Kansas City (UMKC), he is the author of many books, including Super Imperialism: The Economic Strategy of American Empire *(new ed., Pluto Press, 2002).*

Perpetual War: "Grand Strategy" after 9/11

By TARIQ ALI

"Sovereign is he who decides on the exception," Carl Schmitt wrote in different times almost a century ago, when European empires and armies dominated most continents and the US was basking underneath an isolationist sun. What the conservative theorist meant by "exception"' was a state of emergency, necessitated by serious economic or political cataclysms, that required a suspension of the Constitution, internal repression and war abroad.

A decade after the *attentats* of 9/11, the US and its European allies are trapped in a quagmire. The events of that year were simply used as a pretext to remake the world and to punish those states that did not comply. And today while the majority of Euro-American citizens flounder in a moral desert, now unhappy with the wars, now resigned, now propagandized into differentiating what is, in effect, an overarching imperial strategy into good/bad wars, the US General Petraeus (currently commanding the CIA) tells us: "You have to recognize also that I don't think you win this war. I think you keep fighting. It's a little bit like Iraq, actually ... Yes, there has been enormous progress in Iraq. But there are still horrific attacks in Iraq, and you have to stay vigilant. You have to stay after it. This is the kind of fight we're in for the rest of our lives and probably our kids' lives."

Thus speaks the voice of a sovereign power, determining in this case that the exception is the rule.

Even though I did not agree with his own answer, the German philosopher, Jurgen Habermas posed an important question: "Does the claim to universality that we connect with human rights merely conceal a particularly subtle and deceitful instrument of Western domination?"' "Subtle" could be deleted. The experiences in the occupied lands speak for themselves. Ten years on the war in Afghanistan continues, a bloody and brutal stalemate with a corrupt puppet regime whose President and family fill their pockets with ill-gotten gains and a US/NATO military incapable of defeating the insurgents. The latter now strike at will, assassinating Karzai's corrupt sibling, knocking off his leading collaborators and targeting key NATO intelligence personnel via suicide terrorism or helicopter-downing missiles. Meanwhile, sets of protracted behind-the-scenes negotiations between the US and the neo-Taliban have been taking place for several years. The aim reveals the desperation. NATO and Karzai are desperate to recruit the Taliban to a new national government.

Euro-American liberal and conservative politicians who form the backbone of the governing elites and claim to believe in moderation and tolerance and fighting wars to impose the same values on the re-colonized states are still blinded by their situation and fail to see the writing on the wall. Their pious renunciations of terrorist violence notwithstanding, they have no problems in defending torture, renditions, targeting and assassination of individuals, post-legal states of exception at home so that they can imprison anybody without trial indefinitely. Meanwhile the good citizens of Euro-America who opposed the wars being waged by their governments avert their gaze from the dead, wounded and orphaned citizens of Iraq and Afghanistan, Libya and Pakistan … the list continues to grow.

War—*jus belli*—is now a legitimate instrument as long as it is used with US approval or preferably by the US itself. These days it is presented as a "humanitarian" necessity: one side is busy engaged in committing crimes, the self-styled morally superior side is simply administering necessary punishment and the state to be defeated is denied its sovereignty. Its replacement is carefully policed both with military bases and with a combination of No's and money. This 21st Century colonization or dominance is aided by the global media networks, an essential pillar to conduct political and military operations.

Let's start with homeland security in the US Contrary to what many liberals imagined in November 2008, the debasement of American political culture continues apace. Instead of reversing the trend, the lawyer-President and his team have deliberately accelerated the process. There have been more deportations of immigrants than under Bush; fewer prisoners held without trial have been released from Gitmo, an institution that the lawyer-President had promised to close down; the Patriot Act with its defining premises of what constitutes friends and enemies has been renewed, a new war begun in Libya without the approval of Congress on the flimsy basis that the bombing of a sovereign state should not be construed as a hostile act; whistleblowers are being vigorously prosecuted and so on—the list growing longer by the day.

Politics and power override all else. Liberals who still believe that the Bush administration transcended the law while the Democrats are exemplars of a normative approach are blinded by political tribalism. Apart from Obama's windy rhetoric, little now divides this administration from its predecessor. Ignore, for a moment, the power of politicians and propagandists to enforce their taboos and prejudices on American society as a whole, a power often used ruthlessly and vindictively to silence opposition from all quarters—Bradley Manning, Thomas Drake (released after a huge outcry in the liberal media), Julian Assange, Stephen Kim, currently being treated as criminals and public enemies, know this better than most.

Nothing illustrates this debasement so well as the assassination of Osama Bin Laden in Abbotabad. He could have been captured and put on trial, but that was never the intention. The liberal mood was reflected by the chants heard in New York on that day: *U-S-A. U-S-A. Obama got Osama. Obama Got*

Osama. You can't beat us (clap-clap-clap-clap-clap-clap) You can't beat us. Fuck bin La-den. Fuck bin La-den.

These were echoed in more diplomatic language by the leaders of Europe, junior partners in the imperial family of nations, incapable of self-determination. Cant and hypocrisy have become the coinage of political culture.

Take Libya, the latest case of "humanitarian intervention." The US-NATO intervention in Libya, with United Nations security council cover, is part of an orchestrated response to show support for the movement against one dictator in particular and by so doing to bring the Arab rebellions to an end by asserting western control, confiscating their impetus and spontaneity and trying to restore the status quo ante. As is now obvious the British and French are boasting of success and that they will control Libyan oil reserves as payment for the six month bombing campaign.

Meanwhile, Obama's allies in the Arab world were hard at work promoting democracy.

The Saudis entered Bahrain where the population is being tyrannized and large-scale arrests are taking place. Not much of this is being reported on al-Jazeera. I wonder why? The station seems to have been curbed somewhat and brought into line with the politics of its funders. All this with active US support. The despot in Yemen, loathed by a majority of his people continues to kill them every day by remote control from his Saudi base. Not even an arms embargo, let alone a "no-fly zone" have been imposed on him. Libya is yet another case of selective vigilantism by the US and its attack dogs in the west. That the German Greens, amongst the most ardent European defenders of neo-liberalism and war, wanted to be part of this posse reveals more about their own evolution than the intrinsic merits or demerits of intervention.

The frontiers of the squalid protectorate that the west is going to create are being decided in Washington. Even those Libyans who, out of desperation, backed NATO's bomber jets, might—like their Iraqi equivalents—live to regret their choice.

All this might trigger a third phase at some stage: a growing nationalist anger that spills over into Saudi Arabia and here, have no doubt, Washington will do everything necessary to keep the Saudi royal family in power. Lose Saudi Arabia and they will lose the Gulf States. The assault on Libya, greatly helped by Qaddafi's imbecility on every front, was designed to wrest the initiative back from the streets by appearing as the defenders of civil rights. The Bahrainis, Egyptians, Tunisians, Saudi Arabians, Yemenis will not be convinced, and even in Euro-America more are opposed to this latest adventure than support it. The struggles are by no means over.

The 19th century German poet Theodor Däubler wrote that:

The enemy is our own question embodied And he will hound us, and we will hound him to the same end.

The problem with this view today is that the category of enemy, determined by US policy needs, changes far too frequently. Yesterday Saddam and
Qaddafi were friends and regularly helped by western intelligence agencies
to deal with their own enemies. The latter became friends when the former
became enemies. And so the planetary disorder continues. The assassination
of Osama Bin Laden was greeted by European leaders as something that
would make the world safer. Tell that to the fairies.

Tariq Ali's latest book The Obama Syndrome: Surrender at Home, War
Abroad *is published by Verso.*

Guantánamo, Torture and Obama's Surrenders

By ANDY WORTHINGTON

Looking back on President Obama's record with regard to two of the most damaging legacies of the Bush administration—the existence of the prison at Guantánamo Bay, Cuba, and the use of torture—it is noticeable that the boldest moves were taken within forty eight hours of him taking office, in January 2009.

On his second day in office, Obama cared enough about Guantánamo and torture to issue executive orders promising to close Guantánamo and to uphold the absolute ban on torture. He also suspended the system of trials by Military Commission, used by the Bush administration to prosecute prisoners at Guantánamo, which were widely criticized not only for failing to conform to internationally recognized standards of fairness, but also for securing just three convictions throughout their eight-year history.

Other bold moves undertaken by President Obama took place in his first few months in office. In April 2009, for example, in response to a court order, his Justice Department, under Attorney General Eric Holder, released four "torture memos" written and approved in August 2002 and May 2005 by lawyers in the Justice Department's Office of Legal Counsel.

The first of these, written and approved by John Yoo and Jay S. Bybee, purported to redefine torture so that it could be used by the CIA, and the 2005 updates broadly upheld that decision. As well as respecting the courts, the release of these documents also provided important information for those hoping to hold Bush administration officials and lawyers accountable for their actions, although President Obama had already made clear his belief that, on accountability, "we need to look forward as opposed to looking backward," as he explained to the *New York Times* just before he moved into the White House.

The final bold move of this period was the decision to move a Guantánamo prisoner to New York to face a federal court trial, which took place in May 2009. Ahmed Khalfan Ghailani was a Tanzanian, seized in Pakistan in July 2004, who was held in secret prisons run by the CIA until September 2006, when he was moved to Guantánamo with thirteen other men regarded as "high-value detainees"—including Khalid Sheikh Mohammed, the alleged mastermind of the 9/11 attacks.

Ghailani's transfer to New York, to face a trial in connection with his alleged involvement in the 1998 US embassy bombings in Africa, was important for establishing, in the face of criticism from mainly Republican supporters of the Military Commissions, that Guantánamo prisoners could be successfully tried in federal court. In Ghailani's case, there was also a clear connection to how justice had been pursued before the 9/11 attacks, because Ghailani was indicted for his part in the embassy bombings in 1998, and three of his alleged co-conspirators were tried and convicted in federal court in May 2001, receiving life sentences in October 2001.

In examining Obama's record, however, it is also noticeable that "hope" and "change," in any meaningful sense, regarding issues relating to national security only existed until May 21, 2009, when, on the same day that the Justice Department announced that Ghailani had been transferred to New York, Obama delivered a speech at the National Archives, in which he announced that he was reviving the Military Commission trial system, and also revealed that his advisers had told him that some prisoners in Guantánamo were too dangerous to release—even though there was insufficient evidence to put them on trial—and would have to be held indefinitely without charge or trial.

The concessions to Bush's worldview that were contained in this speech were thoroughly disappointing. Indefinite detention was at the heart of Bush's War on Terror, and the Commissions had been condemned by conscientious lawyers throughout their existence. Moreover, this speech shattered any notion that prisoners at Guantánamo would either be released or charged in federal court, as anyone concerned with human rights and the law had hoped.

Since then, the president and his administration have been noteworthy not for their courage and their principles but for their capitulation to criticism, their absolute refusal to hold anyone in the Bush administration accountable for their crimes, and, finally, a paralysis so complete that, without concerted pressure from the American public on their elected officials, Guantánamo may remain open forever. To understand how this retreat took place, it is important to note further details of the context of the National Archives speech. Firstly, it came just days after Obama changed his mind (after criticism from the Pentagon) about complying with another court order, involving the release of photos showing the abuse of prisoners in US custody in Afghanistan and Iraq, and, secondly (and more significantly, in the long term), it also coincided with the president's decision to scrap a plan that would have contributed enormously to the successful closure of Guantánamo.

This latter plan was conceived by Greg Craig, the White House counsel, who had been largely responsible for the executive orders regarding Guantánamo and torture that were issued when Obama took office. Craig, it seems, understood more clearly than anyone else in the Obama administration how important it was to make a clear and decisive break with the Bush administration's policies, and his plan, which was close to fruition when it was scrapped by Obama, involved resettling two Uighur prisoners at Guantánamo on the US mainland.

Craig's plan was conceived in order to break a deadlock involving finding suitable homes for cleared Guantánamo prisoners, who could not be repatriated because they faced the risk of torture. However, it was also designed to send out a clear message to US allies that, in closing Guantánamo, the administration was able to acknowledge that the Bush administration had made mistakes, and that, as a result, Obama was calling on other countries to help him rid the world of the stain of Guantánamo by taking other cleared prisoners who could not return home.

The Uighurs—the subject of Greg Craig's settlement plan—were Muslims from China's oppressed Xinjiang province, and the seventeen Uighurs in Guantánamo at the time had won their habeas corpus petition in a US court in October 2008, after the Bush administration abandoned its claim that they were "enemy combatants." The seventeen men had mostly been seized by opportunistic Pakistani villagers, and sold to US forces after they fled from a settlement in Afghanistan's mountains, where they had been living.

Greg Craig secured support for his plan from Secretary of State Hillary Clinton and Defense Secretary Robert Gates. But Obama quashed it, after Republicans in Congress heard about it and threatened to use their influence to stir up damaging stories about Obama releasing "terrorists" into America's heartland. The capitulation left the Uighurs stranded (although some were later re-housed in Bermuda, Palau and Switzerland), and also, as Greg Craig knew, made the job of finding new homes for other cleared prisoners in other countries more difficult. Furthermore, Republicans—and members of Obama's own party—followed up on this successful attempt to intimidate the president by passing a law explicitly preventing him from bringing any cleared prisoner to the US mainland.

Most importantly, however, Obama's capitulation—especially on the Uighur issue—confirmed that he would succumb to criticism on national security issues, and would not stand up and fight back by pointing out the many crimes and failures of the Bush administration. As a result, capitulation has followed capitulation.

In November 2009, for example, Eric Holder announced that Khalid Sheikh Mohammed and four other "high-value detainees" accused of involvement in the 9/11 attacks would follow Ahmed Khalfan Ghailani to New York, to face a federal court trial. However, when a backlash started, Obama gave in yet again refusing to press the advantage gained by having already moved Ghailani to New York, and refusing to do anything more with Khalid Sheikh Mohammed and the other men.

Part of the problem was that, when Holder announced the 9/11 trial, he also announced that five prisoners would face trials by Military Commission, leaving an option open for critics of federal court trials that should have never have been allowed to exist. In addition, by refusing to move forward on the 9/11 trial, Obama not only made Holder look like a man who was not in charge of the Justice Department—as he told Jane Mayer of the *New Yorker* in February 2010 that trying Khalid Sheikh Mohammed in federal court would be "the defining event of my time as attorney general"—but also paving the way for Khalid Sheikh Mohammed and the four others to be put forward for Military Commission instead, as happened in April this year.

By January 2010, when the hysteria about the proposed 9/11 trial was at its height, Obama's inability to respond to criticism with anything other than capitulation meant that—when Umar Farouk Abdulmutallab, a Nigerian, was seized after trying and failing to blow up a plane bound for Detroit on Christmas Day 2009, and it was claimed that he had been recruited in Yemen, Obama caved in to outrageous demands that no Yemenis should be released from Guantánamo. A moratorium on the release of any Yemenis was announced, which is still in place and shows no sign of being brought to an end.

This proposal was unjust and counterproductive for a number of reasons. In the first place, it essentially contradicted the findings of the Guantánamo Review Task Force, consisting of sixty career officials and lawyers in government departments and the intelligence agencies, who spent a year reviewing all the Guantánamo cases. The Task Force had just published its final report, recommending that fifty nine of the Yemenis be transferred to their home country. It was also clearly unjust to suggest that any of these men had any connection with a purported Al Qaeda cell in Yemen, and, in addition, it was a thunderous insult to the Yemeni people, suggesting that, collectively, they had some sort of allegiance to terrorism, when this was clearly not the case.

Obama's opponents in Congress (who include members of his own party, as well as Republicans) have continued to insist that they have the right to interfere with the president's plans for the disposition of the Guantánamo prisoners, by passing legislation preventing any prisoner from being brought to the US mainland for any reason except to face a trial, and, therefore preventing the president from using funds to close Guantánamo by buying a prison in Illinois and moving the prisoners there.

In December last year, lawmakers inserted passages into the annual defense authorization bill that went even further, banning the use of funds to bring any Guantánamo prisoners to the US mainland, even to face trials, and specifically mentioning Khalid Sheikh Mohammed by name—thereby, ensuring that a trial by Military Commission would be the only way for the administration to proceed with the mooted prosecution of Khalid Sheikh Mohammed and his alleged accomplices.

Lawmakers also reiterated their ban on the use of funds to buy a prison on the US mainland for the Guantánamo prisoners, and prevented the president from releasing any prisoner unless the defense secretary assured Congress that it was safe to do so. This provision was designed specifically to restrict the president's ability to act freely on the recommendations of the Guantánamo Review Task Force, preventing the release of prisoners to countries regarded by lawmakers as dangerous, including Afghanistan, Pakistan, and—yet again—Yemen.

These passages were an unwarranted and unconstitutional assault on the president's powers, but Obama once more failed to act, reinforcing his critics to such an extent that, in their most recent discussions, lawmakers announced their intention to attack the president's right to review prisoners' ongoing detention without Congressional interference. This referred to an executive order, issued by Obama on March 7, 2011, which authorized periodic reviews of the cases of the Guantánamo prisoners designated by the Task Force for indefinite detention without charge or trial (46 of the remaining 171 prisoners, at the latest count).

Also included in the attacks was, for the first time, a fundamental assault on the president's right to prosecute foreigners seized in connection with terrorist offences in federal court, which was a particularly alarming development.

While the fallout from these assaults had yet to be decided at the time of writing, elsewhere it was clear that Obama's other capitulations—which were at least as far-reaching—involved categorically refusing to hold any Bush official or lawyer accountable for implementing torture. At the start of 2010, a Justice Department "fixer," David Margolis, was allowed to override the damning conclusion of a four-year internal investigation into John Yoo and Jay S. Bybee, who wrote and approved the 2002 "torture memos," in which Margolis replaced the report's conclusion—that both men were guilty of "professional misconduct"—with a mild rebuke for their "poor judgment."

In the courts, too, Obama has resisted all calls for accountability, invoking the little-known and little-used "state secrets" doctrine to block any attempt to even discuss torture in a US courtroom. The most blatant example of the Obama administration's blanket misuse of the "state secrets" doctrine is in the case of five men subjected to "extraordinary rendition" and torture, who tried to sue Jeppesen Dataplan, Inc., a Boeing subsidiary responsible for acting as the CIA's torture travel agent. Although the five men won an appeal to a three-judge panel in the Ninth Circuit Court of Appeals in April 2009, that was overturned by a full panel in September 2010 and by the Supreme Court this year.

In addition, the president has also expanded his abuse of the "state secrets" doctrine to defend two alarming innovations that are entirely his own: a massive increase in drone killings in Pakistan and a decision to endorse the assassination of US citizens anywhere in the world.

In conclusion, Obama's failures to hold anyone accountable for torture have contributed to continuing acceptance of torture within the US, and, on the closure of Guantánamo, his inability to insist that some principles are too important to involve compromise, has led to a situation in which he has not only compromised horribly on the 9/11 trial, but also appears to have accepted that he can deflect further criticism of his failure to close the prison by relying on the Authorization for Use of Military Force (AUMF).

Passed by Congress the week after the 9/11 attacks, the AUMF justifies the detention of prisoners at Guantánamo, although it remains a deeply

troubling piece of legislation, perpetuating the false notion that the Guantánamo prisoners are neither prisoners of war nor criminal suspects but the
"enemy combatants," invented by the Bush administration. As such, although
they are no longer described as "enemy combatants," they are still in a unique
and uniquely disturbing position, which is still akin to a legal black hole,
despite the fact that they were granted constitutionally guaranteed habeas
corpus rights by the Supreme Court in June 2008.

If Obama was committed to justice, and to consigning to history the
crimes of the Bush administration, he would have sought to repeal the
AUMF, as well as either releasing the remaining Guantánamo prisoners or
charging them in federal court, and not intervening to prevent calls for Bush
administration officials and lawyers to be held accountable for their actions.
As it stands, however, it is just one more failure in a litany of failures that
display him as a president who failed to stand up to his critics and, time after
time, caved in.

Andy Worthington is a freelance investigative journalist. He is the author of
The Guantánamo Files: The Stories of the 774 Detainees in America's
Illegal Prison *and co-director, with Polly Nash, of the documentary film,*
Outside the Law: Stories from Guantánamo.

Obama and the Economy
By MIKE WHITNEY

When Barack Obama took office in January 2009, the economy was a shambles. The workforce was shedding 750,000 jobs per month, the equities markets were plunging, and GDP was contracting at an annual rate of 6 percent. Exports, retail sales, manufacturing and consumer spending were all falling faster then they had during the Great Depression. Obama had no time to celebrate his victory or ease his way into his new job.

On February 19, 2009, less than a month after he had been inaugurated, Obama launched The American Recovery and Reinvestment Act (ARRA), a $787 billion fiscal stimulus bill that was designed to lower unemployment, boost growth, and reduce the amount of slack in the economy. By the fourth quarter of 2009, GDP had climbed to 5 percent while unemployment slowly began to retreat from its peak of 10.1 percent. The hemorrhaging of jobs slowed to a trickle, and the economy returned to positive growth in just six months.

Unfortunately, the stimulus package was too small to have the long-term effects that many had hoped for and, by June 2011, unemployment started to rise once again and the economy began to teeter. Liberal economists, like Paul Krugman, Joseph Stiglitz and Dean Baker, called for a second stimulus warning of another slowdown, but Obama just brushed them off. He'd already moved on to other matters, like trimming the deficits and paring back long-term entitlement spending. The deepening job crisis, which left 14 million Americans out of work, was put on the back burner, while reducing spending on popular social programs and balancing the budget became the top priority.

For those who follow the financial news closely, Obama's volte-face on fiscal stimulus was not really much of a surprise. In fact, there were indications early on that Obama was not the died-in-the-wool liberal his critics had made him out to be. Even his brief stint as a community organizer smacked of political opportunism, as did his vacillating voting record in the US Senate. Obama seemed less attached to any set of principles than he was to the idea that doctrinal flexibility and grandiloquence were the fast track to political stardom. Even so, his supporters still thought of him as a progressive, which is why so many of them were disappointed when he selected his team of economic advisors. Here's a bit of what he said on November 23, 2008:

> We'll need to bring together the best minds in America to guide us.... And that is what I've sought to do in assembling my economic team. I've sought leaders who could offer both sound judgment and fresh thinking, both a depth of experience and a wealth of bold new ideas— and, most of all, who share my fundamental belief that we cannot have a thriving Wall Street while Main Street suffers.

And who were those leaders who would provide "both sound judgment and fresh thinking"? Lawrence Summers and Timothy Geithner. From the moment the announcement was made, it was clear that Obama's promise of "change" was just empty rhetoric. Geithner and Summers were not only trusted allies of Wall Street, they were also steadfast proponents of deregulation and laissez-faire capitalism, the likes of which paved the way to the crash of 2008.

As Treasury secretary under President Bill Clinton, Summers pushed the Gramm-Leach-Bliley Act through Congress, which repealed parts of the Glass-Steagall Act and removed the firewall between commercial and investment banks. Once those critical safeguards were lifted, the banks were free to use savings deposits in high-risk speculation. Gramm-Leach-Bliley also allowed commercial banks to get into the mortgage-backed securities game, which helped inflate a multi trillion-dollar housing bubble that eventually burst, sending housing prices down more than 30 percent.

Summers also had a hand in the passing of the Commodity Futures Modernization Act, which deregulated derivatives trading. The CFMA led to an explosion of exotic debt instruments, which suddenly plunged in value in late 2007, when French bank Paribas PNB stopped redemptions on its cache of mortgage-backed assets. That was the incident that sent the dominoes tumbling through the financial system, taking down hundreds of banks and brokerages and wiping out nearly $50 trillion in capital. If the CFMA had not been passed, then derivatives trading would have been regulated, contracts would have sufficiently capitalized, and the financial crisis would never have happened. While there's plenty of blame to go around, Summers's role in the meltdown cannot be overstated.

Timothy Geithner's resumé was nearly as bad as Summers. Aside from forcing AIG to keep quiet about billions of dollars of payments that the US Treasury made to several Wall Street banks and helping former Treasury Secretary Henry Paulson put together the vastly unpopular $700 billion bank-bailout bill (Troubled Asset Relief Program), Geithner was also a key figure in the Lehman Brothers "Repo 105" scandal. As head of the Federal Reserve Bank of New York at the time, Geithner allegedly helped Lehman to conceal $50 billion in red ink off its balance sheet, in order to mislead investors about the bank's true financial condition.

Obama would never have picked Geithner and Summers if he was serious about change. This was just more of the same, which is exactly what Wall Street wanted, a close-knit group of top presidential advisors who would do their bidding from inside the White House, assisting the big banks whenever possible and subverting reform at every turn.

The influence of Geithner and Summers can be seen in all of Obama's economic decision making, but particularly in his handling of the stimulus. The administration had been warned repeatedly by a number of top-notch economists that the stimulus was not big enough to make up for the gigantic loss in aggregate demand caused by the downturn. They were also cautioned that it would be politically impossible to approve a second round of stimulus because of growing concern over the ballooning budget deficits. That's why it was imperative that they get it right the first time, so they wouldn't have to go back to Congress looking for a second helping.

But Summers wasn't interested in what other economists had to say; he wanted a smaller stimulus package. And, as director of the National Economic Council, he had the final say-so. Thus, the Summers plan was implemented, and, sure enough, two years later, the funds began to run dry just as the economy was showing signs of a rebound. Summers' critics had been right after all: there wasn't enough money for the economy to reach "escape velocity" and shake off the grip of recession. As we know now, nearly $200 billion of the ARRA were earmarked for ineffective tax cuts (demanded by the GOP), while another $100 billion paid for an extension to the Alternative Minimum Tax. That means the spending component was just $500 billion spread over two years, barely enough to cover long-term unemployment benefits, food stamps, state assistance, and a few construction projects. But not nearly enough to reduce the output gap, put 14 million people back to work, or put the economy on a path to a self-sustaining recovery.

As the stimulus dwindled in late 2010, the signs of economic weakness began to re-emerge and, by early 2011, the US economy was sliding back toward recession. GDP had dropped to below 1 percent for the first six months of 2011, while unemployment still topped 9 percent. Businesses stopped hiring, and the economy began to stall.

In June 2011, Summers—who had left the administration some months earlier for a job in the private sector—admitted his mistake in an op-ed in the *Financial Times*, where he called for more stimulus and warned of a "lost decade" if his advice was not heeded. Here's an excerpt from the article:

> Substantial withdrawal of fiscal stimulus at the end of 2011 would be premature. Stimulus should be continued and, indeed, expanded by providing the payroll tax cut to employers as well as employees ... We averted Depression in 2008/2009 by acting decisively. Now we can avert a lost decade by recognizing economic reality.

Summers's comments suggest that he merely miscalculated the amount of support the economy would need to stage a rebound, but that's not entirely true. As Paul Krugman has pointed out, figuring out how big the stimulus needed to be was pretty straightforward, especially for someone with Summers's background. As Krugman's states on his *New York Times* blog, "Conscience of a Liberal":

The case for a much bigger stimulus came out of basic textbook macro-economics, and could be justified by fancier but still standard models as well. The argument for doing much less was, by contrast, based on a combination of seat-of-the-pants intuition and political symbolism: policy makers believed, based on no evidence, that a big stimulus would unnerve the bond market and/or that a temporary boost would be enough to restore all-important confidence, or that it was politically crucial that the number be well under the magic $1 trillion mark.

In other words, wisdom—as perceived—came from rejecting actual economic analysis in favor of feelings, and not waking up to the fact that the analysis was right until a couple of years of massive unemployment later.

So, Summers knew how much stimulus was needed, but he chose to "go small." Why? Mainly because the outcome was what he wanted from the onset. Yes, he wanted to avoid another Great Depression, but he also wanted to force cutbacks at the state and federal level, while putting extra pressure on the unions. That would lead to lower labor costs and more privatization of government assets and services, which is exactly what anyone would hope for if they were advancing a pro-big-business agenda.

As it turns out, Summers never veered from the neoliberal dogma that guided him during the Clinton years, when he preached the three "-ations": "privatization, stabilization, and liberalization." The size of the stimulus merely confirms that his calculations were made with different objectives in mind.

Still, that doesn't mean that the $787 billion was wasted. Quite the contrary. According to a report in June 2011, by the nonpartisan Congressional Budget Office, the ARRA increased the number of people employed by between 1.2 million and 3.3 million, and lowered the unemployment rate by between 0.6 and 1.8 percentage points in the first quarter of 2011. The stimulus also raised GDP by between 1.1 percent to 3.1 percent in the same period.

The reason that Republicans were able to score points by blasting the stimulus was because the economy never returned to the pre-bubble level of activity. But that's an impossible standard to meet. It would require a massive re-leveraging of the shadow banking system and another asset-price bubble that would allow working people to borrow $500 billion a year off the exaggerated value of their assets, as they did during the housing bubble via mortgage-equity withdrawals. That type of bubble-driven profligacy is no longer possible, nor does it create a sustainable growth path for the economy.

The bottom line is that the Obama team saw the stimulus as a means to an end. Summers and Co. didn't want a strong rebound. What they wanted was an economy that was healthy enough to keep breathing, but too feeble to resist the attacks of Wall Street and big business. And Obama was a big part of their plan. He was fingered as the pitchman for structural adjustment and belt-tightening. He'd use impressive rhetorical skills and power of persuasion to preach the gospel of austerity and to clear the way for slashing entitlement programs.

"Government has to start living within its means, just like families do. We have to cut the spending we can't afford, so we can put the economy on sounder footing and give our businesses the confidence they need to grow and create jobs," Obama declared on July 2, 2011.

It was just more "small government" claptrap, the same song the GOP faithful have been singing for thirty years. Obama claimed that cutbacks to Medicare, Medicaid and Social Security would be necessary to restore investor confidence and to keep the bond vigilantes at bay. He said that "everyone must make sacrifices," knowing full well that working people and retirees would suffer the brunt of the cutbacks, while more money would be diverted to Wall Street.

None of this was new ground for Obama. He'd given similar speeches in the past, but no one cared to listen. They were too enamored with his eloquence, his self-confident demeanor, and his rock-star charisma. But the fact is that Obama had been preaching austerity for a long time, even before he replaced Bush. Here's an excerpt from a speech he delivered in 2008:

> Our economy is trapped in a vicious cycle: the turmoil on Wall Street means a new round of belt-tightening for families and businesses on Main Street … We'll have to scour our federal budget, line by line, and make meaningful cuts and sacrifices as well.

This speech was given before Obama had even become president. It shows that he had been zeroing in on Medicare, Medicaid and Social Security from the very beginning, even before the deficits had become an issue. This explains why corporate America and big finance kept his campaign chest overflowing in 2008—because he was reading from a script that they had written. It also explains why he was so eager to reach an agreement with Republicans on cutting $4 trillion from the budget over the next decade—because they share a common vision of the future: a future where high stakes speculators and business tycoons dictate policy, a future where the chasm between the "haves" and "have-nots" gets wider by the day, a future where working people have to fend for themselves in a hostile environment devoid of public assistance or safety nets.

Obama's dark vision for America is the same as George W. Bush's. The only difference is that Obama has been able to operate almost entirely under the radar, mainly because his supporters refuse to open their eyes and see what they're dealing with.

Mike Whitney is economics correspondent for CounterPunch. *He lives in Washington State.*

The Audacity of Dope

By Fred Gardner

Leaders of pro-cannabis reform groups angrily accuse Barack Obama of having misled and betrayed them. Nary a word of self-criticism, as the move-ment/industry reacts to escalating repression from the federal government.

On October 13, at 6 a.m., DEA raiders stormed into the bedroom of Matt Cohen and his wife, Courtenay, yelling and brandishing automatic weapons. The couple live in Redwood Valley, Mendocino County, and run a collective called Northstone Organics that grows cannabis for and delivers it to some 1,700 members in the Bay Area and Los Angeles.

The Cohens were handcuffed, while the narcs ransacked their house and chopped down their ninety-nine plants, all zip-tied to show that they had been authorized and inspected by the sheriff's office. "If we're not legal, nobody's legal," Cohen said. "We, actually, are a legitimate not-for-profit corporation ... we worked with the county to get where we are, and there are illegal growers all around us."

Only six days earlier, California's four US attorneys had held a press con-ference in Sacramento, to announce that letters were being sent to landlords who rented to dispensaries and growers, threatening them with criminal prosecution and forfeiture of their property. The feds claimed to be targeting "egregious" profiteers, but as the raid on Northstone Organics showed, they're also taking down the most exemplary collectives. (If the feds only targeted egregious profiteers, the medical marijuana industry would thrive. They have to take down the righteous in order to scare people into folding. The classic example was the 2002 DEA raid on WAMM, a Santa Cruz garden grown mainly for hospice patients.)

Many other Prohibitionist measures have been renewed or initiated by the administration in 2011. Some examples:

• The Department of Housing and Urban Development's general counsel asserted in a memo, "Any state law purporting to legalize the use of medical marijuana in public or other assisted housing would conflict with the admis-sion and termination standards found in the Quality Housing and Work and Responsibility Act of 1999." The memo was issued on January 20, the anniversary of Obama's inauguration.

• The US Department of Justice sent letters to officials in California, Ari-zona, Colorado, Montana, Rhode Island, Vermont, Hawaii, New Hamp-shire, Maine, and Washington threatening to prosecute those who imple-mented cultivation and distribution programs. The Washington legislature had recently passed a measure, supported by Gov. Christine Gregoire, that authorized dispensaries. After a warning from federal prosecutors, Gregoire decided to veto it.

• The Drug Enforcement Administration raided and closed down dispensaries, most dramatically, in Montana, where voters had passed an initiative in 2004 (by a 62–38 percent margin), and some 80,000 residents were using marijuana legally. On March 14—the very day state legislators were debating a bill to repeal the law the voters had created—DEA agents raided twenty-six dispensaries in thirteen Montana cities. In Michigan, the DEA spent two days raiding dispensaries after a circuit court judge in Isabella County ruled that patient-to-patients transfers are illegal.

• The DEA, after a nine-year stall, rejected a petition to move marijuana from Schedule I (the category for dangerous drugs with no medical use) to Schedule III, IV or V.

• The Bureau of Alcohol, Tobacco and Firearms ordered gun and ammunition dealers to not sell to medical marijuana users. On September 21, an ATF official named Arthur Herbert sent out a memo—supposedly in response to "a number of inquiries about the use of marijuana for medical purposes, and its applicability to federal firearms laws"—advising dealers that "Federal law makes it unlawful for any person to sell or otherwise dispose of any firearm or ammunition to any person knowing or having reasonable cause to believe that such person is an unlawful user of or addicted to a controlled substance."

• The Federal Deposit Insurance Corporation instructed financial institutions to stop dealing with cannabis-related businesses. Wells Fargo, Bank of America, CitiCorp and others closed the accounts of dispensaries rather than face costly, exhaustive audits by the FDIC to assure compliance with the Bank Secrecy Act.

• The Internal Revenue service presented Harborside Health Center with a $2.4 million bill for back taxes from 2007–08. The IRS disallowed deductions for rent, payroll, employees' health insurance and other standard expenses because the business itself involves "the trafficking of controlled substances."

Harborside director Steve DeAngelo says "The Harborside audit is part of a nationwide IRS program which has targeted dozens of medical cannabis providers, claiming we are drug-trafficking organizations. If successful, this program could tax legal cannabis providers out of existence."

* * *

On October 8, 2011, Ethan Nadelmann, executive director of the Drug Policy Alliance, was quoted by Bob Egelko in the *San Francisco Chronicle* as saying:

Barack Obama is betraying promises made when he ran for president and turning his back on the sensible policies announced during his first year in office.

Four days later, on October 12, 2011, Rob Kampia, executive director of the Marijuana Policy Project, wrote on the *Huffington Post*:

During his run for the presidency, Barack Obama instilled hope in medical marijuana supporters by pledging to respect state laws on the matter. And for the first two years of his term, he was generally faithful to his promise. Yet suddenly, and with no logical explanation, over the past eight months he has become arguably the worst president in U.S. history regarding medical marijuana.

By accusing the president of breaking campaign promises and suddenly changing his line on marijuana, the reform honchos absolve themselves of responsibility for having misinterpreted and/or intentionally misrepresented what he said, and failing to provide useful intelligence—i.e., warnings—to growers and dispensaries. The truth is, Barack Obama never expressed unambiguous support for medical marijuana. They—Nadelmann and Kampia—loudly proclaimed that he had.

While running for president, Sen. Obama was drawn out twice on the subject, both times by reporters in Oregon. On neither occasion did his reply indicate that he had been briefed on the topic, or given it much thought. In March 2008, Obama told Gary Nelson of the Medford *Mail Tribune*: "My attitude is that if it's an issue of doctors prescribing medical marijuana as a treatment for glaucoma or as a cancer treatment, I think that should be appropriate, because there really is no difference between that and a doctor prescribing morphine or anything else.

I think there are legitimate concerns in not wanting to allow people to grow their own or start setting up mom-and-pop shops, because at that point it becomes fairly difficult to regulate. Again, I'm not familiar with all the details of the initiative that was passed [in Oregon] and what safeguards there were in place, but I think the basic concept that using medical marijuana in the same way, with the same controls as other drugs prescribed by doctors, I think that's entirely appropriate...

I would not punish doctors if it's prescribed in a way that is appropriate. That may require some changes in federal law. I will tell you that—I mean I want to be honest with you, whether I want to use a whole lot of political capital on that issue when we're trying to get health care passed, or end the war in Iraq, the likelihood of that being real high on my list is not likely... What I'm not going to be doing is using Justice Department resources to try to circumvent state laws on this issue, simply because I want folks to be investigating violent crimes and potential terrorism. We've got a lot of things for our law enforcement officers to deal with.

In May 2008, James Pitkin of the *Willamette Week* asked, "Would you stop the DEA's raids on Oregon medical marijuana growers?" To which Obama replied: "I would, because I think our federal agents have better things to do, like catching criminals and preventing terrorism. The way I want to approach the issue of medical marijuana is to base it on science, and if there is sound science that supports the use of medical marijuana, and if it is controlled and prescribed in a way that other medicine is prescribed, then it's something that I think we should consider."

Let's dissect these comments from a suspicious rather than a hopey-changey perspective. (And why shouldn't a medical marijuana user be suspicious of the Democratic candidate for president? Clinton's Justice Department responded to the passage of Prop. 215 by threatening to revoke the license of any California doctor who approved cannabis use by patients. Jimmy Carter's DEA paid Mexico to spray the campesinos' US-bound herb with Paraquat.) Obama says he sees the logic of "not wanting to allow people to grow their own or start setting up mom-and-pop shops." Why didn't Nadelmann choose to quote and paraphrase ad nauseam that ominous comment? Or, at least bring it to the attention of the rank and file?

Obama tells Nelson he would like to see medical marijuana used "In the same way, with the same controls as other drugs prescribed by doctors." That means: after clinical trials have been conducted and data from those trials have been reviewed and approved by the Food and Drug Administration. This has been the White House line on medical marijuana since January 1997, when someone explained to Drug Czar Barry McCaffrey that it couldn't be dismissed as "Cheech-and-Chong medicine," and that a more sophisticated stall in the name of science was called for until the drug companies could figure out how to synthesize and market the useful compounds in the plant.

Obama says he understands that "some changes in federal law"—rescheduling—would be required in order for doctors to prescribe medical marijuana, but frankly acknowledges not wanting to spend "a whole lot of political capital on that issue."

From a suspicious Californian's perspective, Obama's often quoted half-sentence, "What I'm not going to be doing is using Justice Department resources to try to circumvent state laws on this issue...," is reassuring only if and when state and county prosecutors accept the legality of dispensaries. What Obama says next is dismaying, "simply because I want folks to be investigating violent crimes and potential terrorism." His vaunted "support" for medical marijuana on the campaign trail comes down to a matter of budgetary limitations.

Obama's answer to Pitkin is a more succinct version of his comments to Nelson. It is an expression of support for the prevailing corporate-friendly regulatory process, not the medical marijuana movement/industry.

* * *

Barack Obama took office on January 20, 2009. Two days later, DEA agents raided a South Lake Tahoe cannabis dispensary run by Ken Estes, a wheelchair-bound entrepreneur. They seized about five pounds of herbal medicine and a few thousands dollars. No arrests were made. "It was a typical rip-and-run," says Estes.

On February 3, four cannabis dispensaries in the Los Angeles area were raided simultaneously by DEA squads. "They took everything," said a member of the Beach Center Collective in Playa del Rey, "right down to the television. The computer, patient files, medicine, cash in the register. That's it, we're done. It's just too bad. Our patients have epilepsy, cancer, MS, diabetes. Two of our patients have one leg. They're gonna have to travel a lot farther and go to places that aren't as safe for them." Activists led by Americans for Safe Access protested at a rally in Los Angeles, and the White House was deluged with emails quoting Obama's "promise" not to circumvent state laws.

On February 11, DEA agents took part in a raid on the MendoHealing Cooperative farm in Fort Bragg, California.

On February 25, Attorney General Eric Holder held a press conference with Acting DEA Administrator Michele Leonhart, to discuss drug-related violence in Mexico. The fact that he hadn't replaced her was far more significant than an exchange that occurred twenty minutes in. A reporter asked: "Right after the inauguration, there were some raids on California medical marijuana dispensaries. Was that a deliberate decision by you, by the Justice Department? Is that a prediction of policy going forward? Do you expect those sorts of raids to continue despite what the president said during the campaign?"

Holder replied, "Well, what the president said during the campaign, you'll be surprised to know, will be consistent with what we'll be doing here in law enforcement. He was my boss during the campaign. He is formally and technically and by law my boss now. So, what he said during the campaign is now American policy." Given how much the reform honchos would make of it, Holder's response is worth checking out on YouTube (search "Holder marijuana"). He's been in office less than a month, the press conference was called on another topic, he's ad-libbing, it's obvious that he doesn't know what promises, exactly, his boss may have made regarding medical marijuana, but he gamely commits to carrying them out.

Kampia's Marijuana Policy Project immediately sent out a press release linked to a video clip on its website, under the headline, "Holder Says 'No More DEA Raids' in Press Conference." But Holder never spoke those words! The quotation marks are duplicitous. Why would the reform leaders lie about the administration's position? Four guesses.

1. Claims of success facilitate fundraising. If Holder really had said, "No more DEA Raids," the reform groups would be entitled to some credit. 2. Dispensary owners and other cannabis-industry entrepreneurs (an increasingly important source of funding for the reform groups) had ambitious expansion plans. 3. Their ability to attract investors was directly linked to how permissive the administration was perceived to be. The reform honchos pride themselves on their "media messaging" skills, and believe that how an event gets spun is as or more important than what actually went down (i.e., reality). They evidently thought that by claiming the Obama administration was reining in the DEA, they would create a bandwagon effect and it would somehow come to pass. 4. Disrespect for the rank and file, who trust the Drug Policy Alliance and the Marijuana Policy Project to provide them with accurate intelligence from the corridors of power.

One person evidently misled by news of Holder's February 20 press conference was Thomas P. O'Brien, US attorney for the Southern District of California. O'Brien directed prosecutors in his office to stop filing charges, issuing subpoenas, and applying for search warrants in cases involving medical marijuana dispensaries. A week later, he rescinded his own order. He must have seen and believed a story that Holder intended to end such prosecutions, and complied in hopes of keeping his job. (US attorneys traditionally submit pro forma letters of resignation, enabling a newly elected president to replace them at will.)

On March 18, AG Holder told reporters, "The policy is to go after those people who violate both federal and state law. To the extent that people do that and try to use medical marijuana laws as a shield for activity that is not designed to comport with what the intention was of the state law, those are the organizations, the people, that we will target. And that is consistent with what the president said during the campaign."

Once again, the reform leaders claimed a huge win. "Today's comments clearly represent a change in policy out of Washington," Nadelmann told the *Los Angeles Times*, "He [Holder] is sending a clear message to the DEA."

But the Drug Warriors weighed in with a different interpretation (which would prove to be more accurate). The US attorney's spokesman in Los Angeles, Thom Mrozek, told the *Los Angeles Times* that Holder had vindicated their longstanding approach: "In every single case we have prosecuted, the defendants violated state as well as federal law." The *Los Angeles Times* story summarized Holder's line thus: "Holder said the priority of the new administration is to go after egregious offenders." That hardly represents a change in policy. The Bush DOJ also claimed to be targeting "egregious" offenders, but they raided WAMM, the Santa Cruz hospice operation whose leaders are saintly. If law enforcement only took down the "egregious," the industry would thrive. They have to actually take down the exemplary as well.

On March 20, the *New York Times* ran a piece by Solomon Moore headlined, "Dispensers of Marijuana Find Relief in Policy Shift" (a subtle pun). Ethan Nadelmann was quoted saying that the feds now recognize state medical marijuana laws as "kosher." But DEA spokesman Garrison Courtney "pointed out that the attorney general's statement indicated that the federal authorities would continue to go after marijuana dispensaries that broke state and federal laws by selling to minors, selling excessive amounts, or selling marijuana from unsanctioned growers."

On March 23, in Los Angeles, US District Court Judge George Wu delayed the sentencing of Charles Lynch and asked the US attorney to provide a written summary of the Justice Department policy. Lynch, who operated a dispensary in Morro Bay, had been convicted of cultivation for sale, conspiracy to distribute, and selling marijuana to a minor. He contended that he was operating legally under California law and with the support of city officials.

On April 8, 2009, Joe Russoniello, US attorney for the Northern District of California (a Bush appointee whom Obama would keep in office through August 2010), stated at a Hastings Law School forum that all medical marijuana dispensaries are profiteering operations in violation of state law and, therefore, "fair game" for DEA raiders. Russoniello seemed "very specific and confident, as if he had just seen a policy memo," according to attorney Joe Elford, who debated him at the event. Russoniello's clear statement of the political/legal realities was not publicized (except by your correspondent). Turns out, he was our most accurate source of information.

On April 17, US Attorney O'Brien forwarded to District Judge Wu the letter he requested, clarifying Justice Department policy in the Lynch case. The letter from H. Marshall Jarrett, director of the office that oversees all US attorneys, said, "Based on the facts of this case, the Office of the Deputy Attorney General concurs with your office that the investigation, prosecution, and conviction of Mr. Lynch are entirely consistent with Department policies as well as public statements made by the Attorney General. Accordingly, you should seek to proceed with the sentencing recommendations [five years] which your office has filed with the court."

At this point—not quite three months into his term—Obama's position has been made clear: all California dispensaries and growers are subject to DEA raids, all are making profits in violation of state as well as federal law, and prosecutors should go after the "egregious" successes, not gravely ill individuals.

Many leftists and liberals feel betrayed by Obama. *CounterPunch* is filled with examples of specific, broken promises. But in terms of marijuana policy, we should not mistake our deep disappointment (dashed hopes) for betrayal (being lied to). We were lied to by our own opportunistic leaders, not by Obama.

Fred Gardner edits O'Shaughnessy's: The Journal of Cannabis in Clinical Practice.

Black Backlash Against Obama

By LINN WASHINGTON, JR.

After spending much of her ninety-four-years as a civil rights activist this Washington, DC resident is understandably supportive of the Barack Obama presidency because she like many African-Americans never thought she'd ever see a black man sitting in that Oval Office seat designated for the most powerful person on earth.

This ninety-four-year-old bristles at the extraordinary amount of criticisms unleashed against Obama telling a niece that she'd like to take a sharp sword and stick Obama critics "in the butt!"

Many blacks are touchy about criticisms directed toward Obama, feeling—with factual basis—that Obama receives unfair criticisms, particularly from right-wing conservatives.

For example Michelle Bachmann, the extremist Republican congresswoman with presidential aspirations, blasted Obama, blaming him for historic high levels of black unemployment, a rate consistently double that of whites during this so-called Great Recession which actually is a full-blown depression for minorities and many whites.

Of course Bachmann's partisan slam was silent on small yet salient facts like Obama inheriting the jobs killing recession from his Republican Oval Office predecessor, who Bachmann blindly supported.

And, Bachmann's blast blithely dismissed the fact that she and her Republican confederates on Capitol Hill have persistently opposed efforts by congressional progressives to pass jobs creating initiatives that would significantly increase employment among all jobless Americans, including blacks.

Capitol Hill progressives including the Congressional Black Caucus have long sought creation of public service jobs for unemployed Americans like those federal initiatives utilized during the Great Depression of the 1930s and the recession of the early 1970s.

Interestingly, if that ninety-four-year-old desires taking a sword to the backside of Bachmann and other Obama bashers she also must wield it against some black Obama critics, including those she's revered like Congressman John Conyers (D-Mich).

Conyers is the second most senior member in the US House and was the first congressman to publicly support Obama's presidential candidacy.

Conyers' tough criticisms of perceived shortcomings in Obama's presidency, particularly tepid attacks on unemployment, have earned the Detroit congressman icy antipathy from Obama, who Conyers once mentored.

Obama's jobs creating emphasis has been principally through public works infrastructure renovation projects funded through his federal stimulus initiative. However that approach largely bypasses blacks because of historic discrimination in the building trade unions that perform infrastructure work.

Obama's American Recovery and Reinvestment Act (ARRA) stimulus did pump billions into state and local government coffers that helped retain public sector employees, many of whom are black. But the Obama Administration has failed to institute aggressive jobs creation initiatives during its first two and a half years.

Despite America's first black president enjoying solid support in black communities coast-to-coast criticisms from that seemingly secure sector of Obama's voting base are increasing.

Famed figures like Princeton University Professor Cornell West and iconic actor/activist Harry Belafonte plus folks from the faceless rank-&-file are leveling sharply phrased critiques of Obama's failure to specifically address crisis-proportion problems in a long-suffering segment of American society: the black community.

"President Obama hasn't talked about poor people who are suffering. He is always talking about the middle class," said Daryl Brooks, a community activist in Trenton, NJ who aligns himself with the Tea Party out of frustration with black and other political leaders ignoring inner-city concerns.

In July 2011 when Obama seemingly accelerated his rightward drift embracing deficit reducing austerity loudly advocated by conservative Republicans, the Pew Research Center released a report detailing that by 2009 only 15 percent of whites households had a net worth of zero or less compared to about a third of the black and Hispanic households.

"The highest unemployment rates in the industrialized world are among African-American youth. The federal and state governments are not addressing this major problem," said Brooks, who also criticizes New Jersey's Republican Governor Chris Christie, a politician receiving praise from conservatives countrywide for his attacks against teachers' unions, deep budget cuts that savage the poor and tax breaks for millionaires.

Countering escalating criticisms of Obama in black communities, the President's prominent black supporters like civil rights leader Rev. Al Sharpton echo the rationale advanced by Obama himself that he is the president of all Americans so his addressing issues specific to African-American would be inappropriate.

However, that view side-steps the reality that Obama has addressed specialized issues important to specific groups, including gays and women.

Obama's even repeatedly addressed issues important to his Republican political adversaries.

Obama's embrace of Republican demands for deficit reducing austerity by slashing services to the most needy chagrins many, beyond black communities already enduring disproportionate pain from the GOP's ruthless onslaught against the middle and working classes.

Black-owned businesses, historically marginalized in federal contracting, have received a paltry 3.5 percent of federal contracts funded through Obama's ARRA stimulus between February 2009 and November 2010 compared to white-owned businesses receiving 81.3 percent of stimulus-funded contracts during that period, according to calculations by Ohio State University's Kirwan Institute for the Study of Race and Ethnicity.

That figure for black firms receiving federal stimulus-funded contracts is lower than the percentage of black-owned businesses in America. Latino and Asian owned businesses also have fared poorly in receipt of ARRA funded contracts, according to Kirwan calculations.

The President of the United States has a legal duty to address discrimination inclusive of contracting inequities that adversely impact identifiable groups.

The failure and/or inability of the Obama Administration to deal with such discrimination causes black critics like Dr. West to conclude that this president—like his white predecessors—treats blacks differently.

Black bashers of Professor West, from Sharpton to former West colleague Dr. Melissa Harris-Perry (the professor/media commentator) and syndicated radio personality Tom Joyner are particularly incensed with slams from West like his tagging Obama a "mascot" of Wall Street.

Setting aside the tone of West's "mascot" tag, facts do document that Obama received huge financial contributions from mega-financial/corporate entities during his 2008 presidential campaign, with ten of Obama's top twenty contributors coming from that sector, including Wall Street giant Goldman Sachs and corporate titan General Electric.

And facts also document that the Obama Administration embraced Bush's controversial Wall Street bailout without seriously extracting tough (and overdue) reforms in return for the tax-payer rescue even after Wall Street executives lavished bonuses on themselves with bailout money.

That lack of thorough financial sector reform was an unseemly break for Wall Street, particularly its financial fraudsters, whether or not it was payback for those campaign contributions.

Facts further document that the Obama Administration (like its predecessors) has been more aggressive in cracking down on "street crimes'" than on the more grievous economy wrecking crimes committed by the corporate-financial elite.

During 2010, the second year of Obama's presidency, federal prosecutors secured the convictions of 3,838 blacks for crack cocaine law violations, producing prison sentences averaging nearly ten years.

However, that same year the feds continued wrist-slap enforcement on corporations facing criminal charges for far-reaching offenses including fraud and environmental pollution. None of the corporate culprits responsible for those crimes received prison terms, according to US Sentencing Commission data.

Yes, corporate offenders in 2010 paid fines averaging $16.3 million, but some black drug law offenders last year received substantial fines plus long prison sentences.

An East St. Louis, Ill. businessman received a life sentence plus a $2.25-million fine for distributing three thousand pounds of cocaine between 2004 and his arrest in April 2008.

Wachovia—once the nation's sixth largest bank by assets—received in March 2010 what amounted to a year-long probation when Obama Administration federal prosecutors entered into a deal settling a criminal proceeding against Wachovia for its facilitating illegal money transfers from Mexico totaling $378 billion, a staggering sum that included billions traced directly to violent Mexican drug cartels.

The amount of cocaine trafficking that sent that Illinois man to prison for life—one and a half tons—was smaller than a single twenty two ton cocaine shipment referenced in the Wachovia settlement document.

While no Wachovia personnel involved in this drug-tainted money laundering went to prison, during 2010 the US government won convictions against 806 persons involved in money laundering sending nearly 77 percent of those offenders to prison.

Apparently for Obama prosecutors, a too-big-to-fail bank was too-big-to-jail.

Wells Fargo purchased Wachovia in early 2009, a few years after the money laundering infractions. Wells purchased Wachovia for $12.7 billion, shortly after Wells Fargo received $25 billion in federal bailout funds. That purchase helped make Wells Fargo America's second-largest bank.

Quibbling with the words Cornell West uses in his critiques does not erase the Obama Administration's substantive failure to seriously tackle the onerous scourge of high unemployment, particularly among blacks.

Yes, mass unemployment during this recession ravages Americans of all races. However, this dire malady is peculiarly pronounced in the black community.

While the national unemployment rate in June 2011 registered 8.6 percent among whites, the rate for blacks was nearly double at 16.2 percent, according to federal figures—figures that curiously under-count actual levels of unemployment.

Black unemployment in inner-city sections of Philadelphia, for example, is nearly 50 percent according to community activists who tabulate their figures from street-level contacts, not sophisticated statistical samplings. Most of these jobless endure long-term unemployment predating Great Recession related layoffs.

Unemployment drives other crippling conditions like mortgage foreclosures that have disproportionately impacted blacks in the wake of the housing market downturn. Civil rights leader Rev. Jesse Jackson, during a

June 2010 address to black newspaper owners, termed foreclosures and home value drops the largest loss of black wealth in history.

Obama selected the CEO of GE to be his "Jobs Czar."

That's the same GE that has cut and/or off-shored jobs through closing factories in the US in recent decades. In July 2011 GE announced moving its hub for medical X-Ray business to China.

And, this is the same GE that rakes in billions of dollars in profits while avoiding all federal tax payments by adroitly exploiting tax code loopholes, loopholes unavailable to middle and low-income wage earners struggling with their tax burdens.

Given the soaring joblessness among Americans of all races, Obama's Job's Czar is not doing a bang-up job.

"If a White House had been as dismissive of African-American's interest as Obama has been, Blacks would have been ready to march on the White House," wrote respected journalist George Curry, who in mid-2011 moderated a discussion between Rev. Sharpton and Prof. West about their differences on Obama.

Often divorced from critiques of Obama is the fact that he faces an unprecedented dilemma beyond strident obstructionism from Republicans who are willing to sacrifice the well-being of whites to undermine this President. Obama is caught on the horns of America's legacy of individual and institutional racism ... a dilemma not endured by any other Oval Office occupant.

"Seeing the president as one of them, many African Americans expect the president to do more for them," observed blogger Debbie Hines, a lawyer. "Others view that there is a balance to the president being able to overtly address their concerns mainstream and risk alienating other segments of society."

President Obama will receive criticism from many whites if any programmatic initiative appears to them to specifically or disproportionately benefit blacks.

Some conservatives blasted Obama's health care reforms by calling them reparations for blacks despite Obama's publicly stated opposition to the concept of reparations for slavery (a stance that riles some blacks).

In fact, Obama's health reforms specifically sought to corral rapidly rising health costs that are killing America's economy. He did not seek to covertly compensate blacks who are "sick" of racism.

Obama publicly admits that his health reforms did benefit many blacks but within the context of his governance posture of "a rising tides lifting all boats" ... which many contend is a rework of despised (and ineffective) "trickle down economics" of the Ronald Reagan presidency.

Obama has directed monies to historically black colleges as part of his efforts to improve education including expanding Pell Grants for all college students. Obama did support paying the court settlement for the long-festering race discrimination suit black farmers filed against the US Department of Agriculture, ending a long-festering injustice and incurring more bigot-tainted barbs from Congresswoman Michelle Bachmann.

During the 2008 presidential campaign, whites (conservatives and many liberals) banged Obama around for his association with his long-time Christian pastor, the Rev. Jeremiah Wright.

Those critics tarred Obama for Wright's alleged "radical" theology—a theology ironically based on social justice, the care-for-the-poor principles advocated by Jesus.

Lashing Obama as a socialist causes real socialists like Ken Heard of Philadelphia to chuckle.

"Anytime someone calls Obama a socialist or Clinton a communist, shows they don't know what they're talking about," said Heard who is active in the Philadelphia branch of the Black Radical Congress. "Obama and Clinton are both centrists and defenders of capitalism. They are not even members of the Democratic Party's left-wing."

Consistent with Obama's damned if he does/damned if he doesn't dilemma, his attempts to mitigate white criticism result in his angering many blacks, who understandably feel he is ignoring long festering issues like structural unemployment and mass incarceration.

Much of the mass incarceration across America impacting blacks arises from this nation's Drug War, which marked a dubious 40th Anniversary on June 17, 2011. Half of the 216,706 inmates in federal prisons at the end of June 2011 were drug law offenders according to the federal Bureau of Prisons. Blacks comprise 38 percent of the federal prison population; triple their rate in America's population.

Federal studies repeatedly document that more whites use crack cocaine than blacks. Yet, blacks comprised 78.5 percent of those convicted in federal courts for crack offenses in 2010 compared to the 7.3 percent white rate, according to US Sentencing Commission statistics.

Obama did fulfill a campaign pledge to reduce the imbalance between powder cocaine and crack cocaine sentences reaching a compromise with Capitol Hill in 2010. That compromise reduced but did not eliminate the sentencing disparity that resulted in many black crack users receiving longer sentences than white powder cocaine dealers.

Despite inheriting an unprecedented economic mess Obama has wasted mega-money on military activities like escalating his predecessor's quagmire in Afghanistan.

Further, in mid-March 2011, the Noble Peace Prize winning Obama eagerly joined the French-British assault on the leader of Libya—a fiasco for the US that drained $715 million in federal funds during three months according to a report the White House sent Congress in late June 2011.

The money Obama's squandered on attempting to oust Libya's Qaddafi could have covered the entire $629 million deficit facing the School District of Philadelphia. That deficit produced the layoffs of 3,400 district employees at the end of June 2011, a substantial number of those layoffs falling on blacks.

Journalist George Curry rightly notes that many blacks "do not want to hear anything bad about Barack Obama even if it's true." This deaf-to-Obama-foibles stance taken by many blacks is not substantially different from whites who blindly idolize Ronald Reagan.

That late president dangerously ran-up the national debt during the 1980s and initiated much of the deregulation responsible for many of the structural fiscal problems facing the country today—problems Reagan idolizers duplicitously blame on Obama.

The unquestioning support Obama enjoys among many blacks is curiously similar to the stance adopted by many Jewish Americans who reflexively attack any criticism of Israel. "Those public supporters of President Obama who defend him at all costs are clearly doing Black people a major disservice," stated a commentary posted on *Black Agenda Report*, a website long critical of Obama. "President Obama and his administration have taken the black vote for granted and feel no need to acknowledge or act on any issues on our behalf."

Daryl Brooks, the Tea Party member, offers a relevant observation for blacks, "We have to challenge the President on issues. We can like him but we can't give him a free pass because he's black."

Linn Washington, Jr. is a professor of journalism at Temple University in Philadelphia.

Occupy the System

By JEFFREY ST. CLAIR and JOSHUA FRANK

It's not too cool to be ridiculed
But you brought this upon yourself
The world is tired of pacifiers
We want the truth and nothing else

And we are sick and tired of hearing your song
Telling how you are gonna change right from wrong
'Cause if you really want to hear our views
"You haven't done nothing"!

—Stevie Wonder, "You Haven't Done Nothing"

There is an anger running rampant across the country. Some on the right are calling it class warfare. People are enraged. Jobs are scarce, the rich continue to get richer while the poor continue to struggle to make ends meet. Indeed, it should be classified as economic warfare, Americans are sick and tired of being pushed around. It is time to shove back.

Herman Cain is right. The problem resides in the White House. Herman Cain is wrong. The problem resides on Wall Street. They are, in fact, the same problem: a goutish economic system that enriches the wealthy and impoverishes everyone else, a system that pillages the natural world and tramples on basic human liberties, a system that treats corporations as people and people as commodities.

The victims of neoliberal economics are easy to spot. So too are the perpetrators and profiteers of privatized markets. In many ways the occupations sprouting up around the country remind us of the outpouring of opposition to the WTO that jammed up the streets of Seattle in the late-1990s. Like that organic movement, the current protests are grassroots, and fueled not by overt political motivations, but by a sense of justice.

Like the Battle for Seattle, Occupy America is taking place during a time when a Democrat resides in the White House. There is little question that President Clinton recklessly pursued a free trade agenda that endangered the American workforce and ravaged the environment, prompting strong criticism of all the WTO embodied. But today President Obama's motivations are a bit more cavalier. While he speaks of job creation and jumpstarting the struggling economy, he simultaneously ensures his pals on Wall Street that their power and profits will remain intact.

President Clinton, like his predecessor, is largely responsible for the dire economic situation we now face. It was Clinton and his Treasury Secretary

Robert Rubin that pushed for increased deregulation, which ended up shifting jobs, and entire industries, overseas.

Rubin even pushed for Clinton's dismantling of Glass-Steagall, testifying that deregulating the banking industry would be good for capital gains, as well as the folks on Main Street. "[The] banking industry is fundamentally different from what it was two decades ago, let alone in 1933," Rubin testified before the House Committee on Banking and Financial Services in May of 1995.

"[Glass-Steagall could] conceivably impede safety and soundness by limiting revenue diversification," Rubin argued.

While the industry saw much deregulation over the years preceding Clintontime, the Gramm-Leach-Biley Act of 1999, which eliminated Glass-Steagall, extended and ratified changes that had been enacted with previous legislation. Ultimately, the repeal of the New Deal era protection allowed commercial lenders like Rubin's Citigroup to underwrite and trade instruments like mortgage backed securities along with collateralized debt and established structured investment vehicles (SIVs), which purchased these securities. In short, as the lines were blurred among investment banks, commercial banks and insurance companies, when one industry fell, like big mortgage lenders, others could too.

What Clinton began, President Bush only escalated with an extreme capitalist vigor. Alan Greenspan stayed as head of the Federal Reserve, continuing to press forward with his callous libertarian agenda of deregulation and damaging austerity measures. When Greenspan retired, Ben Bernanke, another Wall Street ally, took the Bank's helm, and was kept in place by the dutiful Obama.

President Obama wasted little time bailing out the greed-infested financial sector. When he took office in 2009 Obama nominated Rubin-trained economist Timothy Geithner, former president of the Federal Reserve Bank of New York, to serve as Treasury Secretary. Geithner, if anything, is an insider among insiders and Wall Street's main man in DC.

It was certainly not the hope and change Obama supporters had voted for, especially in a time when the economy was suffering and jobs were scarce. Obama's modest stimulus program did little to sustain job growth and was nowhere near the scale of the New Deal's robust Works Progress Administration. In short, Obama has been an economic disaster for the majority of Americans, sans the Wall Street crowd that continues to profit and is protected by the government under the guise of "too big to fail."

Did you really expect something different from the man who begged Joe Lieberman to serve as his mentor in the senate?

It's this entrenched, systematic refusal to challenge the status quo that is driving the animosity and outrage across the country. Wall Street is being upheld, and indeed enabled, by both the Democrats and Republicans, including, at the top of the stinking pile, President Obama and his administration.

The Democrats are a prosthetic bunch, a hollow shell for the detritus of New Deal liberalism, that maintains popular allegiance through blind inertia. For the past thirty years at least, the Democrats have functioned less as a political party driven by a tangible ideology than as a low-fat franchise of Wall Street and the defense contractors. From war to neoliberal economics, the new Democrats have pursued brutal policies, often inflicted most grievously at the party's most devoted constituents: Hispanics, blacks, labor and the unemployed.

There's a Wilsonian quality to Obama: trim, aloof, pedantic and shank-you-in-the-back dangerous. Obama has never wanted to be seen socializing with the poor or working class stiffs. He doesn't even want them in his orbit, except as props behind his scrolling teleprompter. In his first three years in office, the closet the president came to such a pedestrian parlay was his famous beer summit with the Cambridge cop who manhandled Professor Henry Louis Gates. Come to think of it, that meeting was a twofer, since it was also one of Obama's few close encounters with a voice from black America as well.

Making the connection between the continued economic disparities on Main Street and the policies that fuel this divide is paramount to bringing about real systematic change. As such, it's time to Occupy Washington and make this, not only an electoral issue, but also a very genuine threat to our government's consolidated power.

Obama's first term has revealed the utter vacuity of our political system and the prodigious level of corruption eating away at the sinews of US empire. Democracy itself is being degraded. From bank bailouts and war to indemnification of corporate criminals and assassination orders against American citizens, the most urgent matters of government are now hatched without public debate in the secret chambers of power. The majestic hypocrisy of the Democrats in a time of deepening economic and environmental crisis has inflamed the spectrum of outrage now sweeping America. But where does the movement go from here?

The 99% movement needs to forsake protest for a sustained resistance and disruption of the status quo. After all, the object isn't reform—we're far, far beyond that—but radical, systemic change. Its structure should remain enigmatic, diffuse, protean—too slippery to be captured and co-opted by Democrats looking to hijack its momentum. In order to maintain its integrity and political power, the 99% movement must publicly shun any perilous alliance with Democratic front groups such as MoveOn and the Natural Resource Defense Council. It should reject the coruscated cant of faux leftists like Bernie Sanders and Rachel Maddow and instead give full-voice to the intrinsic rage of the outsiders, the disenfranchised and destitute, the left behind, the new American preterite.

It's time for the nation to hear the spooky vibrations of a home-grown and organic movement on the march, a swarming mass of discontent that will make the financial aristocrats and their low-rent political grifters tremble in their sleep. If they can sleep at all.

Let's run the bastards out of town.

Index

Support AK Press!

AK Press is one of the world's largest and most productive anarchist publishing houses. We're entirely worker-run and democratically managed. We operate without a corporate structure—no boss, no managers, no bullshit. We publish close to twenty books every year, and distribute thousands of other titles published by other like-minded independent presses from around the globe.

The Friends of AK program is a way that you can directly contribute to the continued existence of AK Press, and ensure that we're able to keep publishing great books just like this one! Friends pay a minimum of $25 per month, for a minimum three month period, into our publishing account. In return, Friends automatically receive (for the duration of their membership), as they appear, one free copy of every new AK Press title. They're also entitled to a 20% discount on everything featured in the AK Press Distribution catalog and on the website, on any and every order. You or your organization can even sponsor an entire book if you should so choose!

There's great stuff in the works—so sign up now to become a Friend of AK Press, and let the presses roll!

Won't you be our friend? Email friendsofak@akpress.org for more info, or visit the Friends of AK Press website: http://www.akpress.org/programs/friendsofak